Patrick Kennedy
b. 1858 d. 1929
m. Nov. 23, 1887
Mary A. Hickey
b. 1857 d. 1923

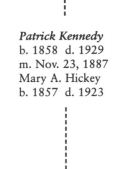

Joseph P. Kennedy
b. 1888 d. 1969
m. Oct. 7, 1914
Rose Fitzgerald
b. 1890 d. 1995

Francis Kennedy
b. 1891 d. 1892

Mary L. Kennedy
b. 1892 d. 1972
m. Oct. 12, 1927
George Connelly
b. 1898 d. 1971

Margaret Kennedy
b. 1898 d. 1974
m. June 14, 1924
Charles J. Burke
b. 1899 d. 1967

Eunice Kennedy
b. July 10, 1921
m. May 23, 1953
R. S. Shriver
b. Nov. 9, 1915

Patricia Kennedy
b. May 6, 1924
m. April 24, 1954
Peter Lawford
b. 1923 d. 1984

Robert Kennedy
b. 1925 d. 1968
m. June 17, 1950
Ethel Skakel
b. April 11, 1928

Jean Ann Kennedy
b. Feb. 20, 1928
m. May 19, 1956
Stephen E . Smith
b. 1927 d. 1990

Edward Kennedy
b. Feb. 2, 1932
m. Nov. 29, 1958
Virginia J. Bennett
b. Sept. 9, 1936
m. Aug. 21, 1992
Victoria Reggie
b. Feb. 26, 1954

The SINS of the FATHER

The SINS of the FATHER

JOSEPH P. KENNEDY
and the Dynasty He Founded

RONALD KESSLER

WARNER BOOKS

A Time Warner Company

Warner Books, Inc., 1271 Avenue of the Americas, New York, NY 10020

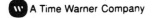 A Time Warner Company

Printed in the United States of America
First Printing: March 1996
10 9 8 7 6 5 4 3 2 1

LC: 95-61889

ISBN: 0-446-51884-0

Book design by Giorgetta Bell McRee

For Pam, Greg, and Rachel

CONTENTS

ACKNOWLEDGMENTS

This book was the inspiration of my agent, Robert Gottlieb. More than thirty years have elapsed since the publication of Richard J. Whalen's *The Founding Father*, the only major book on Joseph P. Kennedy. The only other biography, *Joseph P. Kennedy* by David E. Kostoff, was published in 1974. Since then, much more material has become available in archives, and people have become more willing to tell what they know. Robert's idea was brilliant. I am deeply grateful to Robert, the executive vice president of the William Morris Agency, for sharing his idea with me, and for his terrific support throughout.

Laurence J. Kirshbaum, president and chief executive officer of Warner Books, and Maureen Egen, vice president and publisher, immediately recognized the potential of the subject and gave me the resources to pursue it properly. As my editor, Maureen has been a joy to work with—tremendously enthusiastic and supportive during the research phase and incredibly skilled at honing the final product.

My wife, Pamela Kessler, collaborated with me on the book by doing the archival research. A former *Washington Post* reporter and the author of *Undercover Washington,* a book on the spy sites of Washington, she applied her considerable investigative skills to finding dozens of sources of documents that had never been consulted before, deciphering nearly illegible handwriting in diaries, and fitting the often disparate pieces of the puzzle together. All of the revelations in the book from documents are hers. She then applied her talents to doing the initial editing of the manuscript. Finally, she came up with the title of the book. As my wife, friend, and trusted adviser, Pam could not be more supportive or loving.

My children, Rachel Kessler Englehart and Greg Kessler, were sources of love, pride, and emotional support. Rachel also helped out by preparing a chronology. My stepson, Mike Whitehead, was his usual gracious and charming self. My mother, Minuetta Kessler, and stepfather, Dr. Myer M. Kessler, let me stay with them in Belmont, Massachusetts, on my monthly trips to Boston and Cape Cod. My sister, Jean Brenner, a nurse practitioner, and my brother-in-law, Mark J. Brenner, M.D., analyzed prescription and medical records and gave me guidance on medical issues.

As managing editor of the *Boston Herald,* Dave Farrell hired me thirty years ago as a police reporter, investigative reporter, and editorial writer. For more than two decades, he was perhaps the leading political columnist in Boston, first at the *Boston Herald* and then at the *Boston Globe.* I was gratified that he offered to help me on the project, even taking old sources out to lunch to convince them to talk with me. As a result, key people who had never before discussed Joe Kennedy opened up. Dave then applied his unique knowledge of Boston politics, the Kennedys, and the Boston Irish to reading the manuscript. Besides insuring that the finished product would be accurate, his remarkable skill as an editor brought out areas that needed further illumination.

As he has in the past, my friend Daniel M. Clements read the manuscript as well, offering insightful advice that I followed. Irwin M. Borowski, a former associate chief of enforcement of the Securities and Exchange Commission, also read the manuscript and pointed out areas that needed clarification, as did several other experts who cannot be named.

I am fortunate to have so many talented supporters. Without them, I could not have done this book. To them, I give my thanks.

Those who were interviewed or who helped in other ways include:

Joseph Aboody, Rupert Allason, M.P., Frederick "Rick" Allen, Anne Anable, Richard Atkins, James L. Auchincloss, Gertrude Ball, Joseph Bellino, George Bookman, Irwin Borowski, Jean N. Brenner, Dr. Mark J. Brenner, William S. Brodrick, Dr. Bertram S. Brown, Charles J. Burke, Mortimer M. Caplin, Christopher Carberry, Igor Cassini, Oleg Cassini, Nicholas J. Chase, Nancy Tenney Coleman, Harold E. "Hal" Clancy, Daniel M. Clements, Ned Comstock, the late John Costello, John J. Craven Jr., Robert T. Crowley, Lloyd N. Cutler.

Rita Dallas, Mark Dalton, Raymond W. Daum, John H. Davis, Elizabeth Deane, Elizabeth de Bedts, Carmen dell'Orefice, Margaret dell'Orefice, Janet Des Rosiers, Ann Downey, Morton Downey Jr., Peter Drummey, the late Orval DuBois, William Dufty, Andy Edmonds, Frank Fallaci, Christine Farber, Joseph D. Farish Jr., Dave Farrell, John T. Fawcett, Raymond G. Faxon, Dan H. Fenn, William J. Foley, Otto Fuerbinger.

Father Adelard J. Gagnan, Anthony Galluccio, Stanley B. Galup, Ann Gargan, Joseph F. Gargan, Antoinette Giancana, K. Dun Gifford, Mary Gigante, Sam Gill, Theodore Gittinger, C.Z. Grant, Tom Griffith, Nigel Hamilton, Rear Admiral John Harlee, Oscar W. Haussermann Jr., Lawrence J. Heim, Luella R. Hennessey, Burton Hersh, C. David Heymann, Pat M. Holt, the late William J. Hopkins, Page Huidekoper, Henry James Jr., Janet Jeghegian, Laura Jereski, William "Will" Johnson, Joseph Jones.

Richard D. Kaplan, Stanley A. Karnow, Dmitri Kessel, Willi R. Korte, Robert Lacey, James K. Langan, Evelyn Lincoln, the late Joseph M. Linsey, Joseph LoPiccolo, Peter Lucas, Henry Luce III, Dr. James L. Luke, Richard Lyons, Peter Maas, Pat Maniscalco, Kerry McCarthy, Mary Lou McCarthy, Ronald T. McCoy, the late Nellie McGrail, Edward F. McLaughlin Jr., Priscilla Johnson McMillan, William J. McMullin, Hank Messick, Jeffrey S. Miles, William H. Miles, Melody Miller, Dan T. Moore, Dr. Nicholas Morgan, Robert M. Morgenthau, Francis X. Morrissey, William J. Mulcahy, Patrick Munroe.

Larry G. Newman, Robert Pack, Dr. Rene S. Parmar, Françoise Pellegrino, Mary Pitcairn, Margot Prendergast, Cynthia Stone Ray, James A. Reed, George E. Reedy, Michael Reynolds, Donald A. Ritchie, Chalmers M. Roberts, William F. Roemer, Benjamin Rosales, Dr. Saul Rotter, James A. Rousmanière, Ralph Salerno.

Richard Segura, Dr. Melvyn I. Semmel, Donald Senich, Joseph Shimon, Dr. Morris C. Shumiatcher, Q.C., Kane Simonian, Martin T. Sixsmith, George A. Smathers, James H. Smith, Liz Smith, Augustus "Gus" Soule Jr., Charles "Chuck" Spalding, Dennis Spear, Edward J. "Ned" Spellman, Judge Stanley Sporkin, the late Lucy P. Steinert, Daniel Strohmeier, Marianne Strong, Arthur Stryker, William Sutton.

John E. Taylor, Edward Thompson, Joseph Timilty Jr., Robert Tonis, Walter J. Trohan, Kenneth Turan, Helga Mayerhofer Wagner, Frank Waldrop, Thomas J. Walsh, the late William Walton, Dr. Robert D. Watt, the late Dr. James W. Watts, Paul R. Wieck, David Wigdor, Terryl Williams, Thomas Winship, F. Mark Wyatt.

The SINS of the FATHER

PROLOGUE

"I just bought a horse for $75,000," Joseph P. Kennedy confided to the cardinal over lunch. "And for another $75,000, I put Jack on the cover of *Time*."

Joe Kennedy, then sixty-nine years old, always appeared to be smiling, but this time he really was.

Joe was "very proud of the fact that he had spent $75,000, and now he would not have to spend as much [on advertising]," recalled Edward J. "Ned" Spellman, the nephew of Francis Cardinal Spellman, both of whom were present at the lunch at the cardinal's residence at 452 Madison Avenue in New York.

A few weeks later, John F. Kennedy's beaming countenance appeared for the first time on *Time*'s cover. Jack Kennedy—the "Democratic Whiz of 1957"—had just begun his bid for the presidency, and the glowing story accompanying the December 2, 1957, cover gave him a tremendous boost. The story described Jack's father as a former ambassador to Great

Britain, a former chairman of the United States Securities and Exchange Commission, and a former chairman of the United States Maritime Commission. He was the purveyor of a fortune estimated at $100 million, made in part during a few hours' selling short during the stock market crash of 1929, the story said. It gave no hint of the way he made his money initially—as a bootlegger in partnership with organized crime figures during Prohibition. His days as a moviemaker in Hollywood and premier liquor distributor did not rate a mention either. Neither did Joe's well-documented anti-Semitism, his efforts to appease Adolf Hitler, or his manipulation of the stock market.

In that respect, *Time* was not alone, for Joseph P. Kennedy led a charmed existence. With his piercing sky blue eyes, round spectacles, freckles, and reddish blond hair, Kennedy mesmerized the press, just as his son Jack would do. Until his death in 1969 at the age of eighty-one, Joe would be described in print as a Horatio Alger hero and chaste Roman Catholic, a man who had risen from the home of a saloon keeper in East Boston to become one of the richest men in America. Usually, he would be pictured with his wife, Rose, and one or more of his nine children, his 190 pounds fitting trimly into a six-foot frame. The pictures never showed his well-sculpted, green-eyed Hyannis Port secretary, Janet Des Rosiers (pronounced Day Ro-see-ay), who was his mistress for nine years.

Joe Kennedy managed to compartment his life so perfectly that even his closest aides did not know every facet, let alone his corruption, his duplicity. He had an ability to show different sides of himself to different people. Like the mystery of the Holy Trinity, his life remained a cipher, immune from scrutiny even by his own children. Better than any Mafia chieftain, Joe covered his tracks. But if the methods were clandestine, the results were clear to everyone.

By spawning America's own version of the British royal family, Joseph P. Kennedy founded a dynasty that produced the first Catholic president, three senators, an attorney general, three congressmen, and future presidential contenders who are likely to continue to shape American history. But Joe Kennedy did more than *create* America's preeminent political family. Unlike John Adams, the farmer whose dynasty included two American presidents, Joe Kennedy *orchestrated* his sons' destinies. It was his edict that they rise, like salmon swimming upstream, to the top of American government. As a silent partner, Joe Kennedy provided all the cash and connections they needed to take advantage of their natural gifts, and he financed and directed their campaigns.

Once they achieved high office, Joe Kennedy continued to dominate and direct his sons' actions, shaping the myths that continue to enshrine the family and have turned it into a national obsession.

Jack Kennedy's friend Charles Spalding recalled that as a marine helicopter lifted him from Joe Kennedy's white-shingled, two-story home in Hyannis Port, Jack pointed at his father sitting in a wheelchair below. "He made the whole thing possible," the president said.

He did that and more.

"Joe was always watching what made power and gentility; he wanted both," said Thomas G. Corcoran, the assistant to President Franklin D. Roosevelt who at one point was Kennedy's lawyer. "He studied where power came from . . . power came from money, and he was out to get it."

But if Joe Kennedy achieved power beyond his wildest dreams, it would come at colossal cost.

1

NODDLE ISLAND

When Joseph P. Kennedy died on November 18, 1969, the *Boston Herald* editorialized that in mourning his passing, the nation "pays homage to a man whose life story far surpasses the fictional heroes of the Horatio Alger era into which he was born." The paper continued: "In his own right and on his own terms, Joseph P. Kennedy rose from modest beginnings to the pinnacles of financial power and political eminence by adhering to old-fashioned American virtues that have been somewhat discounted in today's society: devotion to family, loyalty to friends, strength of character, and the will to win."

Not to be outdone, the competing *Boston Record-American* ran a series on Joe Kennedy's life. The first article appeared under the subhead "Saloon Keeper's Son to Multimillionaire." The concluding article appeared under the subhead "He Believed in Faith, Hope, and Charity."

Fifty miles south of Boston, the *New Bedford Standard-*

Times noted editorially that "Richard Cardinal Cushing, his friend for many years, will celebrate a white mass. . . . This is how Joseph P. Kennedy, a deeply religious man, would have wanted it."

Indeed it was. For the eulogies followed exactly the line that Joseph Kennedy had fashioned for himself. No tale of Joe's life was complete without reference to the potato famine in Ireland; the impoverished life of a saloon keeper's son in East Boston; the struggle to pay the bills at Harvard College; and the miraculous feat of becoming president of a bank at the age of twenty-five.

To be sure, there was a fragment of truth to it. Joe's grandparents, Patrick Kennedy and Bridget Murphy, had emigrated from Ireland after the fungus *Phytophthora infestans* began turning the potato crop rotten in 1845. From 1846 to 1849, a million Irish peasants died, and another million fled to North America, with others crossing the Irish Channel to Great Britain. But while the blight caused massive starvation, Patrick's family—which included a sister and two brothers—was relatively well off. Patrick's father, who was also named Patrick and was married to Mary Johanna, was a tenant farmer in the town of Dunganstown, County Wexford. The town was six miles down the mist-covered River Barrow from New Ross, a seaport of fifteen thousand people. The family tilled twenty-five acres of relatively fertile land and lived in a one-story cottage of stone and clay. The cottage had four rooms, each with its own door to the outside. Besides growing sugar beets, potatoes, and barley for malt, the Kennedys raised cattle and sheep.

Then under British rule, Ireland was exploited for its produce and livestock. Most of the landlords were English, and they extracted high rents. As the potato blight cut into production, the landlords raised rents still higher. This was the dilemma the Kennedy family faced. Moreover, since Patrick was the youngest son, the farm would not pass to him when his father died. Instead, it would pass automatically to his older brother, John. Patrick decided to leave Ireland not because he was starving but because—like the millions of other immigrants who came to America from many lands—he saw a brighter future in the United States.

Patrick made his way to Liverpool, England, and booked passage on the SS *Washington Irving*. The forty-day journey was perilous. About 6 percent of the Irish who came to America during the period died on board of cholera, dysentery, yellow fever, smallpox, or measles.

Patrick landed on April 21, 1849, on Noddle Island. At the confluence of the Charles and Mystic Rivers and Boston's inner harbor, Noddle Island consisted of 633 acres. It had been incorporated by Boston in 1636, just six years after Boston itself was established as a settlement. A third of a mile northeast of downtown Boston across the water, Noddle Island was still mostly grazing land when the East Boston Company began developing it in 1833. The company laid out streets named for battles in the Revolutionary War—Lexington, Saratoga, Eutaw, Trenton. Using fill, the city connected the island to other nearby islands, and the larger area became known as East Boston. Eventually, East Boston would be connected by filling in the waterfront to the mainland.

By the time Patrick Kennedy landed, East Boston had a population of 16,618 and 1,897 homes, eleven churches, ten schoolhouses, and twenty-four companies. These included a bakery, an iron forgery, a sugar refinery, and a timber company. One of the businesses was American Stave and Cooperage Company on Chelsea Street. Here Patrick began working as a cooper making barrels. At the time, many goods and foodstuffs—from molasses to sugar—were shipped in barrels.

Having established himself in the new land, Patrick quickly found himself a wife. No one is sure how or when he met Bridget Murphy, who was also born in Ireland. While many in the Kennedy family believe they met on the voyage to America, there is no record of a Bridget Murphy making the crossing with Patrick Kennedy. In her memoirs, Rose Kennedy said the two met once they had arrived in Boston.

In any case, the two were married on September 26, 1849, at the Cathedral of the Holy Cross in Boston.

Industrious and personable, Bridget Murphy got a job as a hairdresser at Jordan Marsh Company in downtown Boston, which she commuted to on a ferry that cost a penny. Later, she opened a notions or variety shop near the ferry landing on Noddle Island. She became known as well for her willingness to help other Irish immigrants. Those who needed help locating jobs or housing found their way to her shop.

On January 14, 1858, Bridget and Patrick had their fourth child, Patrick Joseph Kennedy. Known as P.J., he would be Joe Kennedy's father. On November 22, 1858, the senior Patrick died of cholera, leaving Bridget to raise their family.

With blue eyes, a rosy complexion, reddish hair, and a handlebar mustache, P.J. Kennedy grew up to look like a barroom brawler. Initially, he worked as a stevedore on the East Boston waterfront. With John J. Quigley, a water inspector, he then opened a saloon. Located at 81 Border Street, it was just down the street from P.J.'s home at 25 Border Street.

"They are universal places, like churches, hallowed meeting places of all mankind," Iris Murdoch, the British novelist, has said of bars. P.J. used his bar as a launching pad for his political career. A man who rarely drank, he listened to his customers and was always ready to help out with the loan of a dollar or a gift of coal. P.J. got to know everyone in the neighborhood, and soon he was ready to trade his popularity for votes.

On November 3, 1885, at the age of twenty-seven, P.J. was elected to the Massachusetts House of Representatives from Ward 2 in East Boston. He was said to have received strong backing from the liquor lobby, which was worried about the temperance movement.

Soon, P.J. Kennedy opened a second bar at 2 Elbow Street and eventually a retail liquor store at 985 Tremont Street in Boston's South End.

While P.J. cultivated the image of a quiet man whose greatest malediction was to call a man a "loafer," he had a vicious side. Joseph L. Kane, a cousin, was close to him and had managed Maurice Tobin's campaign against James Michael Curley for mayor. Kane confided to his friend Kane Simonian that, in temperament, P.J. was ruthless.

♦ ♦ ♦

Two years after his election to the legislature, on November 23, 1887, P.J. and Mary Augusta Hickey of Brockton, both twenty-nine, were married at the Church of the Sacred Heart. She was the daughter of another saloon keeper and had three successful brothers—Charles Hickey, the mayor of Brockton; Jim Hickey, a police captain; and John Hickey, a doctor in nearby Winthrop.

The following year, on September 6, 1888, P.J. and Mary had their first child, Joseph Patrick Kennedy, the third generation of the Kennedy family to live in Boston. In America, it was not unheard of for an immigrant, such as Andrew Carnegie, the son of Scottish weavers, to rise to great wealth. Yet Joe Kennedy was not an immigrant; nor was his father, P.J. Kennedy. It was his grandfather Patrick who had immigrated from Ireland. Thus Joe's privileged environment had no connection with the modest circumstances of his grandfather or with Ireland's potato famine.

To be sure, the Cabots, the Lowells, and the Lodges still controlled Boston's financial institutions. But politically the Irish had already taken over. The Irish now represented more than a third of Boston's population. The blatant discrimination characterized by "No Irish Need Apply" warnings in classified employment ads had all but disappeared. Nearly every immigrant to America had fled hardship and faced discrimination upon arriving. Most did not dwell on the humiliations. But throughout his life, Joe would take perverse pleasure in describing how he had bested the Brahmins at their own game, as if no one else had persevered against such obstacles. Joe would cite his Irish heritage when it suited his purposes, as when he claimed publications were attacking him because of his origins. Yet at other times, he denigrated the Irish. At a St. Patrick's Day Dinner sponsored by the Irish Clover Club at the Hotel Somerset in Boston in March 1937, he said that too many Irish did not have the "family tradition adequate to win the respect and confidence of their Puritan neighbors."

By the time Joe was born, Joe's family lived at 151 Meridian Street in East Boston in a comfortable, three-story dark-red-brick house that would today be known as a town house. Having served five terms as a state representative, P.J. Kennedy was elected to the Massachusetts Senate. He then became city wire commissioner, responsible for electrifying Boston. P.J. was not only powerful politically, he was wealthy. He invested in Suffolk Coal Company and, four years after Joe's birth, P.J. invaded that most sacrosanct territory of the Brahmins, the banks.

P.J. Kennedy became an incorporator and vice president of Columbia Trust Company with offices at 20 Meridian Street. Just nine blocks south of his home, Columbia Trust boasted fireproof offices of brick and iron with a vault that rested on a solid stone foundation surrounded by solid brick and three feet of stone masonry. In March 1895, the bank opened for business with capital of $130,300 and surplus of $50,000. Later, P.J. was an organizer of Sumner Savings Bank as well.

In the same year that he helped found Columbia Trust, P.J. was a delegate to the Democratic National Convention, where he helped nominate Grover Cleveland for president, and was himself reelected to the Massachusetts Senate. P.J. would go on to become acting fire commissioner and would twice be reappointed wire commissioner. In 1899, he was named one of four Boston election commissioners. Most important, he became a member of what was called the Democratic board of strategy, which carved up political spoils and manipulated Boston's Democratic party from Room 8 of the Quincy House on Brattle Street. Besides P.J., it consisted of

Joseph J. Corbett of Boston's Charlestown section, city clerk James Donovan of the South End, and later Boston mayor John F. "Honey Fitz" Fitzgerald of the North End—all powerful ward bosses.

P.J., like Martin Lomasney, operated a mini-welfare state. Known as "the Mahatma," Lomasney had built a political machine called the Hendricks Club. A bachelor, Lomasney was a thickset, well-muscled man who devoted his life to "his" people—the people of the West End. By putting them on city payrolls or giving them contracts, he relieved thousands of "the inquisitorial terrors of organized charity," as he put it. In turn, the ward heelers made sure he stayed in office, even if that required graft and election fraud, just as they made sure P.J. was reelected.

In one of his earliest memories of his father's political activities, Joe recalled a couple of ward heelers telling P.J. one day, "Pat, we voted 128 times today."

"Pat Kennedy [P.J.] was an old-time politician," said Kane Simonian, a former executive director of the Boston Redevelopment Authority. "He was a Robin Hood type. Take care of the poor, give them Christmas baskets, take care of everybody, while at the same time he robbed everybody blind for their influence." P.J. was "very entrepreneurial," Simonian added. "He made money on contracts. They didn't have all these laws on ethics. He had a lot of contracts to give out on construction. He could do all kinds of favors and add on extras," he said. "He electrified Boston and robbed the city blind."

Indeed, when he died, P.J.'s assets were listed at $57,000. The real figure, according to James M. Landis, who worked for Joe, was more than $100,000—equal to $845,000 today.

P.J. symbolized the Irish character described by George E. Reedy. That character, he wrote in his book *From the Ward to the White House: The Irish in American Politics*, was forged from decades of living on the edge of extinction. "Those who survived were lean and mean. They were quick of wit and masters of dissembling. They understood political leverage and knew when to attack, when to retreat, and when to hide."

Thus by the time Joe Kennedy was ten, his father was a banker and one of the most powerful politicians in Boston. Far from being disadvantaged, Joe lived in a stately brick mansion at 165 Webster Avenue, just a mile and a quarter south of where he was born. With ten windows overlooking Boston's inner harbor, the Kennedy home on Jeffries Point gave Joe a panorama of Boston's financial district across the water. From this perch, he could watch the imposing ships as they moved through the harbor. If the ships were a daily lesson in the importance of commerce, they also suggested that there was a bigger world outside of Boston.

"There is hope from the sea, but none from the grave," according to an Irish proverb. Whether in tranquil Hyannis Port or racier Palm Beach, for all his life Joe looked to the sea. Like his father, Joe would have a yacht with a skipper. And like his father, he would winter in Palm Beach and have maids and cooks to attend to his needs.

"Joe did not come in on a raft," said Mary Lou McCarthy, the daughter of Joe's sister Loretta. "His life was very comfortable." The family had "servants and teams of horses, lovely clothing, and European travel. Joe had that kind of comfortable life growing up."

But Joe wanted more than that. The Irish invented classifications for themselves like "shanty" for the luckless and "lace curtain" for the more successful. Joe always seemed to know what he wanted. Lace curtains were not good enough. And more than money, he wanted power.

2

FAILING GRADES

As the family's only son, Joe was revered. His two younger sisters, Mary Margaret—known as Margaret—and Loretta, looked up to him. (A younger brother, Francis Benedict, was born in 1891 and died of diphtheria the following year.) Joe had a magnetic personality, one that drew people to him and made them want to join him. He had a booming, authoritative voice that made people think he knew what he was talking about, even if he didn't.

"When Joe talked with you, he didn't converse with you. He intimidated you," a confidant said. "Joe always put people on the defensive. He would come in and say something or ask a question so you had to justify yourself."

If Joe's father, P.J. Kennedy, looked like a ruffian, Joe had a more refined, intellectual appearance. His broad smile, revealing regular white teeth, seemed painted on his face and was infectious. Much later, Paul B. "Red" Fay Jr., one of Jack's friends, recalled playing golf with Joe.

"You know, that guy thinks I'm smiling," Joe said to Fay when another golfer waved to him.

At the same time, Joe, like his father, had an Irish temper, which he used to coerce. He inherited what are known within the family as "Hickey eyes," since they came from his mother's side of the family. When Joe was furious, those eyes became an icy, translucent steel gray. The pupils became so dilated they almost disappeared. The effect was scary. Lacking any core, his eyes could see out but appeared to prevent anyone from seeing in.

All his life, Joe would employ his volatile temper to get what he wanted. He was proud of his aggressive demeanor. Joe would later send his son Ted a photo of himself taken when he was around seven. "What I would particularly like you to observe is the piercing eyes, the very set jaw, and the clenched left fist," Joe wrote proudly in a note attached to the photo. "Maybe all of this meant something!"

Psychologists say bullies often come from families where they experienced bullying themselves. The defenseless kids who end up as victims remind bullies of their own defenselessness against abuse at home and the shame it caused them. "They bully as if to say, 'You're the victim, not me,'" according to psychologist Nathaniel Floyd.

Joe's father, P.J., was known as a strict disciplinarian. Whether that extended to abusive behavior toward his son can only be speculated upon. Certainly Joe did not display any warmth toward his father. While Joe gave lip service to respecting him, he did not attend his funeral. He claimed at the time of his father's death he was too busy in Hollywood with the bewitching movie star Gloria Swanson. His relationship with his mother, on the other hand, was warm and loving, and she doted on him.

"As a child, his mother adored him," said Mary Lou McCarthy. "He was the firstborn child, the firstborn son."

While Joe was growing up, Sundays were special. The Kennedys often had guests, and Joe's sister Margaret recalled that their mother would serve her own baked bread, Boston baked beans, relishes, and mincemeat and apple pie, along with cold sliced ham or chicken. After dinner, the family would sing songs around a Steinway baby grand. While he was often off key, Joe would sing such Irish favorites as "Danny Boy," "Molly Malone," or "Peg o' My Heart."

Mary Kennedy was friendly with an Irish family that was having a tough time, so she took in their son, Johnny Ryan. He lived with the family from age eight to sixteen, according to Joe's sister Margaret. "It wasn't a case of charity," she said, "because it was just the kind of thing one Irish family would do for another back then." Perhaps it was also a way of replacing Francis Benedict, the younger brother who had died in 1892.

Joe attended the Xaverian and later Assumption parochial schools. On the side, he had odd jobs as most teenagers do. He sold newspapers after school to sailors, passengers, and shopkeepers on the Cunard Line docks. He also sold peanuts and candy to passengers on the excursion boat the SS *Excelsior* and to sightseers along Long Wharf on the Boston side of the harbor. He worked in a haberdashery, and he ran errands for Columbia Trust Company. At one point, Joe lighted coal stoves for Orthodox Jews forbidden by their religion to work on the Sabbath.

In one of his first partnerships, Joe joined his friend Ronan Grady in raising squab, a delicacy they sold to poultry stores. To increase their store of fledgling pigeons, the two would snatch a few of Grady's pigeons and hop on the back of slow-moving coal wagons, which were drawn by two horses, then alight at Boston Common. There, they would release the pigeons from under their shirts. By evening, the pigeons would return to their coops with two or more guests from among the wild pigeons on the common.

When the Larkin Soap Company offered the reward of a bookcase to the person who gathered the most coupons enclosed in its products, Joe persuaded friends to sell soap throughout East Boston, his sister Loretta recalled. He kept the coupons and won the bookcase. Whether he gave his friends anything in return is not clear. His choice of books to fill the bookcase was telling. Besides the rags-to-riches novels of Horatio Alger, he had a collection of the works of Mark Twain, including *Tom Sawyer*. Like Tom Sawyer, Joe was adept at persuading people to help him even if it was against their own interests.

Joe also organized a local baseball team called the Assumptions, for Our Lady of Assumption Church, which he attended on Sumner Street. The games drew so many people that he hired a ballpark and sold tickets, turning a profit.

While both Joe's parents were high achievers, Mary in particular was determined that Joe would be on an equal footing with the WASPs who dominated Boston society. She insisted that when delivering packages for Columbia Trust, he introduce himself as "Joe" rather than "Joe Kennedy," thus hiding his Irish heritage. More than her husband, P.J., it was Mary who decided that, rather than continue in the Catholic school system, Joe should attend Boston Latin School. Then at Dartmouth Street and Warren Avenue in Boston's South End, Boston Latin was a monument to the Brahmins. Its alumni included Cotton Mather, Benjamin Franklin, John Hancock, and John Quincy Adams.

On September 11, 1901, Joe took the ferry to attend his first day of class in the seventh grade. But he proved to be a poor student. The transcript of his grades in his last four years at Boston Latin shows that while he had a C average in Greek, he had a D plus average in algebra and a D average in English, in elementary Latin, in history, and in geometry. He failed elementary physics, elementary French, and advanced Latin.

In fact, Joe had to repeat his junior year. While that could hardly be concealed from his public record, his overall grades never became public knowledge. When asked how he did in school, Joe would later say he had done "okay."

In the social and sports arenas, Joe did far better. The *Latin School Register* lists him as class president. He was in the School Cadets, a drill team. It would be as close as he would ever get to serving in the military. In 1907, he won the cup offered by Mayor Fitzgerald, his future father-in-law, for having a batting average of .580 in the Seven League School Games in the Boston area.

When Joe graduated on June 20, 1908, the Boston Latin yearbook predicted he would make his living "in a very roundabout way."

Based on his grades, Joe Kennedy should not have been admitted to any college, let alone Harvard. Yet astoundingly, the admissions committee voted to admit him. Ironically, Joe would later use his Irish background as a badge of honor, claiming he had had to fight anti-Irish prejudice. But the truth was that that bulwark of the Boston Brahmin, Harvard College, had grossly bent its own standards to let Joe in.

The only plausible explanation is that the committee knew he was the son of one of the most influential politicians in the state. It is also likely that John F. Fitzgerald, who had been mayor of Boston for more than five years, made a call to the college at P.J.'s request. Fitzgerald and P.J. constantly traded favors. One of Fitzgerald's first acts as mayor was to reappoint P.J. Kennedy wire commissioner. Moreover, Joe had been dating Fitzgerald's daughter Rose. While Fitzgerald was not pushing the romance, he had no objections to it, either.

◆ ◆ ◆

A pretty girl with agate eyes and jet black hair, Rose Elizabeth Fitzgerald was born on July 22, 1890, the first child of John Francis Fitzgerald and Mary Josephine "Josie" Hannon. Like P.J.'s parents, Fitzgerald's parents, Thomas Fitzgerald and Rose Mary Murray, had come over from County Wexford in Ireland. Fitzgerald was born on February 11, 1863, five years after P.J. Despite his short stature—he grew to be five feet, seven inches—Fitzgerald boasted that he could take on any of his school chums. Like Joe, he attended Boston Latin School. He had begun his first year at Harvard Medical

School when his father died. He dropped out to help support the rest of the family. Fitzgerald landed a job as a clerk at the Boston Customs House. He ran for the Boston Common Council and won the critically important support of the ward boss Lomasney. Fitzgerald portrayed himself as the representative of the poor and downtrodden against the established leaders. "Down with the bosses!" was his campaign slogan.

Many thought of Fitzgerald, who invariably sang "Sweet Adeline" at campaign rallies, as a "lovable old windbag," as Joe Kane, Joe's cousin, put it. "The only reason he had a head was to give him a place to park his hat," Kane said.

Fitzgerald, who wore baggy pants, owed his nickname, "Honey Fitz," to his syrupy speeches. He always referred to his section of Boston as the "dear old North End." Nevertheless, he compiled an impressive record. Elected a state senator in 1892, he served simultaneously with P.J. Beginning in December 1895, he served three terms in the United States House of Representatives. With his election on December 12, 1905, he became Boston mayor, serving three terms.

Owing to a little blackmail, Fitzgerald did not run for a fourth term as mayor. He had been seeing Elizabeth Ryan, a prostitute known as Toodles. Then–Roxbury congressman James Michael Curley found out about the affair in the fall of 1913 and sent a letter to Fitzgerald's wife, Josie, threatening to make the affair public if her husband did not withdraw as a candidate. (Curley himself was no altar boy, having been sentenced to federal prison in 1904 for taking a postal exam for someone else.) When Fitzgerald did not withdraw his candidacy, Curley announced through a university professor a series of lectures, including "Great Lovers in History: From Cleopatra to Toodles." On December 17, 1913, Edward E. Moore, the mayor's assistant secretary, announced that Fitzgerald would not be running after all. A ditty began making the rounds: "A whisky glass and Toodles' ass/made a horse's ass/out of Honey Fitz."

Rose was born in the Fitzgerald home at 4 Garden Court Street, a narrow, quiet alley behind Hanover Street in the

North End. The North End had been the center of colonial Boston and was rich with reminders of its role in securing America's freedom from the British—the old North Church and Paul Revere's house.

Rose's father and P.J. often met at each other's homes. The Fitzgeralds vacationed two or three weeks each summer at Old Orchard Beach in Maine. There, when Rose was five, she first met the freckled Joe—then seven. Neither recalled the meeting; they later realized they had met when a photograph surfaced of them posing with their families.

Like her mother, Rose was deeply religious. Having moved to the suburb of Concord, one of her fondest memories was of attending mass there. However, as a congressman from Boston living in Concord, Fitzgerald was accused of being a carpetbagger. So, when Rose was fourteen, the family moved back to Boston. From her home at 39 Welles Avenue in Dorchester, Rose could walk to Dorchester High School on Talbot Avenue in Codman Square.

In the spring of 1906, Joe invited Rose to a dance at Boston Latin School. Significantly, this was six months after her father had become mayor of Boston. Joe was mastering the art of weaving social connections into power.

"My father refused to let me go," recalled Rose. "He disapproved of a girl of sixteen going around to dances in strange places and meeting people who might cause trouble."

Fitzgerald was known as "Little Napoleon," and Rose knew it would be useless to argue. Joe invited someone else. But the next spring, when Rose was almost seventeen and a senior, she invited Joe to a graduation dance at Dorchester High. This time, the dance would be in the afternoon and nearby. Her father let her go.

They continued to see each other at friends' homes, always with adults on the premises. Pushing back the parlor furniture, they would drink homemade lemonade and dance. Rose said her father did not object to Joe. "How could he?" she said. "There was nothing to object to. The only fault that anyone could find with him was that he had to take an extra year at Boston Latin to make up some languages. . . . And he ended up with an academic record good enough to be admitted to Harvard: one of the few Boston boys of Irish descent in that era to go there."

While P.J. Kennedy and Fitzgerald had been at opposite ends of a previous political fight, they were now allies and fellow members of the board of strategy. Rose "never heard, then nor later, either say an uncomplimentary thing about the other," she claimed.

Unlike Joe, Rose earned relatively good grades: In her last year at Dorchester High, she got As in English and French and Bs in Latin, German, algebra II, and chemistry. After being voted prettiest senior, Rose graduated on June 23, 1906. She was just sixteen.

In her choice of colleges, her father again intervened. She wanted to go to Wellesley College, but William Cardinal O'Connell had decreed that every good Catholic should go to Catholic schools. Honey Fitz insisted that she go to the Convent of the Sacred Heart at 264 Commonwealth Avenue in Boston. She later attended the Blumenthal Academy of the Sacred Heart at Vaals, Holland, and Sacred Heart Convent at Manhattanville in New York.

"I am an angel," Rose wrote in a letter after she had been at Blumenthal a few months. "I arise at six o'clock (fifteen minutes earlier than the others) and go to meditation nearly every morning. So you see my piety is increasing."

Having graduated on June 10, 1910, Rose became a special student at the New England Conservatory of Music. She made her debut in Boston Catholic society at a coming-out party at the family home on January 2, 1911. While she was away at college, Joe and Rose had corresponded with each other. Now twenty-two, Joe attended her party.

◆ ◆ ◆

Joe began his freshman year at Harvard on October 1, 1908. At Harvard, being accepted at the right clubs was almost as important as graduating. Joe did not make the most prestigious clubs, like Porcellian or AAD, known as "final" clubs. Membership in these clubs generally guaranteed acceptance after graduation to the ultra-WASPish Somerset or Union Clubs of Boston. But Joe did make the Institute of 1770 and Delta Kappa Epsilon—the Dickey, an inner club within the institute. He also joined Delta Upsilon, Hasty Pudding, the St. Paul Catholic Club, and the Boston Latin Club.

For his initiation into Hasty Pudding, Joe dressed as a ten-year-old girl. Carrying a large doll, he sang "Oh, You Beautiful Doll."

Oscar W. Haussermann, a classmate and friend, said that both Hasty Pudding and ΔKE were perfectly respectable clubs, but Joe was hurt that he had not been chosen for the more elite ones.

While Joe later claimed he did "all right" in college, the truth was his record was less than respectable. In his freshman year, he got Cs in English, German, government, and Latin and a B in economics. The next year, he got a D in economics, a C and a D in history, a B in education, and Cs in German and government. In his junior year, he got Cs in comparative literature and history and Ds in social ethics, German, English, and economics. In his final year, he got Cs in comparative literature, economics, English, government, and history, and a B in public speaking.

On October 14, 1911, Harvard informed Joe's father that the college had had to admonish Joe for failing to hand in his study cards on time without a good reason. "Boys are expected to make out their list of studies and present the card before six o'clock on Friday, the second day of the term," the school wrote to P.J. Kennedy. "We try to make our rules few and simple, holding the boys up merely to the standard that they must observe as men when they get into the world." (By then, P.J. had moved to 159 Locust Street in Winthrop, a fashionable Boston suburb.)

On March 2, 1912, Harvard informed Joe that he could

drop Economics 18, as he had requested. Joe would later boast that Harvard had asked him to drop the course because he was doing so badly. "It was a course in banking and finance, what I was to make my living at," he later told a reporter.

As unimpressive as his grades were, they undoubtedly would have been worse were it not for Joe's practice of slipping bottles of Haig & Haig Pinch Bottle Scotch supplied by his father to his professors. Known today as Haig Pinch, the fifteen-year-old Scotch sells for $300 a case. Like his father, Joe neither smoke nor drank. But he had learned from his father what a free drink could buy. For the rest of his life, Joe carried on the practice of supplying free liquor to people whose influence he sought. Instead of supplying bottles, he would send cases of Scotch. Instead of sending them to Harvard professors, he would send them to the likes of President Franklin D. Roosevelt and *New York Times* columnist and Washington bureau chief Arthur Krock.

In his freshman year, Joe lived in Room 50 at what was then called Perkins Hall. In his sophomore and junior years, he stayed in Room 27 at what was then Holyoke Hall. In his senior year, he roomed in Room 26 and later 28 at Hollis Hall, which is now a freshman dorm. If Joe did not excel academically, he forged connections with other classmates who would help him later in business. He also learned how to take advantage of his political connections to further his financial security. To be sure, Joe's later claim that he worked his way through college was more mythology: His father paid for his college expenses. But Joe was always looking for ways to make more money.

During vacation after his sophomore year, Joe became a partner with his classmate Joseph Donovan in a sightseeing bus they bought for $600. Speaking through a megaphone, Joe related the sights to the passengers while Donovan drove. The Colonial Auto-Sightseeing Company was a financial success in large part because Mayor Fitzgerald increased for

Joe's competitor the fee required to operate buses out of South Station. For two months of work, Joe and Donovan cleared a profit of $5,000.

During the summer after his graduation from Boston Latin, Joe had played on an amateur college baseball team in Bethlehem, New Hampshire. The manager, Henry J. "Harry" O'Meara, told him the *Boston Globe* wanted a stringer to cover tennis, social news, golf, and baseball. Joe took the job, but when Harvard classmate John Conley expressed envy, Joe told Conley he could write the pieces as long as he got the money and the byline.

Now that he was at Harvard, Joe tried out for the baseball team each year. While he promoted the myth of being a baseball standout, according to *The H Book of Harvard Athletics*, there "were no stars" in 1911, the year he lettered in baseball—and just barely lettered, at that. For while Joe had made the freshman team, he could not win a place in his sophomore and junior years. Joe was a slow runner, and his batting eye not as good as it once was. But in the Kennedy household, nothing stood in the way of success—certainly not good sportsmanship.

Knowing that team captain Charles B. "Chick" McLaughlin wanted to open a movie theater after graduation, Joe arranged for friends of his father to promise McLaughlin a license to operate a theater if he would put Joe in the last game of the season against Yale. Joe's appearance in the game would guarantee him a letter. And so, in the top of the ninth inning, with Harvard leading 4 to 1, Yale had two outs and Kennedy was sent in to cover first base. The last Yale batter hit a fly ball and Kennedy caught it, to finish the game. McLaughlin, the winning pitcher, assumed Joe would hand over the game ball to him, as tradition required. Instead, Joe put it in his pocket and walked away.

It was an approach that would mark Kennedy's life. For Joe, it was not *how* you play the game but whether you win or lose.

"Joe was bright, aggressive, and aware of the uses of influence," said his classmate Ralph Lowell. "Joe would do anything to get what he wanted."

◆ ◆ ◆

Rooting for Joe in the stands that day at the Harvard–Yale game was Rose. When she was in town, Joe continued to date her. He invited her to the junior prom at Harvard, but she could not go because her parents had already planned a trip with her to Palm Beach.

"Now remember," Joe would say at the beginning of each season, "you are invited to the Cecilian Club dance, the Newman Club dance at Harvard, the Ace of Clubs dance, and any other dances I can't think of now—remember that I invited you to all of them." When her mother was a chaperone at these dances, Rose would have to attend with her. But then Rose would dance with Joe.

What necking Joe managed to engage in with Rose did not proceed very far. As she wrote in her memoirs, *Times to Remember*, she believed that "to everything there is a season, and a time for every purpose. There was courtship, there was the discovery of love, there was engagement, there was marriage, there was parenthood."

Whether Joe ever loved Rose, or whether he saw her merely as a stepping-stone for his own aspirations, is open to debate. "I don't think any of the Kennedys were capable of deep emotional attachment," said Janet Des Rosiers, Joe's mistress. What is clear is that Rose was never Joe's exclusive love, and that Joe would continue to use her father to gain what he wanted.

Arthur Goldsmith, a Harvard classmate, friend, and later a partner of Joe's in a New York brokerage business, recalled that even as Joe was courting Rose just before his Harvard graduation, he and Joe were dating two young women from *The Pink Lady*, a musical comedy. For Joe, it was important not only to conquer shapely young women, but to be seen with them. It gave him a feeling of power and success. Above all, Joe wanted to be accepted, and this was one of his ways of achieving that.

One day, the four of them ran into Rose while they were roller skating. "He talked himself out of that one," Goldsmith said.

On June 20, 1912, Joe, twenty-three, graduated with 497 others from Harvard. His classmates included twenty-six other Catholics and thirty Jews. Nearly all the rest were Protestants. In response to a Harvard questionnaire, he said he planned after graduation to enter a "manufacturing business." But Hugh Nawn, a classmate at Harvard who was also a suitor of Rose's, recalled that Joe said he wanted to be on his own, perhaps in the banking field.

3

THE BRAHMINS

If Joe Kennedy had learned nothing about financial affairs at Harvard, that would soon change. In September 1912, his father got him a job as a state bank examiner. Willie Sutton said he robbed banks because that was where the money was, and for someone interested in making money—as Joe was— a bank was a good place to start.

As a bank examiner, Joe learned how to read a balance sheet, evaluate credit, and value assets. Even more useful, he learned about the confidential affairs of companies and individuals who had credit lines with major Boston banks. He found out which companies were in trouble and which had extra cash, who was planning new products or acquisitions and who was about to be liquidated.

"That bank examiner's job took him all over the state and laid bare the condition of every bank he visited," said his Harvard classmate Ralph Lowell, who went on to become chairman of Boston Safe Deposit & Trust Company. "He acquired information of value to himself and others."

Just what Joe did with the information Lowell did not say. But one of his later strategies was to obtain inside information about troubled companies from banks, then drive their stock down so he could buy them more cheaply. While still on the state payroll as a bank examiner, Joe made an acquisition that could well have been aided by inside information. With Harry O'Meara, the former manager of the Bethlehem baseball team, and another partner, he bought Old Colony Realty Associates Inc., an investment company at 30 State Street. Joe turned the company from an old-line investment firm into one that made money on the misery of others. Under Joe's direction, the company specialized in taking over defaulted home mortgages. He would then paint the houses and resell them at far higher prices. By the time the company was dissolved during World War I, Joe's $1,000 investment had grown to a third of the firm's $75,000 in assets.

In the summer of 1913, Joe took his first trip to Europe, sailing with two Harvard classmates. Finding that the ship's imperial suite was empty, Joe paid the purser $33 extra per person to give it to him and his friends. They sailed to Europe like kings.

Upon returning, Joe learned—most likely through his job—that First Ward National Bank was planning a takeover bid to acquire Columbia Trust Company, in which his father still held a minority interest. Afraid that other stockholders would vote to sell, Joe borrowed $45,000 from family members and friends to obtain control of the bank and keep it independent.

On November 14, 1913, Joe resigned as an assistant bank examiner. Having worked for the state for only a year, Joe embellished his credentials on the résumé he submitted to newspapers and to Harvard for his class report. There, he claimed he had worked as a bank examiner from 1912 to 1914, instead of to 1913. The pattern of holding jobs for only a year or two, then claiming he had held them longer, would continue for the rest of his life. A later FBI background report on Joe based on examination of employment records found the discrepancies, which in some cases amounted to dates that were off by as many as two years.

On January 20, 1914, Joe was elected president of Columbia Trust. At twenty-five, he was the youngest bank president in the country, or so he told the press. Whether it was true or not, no one knows. Most young executives would rather not highlight their age. But like Joe's tale of beating the Brahmins, Joe chose to portray himself as the underdog and use his age to gain publicity. For Joe was a master at public relations. Witty, direct, and charming, Joe would talk to reporters off the record, making them think he was giving them big scoops, when in fact he was feeding them his own inventions. Now Joe issued press releases bragging about his takeover of the bank without mentioning that Columbia Trust had been owned by his father and his friends.

"Bank President at the Age of 25," said the headline in the *Boston Herald*.

Noting that Joe worked at the bank fourteen to sixteen hours a day, the Hearst newspapers ran a series on Joe the young bank president. This prompted a letter to the editor from a Brooklyn bank clerk, who said he had looked up the bank's financial statement. If it took Joe that many hours to manage the bank, the clerk said, he must be either "stupid or dumb."

Soon, the *Boston Post* and other papers were saying Joe planned to be a millionaire by the age of thirty-five.

"I don't know whether Joe had a press agent in those days, but the *Boston Post* would put his picture on page one at the slightest provocation," said Oscar Haussermann, his Harvard friend.

What the stories neglected to mention was that much of the money Joe borrowed to assume control of Columbia Trust came from other family members who were never repaid. Kerry McCarthy, Joe's grandniece who interviewed some of those people for a research paper she wrote, said, "I found money was loaned to him by family members and not repaid. . . . Since it was family, he didn't feel there was a need to."

Perhaps one reason family members did not demand repayment was Joe's reputation for retaliation. For Joe could turn off his charm just as easily as he could turn it on. Much later, Gertrude Ball, who was Joe's secretary in his New York office for twenty-nine years, would recall that Joe was "mercurial." He could be "extremely charming. If he wanted to turn it on, he could. He would be dictating a letter and someone would come in whom he was happy to see. The smile would go on. The man would walk out and he would be real sober. He could turn it on or off."

The fact that someone had helped Joe—as Chick McLaughlin had helped him win a baseball letter at Harvard—often meant Joe would later turn on that same individual.

"Joe's a hard-headed, practical man, and former friendships don't mean as much to him as they do to other people," said Ralph Lowell, Joe's Harvard classmate.

Early on, Joe had developed a method of operating that was both secretive and compartmented. No one besides Joe knew all of his activities. Years later, Joseph Timilty, who was one of Joe's closest friends, said he was not his confidant. "He never confided in anybody," Timilty said. At the bank, "There was a silencer put on the mouthpiece of his telephone so that people could not hear what was being said," according to Ethel C. Turner, his secretary at the bank.

Joe was tightfisted with the bank's money. Bank examiners in 1918 found only three loans that they classified as being of "doubtful value" or "secured by collateral of doubtful value." During his three-year tenure, deposits would soar to $1,055,759 from $580,654. But loans, which rose to $822,109 from $526,112, did not increase proportionately. This suggests that rather than investing in home mortgages or commercial loans that would benefit local residents, Joe invested the excess funds in bonds or similar obligations. While safer, they did not promote the interests of local bank customers.

A week after Joe became president of the bank, Mayor Fitzgerald appointed him president of the Collateral Loan Company. This was essentially a city-owned pawn shop that lent money to the poor using articles they offered as collateral. Profits were distributed to the needy for fuel in the winter.

Joe cemented the bond to his benefactor by becoming engaged to Rose on June 1, 1914. In deciding to marry Rose, Joe was following an Irish proverb: "Marry a mountain girl and you marry the whole mountain." Joe had tied his destiny to the most powerful man in Boston. Who needed Brahmins when he had the mayor behind him? In introducing himself, Joe would never fail to mention that he was the son-in-law of the mayor of Boston. Fitzgerald was Joe's secret weapon, so much so that in later years, friends would successfully rattle Joe before he was about to tee off at golf by mentioning his father-in-law's help.

◆ ◆ ◆

On October 7, 1914, William Cardinal O'Connell married Joe, twenty-five, and Rose, twenty-four, in an ornate private chapel connected to the cardinal's residence at 25 Granby Street. Rose looked beautiful in a white satin dress trimmed with roses. She wore a two-carat diamond engagement ring. A reception for 450 guests followed at the home of the mayor.

After a two-week honeymoon at the stately Greenbrier Hotel in White Sulphur Springs, West Virginia, Joe and Rose moved into a nine-room, two-and-a-half-story gray frame house at 83 Beals Street in Brookline. A Boston suburb, Brookline was then largely Protestant. Paying $2,000 down, they purchased the house for $6,500. Soon, Joe bought his first car, a black Ford. Rose loved to tell the story of one of their first rides, when he accidentally drove into a poorly marked construction site, wrecking the car.

On Saturday nights, they attended the Boston Symphony together. In later years, Joe would hide his love of classical music, thinking it branded him a sissy. But in the evening, his home would be filled with the sounds of Beethoven or Bach recordings played on a wind-up gramophone.

Almost exactly nine months after their honeymoon, on July 25, 1915, Rose fulfilled the "sacred role" for which the nuns had prepared her. Their first child, Joseph Patrick Kennedy Jr., was born in a cottage they had rented along Nantasket Beach.

Regularly after that, Rose performed the mission spelled out for her in the Catechism, bearing eight more children. For Rose believed sex was for procreation only, while Joe saw it as a way of asserting control and establishing his own self-worth. Joe's philandering was constant and well known. He boasted of his conquests, for example, to Guy Currier, a well-connected Brahmin lawyer who would turn out to be critically important in Joe's rise. Currier was a Renaissance man whose library at 8 Commonwealth Avenue included all the classics, all of which he had read. "He knew art, architecture, jewelry, and ballet," said his granddaughter, Anne Anable. "He had a sense of obligation and would help others who were starting out in their careers."

Impressed by Joe, Currier took him under his wing. He thought Joe might become a lawyer, and he let him use his office. If Currier did not particularly approve of Joe's unfaithfulness, it was not something he dwelled on, for Currier himself had a mistress.

As a friend of Gordon Abbott, chairman of the Massachusetts Electric Company, Currier persuaded him to nominate Joe to the board of the utility. Joe was elected on May 29, 1917. Referring to the legendary Boston Brahmin family, Joe asked James A. Fayne, an associate of his, "Do you know a better way to meet the Saltonstalls?" when Fayne asked Joe why he had chosen to join the board.

Joe was elected the same day that Rose gave birth to John "Jack" Fitzgerald Kennedy, a small, blue-eyed boy, at the family home in Brookline.

A week later, with World War I already in progress, Washington announced plans to draft young men in case the United States entered the war. By August 4, 1917, the government announced that draft resisters would be executed. Most of Joe's friends from Harvard had already volunteered to serve, but Joe had no intention of fighting. Joe had already been placed in Class 1, subject to immediate call-up. Currier came to the rescue, for he was a lobbyist for the Bethlehem Shipbuilding Corporation at Fore River in Quincy, Massachusetts. Citing the fact that Joe was the son-in-law of Mayor Fitzgerald, Currier asked Fore River to hire him. But Joe Kennedy knew nothing about shipbuilding. When Currier could not get the shipyard to hire Joe, Mayor Fitzgerald made it known that he would be pleased if the shipyard took his son-in-law. In October 1917, Joe became assistant general manager at $15,000 a year. Joe resigned his position at Columbia Trust, and his father replaced him.

Now that he was helping the war effort, Joe appealed his classification to the local draft board. When the board turned down Joe's appeal, Joe got top executives at Fore River to wire Washington officials to get him excused.

Then employing two thousand, the Fore River yard was engaged in a frantic effort to build destroyers for use in the war. Soon, the shipyard was smashing production records, constructing thirty-seven destroyers for the war effort.

Joe would later boast that he had directed the efforts and had faced down Franklin D. Roosevelt, then assistant secretary of the navy, over a dispute about payment for ships built for the Argentine navy. According to this story, the Argentineans had not paid for ships previously delivered. Charles M. Schwab, the legendary chairman of Bethlehem Steel, the shipyard's parent company, refused to release any more destroyers until payment had been made. Since it was considered in the interest of the United States to arm the

Argentineans, Roosevelt demanded that the shipyard deliver the new ships. Schwab was said to have sent Joe to tell Roosevelt the ships would not be released. Soon Roosevelt sent United States Navy tugboats to Fore River with an escort of armed marines to take the ships for the Argentineans.

The trouble with the story was that it came from Joe's lips, or from his cronies'. If the navy had indeed confiscated ships built by Bethlehem Steel, it would have been front-page news. In fact, said Daniel Strohmeier, who later was vice president of Bethlehem Steel in charge of shipbuilding, Joe did little beyond collect his salary at Fore River.

"Joe was just accommodated to skip the draft during World War I because of a lot of pressure from his father-in-law, Honey Fitz," Strohmeier said. "I learned this while I was there. He was given some kind of an office job. . . . He didn't impress anybody who lasted longer than he did." Moreover, the former Bethlehem executive said he knew of no dispute with Roosevelt.

Seven months after the armistice was signed, Joe left the shipyard. Having avoided the draft, he had no more need to work there. Joe had come to know Galen Stone, a fellow board member at Massachusetts Electric and a partner in the venerable stock brokerage firm of Hayden, Stone and Company. Joe concocted a story about how he persuaded Stone to hire him because he was so good at selling ships. The truth was that Mayor Fitzgerald promised to swing business to Stone if he hired Joe. Honey Fitz delivered on that promise. For example, Fitzgerald called his friend Bernard Baruch, the financier, to talk about an investment he was considering, then put Joe on the line so Joe could get to know him and presumably obtain some of his brokerage business.

In July 1919, Joe started as a customers' broker, then became manager of the Stock Exchange Department. Located at 87 Milk Street, Hayden, Stone was in the heart of Boston's financial district, within easy walking distance of the Boston Curb Exchange. At the time, it was not unusual for young Irishmen to go into Boston banks and brokerage houses.

"After all, the money of the Irish was as green as anybody else's," said Joe's Harvard friend Ralph Lowell. "What was unusual was for an Irishman to rise—and Joe plainly wanted to rise as far as fast as he could." In that respect, Lowell said, Joe's political connections did not hurt.

Galen Stone taught his protégé how to make huge sums off unsuspecting investors by trading on inside information. Stone sat on the boards of twenty-two companies whose securities he sponsored. One was the Pond Coal Company, of which he was chairman. Stone was about to agree to acquisition of the company by Henry Ford. The company held mineral rights to twenty-two thousand acres of land in Kentucky and supplied soft coal for the production of illuminating gas. Before the public was told about the plan, Joe bought fifteen thousand shares at $16, later selling the stock for $45 a share. In nine months, he made a profit of $675,000 on his investment of $24,000, the rest being borrowed money. While the practice of using inside information was not then illegal, it was unethical. Stone breached his fiduciary duty to his stockholders, while Joe made money because of his privileged position at Hayden, Stone. Joe told his Harvard friend Tom Campbell: "Tommy, it's so easy to make money in the market we'd better get in before they pass a law against it." It was easy if one was willing to breach trust. Yet Joe also told his friend Oscar Haussermann that he had been wiped out three times in those early days.

At the end of 1922, Stone retired, and Joe left the firm on December 30, 1922. Joe took a separate office connected by a flight of stairs to the Hayden, Stone office. Nonetheless, on his résumé, Joe claimed he had worked for Hayden, Stone until 1924, two years later. Timothy A. McInerny, a *Boston Post* editor who later explored buying the paper with Joe, recalled that the sign on Joe's door said, "Joseph P. Kennedy—Banker." While he was no longer connected with the firm, he did much of his trading through Hayden, Stone.

Besides using inside information improperly, Joe made fabulous sums through what were known as stock pools. This was a way of manipulating the market by forming a syndicate and arranging for the members to trade stock back and forth. By bidding the price of the stock higher, the pool members created the appearance that the public was bidding up the price. In fact, the syndicate members retained the profits. When the trading public bit by joining in the action, the syndicate members sold out, leaving the public with losses. Joe called the practice "advertising" the stock.

Occasionally, Joe manipulated the market for a fee at the request of companies. For example, in April 1924, when Checker Cab Company attempted to acquire John D. Hertz's Yellow Cab Company, the Hertz forces asked Joe to ward off the raid. He set up a command post at the Waldorf-Astoria, where he had a ticker installed. For several weeks, Joe arranged trades throughout the country. The disconcerting movement of the stock so confused Checker Cab that it called off the raid. When his campaign had proved to be a success, he received a handsome fee. Because his role made him look like a good guy, he made sure the press knew about it. Later, Hertz became convinced that, on the side, Joe had sold his stock short so that he could profit even more on Yellow Cab.

It was all part of what McInerny said was Joe's chameleon-like nature. "This man is a many-sided fellow," he said. "He exhibits a different side of his nature to different people."

Guy Currier found that out too late. Having helped save Joe from the draft and gotten him on the board of Massachusetts Electric, the Boston Brahmin would later discover that Joe had double-crossed him. He became embittered for the rest of his life.

◆ ◆ ◆

On January 29, 1919, the Eighteenth Amendment was ratified, and the following year, the Volstead Act, as it was known, became effective. It prohibited the manufacture, sale, transportation, or importation of "intoxicating liquors" for "beverage purposes." For Joe, the law represented an opportunity to make huge profits. Having grown up in a family that made its money on liquor, it was natural for Joe to continue in that tradition. It was all part of a continuum: After Prohibition, he would become the largest distributor of Scotch in the country.

Having given up his office next to Hayden, Stone in 1924, Joe operated out of Guy Currier's office or out of his home, which now was a twelve-room house at 51 Abbottsford Road at the corner of Naples Road in Brookline. (The address was later changed to 131 Naples Road.) The Kennedys had paid $16,000 for the home.

Joe ordered liquor from overseas distillers and supplied it to organized crime syndicates that picked up the liquor on the shore. Frank Costello would later say that Joe approached him for help in smuggling liquor. Joe would have the liquor dumped at a so-called Rum Row—a transshipment point where police were paid to look the other way—and Costello would then take over. Costello was allied with men like Meyer Lansky, Joe Adonis, Louis "Lepke" Buchalter, Abner "Longy" Zwillman, Dutch Schultz, and Charles "Lucky" Luciano. They distributed the liquor, fixed the prices, established quotas, and paid off law enforcement and politicians. They enforced their own law with machine guns, usually calling on experts who did bloody hits on contract.

"The way he [Costello] talked about him [Joe]," recalled columnist John Miller, "you had the sense that they were close during Prohibition, and then something happened. Frank said that he helped Kennedy become wealthy."

Ten days before he died, Costello, in his raspy voice, told author Peter Maas the same story. Costello was then considering collaborating with Maas on a book about his life. "Frank Costello said he [Joe] was in the liquor business," Maas said. "At the time, it was illegal. Frank didn't lie. It was during Prohibition."

When the story appeared in the New York Times, Stephen E. Smith, who had married Joe's daughter Jean, said that a check of Joe's records revealed no such relationship. However, Joseph "Joe Bananas" Bonanno, the former Mafia boss, also stated that Joe's people unloaded whisky during Prohibition at Sag Harbor in Long Island, New York. On May 1, 1983, Bonanno made the same claim to Mike Wallace on CBS' *60 Minutes*.

A major Boston liquor distributor said Joe promised a Chicago buddy that if he got Al Capone's business, he would give him a 25 percent cut. The man got the business, but Joe then fired him and hounded him so he could not find another job.

Besides importing Scotch, Joe bought rum from Jacob M. Kaplan. Kaplan, who was from Massachusetts, made molasses and rum in Cuba and the West Indies during Prohibition. Kaplan went on to acquire Welch's Grape Juice Company in 1945.

The profits were princely. The best Scotch cost $45 a case on Saint-Pierre and Miquelon, a group of eight small, craggy islands in the North Atlantic Ocean about sixteen miles south of Newfoundland, Canada. The islands' ice-free ports were perfect for whisky shippers. Since they were under the French flag, the territory imposed no high Canadian duty. The cost of shipping the goods to the local Rum Row—often sleepy towns in Long Island—added another $10 to each case. Overhead, labor, and bribes cost another $10, making the total expense $65 a case or $325,000 for a five-thousand-case shipment. The Scotch was often mixed with other liquids, diluting it by half. It was then repacked and sold to wholesalers for $85 a case. Thus after cutting, the net profit on an investment of $325,000 could be $525,000, a markup of roughly two thirds.

In 1922, Joe supplied the liquor for his tenth Harvard reunion at the Pilgrim Hotel in Plymouth, according to classmate Ralph Lowell. Three years later, Joe amplified his supplies when Columbia Trust Company, now headed by his father, bought Quincy Cold Storage Warehouse, which had supplies of liquor left over from before Prohibition.

Years later, Joe would implicitly confirm that he was a

bootlegger when he boasted as ambassador in London that he knew all about trade with the British: "On and off for 20 years I have more or less successfully traded with the English," he wrote to the State Department in October 1938. During that time, he had no other foreign trade. Thus Joe could only have been referring to his importation of liquor, first during Prohibition and then, beginning in 1930, as a legitimate distributor.

By the mid-1920s, *Fortune* estimated Joe's wealth at $2 million, equal to $15 million today. Yet since Joe had left Hayden, Stone in 1922, he had had no visible job. While he made hundreds of thousands of dollars manipulating the market, only bootlegging on a sizeable scale would account for such sudden and fabulous wealth.

When Rose read the story in a local newspaper, she asked her husband if it was true and, if so, why he hadn't told her they were rich. He brushed her off. "How could I tell you, when I didn't know it myself?" he said. As for Joe's occupation, Rose was not much interested. "My husband changed jobs so frequently I simply never knew what business he was in," she said. "It was mostly developing some movies and then, of course, there was the embassy in London and some jobs with the New Deal in Washington."

4

THE TRIBE

When Joe returned from New York after warding off the takeover of Yellow Cab, he met the latest member of his brood—Patricia, who had just been born on May 6, 1924. Three other children had followed Jack. Rose Marie Kennedy—known as Rosemary—was born on September 13, 1918. Then on February 20, 1920, Kathleen Kennedy, known as Kick, was born. On July 10, 1921, Eunice Mary Kennedy was born. And on November 20, 1925, Robert "Bobby" Kennedy was born. (At confirmation, he took the middle name Francis.)

Just before Patricia was born, Rose had moved back to her father's home on Welles Avenue, a move she would later say was to get some "rest." But it was more like a trial separation, for Joe was almost always away, and she at least suspected his extracurricular activities. During that time, Rose left the children in the hands of a nurse. After three weeks, Fitzgerald told her sternly one snowy night that the time had come to return to her family. "Your children need you, and your husband needs you," he said. "You *can* make things work out."

Before going home, Rose attended a religious retreat. From then on, she would turn to the Catholic church for solace rather than to her father. Within weeks of her return, she almost lost Jack to a bout with scarlet fever.

In the summer of 1922, Joe and Rose rented a house in Cohasset, where the country club rejected Joe for membership. Joe always attributed the rejection to the fact that he was an Irish Catholic. However, Louis Eaton, a former president of the club, said members who had voted against him told him they rejected him because of his "rascality."

Similarly, Augustus W. "Gus" Soule Jr., who helped found the Dexter School, a private school in Brookline where Joe sent his children, recalled how reluctant other trustees were to accept Joe's money when the school was started. Joe was "a trustee of Dexter School, a founding trustee, although he was not very popular because of what he had done in the stock and bond market," Soule said. "People would barely speak to him. But I guess they needed his money, and that was it."

By the summer of 1925, Joe and Rose had rented what was known as the Malcolm Cottage in Hyannis Port. Joe chose the area because he had been told by Charles Falvey, a wealthy Irish Catholic businessman from Brookline whose summer home was in Hyannis Port, that the Hyannis Port Country Club would accept him. "The basic reason Joe Kennedy came to Hyannis Port was that as an Irish Catholic, he could get into the country club," Rose's nephew Joseph F. Gargan said. Eventually, Joe and Rose would buy the house and make it their permanent home.

"The Cape," as New Englanders call it, was then a quiet enclave of wealthy Republican blue bloods. Hyannis Port consisted of some three hundred homes in Barnstable County, owned mostly by scions of the oil, banking, and steel industries. The Malcolm house on Marchant Avenue is a mile and

a half south of Hyannis and some sixty-five miles southeast
of Boston. It sits on 2.43 acres on Nantucket Sound.

Joe ran the family like a football team. He was the coach,
the manager, and the referee. Rose was the water boy, constantly filling the children's minds with trivia. The aim was
to win at everything, no matter what.

Thomas Bilodeau, a friend of Joe Jr.'s, recalled that everything centered on the father, who was "interesting, he had
stories to tell, his life was very exciting to people such as
myself. And the Kennedy boys, at least the two older boys
at the time, worshipped Mr. Kennedy, and their every thought
was upon what he was talking about."

"Everything was figured by how Uncle Joe would react to
it," said Mary Lou McCarthy, the daughter of Joe's sister
Loretta. "He was the yardstick by which we were all measured, whether it was sports, our school work, or our knowledge. 'Would Uncle Joe be proud of us?' Joe had charisma
before anyone used the word charisma."

"When Joe spoke, everyone hopped to," said Edward F.
McLaughlin Jr., a friend of Jack's who later became Massachusetts lieutenant governor. "We were lolling around on
the porch one day. The word came that he [Joe] was landing
at the airport. Everyone had to get a new activity. Everyone
hopped to, playing football. He didn't want to see you sitting
on your fanny. He drilled that into these people."

When Joe was home, he "ran the show. Then on down
the line," Bilodeau said. "Joe Jr. was next in command, and
although Jack might compete with him, and the other boys,
who were young, might argue with him, when Joe Jr. finally
made a decision, the rest of the family underneath him followed that decision." Tag football was played "as though it
was a scrimmage," said Bilodeau. "They just delighted in the
physical contact and the competition."

Yet the Kennedys' prowess at the game was more illusion
than reality. "I myself used to play in the touch football
games down there," said Dave Farrell, then managing editor
of the *Boston Herald*. "It always amused me, this myth about

them and touch football. You would think they were the greatest in touch football. I could have picked up any six kids off the streets in Dorchester where I grew up and kicked the crap out of them. Jack, Ted, and Bobby were not good athletes. But they created this myth that they were marvelous athletes."

Joe's need to control his environment manifested itself most often in his constant insistence that everyone be on time. "Dinner at Uncle Joe's began promptly at 7:15 o'clock, and no one was to be late," said Joe Gargan. "It was not just a point of discipline. The important thing was not to irritate Uncle Joe's favorite cook. One evening when I was somewhat late, Uncle Joe announced to me, 'If that cook leaves, Joey, you're going with her.'"

"Joe was a controlling person," said Mary Lou McCarthy. "He controlled everything. How everyone dressed, their table manners, their attitudes towards learning and religion and government."

One day, Joe asked Gargan to drive his new Cadillac from the dealer's showroom in Boston to Hyannis Port. On the Cape, Gargan, who was eighteen and had had his license a year, had an accident with a pickup truck.

"The right side [of the car] was banged up," he recalled. "When I drove it into the yard, everyone disappeared. They all ran in different directions. I told Aunt Rose about it. When Joe got up and came downstairs, he said, 'I understand you had a little accident with the car.' We looked at it, and the first thing he said was, 'Are you all right, Joey?' He said, 'They are waiting for you to play touch football. You better go down and play. But I expect you to drive it to Boston and get it fixed.'"

At the dinner table that night, Jack said, "Dad, I understand Joey had a little accident with your car."

Turning to Jack, he said, "Jack, if Joey Gargan causes me half as much difficulty as you do, I'll be happy. But I don't want to hear that car ever mentioned in this house again."

The children reported at 7 A.M. to their physical education

instructor for calisthenics. After breakfast, they had lessons in swimming, sailing, and tennis.

Joe entered his children in races when they were as young as six. "And if we won," Eunice recalled, "he got terribly enthusiastic. Daddy was always very competitive. The thing he always kept telling us was that coming in second was just no good." Later, Joe would tell a *New York Herald-Tribune* reporter that he never reproached the children if they came in second. "No," he said, "there is no point in finding fault."

"He didn't like anyone to be second best, and he expected you to prepare yourself better than the other fellow and then try harder than he did," K. LeMoyne Billings, Jack's friend, said. "Any other course of action in his mind suggested stupidity."

Feelings were repressed. Joe wanted the children to "be able to smile no matter how tough things were," Ted Kennedy recalled. "I don't want any sour pusses around here," he would say.

Over and over he told the children, "Kennedys don't cry." He inquired of each child about his or her weight and even found a discreet way to find out if they were having regular bowel movements. Joe listed which museums they should see when the boys visited Europe.

"We didn't have opinions in those days," said Jack of the conversation at the dinner table. "They were mostly monologues by my father. . . . It was mostly talk about some of the personalities that my father ran into and some of those he brought home." Jack said his mother was the "glue that holds our family together."

Right or wrong, family members were fiercely loyal to each other.

"We liked each other more than we liked other people, but I suppose that's natural," said Eunice.

"Years ago, we decided that our children were going to be our best friends and that we never could see too much of them," Rose said.

But Rose was stingy with gestures of affection and away

much of the time. "Mrs. Kennedy didn't say she loved her children," recalled Luella R. Hennessey, the nurse who for four decades took care of the Kennedy children. "It just wasn't said. It was all about respect. She respected them, and they respected her."

Over the years, Rose would become more and more disengaged, taking frequent trips to Paris to buy clothes. She had a prefabricated shack erected on the Hyannis Port property so she could "get away," as she put it. "It's solitary confinement, not splendor, I need," she explained. "Any mother will know what I mean." Jack lamented to a friend, "My mother is a nothing."

◆ ◆ ◆

In contrast to Rose, Joe had an urgent need to be surrounded by people. It was almost, said his mistress Janet Des Rosiers, as if he were afraid to be alone. Throughout his life, he would have a small circle of cronies who followed him wherever he went. Most of them were either on his payroll or derived some other financial benefit from their association.

Joe's closest aide was Edward E. Moore, the former assistant to Fitzgerald, for whom Joe would name his son Ted. Moore had begun working for Joe in 1915, just after Joe and Rose married. Moore had a dry wit and disarming manner. He was Joe's shadow throughout much of Joe's career.

Joseph Timilty, another friend, acted as a beard for Joe when he saw his girlfriends and made payoffs to boost Jack's political campaigns. Timilty had bushy eyebrows and hair parted down the middle. When Joe first met him, he was Boston police commissioner, the son of Joseph P. "Diamond Jim" Timilty, a paving contractor who was a ward leader from Roxbury and was elected a Massachusetts state senator nine times. As Boston police commissioner, Timilty distinguished himself by banning "indecent" magazines and books, including *Life*, and having vendors who sold such publications arrested. A grand jury investigated him for allegedly taking payoffs from racketeers, but it never brought an indictment. Timilty ran for mayor of Boston but was defeated. After his term expired as police commissioner, he became what he called a "houseguest" of Joe's, traveling everywhere with him.

"Timilty was a disgrace," said Robert Tonis, a former FBI agent based in Boston at the time. "I don't think he knew what the hell crime was. He was a big stuffed shirt."

Arthur J. Houghton, a former New York theater manager who had lived in Hollywood, was also on Joe's payroll. Joe first met him in 1917, when Houghton was manager of a New York musical show with "twenty-four beautiful chorus girls," as Houghton put it. Houghton was happy to introduce them to Joe and his friends. In a letter about an impending visit, Joe spelled it out: "I hope you will have all the good looking girls in your company looking forward with anticipation to meeting the high Irish of Boston because I have a gang around me that must be fed on wild meat. Lately they are so bad. As for me, I have too many troubles around to bother with such things at the present time. Everything may be better, however, when you arrive."

Later, Houghton accompanied Joe to London when Joe was ambassador. At least part of Houghton's salary was paid by the Motion Picture Producers' Association. Known as "Huxie," Houghton was Joe's court jester, much as Dave Powers would become Jack's court jester. Silver-haired, sophisticated, and suave, Houghton might be with Joe when he was discussing business with bankers. Having no idea of what they were talking about, Houghton would say solemnly, "What about the debentures?" The bankers would think he knew what he was talking about, and Joe would be amused.

Morton Downey was a third close friend. Joe met him in 1923 in Chicago, where Downey was singing with Paul Whiteman's band, faking playing the saxophone while he sang. Born in Wallingford, Connecticut, Downey had only finished high school. With big ears, long lashes, and a round face, he smoked cigars and bragged that he never finished his engagements until 4 A.M. He claimed that he ate three banana splits a day, and it showed. In his high, sweet tenor, Downey would sing "You'd Be So Nice to Come Home To" or "Danny Boy," "Rose of Travelee," "My Wild Irish Rose," "Where the River Shannon Flows," "It's the Same Old Shillelagh," "Molly Flannigan," or "That's How I Spell Ireland." He would later claim to have sung "When Irish Eyes Are Smiling" more than ten thousand times. He composed songs such as "Wabash Moon," which became his theme song.

At the height of his career, Downey was making $12,000 a week from radio. He became an idol of the airwaves in the 1930s and 1940s. Later, he sang in Coca-Cola commercials. At one point, Joe loaned Downey $500,000 without collateral so he could buy an interest in the Coca-Cola Bottling Company in New Haven, Connecticut. "My collateral is your character," Joe told the singer. The two were so close that Downey later bought a home on Squaw Island half a mile from the Kennedy home in Hyannis Port.

Downey's singing was not the only attribute that attracted Joe. While married to his first wife, Barbara Bennett, a movie star, Downey was known as a ladies' man who was said to have "made every girl in every chorus line" he worked with, according to Walter J. Trohan, a friend of Joe's and Downey's who was chief of the Washington bureau of the *Chicago Tribune*. Like Houghton, Downey passed along some of the gorgeous women to Joe.

"Mort did him favors in the department Joe liked best— girls," a confidant said. "He knew chorus girls." Since the clubs where Downey sang were generally owned by the mob, he knew "all the mob figures," said Ann Downey, his widow. "They owned everything." In 1957, it was revealed that Downey had a 5 percent interest in the Tropicana Hotel and Casino in Las Vegas when Frank Costello was an owner. According to Arthur Stryker, Downey's lawyer and friend, "Frank Costello arranged it [the interest]. When it came out, he gave it away."

Besides their love of young women and Irish songs, Downey

and Joe shared a hatred of Jews. Now that they were successful Irishmen, they needed another minority to ridicule. When
Joe later went to Hollywood, he told friends he expected to
wipe out the Jewish "pants pressers" who ruled Hollywood.

"Joe Kennedy's feeling toward Jews was that the only way
he could be a success was that every day when he got up, he
would focus on one deal involving a Jew, and he would win
the deal. That was his whole driving spirit," said Morton
Downey Jr., quoting what his father had told him about Joe.

Downey Jr. said Joe and his father would refer to Jews by
a code word—"Canadian geese," apparently because of a
perception that Jews have long noses. John T. Galvin, who
worked for Jack's campaign, confirmed that account.

"Dad was known for his indiscreet remarks, but never for
being bigoted or prejudiced," Ted would later say.

◆ ◆ ◆

If the Kennedy family was like a tribe, Joe controlled the
wampum. As another tool of control, Joe insisted that his
children know nothing about his finances or their own.

"We never discussed money in the house," Joe would later
recall. "Well, because money isn't important. It's just not an
important enough matter to discuss."

"I don't know what is going to happen to this family when
I die," Joe later remarked to the children in Palm Beach.
"There is no one in the entire family, except for Joan and
Teddy, who is living within their means. No one appears to
have the slightest concern for how much they spend."

Joe turned to one of his daughters and said she was the
"worst." She began to cry and ran out of the room, accompanied by her husband. When they returned, Jack said to her,
"Well, kid, don't worry. We've come to the conclusion that
the only solution is to have Dad work harder."

Bobby said that "money was a subject that was taboo. If
the subject would come up about the cost of something or

relating to money, it would immediately be diverted," either by Joe or Rose, to a topic that related to family matters.

On January 27, 1926, Joe established the first trust fund for his family, emulating the moneyed Brahmins whom he detested. When Joe first told John J. Ford, one of his trusted lieutenants, about the idea, Ford said, "Joe, you wouldn't want to do that. They have too much pride to accept that."

To Bernard Baruch, Joe claimed that the purpose was to make his children financially independent, so they would be free to "spit in my eye." But this was self-serving hokum. The truth was that it was a way of tying the children to him, for Joe's trustees controlled the way the funds were disbursed. The children had no idea how the trusts worked. All they knew was that their income came from their father's office.

At a "deeper level of consciousness, the trust was a mechanism for binding his children permanently to his own dreams for the Kennedy family," Doris Kearns Goodwin wrote.

Besides avoiding probate costs upon death, yet another reason for setting up such trusts is to "keep things private," according to Benjamin Rosales, a noted trust lawyer in Boston and principal author of *Estate Taxation in Massachusetts*. After death, he said, "You aren't required to file an accounting in the court."

Over the years, the terms of the trusts have been the subject of constant speculation in the press. The terms—revealed here for the first time—provide for the family until all members of the first generation have died. The first trust, amended after Ted was born, provides for ten equal shares for Joe's nine children and for Rose. At the death of Rose, her principal—or corpus—was to be added to the other trust shares. Before the sons were thirty-five, the trustees were to determine how much of the income from the trust to allocate to each. At the age of twenty-five, the sons were to receive a quarter of the unexpended income, with another quarter distributed when they reached age thirty. The remainder of the unexpended income was to be distributed to them at age thirty-five. After that, they were to receive the income generated by their share of the trust for life.

If a son died, a third of his income was to be paid to his widow for life, until termination of the trust, or until her remarriage. The rest of the deceased son's share of the income was to go to his descendants until termination of the trust. If the son left no spouse or children, the income would go to the other living brothers and sisters. If they were not living, it was to go to Rose.

The provisions governing Joe's daughters' shares are similar. However, when they die, their widowers do not receive any income. Like the Brahmins, Joe also insisted on spendthrift clauses for his daughters, restricting their income if they were wasteful.

In distributing the principal, the trust favored the sons. Presumably, Joe assumed the daughters would be taken care of by their husbands, with the exception of Rosemary, who for reasons that will be explained later was to receive income only at the discretion of the trustee. At the age of forty-five, each son was to receive half of the principal. At the discretion of the trustee, a son could receive additional principal after he reached age fifty. The daughters, on the other hand, could receive $15,000 a year in principal up to a limit of 25 percent of the principal by the time they reached the age of twenty-five. The balance of the principal is to go to the last survivor. Upon the death of the last survivor, the trust terminates, and the remaining principal goes to the Joseph P. Kennedy Jr. Foundation.

As Joe acquired more wealth, he established additional trusts with similar provisions in 1936, 1949, and 1959. Significantly, the later trusts provided only for Joe's children, not for Rose.

While the size of the family fortune over the years was often exaggerated (usually with Joe's encouragement), it probably exceeds $350 million today. Its major asset, Chicago's Merchandise Mart, alone spews out $20 million in income a year.

Everything went according to Joe's plan. The children accepted the money and, for the most part, did exactly what they were told to do. Even in Joe's day, it was unusual for a father to maintain such tight control over his children, at least some of whom could be expected to rebel. In Arthur Krock's view, it was the "force" of Joe's personality and "the fact that he made them all rich" that kept the children in line. They knew that they "owed their financial independence to him," Krock said. "They were grateful for it. It meant they did not have to take any job. That was a good strong hold." It meant that if Joe said, " 'Jack, go into politics,' he'd say, 'Yes, sir.' "

Above all, Joe wanted to dominate his environment, leaving nothing to chance. That included his children. "Joe analyzed the increments of power and cut away the fuzz on the edge until the bare bones showed," his lawyer Tommy Corcoran said. "What other end is there but power? What delighted him was to be part of great events, to enjoy the sheer sense of control."

After refusing to be photographed by the press while Jack was running for president, Joe agreed to let Frank Fallaci take this never-before-published photo at Barnstable Airport in Hyannis the day after Jack was elected in 1960. (Frank Fallaci)

Patrick J. Kennedy, Joe's father, was one of the most powerful men in Boston. (John F. Kennedy Library)

Joe inherited "Hickey eyes" from Mary Augusta Hickey, his mother. (John F. Kennedy Library)

Joe got failing grades at Boston Latin School but was admitted to Harvard College apparently because of his connections. (AP/Wide World)

Joe graduated from Harvard College in 1912. (Courtesy of Harvard University Archives)

Joe, middle row, third from left, won a varsity letter by having his father arrange to give the baseball team captain a license to operate a movie theater after graduation. (Courtesy of Harvard University Archives)

Joe and Rose Elizabeth Fitzgerald were married in October 1914. (AP/Wide World)

Joe poses at his Hyannis Port home in 1933 with, from left, top row, Joe Jr., Jack, Rose, Jean, Patricia, Rosemary; bottom row, Bobby, Ted, Eunice, and Kathleen.

Eunice Pringle said Joe paid $10,000 to have her accuse Alexander Pantages of attempted rape so that Joe could buy his chain of movie theaters. (AP/Wide World)

During Joe's three-year affair with Gloria Swanson, he plundered her business. (Courtesy of the Academy of Motion Picture Arts and Sciences)

Joe performed admirably at the Securities and Exchange Commission, where he posed just after being sworn in with his fellow commissioners, from left, George C. Matthews, Ferdinand Pecora, James M. Landis, and Robert E. Healy. (John F. Kennedy Library)

James Roosevelt, left, helped Joe secure the exclusive right to distribute Haig & Haig Scotch in the United States and got him his appointment as ambassador to the Court of St. James's. Here they are on the SS *Manhattan* just before Joe sailed to London in 1938. (UPI/Bettmann)

Joe leaves the ambassador's residence in London to present his credentials to King George VI at Buckingham Palace in March 1938. From left are Colonel Raymond E. Lee, the U.S. military attaché; Herschel V. Johnson, chargé d'affaires; Capt. Russell Wilson, U.S. naval attaché; and Sir G. Sidney Clive, marshal of the diplomatic corps. (AP/Wide World)

Joe's family took London by storm. Left to right are Kathleen, Joe, Rose, Patricia, Jean, and Bobby. Ted is in front. (AP/Wide World)

Joe arrived in New York from London on the SS *Queen Mary* to attend the graduation of his son Joe Jr. from Harvard College in June 1938. (John F. Kennedy Library)

Joe leaves the American embassy in London for Buckingham Palace in November 1938. (John F. Kennedy Library)

5

ROBBER BARON

By the mid-1920s, the American film industry was turning out eight hundred films a year and employed as many people as did the auto industry. This was "a gold mine," Joe told several friends. "In fact, it looks like another telephone industry."

Joe began by advising William Gray, a flamboyant horse trader who owned a chain of thirty-one small movie houses in New England. With Joe's patron, Guy Currier, Joe bought an interest in Gray's firm, Maine and New Hampshire Theatres Company. Eventually, Joe took it over and expanded it. But Joe saw that the way to make real money was on the production side. Moreover, he was attracted to the glamour of Hollywood. Not only could he influence the way films were made, he could meet dazzling young women.

Through Hayden, Stone, Joe had dealt with the Grahams Trading Company of London, which owned a majority of Robertson Cole Picture Corporation, producers of nearly fifty films a year. Through Film Booking Office, its operational subsidiary, the company also distributed films. In return for a commission of $75,000, the trading company gave Joe an option to sell FBO for $1.5 million. He was also to advise FBO for $4,500 a month.

Instead of selling FBO to another party, Joe put together a consortium so that he could buy a controlling interest himself. The others in the deal included Currier; Boston businessman Louis Kirstein, founder of Filene's department store; Frederick H. Prince, one of Currier's clients and the son of a former Boston mayor; and Joe's father-in-law, "Honey Fitz" Fitzgerald. On the weekend of February 7, 1925, the irrepressible Honey Fitz leaked the story of the sale to the Boston papers. "Fitzgerald a Film Magnate," the *Boston Post*'s banner headline said. Joe, who never missed an opportunity to get favorable publicity, was miffed. Boston never gave him credit, he thought.

In the middle of March 1926, Joe boarded the *Twentieth Century Limited* for the three-day trip to Los Angeles. The train had a barbershop, valet and maid service, and twin dining cars complete with violinists. As chairman and president of FBO, Joe brought in his personal assistants to run the company—Eddie Moore, John Ford, Pat Scollard, and E.B. "Ed" Derr. Tight-lipped and loyal, they worked together as an efficient team.

Joe asked his Harvard friend Oscar Haussermann to become chief counsel of FBO. From observation, Haussermann knew what to expect if he became part of Joe's entourage. "You had to be sharp and smart, but not too smart," he said. "Above all, you had to take orders." He demurred.

FBO's chief attraction was Tom Mix, who had starred in *King Cowboy*, *Son of the Golden West*, *The Big Diamond Robbery*, and *The Drifter*. Joe quickly changed the studio's focus to making cheap Westerns and dog pictures that could be turned out in a week for $30,000 to $50,000 each. If they lacked artistic merit, the pictures sold, and FBO profits ballooned.

The following year, Joe began successful negotiations with David Sarnoff of Radio Corporation of America (RCA) to let FBO use RCA's system for making motion pictures with sound. The era of the talking film had just begun with the enormous success of Warner Brothers' *The Jazz Singer*. The first totally sound film, *Lights of New York*, followed in 1928. Although experimentation with synchronizing sound and picture was as old as the cinema itself, the feasibility of sound film was widely publicized only after Warner Brothers purchased the Vitaphone system from Western Electric in 1926.

RCA's sound system, called Photophone, had been developed in collaboration with General Electric Company and Western Electric Company. While Sarnoff had initiated the negotiations, Joe realized that the talkies would overtake silent films, just as he later foresaw that television would become critically important in the political process.

Now that Joe headed a studio, he wanted to buy a theater chain to distribute his pictures. For this, he chose the Keith-Albee-Orpheum Theaters Corporation. Known as KAO, the chain had seven hundred movie theaters in the United States and Canada, with more than 2 million patrons daily. Joe offered $4.2 million, raised by a syndicate of investment bankers including Elisha Walker, president of Blair and Company. Walker was a favorite partner of Joe's in stock manipulation deals. He also was a trustee of one of the trusts Joe had set up for his children. Born in New York, he was nine years older than Joe but had almost twenty years' more experience in investment banking.

Edward Albee, the founder of KAO, refused to sell out. Finally, relying on Joe's promise that he would continue to expand the chain, Albee agreed to Joe's offer. But once the papers were signed on May 10, 1928, and Joe was chairman, Joe said bluntly, "Didn't you know, Ed? You're washed up. Through."

Joe solidified his position in the movie industry by suggesting to Wallace B. Donham, dean of the Harvard Graduate

School of Business Administration, that Harvard sponsor a lecture series on the industry. Joe would invite such figures as Adolph Zukor, Marcus Loew, Cecil B. DeMille, and Harry Warner.

On March 14, 1927, Joe introduced the speakers at the symposium. "The motion picture industry has attained a standing and a volume that makes it impossible for serious students of industrial nations to overlook it," he said. "Already it is the fourth largest industry in the country. Yet it is an industry that has developed only within the last ten or twelve years. . . ."

In February 1928, Elisha Walker asked Joe to serve as special adviser on the board of Pathé Exchange Inc. In 1910, Pathé had begun production of a weekly newsreel. In 1914, the company shot many of the scenes for Pearl White's serial *The Perils of Pauline*. That involved the camera magic of filming a set inside a thirty-by-forty-foot swimming pool. Thus trapped, the helpless Pauline could be seen being engulfed by ominously rising water. In reality, the set was being plunged deeper into the pool.

Soon, Joe became chairman of Pathé and began implementing his own advice. Joe had long believed—with good reason—that the movie business was wasteful. Employees in motion picture companies were "vastly overpaid," Joe later said. "It was not an uncommon thing for accountants to receive $20,000 a year when in other businesses they received from $4,000 to $10,000. [I] changed that." Joe began slashing costs. Briefly, he became an adviser to First National Pictures, advising similar cuts. For his work at Pathé alone, Joe received a fee of $500,000.

Joe's cost-cutting advice applied to others, not to him. By May 1928, he was drawing a salary of $100,000 a year each from FBO, from Keith-Albee-Orpheum, and from Pathé.

In October 1928, Joe arranged a deal that brought him $2 million. He merged FBO and Keith-Albee-Orpheum into Radio-Keith-Orpheum, the famous RKO, with assets of $80 million. RCA traded its FBO stock for stock in the new company. Joe named his lieutenant John J. Ford general manager. By forming the movie company, Joe made a national name for himself.

Joe went on to plunder Pathé. In 1931, he arranged for RKO to pay Pathé insiders like himself $80 a share. The rest of the stockholders would receive just $1.50 a share. Favoring insiders to such a degree was nothing more than robbery. Since Joe had acquired the stock for $30 a share, he more than doubled his investment in fewer than two years. Stockholders filed suit, but nothing came of it.

Since Joe was in a position to dictate the terms of the deal, he was able to craft the transaction to enrich himself. Moreover, he took advantage of privileged information from the files of major stockholders in the movie companies who were clients of Currier. As was his practice, Currier had taken a long vacation in Italy. As usual, Joe had the run of his office. While Currier was away, Joe pillaged his files for inside information such as the size of holdings of other stockholders and their financial condition. He then used the information to further his own interests. While the details are lost to history, Currier, like so many who had helped Joe, eventually came to realize that Joe had double-crossed him.

"He did not behave in an honorable way," said Anne Anable, Currier's granddaughter. "My grandfather went off to his villa in Florence, leaving the firm in his hands. He said, 'Sit on RKO and Keith.' Joe saw an opportunity to make money. He did a fandango, and when my grandfather got back, he found its value was down and his fellow investors had been betrayed. . . . That's how he got into RKO. He was still trying to make it up to his friends until he died." Unfortunately, Currier "didn't realize how corrupt he was," Anable said.

Lucy P. Steinert, Currier's daughter, said she "listened to many of their conversations." Joe became "too avaricious. . . . Money went to his head."

More than ten years later, Wisconsin Congressman John Schafer took to the floor of the House to denounce Joe as the "chief racketeer" in the "RKO swindle." Another congressman, William I. Sirovich of New York, said the "inside group" at RKO had committed "fraud" by unloading their stock, "making millions." He called for an investigation of the movie industry, but the probe was halted "on the plea of Joseph P. Kennedy," according to Will H. Hays, president of the Motion Picture Producers and Distributors of America. While Hays did not spell out how that was done, Joe was close to key congressional leaders as well as to President Roosevelt.

In Joe's papers, Doris Kearns Goodwin found letters from anguished stockholders of Pathé. Anne Lawler of Jamaica Plain in Boston said she lost her life savings. "This seems hardly Christian like, fair or just for a man of your character," she wrote. "I wish you would think of the poor working women who had so much faith in you as to give their money to your Pathé."

To the press, Joe pooh-poohed the value of inside information, saying that with enough of it and unlimited credit, "You are sure to go broke." Friends would credit his success to his sense of timing and cool, dispassionate judgment. Often, those judgments originated with Eddie Moore, who constantly talked up his boss. The truth was that few of Joe's stunning stock deals were done without inside information whose use today would land him in jail. In his more candid moments, Joe himself admitted that his wealth had more to do with luck than genius. After playing golf at Oyster Harbors in Cape Cod's Osterville, he told his friend Edward M. Gallagher, "Eddie, six or seven times in my life the pendulum swung my way. If it hadn't fallen favorably to me, life could be quite a bit different."

Far from going broke, Joe made an estimated $5 million in the movie business. He was chairman of FBO for two years and nine months, chairman of Keith-Albee-Orpheum five months, special adviser to First National Pictures six weeks, special adviser to Radio Corporation of America two and a half months, and adviser to Paramount Pictures for seventy-four days.

♦ ♦ ♦

If Joe acted like a robber baron in forming RKO, it was nothing compared with what he did to Alexander Pantages. Born in Athens, Greece, Pantages, a balding man with heavy black eyebrows, had shined shoes and sold newspapers until he bought a run-down theater in Seattle and branched out from vaudeville to movies. Eventually, he owned sixty theaters, most designed by B. Marcus Priteca, including his signature Art Deco movie palace, the Hollywood Pantages, which still stands at Hollywood and Vine. By 1929, Pantages was worth $30 million.

In February 1929, Joe made an offer to buy the Pantages chain, the second biggest in California. That same month, Joe had unsuccessfully tried to see J.P. Morgan, showing up without an appointment at 23 Wall Street and expecting the legendary investment banker to see him about some unspecified matter. He was told curtly that the banker was too busy.

Clearly, Joe's innate arrogance was now rampant, and when Pantages again rebuffed his offers in April and May in Los Angeles, Joe threatened him by boasting of his influence in the banking and movie businesses. Soon, the Pantages Hill Street house, on the northwest corner of 7th and Hill Streets in downtown Los Angeles, found it was being denied first-run blockbuster features from major studios. But that was only the beginning.

On August 9, 1929, Eunice Pringle, wearing a low-cut dress, ran screaming out of the janitor's broom closet at Pantages' theater at 607 South Hill. A theater employee raced to the scene. The seventeen-year-old girl collapsed, screaming, "There he is, the beast! . . . Don't let him get at me!" She pointed to Pantages. A traffic policeman was summoned.

"She's trying to frame me!" Pantages yelled. It was to no avail. Pantages was booked on charges of rape.

At the trial, Pantages, with his foreign accent, did not make a good impression on the jurors. Pringle, with her Mary Pickford girlish frock, won their hearts. Hearst's *Herald-Examiner* called Pringle "the sweetest seventeen since Clara Bow." The *Los Angeles Times* described her as a "full-blown beauty."

"We were both seated," Pringle testified, "and he pulled his chair over close to mine and took my hand. Then he slid his arm along the back of my chair and along my shoulder. He said that he admired me very much and that he wished I would be his sweetheart, and then I told him that I didn't want any sweetheart.

"He was kissing me madly," Pringle said. "He not only was kissing me, he was biting me." Asked where he bit her, she pointed to one of her breasts.

Pantages broke into tears as he denied her story. Again and again in his broken English, he said, "I did not." According to Pantages, Pringle had wanted him to buy a playlet her agent had written. Pantages told her he thought it was "vulgar." She later confronted him at the theater, tearing his shirt and clinging to his legs as he tried to push her away.

The jury found Pantages guilty, and he was sentenced to fifty years in jail. But Jerry Giesler, his lawyer, mounted an appeal, claiming the trial court erred when it excluded testimony about Pringle's morals. Since she was underage, she was legally incapable of consenting to sex. For that reason, the trial court had ruled that any previous sexual activity was irrelevant. But the California Supreme Court disagreed and granted a new trial.

At the new trial, Giesler contended that Pringle had conspired with her agent and lover, Nicholas Dunaev, to concoct the charges. He and his co-counsel reenacted the alleged rape and showed that it could not have occurred in the small broom closet the way Pringle had described it. Giesler was able to show the jury how athletic Pringle was, casting doubt on her claim that she could not have fought off advances by the slightly built Pantages. Even more damaging to the prosecution's case, the manager of the Moonbeam Glen Bungalow Court where Pringle had stayed testified that Pringle lived in the same bungalow as her boyfriend.

On November 28, 1931, the jury acquitted Pantages. But because of the notoriety, Pantages' business had plummeted. A few months after Joe's final $8 million offer, Pantages was forced to sell out to Joe's RKO for $3.5 million.

Two years after the acquittal, Pringle told her lawyer she wanted to come clean. Stories began circulating that she was about to blow the lid off the rape case and name names. Suddenly, she died of unknown causes. The night she died, she was violently ill and red in color, a sign of cyanide poisoning.

On her deathbed, Pringle confessed to her mother and a friend that Joe had set up Pantages. For their perjured testimony, Joe had paid $10,000 to Pringle and her agent and lover, Dunaev. Joe had also promised he would make her a star. Joe never made her a star, and Dunaev never gave her her share of the money.

Did Joe have Pringle poisoned to silence her? No one knows. For one thing, no autopsy was conducted. But Pringle's claim that Joe paid her off to make up the charges against Pantages rings true. It would not have been the first time Joe paid bribes to corrupt the judicial or political processes.

6

GLORIA

Having conquered Hollywood, Joe was looking for an even bigger trophy. He found it in Gloria Swanson.

Swanson needed financing for her movie production company, and a friend suggested she meet with Joe. Since he was connected with Wall Street investment firms, Joe might be able to arrange the support she sought.

Joe and Swanson had lunch together at the opulent new Savoy Plaza Hotel on Fifth Avenue across from Central Park South in New York on Friday, November 11, 1927. At the time, Joe was no more to Swanson than a name on a telegram complaining that her planned film *Sadie Thompson*, to be released later that year, was scandalous.

Sadie Thompson was based on the play *Rain*, which in turn was based on "Miss Thompson," a story by W. Somerset Maugham. A sadistically puritanical minister, played by Lionel Barrymore, tries to reform a prostitute named Sadie Thompson. Instead of saving her, he falls prey to her charms and kills himself. Sadie then goes off with a marine (Raoul Walsh) to find a better life.

While the play had run its course without major objection, Will Hays, who since 1922 had run an internal censorship bureau within the movie trade association, applied far stricter standards to films than were applied to plays. In those innocent days, the fact that a minister was secretly a lecher, and a marine talked like a sailor on leave, was enough to brand the movie unacceptable. Under what was known as the Formula, even the length of kisses was prescribed: A kiss could last no longer than a foot of film.

As a member of the Hollywood establishment, Joe had signed the June 10, 1927, telegram objecting to *Sadie Thompson* along with fifteen other movie magnates, including William Fox, Abe Warner, Marcus Loew, and Adolph Zukor. Addressed to Joseph M. Schenck of United Artists, it warned that releasing the film would jeopardize the gains moviemakers had made in winning public confidence in their ability to censor themselves.

"For this subject to be produced at this time will open up the entire question [of the industry's ability to police itself] again," the telegram said, "and we will lose for ourselves everything that we have gained in public respect and confidence for the past four or five years."

Banned or not, every "actress in America with a brain and a figure still wanted to play Sadie, and every producer had secretly dreamed of filming the work," Swanson noted in her memoirs. Swanson was eminently qualified to play the part herself. Born in Chicago in 1898, she was an only child of Joseph and Adelaide Swanson, descendants of Swedish and German immigrants. By the age of sixteen, Swanson was making movies. In 1919, she signed with Cecil B. DeMille to make six films, mostly postwar sexual adventures under the guise of moralizing. In these movies, she glided through opulent sets and was outfitted in satin and sequins.

By the early 1920s, Swanson, along with Charlie Chaplin and Mary Pickford, was considered one of the world's greatest stars. Swanson defined celebrity; she received ten thousand fan letters a week. By the time Swanson was twenty-eight, when she met Joe, she was the most successful and highly paid actress of the silent screen.

What's more, she was gorgeous. With tantalizing, gigantic blue eyes, long brown hair, full breasts, and shapely legs, Swanson could charm any man. A health nut in an age of excess, she followed the teachings of Henry G. Bieler, a Pasadena doctor who prescribed enemas, vegetable broth, and steamed vegetables to rid the body of "poisons."

Swanson was a feminist before the term was invented. She liked to refer to "Mrs. God" and became a self-taught businesswoman as well as an actress. She insisted on more control of her films and formed her own production company. The films were released through Schenck's United Artists. Swanson was a devoted and nurturing mother as well.

By the time she died, she had had six husbands. "Gloria was a fiendishly attractive woman, I would say baby," said William Dufty, her last husband, who was seventeen years younger than Gloria. An author, Dufty, along with Brian Degas, helped her write her autobiography, *Swanson on Swanson*. Dufty and Swanson began an affair in 1965 after he sent her a copy of a book he had translated from the Japanese. Called *You Are All Sanpaku*, it touted the benefits of eating brown rice. In 1975, Swanson went on a publicity tour with Dufty to tout his new book, *Sugar Blues*, on the evils of sugar in the American diet. Dufty became her sixth husband in 1976, just after he turned sixty and just before she turned seventy-seven.

"She had the body of Lolita, with this enormous, Napoleonic head," Dufty said. "She had a good bust, great legs. . . . Gloria was adventurous, she was independent, she was as sexually liberated as any man. There were so many affairs."

When Joe and Swanson met, Rose and Joe were sleeping in separate bedrooms. Marie Greene, who played cards with the Kennedys, recalled that Eunice and Kathleen were astonished when they saw that Greene and her husband, Vincent, slept together in their Brookline home. "They thought that was very odd," she said.

Joe would tease Rose about her narrow views on sex.

"Now listen, Rosie," he would say. "This idea of yours that there is no romance outside of procreation is simply wrong. It was not part of our contract at the altar, the priest never said that, and the books don't argue it. And if you don't open your mind on this, I'm going to tell the priest on you."

But Rose did not change her views. After Ted was born, Rose said no more sex. From then on, the two had a platonic relationship.

For his part, Joe "was a real womanizer," recalled Frederick Good Jr., the son of Rose's obstetrician, Dr. Frederick L. Good. "Wherever you went, he had a girl with him—year in, year out, winter in, winter out."

Now Joe was about to make the ultimate conquest.

From the beginning, Swanson had known that *Sadie Thompson* would provoke protests. Slyly, she had invited Hays to lunch to soften him up. Slobbering over her sexy good looks, Hays had given preliminary approval to making the film. But now that it was about to be distributed, the industry itself was protesting it. In the end, the other moviemakers settled for minor changes in the film, even quibbling about the name of the minister.

When Swanson met Joe, she was in New York to show United Artists' sales and distribution chiefs her daring film. The movie—which would open to enthusiastic reviews—had gone overbudget. Swanson was in debt and thinking about her next film, possibly a sequel. She needed cash.

Since Joe had denounced her film, Swanson did not want to be under any obligation to him. At the Savoy Plaza, Swanson arranged with the maître d' to send her the bill. If Kennedy asked for the check, he was to say that it was compliments of the management.

Swanson had the maître d' call her in her room when Joe

arrived. When she walked into the dining room, Joe was sitting at a table Swanson had reserved. Energetically, he rose and introduced himself.

"He didn't resemble any banker I knew," Swanson recalled. "His suit was too bulky, and the knot of his tie was not pushed up tight. With his spectacles and prominent chin, he looked like any average working class person's uncle. A man of about forty, he still retained a certain boyishness. Apart from his [Boston] accent, his hands were the most noticeable thing about him. They looked unused to work, and there were wide spaces between his fingers. He gestured often and animatedly with them when he talked."

Joe told Swanson that he had impressed his wife and children by telling them he was to meet with the famous star. He asked about her children. Joe was surprised when Swanson ordered steamed string beans and braised celery and zucchini. Joe ordered shrimp cocktail and a steak.

Gloria had brought along outlines of two proposals, one to be financed by Bank of America and the other by Schenck of United Artists. She asked his advice.

Joe looked them over and began asking about her accountant, her offices, and her balance sheet. Nobody in Hollywood understood how to draw up a balance sheet that bankers understood, Joe said. That was what was so fascinating about the movie business, he told her. It was a giant industry, yet nobody seemed to recognize that fact.

Then Joe asked about Swanson's European grosses. She replied that she could never get accurate figures. Her husband, Henri de la Falaise de la Coudraye, was a French marquis, and she had an office in Paris, but she did not trust the numbers she was given. Swanson noted that even in America, theater owners commonly let their friends in free. Since producers were usually paid a percentage of theaters' gross, this cheated them. Why, she said, even Mary Pickford's mother couldn't be in every theater to count the patrons.

"Does she do that?" Joe asked, registering astonishment.

"That's what they say," Swanson said. "But you couldn't prove it by me because she never took me along."

Whacking his thigh, Joe went into spasms of laughter, drawing stares from other diners. He seemed to be enjoying himself so unabashedly that Gloria began laughing, too.

Growing serious again, Joe said the figures Swanson gave him did not adequately portray her financial status.

"Upcoming play dates should be counted as income, don't you see?" he said. "In any other business they would be counted as sales, as accounts receivable. Otherwise your balance sheet for *Sadie Thompson* for this entire year would be just an inventory of costs—all red ink."

Swanson asked where he had learned all this. "At Harvard," he said. "Or I should say I studied business at Harvard." In fact, Joe had taken no business courses and had gotten a D in economics, the only course related to business.

"Tell me," Joe asked with a twinkle in his eye, "how did you ever get Will Hays to say you could make *Sadie Thompson* in the first place?"

It was a sore subject, and Swanson was amazed that Joe would bring it up. On the other hand, perhaps he was paying her a compliment by dealing with her man-to-man, as it were. There was no pretense or false chivalry.

"I just invited him to lunch and asked him," Swanson said demurely.

Again, Joe went into peals of laughter. This time, she did not join in the laughter. If she did, it might imply that she had indeed pulled a fast one on Hays by batting her false eyelashes at him.

"In fact," she said in measured tones as she took out a cigarette, "I think I told all you gentlemen [how it occurred] when I replied to your telegram to Joe Schenck. I know you got your copy, Mr. Kennedy, because your secretary or assistant replied."

Joe reddened, and his embarrassment increased when he realized he had no match with which to light her cigarette.

She held it horizontally until a waiter hurried over to light it.

Joe tried to disassociate himself from the telegram, saying he signed it only because the others had done him a favor.

"May I ask what favor they had done for you?"

"Of course. They attended a symposium on the film industry at Harvard that I sponsored," Joe said, pronouncing it "HAH-vad."

Swanson said she was not entirely clear about what Joe did. "You're a banker and distributor, is that correct?"

"I've also produced," he said, a mildly defensive tone to his voice.

"Really? What?" she asked.

Joe mentioned some cowboy pictures and *The Gorilla Hunt*, which he said was his most successful film. Swanson said she hadn't heard of it. He replied that she never would. When he saw it, he walked out. Yet it made money, he said. They both smiled.

Joe called for the check. As prearranged, he was told it was on the house. After the grand opening, he was going down for defeat, Swanson thought. He recovered by glancing again at the two proposals she had showed him. He advised her to take the one from Schenck, but made no offer of his own. From her viewpoint, the luncheon had been a waste of time. She was sure she would never see him again.

At 5 P.M., the phone in Swanson's hotel room rang. The hotel operator apologized for calling. Swanson had said she did not want to be disturbed. But a Mr. Kennedy had been phoning for two hours, and now he was in the lobby asking to see her. Swanson was bemused; she told the operator to send him up.

Joe asked if Swanson remembered that he had advised her to ask Sidney Kent, a Paramount executive, if Kent would provide figures on that company's European grosses to help her gauge her own.

"Yes, I remember," she said.

"Well, I called him myself, and he will give us everything we need. He's calling me back tomorrow."

This was the first Swanson had heard of "we." But before she could ask what he meant, Joe said he needed to do a favor for Kent in return. Kent was going through a divorce and wanted a postponement on the court date. It so happened that Kent's wife's lawyer, Milton Cohen, was Swanson's lawyer. Could she call him and ask him to reconsider?

Swanson agreed to call, and he pushed her to do it immediately. Cohen agreed to the postponement. When she told Joe, he smiled. It was as if she had just passed a test. He called her a good scout and said he would not forget it.

Joe told her he had found out that she paid for their lunch. Now it was his turn, he said. He invited her to dinner that night.

Swanson rescheduled another date and was in her room when Joe called precisely at 6:30 P.M., just when he said he would call. When she got downstairs, Joe was standing with a man who appeared to be a functionary. After a few words, the man left. Joe reached for a box the man had left on a table. Inside was an orchid. Swanson winced. She hated corsages, and orchids were her least favorite. They reminded her of visiting aunts.

Joe's chauffeur drove them over the Queensboro Bridge to Long Island. During the ride, Swanson mentioned she had turned down a contract for $1 million. She said she was the second or third person in the industry to have signed a $1 million contract, but the first to turn one down.

Joe laughed, and Gloria found herself saying things to amuse him. At one point, she imitated his Boston accent, sending him into long peals of laughter. He wiped his eyes, groaned pleasurably, and asked her to do it again.

At the restaurant, which had an orchestra, a waiter gave Swanson a menu with no prices. Joe was disappointed when she ordered steamed green vegetables, a little rice, and unbuttered dark bread. When the waiter said they had no zucchini,

Joe seemed peeved. After Joe had ordered a big meal, he motioned the captain over. He explained to Swanson that she could have wine poured from a concealed bottle into a teacup. From his tone, she could tell he would not have it himself. Joe seemed pleased when she declined. This time, when she pulled out a cigarette, he was prepared with matches.

Timidly, Joe asked Swanson why she ate such bland food. She told him of her fear that she might have ulcers and the regimen Dr. Bieler had prescribed for her. Joe said he had stomach problems, too, but when she offered to put him in touch with Bieler, he said, "Oh, my, no. I already have the best doctor in Boston working on the case."

They discussed Prohibition, and Joe said that his father had made his money as a saloon keeper. He managed to mention that his wife's father was the former mayor of Boston. Joe gave her a copy of *The Story of the Films*, which reprinted the fourteen speeches given at the Harvard symposium Joe had arranged.

This impressed Swanson. By putting together the symposium, Joe had massaged the egos of all the members of what she called the pinochle club—the Hollywood film-producing establishment. Joe told Swanson that films had tremendous potential to advertise the United States and its products abroad. He seemed to have far more vision than anyone else she had met in the business. Usually she got bored talking about pictures, but not with Joe. He clearly knew how to manipulate people and events.

"Take Boston," he said. "The Cabots and the Lodges wouldn't be caught dead at the pictures, or let their children go. And that's why their servants know more about what's going on in the world than they do. The working class gets smarter every day, thanks to radio and pictures. It's the snooty Back Bay bankers who are missing the boat."

On the way back to Manhattan, Joe said he was interested not only in financing her next picture but in handling all her business arrangements. Together, they could make millions, he assured her. He said *Rock-a-Bye*, the next picture she was considering making, did not sound important enough to interest him. It seemed everything had to be *important*. He reminded her that she had said *Sadie Thompson* brought out her best acting because the story was the best of any movie she'd done. Why not take the next logical step and do a great story with a great director?

"You've convinced me, Joe," she said. "You can almost read my mind. I think we should make a picture together."

"Wonderful!" he said, laughing and clapping his hands like a college boy.

Back at the Savoy, Swanson gave Joe her private telephone number in California. As Joe had requested, she later told her secretary to let Joe and his staff examine her financial records. The secretary said two men in fedoras had already been to the office and had examined everything.

"To me, they looked like gangsters," the secretary told Swanson.

In early December, Joe arrived in Beverly Hills and installed himself in a rented house with tennis court on Rodeo Drive. Swanson invited him to dinner at her home, a cream-colored, two-story mansion at 904 Crescent Drive in Beverly Hills. The home was a fitting place for America's reigning sex goddess. It had twenty-two rooms, an elevator, and five baths. In the garage were a Pierce-Arrow and a Cadillac.

Swanson had four butlers and staged sumptuous dinner parties with a liveried footman stationed behind each guest's chair. Swanson would later say, "In those days, the public wanted us to live like kings and queens. So we did. Why not? We were in love with life. We were making more money than we ever dreamed existed, and there was no reason to believe it would ever stop."

Joe introduced Swanson that night to what she called his four horsemen—Eddie Moore, Charlie Sullivan, Ed Derr, and Ted O'Leary. When Gloria's children asked them to play spin the bottle, they all got down on the floor and played. In those days, the person to whom the bottle pointed had to do whatever he was told to do, like smearing honey all over another guest's face. Kissing was not among the expected penalties.

When Swanson wrenched her knee playing the game, they all sprang into action: One member of Joe's team took her children upstairs to be with their governess. A second one told the cook to hold dinner. Another called a doctor and asked him to meet them at the nearest hospital. The fourth picked up Gloria and carried her into Joe's waiting chauffeured car. Within an hour, her knee had been x-rayed and bandaged, and they were back at the house for dinner.

Joe was intent on getting Erich von Stroheim as director of their first movie. Born in Vienna, he created unforgettable films like *The Merry Widow*, with sets that surpassed even DeMille's for sheer opulence. He was noted for his attention to detail. For example, in *The Merry Widow*, all the soldiers wore silk underpants with the monogram of the Imperial Guard. Louis B. Mayer once called him "the greatest director in the world."

When Joe and Swanson met with Stroheim, he proposed a film he had been working on, then called *The Swamp*. Its heroine, Kitty Kelly, was an Irish Catholic convent girl who encounters a dashing young prince and winds up owning an East African brothel. Later, Swanson asked Joe if he was aware Stroheim had a growing reputation for being arrogant, a spendthrift, and a temperamental perfectionist.

"Yes, I am," Joe said. "But I also know he's our man. I can handle him."

A week later, Joe invited Swanson to his home for dinner. Like all of his homes, this one was well staffed with two Irish maids, a butler, a gardener, and a cook. Over an elaborate dinner, Joe invited Gloria and her husband to visit him at Palm Beach after the Christmas holiday. Meanwhile, Joe had Swanson sign papers setting up their joint company, Gloria Productions Inc. He had Moore dissolve her existing company. When Swanson's lawyer, Cohen, found out about the new arrangement, he quit as her lawyer, noting that he had not been consulted.

When Swanson and Henri arrived by train in Palm Beach in January 1928, she saw Derr and Moore waiting on the platform in tropical suits, white shoes, and straw hats. Henri jumped off the train to make arrangements for the luggage, while Joe bounded through the train and found Swanson in her drawing room.

"He pushed me back into the drawing room, said a few excited words, and kissed me twice," she recalled. Then he released her and straightened up, scraping his head on an overhead rack and knocking off his spectacles. Swanson laughed as Joe fell to the floor to retrieve his glasses. When he had again pulled himself up to his full height, his pants' knees were dirty, and he had lipstick smeared on his face.

"I missed you," he said without embarrassment.

"I missed you too," she said steadily, although she later confessed that her body was shaking.

Swanson invited Joe to meet her husband. "Oh, there he is," he said, looking out the window. He said it in a cheerful, open way.

Swanson checked into the Hotel Poinciana in downtown Palm Beach and began attending a round of parties and dinners. One afternoon, Moore took Henri deep-sea fishing. Back at the hotel, Swanson was stretched out on her bed when the phone rang. It was a florist asking her what color orchid she desired that evening. Swanson replied that she hated orchids and corsages.

"What you can do is save me two or three red carnations," she said. "Just two plain carnations."

Just then, she noticed that Joe was standing at the doorway, a maid having left the door open.

"Well, now you know," Swanson said to Joe, who had ordered the corsage.

Joe didn't reply. He stood there in his white flannels, argyle sweater, and two-toned shoes, staring at her. Then he entered the room and closed the door behind him.

"He moved so quickly that his mouth was on mine before either of us could speak," Swanson said. "With one hand, he held the back of my head, with the other he stroked my body and pulled at my kimono. He kept insisting in a drawn-out moan, 'No longer, no longer. Now.' He was like a roped horse—rough, arduous, racing to be free. After a hasty climax, he lay beside me, stroking my hair. Apart from his guilty, passionate mutterings, he still had said nothing cogent."

Since the kiss on the train, Swanson had expected this. After an hour, well before the fishermen returned, he got up and dressed.

"No more orchids," he said, and they both laughed.

Back in California, they would have sex at his home, then Joe's team of horsemen would drive her home. As she noted in her memoirs, more than her husband, Joe now owned her. His control of Swanson's life even extended to the French war orphan Swanson had adopted so that her daughter would have a brother. Joe kept insisting that he should be baptized. She finally gave in. The child happened to be named Joseph, but that was not good enough. Joe wanted his middle name to be Patrick. She gave in on that, too, and made Joe the boy's godfather. "All in all, this made him very happy," she said.

♦ ♦ ♦

Joe insisted that Swanson and her children, who lived with her in New York, visit his wife and children for a Halloween party. By 1927, Joe had decided that Boston was too insular, and he had moved to New York. "Boston was a small, clear puddle; New York was a big, muddy one, and that's what suited Joe," said Ralph Lowell, his Harvard chum.

Joe attributed the move more to the slights he felt he had suffered. Joe told Lowell of his treatment by the Cohasset

Country Club, which had snubbed him. "Those narrow-minded, bigoted sons of bitches barred me because I was an Irish Catholic and son of a barkeep," Joe said years later. "You can go to Harvard, and it doesn't mean a damned thing. The only thing these people understand is money."

"Joe felt he'd been high-hatted by the silk hats," Lowell said. "Under that rough hide, there's an extremely sensitive human being." After he left, "Joe never gave a damn about Boston," Lowell said. If the slights were more imagined than real, it did not keep Joe from bad-mouthing Boston, which he said was "no place to bring up Catholic children." Joe hired a private railroad car and moved the family in September 1927 to 5040 Independence Avenue on the corner of 252nd Street in Riverdale, New York.

If Swanson was shocked that Joe wanted her to meet his wife and children, it was clearly part of Joe's strategy: He wanted to have his cake and eat it, too. Through much of his life, he would have a mistress while maintaining a seemingly happy family life.

On November 6, 1928, for example, as if nothing were amiss, Joe and Rose purchased the Beulah Malcolm cottage they had been renting on Marchant Avenue in Hyannis Port. Overlooking Nantucket Sound, it was rounded by wide porches and was later remodeled to include a total of fifteen rooms and a moving picture theater.

"Please," Joe said when Swanson expressed reservations about going to the Halloween party. "I promised."

Here were all the man's contradictions in a nutshell, she thought. "While he was in control, he saw nothing as impossible or out of the question," Swanson said. "I couldn't even argue with him, because it would have done no good. I finally said the children could go, but I would not, and he accepted that as the best compromise that could be reached."

Swanson paid several visits to Hyannis Port as well.

"Soon after Mrs. Kennedy left for Europe, always so beautifully dressed, sooner or later Gloria Swanson would swing by," recalled Nancy Tenney Coleman, a childhood friend of the Kennedy girls. "We didn't think of it as anything other than exciting, the big red Rolls and two dogs and the chauffeur jumping out."

◆ ◆ ◆

Joe and Swanson decided that the movie Stroheim had proposed should be called *Queen Kelly*. Shooting began in November 1928 on the Pathé lot. Joe gave his girlfriend an elaborate bungalow with a living room and grand piano, a full kitchen, and a big bedroom. But Swanson soon became appalled at how finicky the director was. He would shoot scenes over and over. Thousands of feet of unused film were piling up. Then, in reviewing the footage, she found that scenes and characters that were supposed to relate to each other did not.

One afternoon, in his usual painstaking way, Stroheim began instructing an actor to dribble tobacco juice from his mouth into Swanson's hand. Swanson became infuriated and walked off the set, never to return.

Swanson called Joe and told him something was terribly wrong. "Our director is a madman," she said. "It's ruined!" Joe met her in her bungalow. He had seen some of the film and now slumped in a chair, cursing Stroheim.

"He held his head in his hands, and little, high-pitched sounds escaped from his rigid body, like those of a wounded animal whimpering in a trap," Swanson recalled. Finally, Joe moaned, "I've never had a failure in my life." Then he rose and went into a searing rage. He yanked Swanson into his arms, and soon her face was wet with his tears. Swanson thought it was odd that he hadn't had a failure. Better late than never, she thought.

"Don't cry," she said. "We'll try to save it."

They had spent $600,000 on the film, which was now useless.

For weeks after that, Joe was depressed. Swanson, more accustomed to crises, asked friends for advice. Edmund

Goulding, an English director, told her she should shelve the project. Talking pictures would soon overtake the silent screen anyway, he said. Even though it was still a novelty, he suggested they make a sound movie.

When Swanson talked to Joe about it, he liked the idea, too. With Goulding, Swanson came up with a script. The talkie would be a drama of mother love called *The Trespasser*.

A few days later, Swanson walked in on Joe when he was in the middle of a phone call. He was agitated, and Swanson gestured toward the door, asking him if he wanted her to leave. He motioned for her to stay. From what Swanson could glean, Joe was offering to donate money to a hospital if it would guarantee that it could cure Rosemary. Apparently, Joe did not get what he wanted, because he finally slammed down the receiver.

"What's the matter with Rosemary?" Swanson asked innocently. No matter what it was, she said, Dr. Bieler could help.

For the first time, Swanson experienced Joe's anger.

"It was frightening," she remembered. "His blue eyes turned to ice and then to steel. He said they had taken Rosemary to the best specialists in the east. He didn't want to hear about some $3 doctor in Pasadena who recommended zucchini and string beans for everything." He warned her that if she continued to recommend Dr. Bieler to people, they would think she was a quack.

"But, Joseph," she said, "it's not only what you eat that helps your body heal itself. It's what you stop eating."

"I don't want to hear about it!" he screamed. "Do you understand me? Do you understand me?"

Joe soon calmed down, and later Swanson asked Eddie Moore what was wrong with Rosemary. Moore looked unhappy. He said it was a sore subject with the boss. Finally, he tapped the side of his head with the tip of his index finger several times. Softly, he said, "She's . . . not quite right."

◆ ◆ ◆

For some time, Joe's father, Patrick J. Kennedy, had been ill. His wife, Mary, had died on May 20, 1923, and he had been living at 97 Washington Street in Winthrop with his daughter Margaret and her husband, Charles Burke. From his hospital bed, P.J. ordered his daughter to destroy all his papers and records. At the age of seventy-one, he died on May 18, 1929, of carcinoma of the liver.

Entranced by Swanson and Hollywood, Joe would not leave California to attend the funeral. His son Joe Jr., then thirteen, stood in his father's place and escorted Rose to the wake at the Washington Street house.

"State and city officials, bankers, politicians, and men and women from all walks of life crowded the St. John the Evangelist Church" in Winthrop to pay final tribute to him, according to the May 21, 1929, *Boston Post.*

"You can't realize," Joe wrote to Attilio H. Giannini, president of United Artists and brother of the president of the Bank of America, "what a shock it was not to return before this thing happened. He was a great man and a great father."

But Kane Simonian, a friend of Joe's cousin Joseph Kane, recalled, "Joe Kane got in an argument with Joe and said, 'You son of a bitch, you didn't even go to your father's funeral. You were too busy on the West Coast chasing Gloria Swanson around.'"

According to Simonian, Joe replied, "I couldn't leave. If I left for two days, the Jews would rob me blind." Simonian added, "Joe Kennedy didn't attend his father's funeral. . . . When someone doesn't go to his father's funeral, you can believe he would do anything."

Indeed, nothing so much illuminates Joe's character as his decision to remain in California while the rest of the family and many of Boston's most notable citizens paid their last respects to the man who had been responsible for many of Joe's early successes. From Joe's entry into Harvard and his job as a bank examiner, to his designation as president of Columbia Trust at the age of twenty-five, P.J. had stood behind his son. Now that his father could do nothing more

to help him, Joe was too busy in Hollywood to say good-
bye.

◆ ◆ ◆

By August 1929, *The Trespasser* was almost finished. The
United Artists sales force wanted to hold the world premiere
in London in September. Joe proposed meeting Swanson there
and returning to America on the same ship.

Swanson pointed out that they could not travel together
alone, but Joe said, "We won't be alone." He lowered his
voice and began talking in even tones, as if soothing an ill
patient. "Rose is coming," he said. "She's never been to
Europe," he claimed falsely, "and I've promised her this trip.
Please, Gloria, she wants to meet you."

Swanson was outraged. In effect, Rose would be Joe's
beard, allowing him to take Swanson along. Joe added that
his sister, Margaret Burke, would also come. "Gloria, listen
to me. You two are going to have to meet sometime, and
this is the perfect time. . . ."

Gloria knew it was useless arguing. She agreed but insisted
on bringing a friend along. They would meet Henri in Paris.

On August 20, 1929, Joe and Rose took the luxurious liner
Ile de France to London. They met Gloria and Henri and
traveled with them to Paris. Swanson, Joe, and Rose returned
to the United States on the same ship.

Swanson could not tell if Rose knew what was going on
and, if she did, whether she resented it. Rose treated Swanson
and her friend as if they were debutantes who needed constant
chaperoning. Rose admired Swanson's clothes and worried
that she was dieting too much.

"Gloria and I both needed some things to wear," Rose
recalled. "Gloria had to have something not only becoming
but spectacular. . . ."

When a man at another table began staring at Gloria, Joe
jumped to his feet and told him to mind his own business.
Rose agreed with what he had done, saying she could not

understand how Gloria could stand being on constant public display.

Swanson discovered that her husband was also having an affair when she opened an envelope meant for him. The writer had mistakenly used the French feminine form of his title instead of the masculine. When she opened the envelope at her hotel in Paris, Swanson found a love letter from movie star Constance Bennett, sister of Morton Downey's wife, Barbara Bennett.

Henri had been aware of Swanson's relationship with Joe. But Swanson was furious with Henri and announced she intended to divorce him at once.

"Poor Gloria," Rose said. "It was a very difficult time for her, and I felt very sorry to see her so hurt." When Joe and Gloria appeared together on the deck of the ocean liner going home, rumors began that they were having an affair, Rose recorded. But she knew that she "never had a thing to worry about, and I only felt sorry for poor little Gloria."

Gloria asked herself in disbelief, "Was she a fool . . . or a saint? Or just a better actress than I was?"

For all her flakiness, Rose knew what was going on. She told her grandniece Kerry McCarthy as much, referring to the relationship as "a flirtation, a short-lived love affair." To McCarthy, Rose said, "Your uncle thought she was fascinating for a year, and then he realized she really is very ignorant." Said McCarthy, "Aunt Rose just thought it was funny and pitiful."

Years later, Swanson was shocked when her press agent called her and told her that Rose Kennedy had phoned and said she wanted to call Gloria to "check some things out" for the book she was writing, Dufty recalled. Rose never called, but the fact that Rose was about to tell her version convinced Swanson—who had denied that she had had an affair with Joe—to tell all in her 1980 autobiography.

After Rose wrote her memoirs, Cynthia Stone Ray, who became Rose's secretary after Jack's assassination, talked with Robert Coughlan, a former *Life* writer who collaborated with Rose on the book. Coughlan asked Rose's secretary, "Do you think we'll ever get an autobiography?" meaning Rose had not told the truth about her life. Stone said no; Rose told a version that she wanted to believe. "I think she knows the truth [about Joe's affairs]. But she will not acknowledge it," Stone said.

When a Hyannis Port neighbor discussed with Rose how wives can use "iciness" to manipulate their husbands, Rose admitted that she used the tactic to make Joe give her everything she wanted. "Clothes, jewels, everything," she said. "You have to know how to use that iciness."

"Poor little Gloria" was Rose's code. It meant: "I don't care who Joe sleeps with. The others will never marry him, will never have his name, his money, or the luxury that go with being Mrs. Joseph P. Kennedy."

7

CRASH

In May 1929, Joe's patron, Guy Currier, once more had to rescue him. Currier did not yet know of Joe's treachery. Currier's realization that Joe had been plundering his files for inside information on major stockholders of Hollywood studios would not come until the summer of 1929. Now Currier warned Joe that the market was overheated.

Currier expressed his concern to his friend Louis Kirstein. "It looks to me that there is an even chance that we are in for some degree of business depression," he wrote. "Present money conditions are slowing up building and will restrict public works. . . . On the whole, it is not an attractive time to go into new matters."

While juggling Gloria Swanson and Hollywood studios, Joe had continued to play the market. Now he began selling his holdings in such companies as Anaconda Copper and Eastern Steamship, purchasing municipal bonds or simply placing his money in the bank. On February 20, 1929, Joe's family had expanded once again when Jean Ann Kennedy was born. Even though the Kennedys now lived in New York, Rose went to Boston to have the baby so her longtime obstetrician could deliver it. Joe decided it was time to buy a bigger house instead of renting one. On May 4, 1929, Joe and Rose bought a six-acre estate at 294 Pondfield Road in Bronxville, New York, a town notorious for its exclusion of Jews and nonwhites. They paid Joseph A. Goetz $250,000 for the twenty-one-room brick colonial home, originally built for Adolphus Busch, who founded Anheuser–Busch with his father-in-law.

As Black Tuesday approached, Joe liquidated his longer-term investments but continued to make money on the declining market by selling short. Usually an investor purchases stock and later sells it, earning a profit if the stock has gone up. Short sales reverse the process. The investor who believes the price of a stock will go down borrows stock—say at $10 a share—from a broker for a fee. He sells the stock to a buyer and receives payment of $10. If the price falls to $8, he buys new shares at the lower price of $8 and gives them back to the broker to replace the shares he borrowed at $10. He then gets to keep the $2 difference as his profit. On the other hand, if the price of the stock goes up, he loses money.

By selling short, Joe made sums estimated at more than $1 million, contributing in a small way to the crash by forcing prices down. While Joe later denied selling short, he also occasionally "hinted broadly that the legend is true," according to the *New York Post*.

On the Thursday before the crash, the stock market suffered the most disastrous decline in its history. A bankers' pool organized by J.P. Morgan & Company's Thomas Lamont purchased $240 million in stocks to stabilize the market. The market rallied, but then another staggering decline took place on the following Monday.

As soon as trading began at 10 A.M. on Tuesday, October 29, 1929, it was clear that the day would be even worse. Immense blocks of stock were dumped on the market. By noon, more than 80 million shares had been sold, shattering all previous trading records. The members of the New York Stock Exchange governing committee held a secret meeting in a smoke-filled room beneath the floor to debate whether to close the exchange. By the end of the day, $15 billion in stock values had been lost. Altogether, since September, $30 billion out of $80 billion in stock listed on the Big Board had vanished—a sum equal to what the United States spent to fight World War I.

The fact that the market was unregulated was largely responsible for the crash. Salesmen had made wild claims to a gullible public. Stock pools such as those perfected by Joe had defrauded legitimate investors. Reporters and columnists often had acted as shills for companies peddling stocks in return for payoffs.

The crash set off a worldwide financial panic and depression that would last three years. By 1932, 12 million Americans were jobless. Governments responded with strict tariff restrictions that dried up world trade. In Germany, where 5.6 million were out of work, the depression contributed to the rise of Adolf Hitler. The panic would lead to the creation of the Securities and Exchange Commission, which Joe would head.

Joe later said that he had figured out that the market was overheated because Pat Bologna, who had a shoeshine stand at 60 Wall Street and later 70 Pine Street, was in the market with relatively large sums and had lots of inside tips.

"When the time comes that a shoeshine boy knows as much as I do about what is going on in the stock market . . . it's time for me to get out," he later said. "Only fools hold out for top dollar."

But the story of the shoeshine boy was baloney. Joe told the story to show how astute he was. In fact, it was Currier— the same man Joe would soon double-cross—who had saved him from disaster by warning him to get out of the market. Nor was Joe the only investor to avoid the crash. Lots of people got out: David Sarnoff, Bernard Baruch, Paul M. Warburg, and the partners of Kuhn, Loeb and Company all sold before the crash.

Considerably richer because of his short selling, Joe gleefully told Gloria Swanson he had sold off his Wall Street holdings before the bottom dropped out of the stock market. He said he was now waiting to pick up the pieces left by "dumb people."

◆ ◆ ◆

The Trespasser opened successfully in New York in November 1929. Critics hailed it as not only a captivating picture but an important one. Joe was jealous. Even though he was a partner in the film's production, he viewed the film as Gloria's, not his.

Before Swanson left for the Chicago premiere of the film, Ted O'Leary, one of the four horsemen, called Swanson in New York. He said an "important person" wanted to see her. Joe was out of town, and she had become accustomed to doing whatever one of the horsemen told her to do. "Fine," she said.

O'Leary picked her up at her hotel in the late afternoon. On the drive to another hotel, she asked the name of the person. "O'Connell," O'Leary said. When that did not satisfy her, he added, "A friend of the Kennedys."

At the door to the man's hotel suite, a young man in a clerical collar said, "Thank you for coming. His eminence will be with you in a moment."

Swanson looked at O'Leary, who avoided her glance. Then a man in red appeared, and O'Leary introduced him as Cardinal O'Connell of Boston. He was the same cardinal who had married Joe and Rose fifteen years earlier.

The cardinal complimented Swanson on achieving so much success at an early age. But she could tell he was not about to discuss her movie career. He said he would like to talk with her about her association with Joseph Kennedy.

Swanson said she had a business relationship with Joe.

Derr had power of attorney, and any business discussions should be held with him.

The cardinal straightened himself in his chair. It was not their business relationship, but rather their personal one that he wanted to discuss.

"There is nothing to discuss," said Swanson, rising and moving toward the door.

O'Connell moved in front of her and fixed her with his eyes.

"You are not a Catholic, my child," he said. "Therefore, I fear that you do not grasp the gravity of Mr. Kennedy's predicament as regards his faith."

"That is true," she said, "but Mr. Kennedy *is* Catholic. Therefore, shouldn't you be talking to him?"

Now the cardinal spoke in stentorian tones.

"I am here to ask you to stop seeing Joseph Kennedy. Each time you see him, you become an occasion of sin for him."

Swanson suggested that Joe might have discussed their relationship in confession. If so, the cardinal had no right to discuss it. If he had not revealed it, she said, there was nothing to discuss.

The cardinal replied that Joe had asked some of the highest church officials if he could live apart from his wife and maintain a separate household with her. That was impossible, the cardinal said. Meanwhile, Joe was exposing himself to "scandal" every time he was seen with Swanson in public.

"Then tell him so," she said.

"Have you no feeling for his family?" he asked.

"Of course I do, just as I have for my own," she said.

Now his voice became calmer. "As a Catholic, there is no way Joseph Kennedy can be at peace with his faith and continue his relationship with you," he said. "Please consider that very carefully."

"I shall," Swanson said, putting on her gloves. She repeated that the cardinal should be talking with Joe, not with her.

Swanson let herself out. She wondered who had put the

cardinal up to this. Rose? Joe? Their families? A friend? She was baffled.

Geraldine Hannon, Rose's niece from her mother's side of the family, told Doris Kearns Goodwin that she overheard a loud argument one sunny summer afternoon at the Fitzgerald home. Fitzgerald was confronting Joe about his affair with Gloria. He threatened to tell Rose if he did not cut it off. Joe, in turn, threatened that if Fitzgerald told Rose, he would marry Gloria.

Years later, Nellie McGrail, the family cook, recalled Rose telling her that Joe had offered to give her father a Rolls-Royce. Fitzgerald "wouldn't take it," McGrail said. "He said, 'If I take that, they'll say that it came from widows and orphans.'"

Quite likely, Fitzgerald had asked the cardinal to intervene in Joe's affair with Swanson. As Joe's father-in-law and as a former mayor of Boston, Fitzgerald had both the clout and the standing to galvanize the cardinal.

Downstairs, Swanson asked O'Leary why he had not warned her.

"I knew if I did, you wouldn't come," he said. "I'm sorry. Orders."

"Whose? Joe's?"

"Oh, no," he said. "All I can tell you is that Cardinal O'Connell contacted me."

◆ ◆ ◆

Still determined to create his own movie, Joe commissioned John and Josephine Robertson to write a comedy. Swanson decided it was awful. Joe wanted his name on a film, but she realized he had little taste or talent to make it happen. She didn't have the heart to tell him, and she went along when Joe invited some writers to dinner to try to come up with a title. When Sidney Howard, a Pulitzer Prize–winning playwright, suggested *What a Widow*, Joe was ecstatic. Slapping his thigh, he ordered that the man be given a Cadillac.

The story spread through Hollywood. Months later, Irving Waykoff, Swanson's accountant, asked her why the Cadillac had been charged to her personal account instead of to Joe's. Since Waykoff was the only one of Swanson's original employees Joe had allowed to remain on her payroll, he remained loyal to her.

Swanson brought it up one night in November 1930 when she was having dinner with Joe at his Rodeo Drive home. When the conversation turned to the new film, Swanson remarked, "By the way, Joe, Irving Waykoff tells me I paid for Sidney Howard's Cadillac out of my personal account. How come? You gave Sidney Howard the car; I didn't. He thanked you for it, not me. So I think it's only fair that you pay for it."

Unaware of Joe's deviousness, Swanson had tried to attribute the matter to a bookkeeping error. But to Joe, Swanson was questioning his honesty, a highly sensitive area. He became agitated and choked on his food. He looked at Swanson the way he had looked when she had suggested he take Rosemary to see Dr. Bieler. When he regained his composure, he stood up and left the room.

After thirty minutes, Joe had not come back. Eddie Moore offered to drive her home. As he fielded her questions, Moore was guarded. A few days later, Swanson heard through the grapevine that Joe had left for the East Coast.

Soon Swanson received a letter from Derr stating he no longer had her power of attorney. This was the only notice she received that her three-year affair was over. On top of that, *What a Widow* was a bomb.

Now Waykoff told Swanson that Joe had been milking her, charging to her account a fur coat that Joe had given her as a present, not to mention the bungalow he had purportedly given her. It took a year to untangle the books. Swanson eventually realized that because of the way Joe had structured their deals, she had wound up holding the bag for millions of dollars in unpaid federal income tax. Yet Joe had no shame. He would not give her information that would help unsnarl the mess.

Gertrude Ball, Joe's secretary, recalled that in the early 1950s Swanson tried to see Joe at his office at 230 Park Avenue in New York.

"She wanted to see Mr. Kennedy, and he didn't want to see her," Ball said. "She stayed in the office for a whole day in the reception room. It was over money she wanted. I would get phone calls from him asking, 'Is she still there?' I would say, 'Yes,' and he would say, 'Thank you,' and hang up." Joe had a separate entrance to his private office, so during the day he went "out to lunch and came back."

"The question was who took the tax loss on *Queen Kelly*," said Dufty. "It was her money, and he took the tax loss. . . . Gloria would look at the Merchandise Mart [which Joe would later buy] and say, 'There's my money.' "

Yet at other times, Joe would call her to boast of his latest achievement or to tell her cheerfully about his children, even asking to see her again. "When she appeared in a play, sometimes she would say Joe was waiting in the wings to see her," Dufty said. "He was still after her. . . . It was something Joe never gave up on."

Since it wasn't finished, *Queen Kelly* never opened. In 1985, a film company brought together the existing reels and showed it at the Los Angeles County Museum. Ironically, in 1950, Stroheim played Swanson's butler in *Sunset Boulevard*. In the legendary film, considered by many to be the best movie about Hollywood ever made, Swanson was a once-adored aging star obsessed with achieving a return to glory. As the deluded Norma Desmond, she lived with her male servant and former director, Stroheim, who tried to assure her in the movie that she would once again conquer the silver screen. Reconciled with Swanson, Stroheim kept asking that scenes be reshot, much as he had for *Queen Kelly*. In the movie, Swanson watched clips from *Queen Kelly* and uttered haughtily her famous line, "I am big. It's the movies that got small." For Swanson, it was a tour de force, the best role of her career.

Years later, Joe bragged that Swanson was "sexually insatiable" and had orgasms "five times a night."

"I'm sure Joe had the time of his life," Dufty said. "She was ultra-geisha. She would service you incredibly. I never experienced any sense of limitation."

Swanson died in 1983 at the age of eighty-four, ever optimistic. "If I had my life to live over again, I wouldn't," she said. "Life is a privilege. Mistakes should be dropped in the wastebasket. No, I'm not much for the past. I'm concerned about tomorrow and what's going on between dreams."

◆ ◆ ◆

As the stock market slowly recovered, Joe returned to making money on Wall Street. From 1930 to 1933, he operated from a desk at Halle and Stieglitz on Madison Avenue and 52nd Street in New York, sending orders to friends in the offices of J.H. Oliphant or Bache and Company. Records of Joe's transactions show he operated through an account in the name of Edward E. Moore, Esquire.

Joe worked in tandem with Bernard E. "Ben" Smith, known as "Sell 'em, Ben," a notorious bear raider. Together, they used inside information and stock pools to enrich themselves.

"If Joe and Ben Smith found out you had $1 million at Continental Bank and you had a loan from the bank and had a tough time covering it, they would get to work on the market," said Charles Spalding, an investment banker who became friends with Joe through Jack. "They would force your stock down and weaken your position. The bank would yell for collateral and you wouldn't have it. Then they would walk in and say we'll take it off your hands for a little more than you bought it for. . . . They were able to get, from banks or the exchange, information on a weak position."

One example of Joe's manipulations came out in Senate Banking and Currency Committee hearings, known as the Pecora Hearings, after Ferdinand Pecora, the committee counsel. Using Moore to conceal his interest, Joe became a partner in Redmond and Company, a stock brokerage firm that specialized in organizing pools or syndicates designed to manipulate stock prices. One such syndicate bought stock in 1933 in Libbey-Owens-Ford Glass Company because its name could easily be confused with Owens-Illinois Glass Company, which made bottles that would be in demand after Prohibition. In fact, the former company made plate glass.

When the syndicate bought 81,500 shares—including 65,000 shares bought on option—the stock was considered inactive. But from June to October 1933, more than a million shares traded, more than half by members of the syndicate trading back and forth among themselves. As a result of the phony trades, other investors thought the stock was more valuable. The price rose from $20 to $37. In four months, the syndicate members made a profit of $395,283. Joe's share was $60,807. When the members pulled out, the public suffered heavy losses.

With Bernard Baruch, Joe acted on inside information on earnings and dividends of Brooklyn Manhattan Transit Corporation. Joe obtained the information from Herbert Bayard Swope, who was on the board. But Joe sometimes lost his shirt. In the summer of 1932, he joined a group organized by Baruch that held 150,000 shares of BMT, which operated subways between Manhattan, Bronx, Brooklyn, and Queens. The group thought that New York's transit systems would be unified, bringing large profits to BMT. But when the system was unified, the city took it over. Joe lost money on his investment.

Joe participated in these abuses even as federal investigators were swarming over Wall Street trying to expose the conditions that had led to the crash.

"Today people would go to jail" for engaging in such activities, said Irwin Borowski, a former associate director of enforcement at the SEC. But in those days, "There weren't any regulations," said Charles J. Burke, a nephew of Joe's who is senior vice president of the Boston stock brokerage firm of Moors & Cabot Inc. "If you had money, you could manipulate the market any way you wanted. You could force it up or down, if you had enough dollars and knew what you were doing."

For nearly two years, a parade of Wall Street titans would march to the witness stand and describe their roles in the seamy dealings. But while records of Joe's unethical transactions were presented during the hearings, Joe was never called to appear. Later, Joe would pretend that he was as innocent of such activities as a newborn kitten. In his book *I'm for Roosevelt*, Joe wrote, "For month after month the country was treated to a series of amazing revelations which involved practically all the important names in the financial community in practices which, to say the least, were highly unethical." The belief "that those in control of the corporate life of America were motivated by honesty and high ideals of honorable conduct was completely shattered."

◆ ◆ ◆

The Halle office out of which Joe operated was managed by his friend and Harvard classmate Arthur Goldsmith. In his view, Joe had no feelings, no sentiment. As Goldsmith told Richard J. Whalen in a not-for-attribution interview for his book *The Founding Father*, "He has tremendous confidence in his own judgment; if it is disputed, he reacts passionately, then lapses into bitter coolness."

Goldsmith considered Joe a brilliant man at times, but also one who had a self-destructive streak of "insanity." By this, Goldsmith meant that Joe repeatedly broke with old associates over "trivial" matters. "Be grateful and be loyal" Joe often quoted his father as telling him, and he claimed he always lived up to that. In fact, as Goldsmith said, these were two of the few principles Joe adhered to religiously—only in reverse. He was known both for discarding friends when they had served their purpose and for knifing in the back those who had helped him. As one Wall Street wag said, "I don't know why Joe Kennedy turned on me—I never did anything to help him."

Like most of his partners and friends, Joe and Goldsmith eventually came to a bitter parting of the ways, apparently over a simple disagreement.

Goldsmith said Joe used words like "kike," "sheeny," and "mick" unthinkingly, yet waxed eloquent about the fact that some of his best friends were Jews—Baruch, *New York World* editor Swope, David Sarnoff, and Goldsmith himself. Often, the two attended the symphony together. Joe later became friends with Carroll Rosenbloom, owner of the Baltimore Colts, and Arthur Krock of the *New York Times*. Phil Reisman, a golfing pal, was also Jewish. His lawyer, William P. Marin, was a Jew. When confronted with the charge of anti-Semitism, Joe would point out that he was the only non-Jewish member of the Palm Beach Country Club, which he joined because it was near his home.

Thus Joe's claim that some of his best friends were Jewish was well supported. Yet in his mind, his friendships did not conflict with his anti-Semitism. That existed apart from his friendships and was expressed often and vociferously. Prejudice, by definition, is irrational.

While Joe was often described as brilliant, his mind was not capable of perceiving that if many of his friends were Jewish, his hatred of Jews in general was ill-founded. Often, Joe's bellicose manner and self-proclaimed forthrightness were mistaken for brilliance. In fact, while he was shrewd, cunning, complex, and often farsighted, Joe's overall intelligence was only slightly better than average. His writing was hackneyed and illogical; his speech was often inarticulate. If compared with his sons' intelligence, Joe would come out not as bright as Jack, for example, who was noted for his intellectual prowess. Rather, according to friends, Joe's level of intelligence was closer to Ted's and to Joe Jr.'s.

"Joe Jr. was a bully, and I think Jack always felt he [Jack] was brighter than he [Joe Jr.] was," said Charles Spalding, Jack's friend.

8

I'M FOR ROOSEVELT

Having made his mark on Hollywood and Wall Street, Joe came to realize that Washington was where the real power was. As he told his friend Morton Downey, "The people who run the government will be the biggest people in America" in the next generation. Joe had never been interested in the arduous way his father had achieved political power—through meetings in smoke-filled rooms and holding constituents' hands. Rather, now that he was one of the richest men in the country, Joe would buy his way into power.

Joe's entry into politics began when Henry Morgenthau Jr., a friend and neighbor of then–New York governor Franklin Roosevelt, called Joe in 1930 and invited him for lunch. Morgenthau then took him to meet with Roosevelt at the governor's mansion in Albany, according to Joe's friend Arthur Goldsmith. Roosevelt was descended on his father's side from an old New York family of Dutch origin. A Harvard graduate and lawyer, he was a fifth cousin of former Republican president Theodore Roosevelt. In 1921, he was stricken with polio. He could walk only with heavy braces and assistance.

Roosevelt had just won reelection as governor. He was already being talked about as a presidential contender. Privately, Roosevelt encouraged such talk, while publicly denying he was a candidate. A pragmatist willing to obtain support from almost any quarter, Roosevelt saw Joe as both a potential source of major campaign contributions and someone who could swing Wall Street and conservative Democrats his way. Joe and Roosevelt spent the afternoon together and forged a political alliance. Joe would contribute to his campaign and open doors for him on Wall Street; Roosevelt would bring Joe into his inner circle of advisers. Later, Roosevelt hinted that he might include Joe in his cabinet.

"Joe called me one day from California—I think he was staying at Hearst's ranch—and in the course of our conversation, he asked me if I had a notebook," recalled investment banker Jeremiah Milbank, Herbert Hoover's leading fundraiser. "I said yes. 'Well,' he said, 'jot down the name of the next president. You're not hearing much about him now, but you will in 1932. It's Franklin D. Roosevelt. And don't forget who told you.'"

Once the campaign got under way, Roosevelt asked Joe to meet with him on May 8, 1932, in Warm Springs, Georgia. According to his later public account, Joe agreed to contribute $50,000 directly to Roosevelt and later raised another $150,000 toward the campaign—equal to $2.2 million today. In fact, Joe eventually gave Roosevelt a total of $360,000 directly for his first two campaigns, according to Joe Kane, Joe's cousin. In today's dollars, this support came to $3.8 million. Moreover, according to Timothy McInerny, who had worked for Joe, Joe not only contributed to the campaign but was Roosevelt's "money collector" or bag man, collecting cash from those who wanted to hide their identities.

Joe was, according to what he told Harvard College in the twentieth report of the class of 1912, a "capitalist." But now he began a new career—as confidential adviser and behind-the-scenes political operative. Besides the money he represented and the financial advice he could give, Joe had grown up in politics and knew many of the players. What's more, he was close to newspaper publishers who could be critically important. Not only could they support candidates in their papers, they often used their political clout to choose candidates in the first place. Chief among these power brokers was William Randolph Hearst.

Portrayed as corrupted by power in the film *Citizen Kane*, Hearst owned thirty-three newspapers with a circulation of 11 million. Joe often gave Hearst financial advice. The two shared a fondness for illicit affairs. Besides his wife, Hearst kept as his mistress Marion Davies, a former dancer he met in 1918, when he saw her perform in the *Ziegfeld Follies*, an elaborate revue produced annually for twenty-four years. Hearst helped Davies start an acting career.

Hearst controlled eighty-six convention delegates to the Democratic nominating convention; nearly all were from California and Texas. An isolationist, Hearst opposed formation of the League of Nations, the forerunner of the United Nations. In his *New York American*, he ran a signed editorial saying he was for neither Roosevelt nor Alfred E. Smith of New York because they were both internationalists. Instead, Hearst supported John Nance Garner of Texas, the Speaker of the House. Hearst had already sent a glowing biography of Garner to all Hearst outlets. While Garner had no chance of winning, votes cast for him would deadlock the convention.

Before the convention, Roosevelt used Joe as an emissary to sound out Hearst. Joe found Hearst was not implacably opposed to Roosevelt after all. When the convention deadlocked, Joe, who was "working his fool head off," as one friend put it, learned that Newton D. Baker, secretary of war in the Woodrow Wilson cabinet, was being suggested to break the impasse. Joe woke Hearst at 5 A.M. at his estate in San Simeon, California. Joe knew that while Hearst had no love for Roosevelt, he had "undying hatred" of Baker.

"W.R., do you want Baker?" Joe asked.

When Hearst said no, Joe said, "If you don't want Baker, you'd better take Roosevelt, because if you don't take Roosevelt, you're going to have Baker."

Hearst asked if there were other possibilities, like Maryland's governor, Albert Ritchie.

"No, I don't think so," Joe said.

Hearst then agreed to back Roosevelt, and Joe proudly handed Hearst's first campaign contribution to Roosevelt. In return for the vice presidential nomination, Garner, at Hearst's urging, swung his delegates to Roosevelt.

On the evening of July 1, when the California delegation's vote was announced, it was clear that Roosevelt would win the nomination over Al Smith. An organ played "Happy Days Are Here Again," Roosevelt's theme song. Roosevelt broke precedent by flying to Chicago to accept the nomination. In his speech on July 2, he promised to deal aggressively with the economic crisis and give a "new deal for the American people."

Joe would later claim, with some justification, that he won the nomination for Roosevelt.

◆　◆　◆

At 4 A.M., Gloria Swanson picked up the ringing telephone at her hotel in London. The connection was terrible, and Swanson thought it was her mother calling with bad news. Instead, it turned out to be Joe, a man whom she now detested, calling from Chicago.

"It's four o'clock in the morning, Mr. Kennedy, and I'm nursing a baby," she said, referring to her second daughter. "What do you want?" she asked.

"I read about your baby," Joe shouted. "We just had one too," Joe said, referring to Edward Moore Kennedy, who was born on February 22, 1932, at St. Margaret's Hospital in Dorchester. "We named him after Eddie Moore. That isn't why I called."

"I should hope not!" Gloria yelled. "Why did you call?"

"Do you know who's here with me, Gloria? The next president of the United States, Gloria! He just won the Democratic nomination. I want you to say hello to him."

Swanson was stunned at how blatantly opportunistic Joe could be.

"How dare you?" she shouted.

Joe pleaded with her to talk to Roosevelt.

"Wait a second, I'll put him on," he said.

"Don't bother!" she said. "I don't want to talk to him, and I don't want to talk to you!" Swanson yelled. She slammed down the phone.

By then, Michael Farmer, whom she was about to marry, had awakened next to her.

"Who was that?" he asked suspiciously.

"The next president of the United States, presumably," she said. "But I hung up on him."

The next morning, a friend of Swanson's cabled to apologize. She had agreed to give Joe Gloria's telephone number in London when he claimed he would help finance Swanson's next picture. Joe had also mentioned that Roosevelt had promised him a cabinet position, most likely secretary of the treasury, if he were elected in November.

◆ ◆ ◆

On September 13, 1932, Joe boarded the *Roosevelt Special* to accompany the candidate on a thirteen-thousand-mile campaign trip. Joe and other close advisers had already tailed Roosevelt on a fishing trip up the New England coast. Each night in port, they discussed strategy. Now the campaign train, with nearly a dozen cars, was packed with most of the members of what would be called Roosevelt's brain trust—advisers who would play crucial roles in his administration. Among them was James Roosevelt, Roosevelt's oldest son, who would become one of his aides in the White House and in some ways his most influential adviser. Joe was pleased to find himself in Car D, which carried Roosevelt's closest friends and advisers, including James A. Farley, the campaign manager.

Joe supplied the Roosevelt camp with ideas for speeches, including ones on the need to reform the securities industry, and tickets to baseball games along the route. Joe would buttonhole local officials and flatter them by asking for their advice. Always self-effacing, Joe told a Boston reporter when asked about his own aspirations, "There is nothing I want. There is no public office that would interest me."

To others, he confided that he thought very little of Roosevelt. For example, Joe told Roy Howard, founder of the Scripps-Howard newspaper chain, that he had a "very low estimate" of Roosevelt's ability but planned to "fly to whatever port Roosevelt is in for the night" to make sure men like Louis M. Howe and Farley, both close advisers to Roosevelt, didn't influence Roosevelt on areas of interest to Joe.

Inevitably, Joe's loose-lipped criticisms began getting back to Roosevelt through advisers like Howe, who was jealous of Joe's access and who had never liked him. Joe's two-faced approach to Roosevelt would continue throughout their relationship.

On election night, November 8, 1932, Joe took over two floors of the Waldorf-Astoria for friends and family. When the word came that Roosevelt was winning by a landslide, Joe instructed an orchestra to play "Happy Days Are Here Again." Roosevelt had carried all but seven states, with 472 electoral votes to Herbert Hoover's 59.

◆ ◆ ◆

As nearly every other adviser was given a job in the new administration, Joe became anxious, then angry. Having been inaugurated as the thirty-second president on March 4, 1933, Roosevelt called a special session of Congress to enact what came to be referred to as New Deal legislation aimed at spurring economic activity and ending the Depression. Already, Congress had passed an enabling amendment to repeal Prohibition, which both candidates, Roosevelt and the incumbent, Herbert Hoover, had promised to end.

Still, there was no call from the White House. Roosevelt recognized Joe's liabilities—including his notorious record on Wall Street. That, together with opposition from advisers like Howe, had stalled any appointment.

In late March 1933, Joe sent Roosevelt a telegram passing on praise he had heard of the new administration. Roosevelt responded with an invitation to accompany him on the presidential yacht, the *Sequoia*. On May 19, 1933, Joe responded that he was rarely in Washington. Obsequiously, he added, "It is pleasant to any of us to know that we are remembered by those in high places," he wrote. "And you have made your place high—in the respect, admiration, faith, and gratitude of the people you saved from despair or worse. . . ."

Joe told Senator Burton K. Wheeler, to whom Joe also had contributed money, that he might sue the Democratic Party to recover money he had loaned for Roosevelt's campaign. Joe took Raymond Moley, a member of Roosevelt's brain trust, to lunch at Robert's on West 55th Street in Manhattan. Joe reminded Moley that his new "status" in Washington required a standard of living that the government would not support. Joe could solicit funds to make it possible for Moley to live as he should.

At the time, the government had no laws prohibiting such arrangements. So long as outright bribery was not involved, anyone could contribute to the salary of a government worker. However, as Moley himself noted, such a fund, if revealed, would create "nasty" publicity. Joe obviously had more in mind than making Moley's lifestyle more comfortable. He wanted access and control. Moley declined his offer but said that if he ever needed a loan, he would come to Joe.

Having failed to buy his way in, Joe swallowed his pride

and called the White House to say he would be in Washington anyway and would like to see his old friend.

"Hello, Joe, where have you been all these months?" Roosevelt asked disingenuously when he met with him. "I thought you'd got lost."

At the suggestion of Bernard Baruch, Roosevelt broached the idea of making Joe a member of the American delegation to the London Economic Conference, which was charged with drafting a reciprocal trade agreement with South American countries. But Roosevelt's delegate, James P. Warburg, put a stop even to that olive branch. On April 8, 1933, Warburg had lunch with Harrison Williams, who served in the new administration. Williams described Joe as "a completely irresponsible speculator" who had been "passing malicious tales about the president." Warburg responded that he was not interested in "political hacks." Joe's appointment to the delegation was never made.

◆ ◆ ◆

That same month, Adolf Hitler, who had become chancellor of Germany in January, began a campaign against the Jews. Hitler used Germany's severe economic problems to win support from extremists who had fomented violence. He claimed Germany had been "stabbed in the back" by the acquiescence of German leaders to the Treaty of Versailles. As scapegoats, he singled out Jews and Communists. They were responsible for Germany's economic plight.

By November 1932, the Nazis had become the largest single bloc in the Reichstag. After Hitler was appointed chancellor, he quickly destroyed the constitutional government. Squads of brown-shirted stormtroopers carted off critics and tortured or shot them. Over four thousand people in public life were thrown in jail.

On April 1, 1933, persecution of the Jews in Germany became official with a Nazi-initiated boycott of Jewish businesses and shops. On May 10, 1933, Nazi students and some professors burned hundreds of thousands of books, including many by Jews. They cast them into bonfires as part of a "purification" of German culture.

As Joe would later make clear, he thought the Jews had "brought on themselves" whatever Hitler did to them. While Joe rarely read books, he professed admiration for the obscure works of Brooks Adams, whose views on racial purity paralleled Hitler's. Joe was impressed by the way Adams depicted the "cold struggle of the classes," he told Tommy Corcoran.

Ironically, Adams was a quintessential blue blood of the sort Joe hated. He was the grandson of President John Quincy Adams and great-grandson of President John Adams. He had done his undergraduate work at Harvard and married a sister of Henry Cabot Lodge. In Cleveland Amory's *The Proper Bostonian*, Adams was described as a man who could not believe that, knowing who he was, a young woman whom he had carefully chosen to be his wife would turn him down. "Why you perfect damn fool," he is said to have responded when she rejected his marriage proposal.

A historian, Adams articulated a "survival of the fittest" theory much like Hitler's. Eventually, the "energy" of a "race" is exhausted, and it must be replaced by the infusion of "barbarian blood," he wrote.

Nor did Adams have much use for democracy. According to Adams' gloomy scenario, outlined in *The Theory of Social Revolutions* and other works, American democracy had inherent defects. Without near-dictatorial powers, presidents cannot govern effectively. Ultimately, these defects would bring disaster to the country.

Adams predicted that England would fare far worse. The country was in a state of "decay," brought on by "high living," "wasteful" habits, and "intellectual torpor." Its military was weak and yellow-bellied. In contrast, Germany had a strong military and a vigorous population that was better educated.

Such blather was of course proven incorrect by events. During World War II, no military force was braver than that of the English. But Joe did not have the intellectual prowess to see through the silly stereotypes. To see through a stereotype requires thought. One must ask if there are exceptions to the stereotype and, if so, whether the stereotype therefore has any validity. Joe accepted Adams as his intellectual guru, ratifying, as he did, the prejudices that Joe already had.

To be sure, anti-Semitism in the United States, particularly in Boston, was not then uncommon. Blue Hill Avenue, where many Jews lived, was often referred to as "Jew Hill Avenue." A ditty called "The First American" that made the rounds during World War II went: "First American killed in Pearl Harbor—John J. Hennessey/First American to sink a Jap ship—Colin P. Kelly/First American to get four new tires—Abraham Lipshitz." (The fact that Meyer Levin, a Jew, died on the same mission that claimed Colin Kelly's life was not mentioned.)

Occasionally, priests in Boston railed against the Jews from the pulpit. Publications of Charles E. Coughlin, the anti-Semitic priest of the Shrine of the Little Flower in Royal Oak, Michigan, were sold outside churches after mass. President Roosevelt himself made anti-Semitic remarks, saying to reporters off the record, "What do you expect from a Jew?" when Herbert Lehman, governor of New York, came out against one of his plans. Even after war had broken out, a public opinion poll found 24 percent of Americans thought Jews were "a menace to America."

But while many were passively anti-Semitic, Joe was rabidly so. Repeatedly and aggressively, he attacked the Jews, even suggesting to his son Jack that he incorporate a campaign against the Jews as part of his political platform.

Joe, as a capitalist, liked Adams' theories because he saw himself as their beneficiary and they appealed to his prejudices. According to Adams, the "greedy" economic man or capitalist becomes dominant in society. Morality and ethics are of no value. Instead, "Men do not differ in any respect from the other animals, but survive, according to their aptitudes, by adapting themselves to exterior conditions which prevail at the moment of their birth. . . ."

◆ ◆ ◆

For years, Joe and Rose had vacationed in Palm Beach, Florida, usually staying at the Royal Poinciana Hotel. Now that he had decided to become a power in Washington, Joe decided to buy a home in Palm Beach. Just as he made it a lifelong habit to give cases of Scotch at Christmas, he would use his new vacation home to entertain such people as James Roosevelt; Marguerite A. "Missy" LeHand, Roosevelt's mistress and personal secretary; and Arthur Krock.

On June 30, 1933, Joe bought a five-bedroom, red-tiled home at 1095 North Ocean Boulevard for $100,000, along with adjacent property for which he paid $15,000. Built in 1925 and added on to in 1933, the Palm Beach home had a heated pool. Addison Mizner, the island's corpulent mansion architect, had designed the Spanish-style home for Lewis Rodman Wanamaker, the second son of John Wanamaker, founder of Wanamaker Department Stores.

The home was located on the northern end of the island that is Palm Beach, an idyllic sliver of land just half a mile wide by ten miles long. Here, on this "island of privilege," as Cleveland Amory described it, Joe was in his element. He was just minutes from a first-class golf course and could mingle with the moguls and celebrities of the day. Woolworth and Wanamaker, Dodge and Firestone, Pulitzer and Marjorie Merriweather Post all had mansions here. Joe took in the brilliant sunshine, the lush vegetation, the high sculpted hedges, the unlined faces, and the bejeweled, tanned women cruising the shops.

"There is more money, more champagne, more caviar, more Rolls-Royces, and of course, more affluence in Palm Beach than [in] all the rest of America put together," Post, the heir to the cereal fortune, once remarked.

From then on, Joe and Rose arrived at Palm Beach around the first of December and stayed until the first of May, when they migrated back to Hyannis Port.

♦ ♦ ♦

By the summer of 1933, enough states had ratified the amendment repealing Prohibition to ensure that liquor sales soon would be legal. Like any successful businessman, Joe had a knack for moving quickly when he saw an opportunity. Already, he had gotten Washington authorities to grant permits to import ridiculously large quantities of Haig & Haig and Dewar's as medicine. He stockpiled the liquor in warehouses so that when Prohibition ended, he would have more high-quality liquor in stock than anyone else. But that was just the beginning.

Late in the summer of 1933, Joe invited James Roosevelt to his home in Hyannis Port. If FDR had been slow in rewarding him for his campaign help, Joe would use the president's son to make sure he had cornered the market in Scotch once Prohibition ended.

Having attended Harvard but not graduating, James Roosevelt had started an insurance business in Boston, representing Travelers Insurance Company. Balding and pin-headed, he was greedy, dim-witted, and unethical. Once Roosevelt entered the White House, Jimmy would be a constant embarrassment to his father. On July 2, 1939, for example, Roosevelt felt constrained to write to his son to tell him he was a "good deal upset" about his calls to Treasury officials, including Treasury Secretary Henry Morgenthau Jr., concerning the indictment of Joseph Schenck, the movie magnate, for income tax evasion. Schenck, a friend of Joe Kennedy's, was accused of bribing a Treasury agent to falsify his reports on the merger of 20th Century-Fox and MGM. With others, Schenck was said to have conspired to defraud the government of $7 million.

President Roosevelt told his son that any action he took

to try to influence such investigations would be seen as an attempt to interfere politically. It would put "you and the government" in a bad position.

According to James Roosevelt, a friend of his had asked him for help. Since Joe was friends with both Jimmy and Schenck, it is quite possible Joe was acting as Schenck's intermediary. In any case, Jimmy's account in his autobiography is instructive. He wrote that he saw "nothing wrong" with trying to help a friend by bringing his case to the "one man who might pardon him"—Morgenthau. Despite documentary evidence that his father severely chastised him for making calls on Schenck's behalf, Jimmy blithely wrote in his memoirs that "father agreed there was nothing wrong with my pleading a person's case." Schenck was later convicted and went to jail.

Joe knew that Jimmy wanted to be governor of Massachusetts. Joe claimed he would help him. Recognizing that Jimmy was open to trading influence for cash, Joe also began steering insurance business his way, not only from his own companies but from banks and stock brokerage firms that he did business with—among them Hayden, Stone, the National Shawmut Bank, and First National Bank. "I can't tell you how much I appreciate what you did for me," Jimmy wrote to Joe, "and anyway, words mean so little that I hope my actions will sometime make you realize how grateful I always will be."

Two months later, without disclosing the considerable financial benefits he was receiving from Joe, James Roosevelt wrote to his father to push for a spot for him in the administration. "Outside of Massachusetts, there is one person who, as I talked over with you the other night, feels that he has more or less been put aside now that his usefulness has come to an end," Jimmy wrote to the president on July 24, 1933. "I am talking about Joe Kennedy," he wrote. Joe was a "very useful man during the campaign, and when the bills had to be paid, he always came across. I believe today there is still $100,000 owed to him by the national committee."

Joe did not need a Louis Howe or Jim Farley to get to

the president. He had the president's feather-brained son—described by Tommy Corcoran as "naive and inexperienced"—in his pocket. And Joe had more in mind for Jimmy than using him to help him get a government job.

Throughout the country there were food riots, and an angry mob nearly lynched a judge who had approved a mortgage foreclosure, but Joe was unaffected. He took a cruise to England with Jimmy Roosevelt to secure liquor distributorships in London. Jimmy told Joe Kennedy biographer David Koskoff that Joe took him to lunch with the head of Distillers Company Limited, now United Distillers PLC.

During Prohibition, the company had kept the United States supplied with its products by shipping to the islands of Saint-Pierre and Miquelon off the coast of Newfoundland. These shipments—known as "in transit" shipments because the company realized the liquor was destined for other places—totaled 48,165 cases a year during Prohibition. When Prohibition ended, these shipments dropped to 5,180 cases and eventually to 325 cases a year.

Bringing Jimmy Roosevelt to lunch was critically important. If Joe was in business with President Roosevelt's son, as appeared to be the case, he must have the president's ear. On December 5, 1933, Utah became the thirty-sixth state to ratify the Twenty-first Amendment, which repealed the Eighteenth and with it, Prohibition. Through his Somerset Importers Inc., Distillers Company Limited appointed Joe exclusive United States agent for its Haig & Haig Scotch, Gordon's Dry Gin, and Dewar's White Label Scotch.

According to a major Boston liquor distributor, Joe kept Jimmy supplied with chorus girls through Morton Downey, and he promised him a 25 percent cut of the liquor business. But as they were docking in the United States, the distributor said, "Kennedy put his arm around Jimmy and said, 'You know, I've been thinking about it, and with your father as president, if it ever got out that you were in the liquor business, it would be death.' He said, 'I don't think we should do this.'"

In his memoirs, Jimmy, who became his father's secretary in 1937 and later was elected a congressman from California, admitted that he had helped Joe get into the liquor business and had helped him "get what he wanted from father." But he said he had not been offered part of the liquor business.

If Jimmy was impressed by Joe, his younger brother Franklin D. Roosevelt Jr. was not.

"I was on a plane with him when I was a kid," Franklin Jr. told Ralph G. Martin, "and he was telling me foul stories in loud language until a woman behind us leaned forward and said she would appreciate it if he would have the decency to keep quiet in a place where other people couldn't walk away from him if they didn't want to listen. He simply laughed and went right on. I think Jack's father was one of the most evil, disgusting men I have ever known. Oh, I know he was a financial genius, but he was a rotten human being. He once called in my brother Jimmy to work out a deal with [a Scotch distiller], and Jimmy went and worked out the whole deal, then had trouble getting old man Kennedy to pay his expenses. And Kennedy made a pile out of that one."

As Joe set up Somerset, he owned only 2 percent of the company's stock. The rest his family owned. While no one knows why he chose Somerset as the name of the company, it is likely that it was because of his resentment of the Somerset Club, the Yankee fortress in Boston. Francis X. Morrissey, Joe's longtime confidant, agreed. "Unless you were Yankee and had millions of dollars, you couldn't become a member of the Somerset Club," Morrissey said. "It was for the Yank and the very wealthy." Perhaps appropriating the name was Joe's revenge.

Joe did not confine himself to importing liquor. He began buying up rum distilleries in the United States as well. Businessman Armand Hammer learned about an abandoned rum distillery in Newmarket, New Hampshire. The plant had been repossessed by the Reconstruction Finance Corporation, which asked for the $55,000 it had loaned the company as the sale price. Hammer wrote a check for the amount on the spot.

"Well, Doctor Hammer," an official told him, "you're now the owner of a distillery. It's a good thing you acted so promptly, because only yesterday Mr. Joseph Kennedy was in here expressing an interest in the plant. He asked me if we would put it on hold for him, and we asked for a deposit. He said that he would be in here today with a deposit. You've just beaten him to it."

In November 1934, John A. McCarthy, who had been a Boston brewer before Prohibition, claimed in a lawsuit that he told Joe of a plan to secure the New England distributorship of National Distilled Products Corporation. Joe promised to work with him and split the ownership, but then reneged. Joe had misled him, the suit said, because Joe was working for himself. The suit was dropped before a trial.

Soon, Joe was selling 100,000 to 200,000 cases of Haig & Haig and 150,000 cases of Gordon's gin a year. But Distillers Company became disenchanted with Joe's bullying tactics and lack of candor. To run Somerset, Joe appointed Ted O'Leary, his aide since his Hollywood days. A graduate of Dartmouth College, O'Leary had sold municipal bonds and used cars before meeting Joe at a riding club in the Boston area. On October 21, 1935, they met with Sir James C. Calder, chairman of Gordon Dry Gin Company Limited, which was part of Distillers Company, to propose a joint investment in a United States gin distillery. After Joe and the pink-faced, blond O'Leary made their case, Calder told them bluntly that the board of the company "could not be expected to believe all they had to say," according to minutes of board meetings.

By 1939, Distillers Company had learned that Somerset was hoarding liquor supplies. "It has been clearly established that our true figures for the year ended 31 March 1939 were greatly exaggerated by reason of the Somerset Importers Inc. having established an overstocked position," according to the minutes of Haig & Haig Limited, a subsidiary. By January

1939, Somerset's overstock was fifty thousand to sixty thousand cases, roughly a third of a year's supply.

By overstocking and thereby limiting supplies, Joe was able to increase prices. He was also able to obtain commissions and other allowances regardless of whether he sold any Scotch. His commission amounted to as much as $9.75 for a case of fifths. Thus he was making close to $500,000 a year in commissions alone.

Haig appointed Joseph M. Kelly of New York to investigate distribution in the United States. Kelly found that Joe was requiring distributors to buy large quantities of an inexpensive rum called Rionco if they wanted to buy Haig & Haig from him. R.S. Cumming, a Distillers Company official, told the board, "At the present moment, the names of Somerset and Haig & Haig are extremely unpopular in the trade throughout the country," principally because "no one could buy" Haig & Haig or King William, another Scotch made by Distillers Company, "without buying three or four times as much rum." Moreover, Somerset's reputation is "poor" because of "promises regarding supplies which they failed to fulfill." During some months, the company makes practically "no deliveries.

"The number of cases accumulated by Somerset quite frankly staggered me, and I understand as a conservative estimate that their present stock of Haig & Haig and King William amount to approximately 140,000 cases," Cumming said. This was well over a year's supply.

In a May 1944 interview with Joseph Dinneen Sr. of the *Boston Globe*, and Lawrence E. Spivak, then editor of *American Mercury*, a popular magazine, Joe would deny that he hoarded Scotch. "They say that you have cornered the market on Scotch whisky; that you're responsible for its shortage," Spivak said.

In response, Joe called the charge "pure bunk. . . . As far as Scotch whisky is concerned, I have a four-months' supply of liquor in warehouses . . . and I've never had anything larger than a four months' supply."

Cumming, the Distillers Company official, concluded that it would be in the "best interests of the trade in general" if Kennedy quit the business, as "I have never felt with all his influence in the past that he has done much in furthering the interests of Scotch whisky." He added that from the company's point of view and "for Scotch whisky generally, one hopes that Kennedy will sell."

By January 1946, the board was pleased to learn that the Kennedy family had sold 50 percent of its interest in Somerset Importers Inc. to Reinfield Importers and the rest to two other firms. Joseph Reinfeld, who owned Reinfield Importers, was a jovial, avuncular man who ran a saloon before Prohibition in Newark. During Prohibition, he carved out a major portion of the bootlegging market for himself.

The Distillers Company board concluded that Joe's policies had been "detrimental to our interests and bound to result in a loss of goodwill." Reinfeld already had set a policy that all brands would be sold "on their individual merits," the board noted, "and he plans to liquidate the considerable inventory." To avoid flooding the market, he planned to sell Joe's overstock slowly.

The overstock meant that Joe could sell out for a much higher price. The total price was $8 million, compared with the $100,000 he had initially invested to form the company. For his efforts in developing the company, Joe paid O'Leary $25,000 in severance.

"I don't think the parting was too cordial," said Richard P. O'Leary, his son. "There was a general understanding that my father would get a share of the business. He was responsible for the success of the business. Joe was off doing other things."

The two never spoke to each other again.

◆ ◆ ◆

Joe and Rose sent their children to boarding schools, the girls to Catholic ones and the boys to secular ones. In effect,

Joe had decided, "I'll send my girls to Catholic colleges to believe, my men to the market place to know better," Thomas Corcoran, a Catholic, said.

Even before they were sent away, Jack recalled that his father "was away a lot" so that "he was a more distant figure" than his mother. Yet when he was with the children, "He was this extraordinary figure that was trying to keep the blowtorch on you, in terms of your own kind of abilities, and was quite willing to point out your deficiencies and challenge you to do better," Ted said.

Rose was "a little removed," Jack recalled, perhaps a defense mechanism when one has nine children. At the time Jack lay seriously ill in the hospital in Connecticut for more than a month in February 1934, Rose had gone abroad seventeen times in the previous four years, Nigel Hamilton, author of *JFK*, calculated. Yet she did not see Jack once that month.

Charles Spalding, Jack's friend, said Rose never touched Jack. "I think half of this activity with girls was making up for what he didn't have at home," Spalding said. "She would get pregnant once a year and that would be it. She never touched him as a mother. I have never seen a house where so much is done by the father." But that was the way Joe wanted it. "Joe was determined to capture each of the kids himself," Spalding said. "He wanted to be the biggest item in all their kids' lives."

"She was a loner," Red Fay, another of Jack's friends, said of Rose. "Like at a cocktail party, she'd never be involved in it, she'd never be a part of the conversation." Fay felt Jack had lacked a warm, loving mother.

To Joe, Rose was but another courtier, there to make his life more comfortable. They had a curious idea of togetherness. For her fortieth birthday, Rose went to Paris, and the two exchanged telegrams. "What a thrill he [Joe] gave me when he cabled me on my fortieth birthday in Paris, calling me 'The Eighth Wonder of the World,' " Rose wrote. Again on October 6, 1934, Joe and Rose celebrated their twentieth wedding anniversary by exchanging telegrams. From the Ritz in Paris, Rose wired, "Thank you. Twenty years. Rare happiness. All my love always, Rose." Joe responded: "I cannot tell you how happy these years have been for me and what a marvelous person you have been through it all. . . . I love you now more than ever."

Of all his sons, Joe most identified with Joe Jr. A sturdy young man with dark blue eyes, he had inherited a ruffian appearance from his grandfather. Like his father and grandfather, he liked to intimidate. Jack, who was now a junior at Choate School in Wallingford, Connecticut, would later describe Joe Jr. as "a slight bully as far as I was concerned."

Joe Jr. absorbed his father's virulent anti-Semitism. Having graduated from Choate, Joe Jr. was sent to London to study with Harold J. Laski at the London School of Economics. During a break from school in April 1934, he traveled to Germany. By then, public eating facilities, theaters, and shops in Germany displayed signs saying "Jews not Welcome." Jewish mothers could not buy milk for their infants. Jews who were sick could not obtain prescriptions.

SS leader Heinrich Himmler started a state breeding program to produce an Aryan "super race." He urged young women of "pure blood" to volunteer to be impregnated by SS officers to produce blond, blue-eyed "Nordic beings" for the Reich. The Nazi Party Congress forbade intermarriage with Jews and proclaimed that sexual intercourse between Jews and Aryans would be punishable by death.

Joe Jr. wrote to his father on April 23, 1934, that Hitler had taken advantage of a widespread dislike of the Jews, a dislike which was "well-founded." After all, Joe Jr. said, the Jews' methods are "unscrupulous," and since lawyers and prominent judges are Jews, "if you had a case against a Jew, you were nearly always sure to lose it."

Joe Jr. told his father Hitler was "building a spirit in his men that could be envied in any country." The brutality, bloodshed, and marching were necessary, he said, and the sterilization law was a "good thing."

"I don't know how the church feels about it but it will do away with many of the disgusting specimens of men who inhabit this earth," Joe Jr. wrote. The only problem would be if "something happened to Hitler," allowing "one of his crazy ministers" to come to power.

9

THE FOX IN THE CHICKEN COOP

In late June 1934, Roosevelt's adviser Raymond Moley sat next to newspaper publisher Roy Howard on a flight to Washington. Having directed the drafting of the legislation creating the Securities and Exchange Commission, Moley told Howard that he had recommended to the president that he name Joe as chairman.

In a memo to the president, Moley had said Joe Kennedy would be the "best bet" for the job. Moley cited Joe's "executive ability, knowledge of habits and customs of business to be regulated, and ability to moderate different points of view." What he did not write down, but pointed out to Roosevelt, was that Joe's financial support had been critically important, especially in a Depression year.

Howard could not believe what he was hearing. Joe symbolized everything the SEC had been set up to eradicate. Whether Joe's earlier offer to make Moley financially secure had affected his judgment can only be speculated upon. But

Howard did not waste time trying to analyze Moley's motives. As soon as they landed, he telephoned Joe at his hotel in Washington.

Threatening to attack him in his newspapers, Howard asked him to withdraw his name from consideration. When Joe refused, Howard dictated an impassioned editorial for his *Washington News* opposing the appointment. The editorial said the president "cannot with impunity administer such a slap in the face to his most loyal and effective supporters" by appointing Joe to the sensitive post.

With the word now out that Joe was being considered, a storm of criticism erupted. Even though the press had never exposed him, everyone in Washington knew that Joe had made his money through bootlegging and stock market manipulation. Just eight months earlier, Joe had made a killing by participating in the Libbey-Owens-Ford Glass Company pool, a fact that the Pecora Committee would disclose the following month.

Roosevelt brought the issue to a head on the evening of June 28, 1934, when he asked Moley, Joe, and Bernard Baruch to meet with him. It was a steamy Washington evening. Moley noticed the editorial lying on Roosevelt's desk. The president asked the others to sit down. He then pulled out Moley's memo.

"Kennedy," Roosevelt said without looking at Joe, "is first on the list here. I propose to give him the five-year appointment and the chairmanship."

After waiting a year for this moment, Joe pretended to Roosevelt that he did not want the job because of the "injurious criticism" it would provoke.

In the days before FBI background checks, government appointments were made without the benefit of hard investigations into nominees' characters. Instead, Moley said to Joe, "I know darned well you want this job. But if anything in your career in business could injure the president, this is the time to spell it out. Let's forget the general criticism that you made money in Wall Street."

"With a burst of profanity," Moley recalled, Joe "defied anyone to question his devotion to the public interest or to point to a single shady act in his whole life." Joe said he would create an SEC that would be a "credit to the country, the president, himself, and his family—clear down to the ninth child."

Roosevelt believed it took a thief to catch a thief, as he later put it to his adviser James Farley. He ignored Louis Howe's countervailing advice. Not only did Roosevelt have a debt to Joe, he wanted his financial support for his next campaign. Roosevelt had not become president by refusing to make political compromises.

Joe had wanted to be treasury secretary, but "Joe was a strong man, and Roosevelt wanted a weak secretary of the treasury," Thomas Corcoran said. "Roosevelt didn't want any strong men in his cabinet." Yet "Joe had the sense to recognize the opportunity," Corcoran said. "There was stature with the SEC."

Joe accepted the appointment. Besides Joe, Roosevelt appointed James Landis, Ferdinand Pecora, Federal Trade Commission member George C. Matthews, and FTC chief counsel Robert E. Healy to the five-member commission. Along with Corcoran and Roosevelt confidant Benjamin V. Cohen, Landis had been assigned by Moley to draft the Securities Exchange Act of 1934, which set up the SEC. Passed on June 6, 1934, the act combined previous legislation requiring disclosure of information about securities to the Federal Trade Commission and a companion piece of legislation to improve the operation of stock exchanges.

As a member of the FTC, Landis had already administered the Truth-in-Securities Act. A former law clerk for Justice Louis D. Brandeis and a Harvard Law School professor, Landis had originally been considered for the job of SEC chairman. But Moley, who had guided the Securities Exchange Act to passage, argued that Landis should be a member of the commission. Joe, he argued, would be better able to win the confidence of business.

While the commissioners chose their own chairman, Roosevelt signaled that he wanted Joe to be chairman by giving him a five-year appointment. The others were appointed for terms of one, two, three, and four years, respectively. In case they didn't get the message, the president sent a note to the commissioners stating that his "preference" for the top job was Joe.

After Roosevelt announced to his cabinet Joe's appointment, Harold L. Ickes, a former Chicago newspaper reporter who was then Roosevelt's public works administrator, wrote in his diary, "The president has great confidence in him [Joe] because he has made his pile, has invested all his money in government securities, and knows all the tricks of the trade." Ickes added, "Apparently, he is going on the assumption that Kennedy would now like to make a name for himself for the sake of his family, but I have never known many of these cases to work out."

As expected, when it was announced on June 30, 1934, the appointment was greeted with amazement. *The New Republic* called Joe a "grotesque" choice. It was "incredible" that a president would "so far defy public opinion" as to choose someone like Kennedy, the magazine said. But *New York Times* columnist Arthur Krock helped defuse the criticism in his column, which had more impact in Washington than any other political column.

"J.P. Kennedy Has Excelled in Varied Endeavors," read the headline over his "In the Nation" piece. Krock called Joe a "famous baseball player" at Harvard who was "invited" to take over Columbia Trust. He "ran" the Fore River shipyard, and he "resolved" the warring interests of Hollywood. Joe "has never been in a bear pool" in his life or "participated in any inside move to trim the lambs," Krock averred. Joe served as Roosevelt's "campaign, business, and financial manager, with amazing success."

As the piece suggests, Krock had already become one of Joe's unofficial flacks. Krock first came to Washington in 1910 as a reporter for the *Louisville Times* and *Louisville*

Courier-Journal, which had consolidated under the same ownership. On Bernard Baruch's suggestion, Adolph S. Ochs, the publisher of the *New York Times*, hired him in 1927. In 1932, Ochs asked Krock to reorganize the Washington bureau.

Krock insisted that colleagues he had worked with for decades address him as "Mr. Krock." "I'm sorry, but that's the way I am," he said. Roosevelt often made fun of him, pulling out a letter Krock had written after the inauguration listing the special privileges he expected to be granted.

Krock used his position to ingratiate himself with those in power, often obtaining inside scoops that he presented in a turgid writing style. He met Joe in 1932 on Roosevelt's campaign train during a stopover in Chicago. While he avoided Joe's efforts to put him on his payroll, he accepted extensive gratuities, including cases of Haig & Haig Pinch Bottle and lengthy vacations in Joe's Palm Beach home, where Joe's chefs prepared all meals.

After the column appeared, a reader took Krock to task. "The unrestrained amusement of brokers and investment bankers over the attempt you and Joseph Kennedy are making to build Mr. Kennedy up to the stature of a big man shows that Wall Street, in spite of all its tribulations, has not yet lost its sense of humor," the writer said. She asked Krock to "look at all Mr. Kennedy's mergers and manipulations today. What happened to the poor suckers who invested their savings in his movie bonanzas?" She predicted Joe would "play ball" with the money changers.

When Joe later thanked Krock for his support, Krock wrote back that he "called the public attention to you in an effective way. But that is all I concede."

On July 2, 1934, Joe was sworn in at the SEC. Landis was not sure he would like Joe, but Joe won over the soft-spoken man when he dropped into Landis' office at the FTC to obtain his ideas. Joe's apparent forthrightness impressed Landis. He concluded that Joe should be chairman: He would have the power to withstand pressures from Wall Street. Joe turned his charm on the other members as well—including Pecora, who had exposed his practices to the world.

"I'm no sucker," Joe told them. "They [the other members] know more about this law than I ever hope to know." To Cohen and Corcoran, he said one morning at a sidewalk café, "Why do you fellows hate me?" Spurred on by Landis, the commissioners elected Joe unanimously, as Roosevelt had ordained.

Joe rented Marwood, a spectacular thirty-three-room French Renaissance mansion overlooking the Potomac River in Potomac, Maryland. Built by Samuel Klump Martin III, it had gold-plated bathroom fixtures, a movie projection room in the basement, and a large swimming pool. Joe installed an elevator to make it easier for the polio-stricken Roosevelt to visit.

If one of Joe's failings was his lack of loyalty to those who had helped him, he now turned that trait to his advantage. He did not care if his former cohorts hated him because of his enforcement efforts. Joe had ambitions for himself and for his sons that transcended the SEC. This would be a way to make a name for himself and for his family. As Joe later described it to SEC lawyer Milton Katz, his job entailed forcing "their mouths open and go[ing] in with a pair of pincers and just tak[ing] all the gold out of their teeth." Joe was perfectly capable of becoming Wall Street's dentist.

If behind every bully is an insecure man, Joe's insecurities never affected his appointments. Joe never felt threatened by others' accomplishments or credentials. To the contrary, the more impressive their background, the more Joe wanted them as his employees. As Jack, Bobby, and Ted would later do, Joe chose only first-rate people to work for him—a tradition that has continued at the SEC.

Joe asked William O. Douglas, then a Yale University School of Law professor, to meet with him at his office at 8 A.M. on October 10, 1934. Douglas was considered one of the leading experts on corporate finance. Joe told him he wanted his help with a commission study on how stockholders should be protected during bankruptcy proceedings. Joe said Douglas would have an annual budget of $50,000, would be responsible to him, and would have an office and a secretary. He wanted him to start at once.

"He spoke these words rather brusquely and then turned to some papers on his desk," Douglas recalled. "Then, seeing that I was still there, he said, 'Well, what in the world are you waiting for?' "

Taking a leave of absence from Yale, Douglas recruited such heavies as Thurman Arnold and Dean Charles E. Clark of Yale Law School to perform part-time work for the commission. After Douglas had worked for Joe for a year and returned to Yale, Joe was influential in getting Roosevelt to appoint him to the SEC and then to its chairmanship. This led to Douglas' appointment by Roosevelt as an associate justice of the Supreme Court in 1939.

To Douglas, Joe was a "two-fisted, tough, hard-driving administrator" who "backed up his subordinates." He viewed his subordinates as "partners in a cooperative enterprise."

As his chief counsel, Joe hired John J. Burns, another former Harvard Law School professor who was the first Catholic to join the faculty. Joe tended to browbeat the other commissioners into consensus and was not always interested in staying within the boundaries of the SEC law. But with Burns as chief counsel, the other members managed to keep Joe in check.

Joe relied heavily on Landis as well. "I knew the details of the law," Landis recalled. "He knew what he wanted to do but was sometimes incapable of articulating the right things to do. Sometimes he'd want to do something not authorized by the law."

"He got a lot of his strength from Jim Landis," said Orval L. DuBois, who was recording secretary at the SEC and later became secretary of the commission. "I thought he relied a lot on Landis, who succeeded him as chairman."

As was his habit, Joe brought in Eddie Moore as his personal assistant. He went on the government payroll at $1 a year, allowing him access to the SEC's files.

To set up the SEC's regional offices, Joe hired James Fayne, a partner at Hornblower and Weeks. During Kennedy's fourteen-month tenure, the commission hired 692 employees and opened offices in New York, Boston, Atlanta, Chicago, Fort Worth, Denver, San Francisco, and Seattle.

Fayne continued to work for Joe after both had left the SEC. He had no illusions about the man. "If he likes you, you're the tops, no matter what anybody else thinks of you," Fayne said. "If he stops liking you, you simply don't exist anymore." Sometimes people got terribly hurt, Fayne said, but it didn't affect Joe; he had seen so many come and go. The schism sometimes occurred with friends, but Joe remained "entirely indifferent" to it.

As one example, after Burns had worked loyally for Joe at the SEC and later at the Maritime Commission, Joe hired him as a lawyer but quibbled over his fees. After Burns died in 1957, Landis asked Joe for a contribution to a memorial room honoring him at Harvard Law School. Joe curtly refused to contribute.

Besides hiring top-flight people, Joe enlisted the aid of well-connected experts. He could call up the president of Standard Oil Company, for example, and ask him to send his comptroller around for a chat.

Early on, Joe and the other commissioners visited the New York Stock Exchange. With President Richard Whitney escorting them, they wandered around the trading posts, asking questions.

In his speeches, Joe reminded Wall Street of the Better Business Bureau aspect of the SEC. Over and over, he sounded the theme that the agency protected businessmen from fraudulent operators and swindlers. It thus bolstered the public's confidence in the securities markets.

At the time, the country had dozens of stock exchanges, and one of the commission's first acts was to require them to register and comply with SEC rules. The commission refused to register four notoriously rigged exchanges, including the Boston Curb Exchange.

During Joe's tenure, the SEC investigated 2,300 cases of possible securities fraud. However, the cases all involved small operators. During the first year, not one major member of the New York Stock Exchange was prosecuted or the subject of a proceeding.

Initially, the commission required disclosure statements, but Joe decided they were far too lengthy. Under his direction, a new form A-2 was developed for use only by firms that had previously sold securities. "This is our answer," Joe said, "to our pledge to make less onerous, less expensive, and more practical the registration of securities."

The idea was to require companies to honestly disclose information that might affect their prospects so the public could more accurately gauge the value of their securities. What was known as a "capital logjam" due to lack of confidence in the market soon lifted when Swift and Company of Chicago registered a $43 million bond issue. The registration statement was only fifty-nine pages, compared with two thousand pages for a recent filing by Republic Steel under the old system. Two days later, Pacific Gas and Electric registered a $45 million issue. The total of $2.7 billion in securities sold during 1935 was four times greater than the total for 1934.

The SEC issued rules curbing short selling, one of Joe's favorite ways of making money. The chief problem was that the practice, if unchecked, could drive down the price of a stock indefinitely. A new rule banned short sales at a lower price than the last price quoted. Thus short sales could take place only on the "uptick," or when the price of a stock was rising.

Dan T. Moore, who was in charge of registrations by foreign entities at the SEC, said Joe could tell simply by looking at the stock ticker if syndicates were manipulating stocks. "He would hold the ticker in his hand and would say, 'Somebody's running a pool,' and we would send people to New York and find he was almost always right."

Soon, men like Elisha Walker, Joe's former partner in stock market pools, found that Joe was avoiding them. Yet to suggest that Joe had become angelic would be naive. While no evidence has come to light to show that Joe abused his position to make money, there is evidence that he thought nothing of using his government position and access to Roosevelt to benefit his own family, as when the Treasury Department fired James T. Fitzgerald, Rose's uncle.

During Prohibition, Honey Fitz's brother had bought a building on Atlantic Avenue in Boston and turned it into a speakeasy drugstore, which dispensed liquor as medicine. After Prohibition, no doubt through Honey Fitz, he became district supervisor of the Treasury Department's Alcohol Tax Unit. On June 19, 1935, Joe met with Morgenthau, the treasury secretary, to protest his firing. Joe brought along his friend, Congressman John W. McCormack from Massachusetts. Joe had little respect for the intelligence or judgment of his wife's family. He would object whenever Rose wanted her relatives to come over. Usually, she had to visit them at their homes. But Honey Fitz clearly had leaned on him to help him out.

Quickly, Morgenthau recounted the case against Fitzgerald. When first hired, he had falsely listed his age as sixty-five. Since he was seventy-three at the time, he never would have been hired had he told the truth. Morgenthau said Fitzgerald had requested that liquor dispensers under his regulation hire his friends. When dealing with other government agencies, he was "curt, impolite, arrogant, and hostile." Further, Fitzgerald issued permits to companies even though they had not complied with government rules.

Joe staged one of his temper tantrums, asserting that the Treasury Department had not fairly treated his relative. In an aside to a Treasury aide, McCormack later said he owed it to Joe to fight for Fitzgerald, but really "did not care" whether he was rehired or not.

To placate Joe, Morgenthau decided to extend Fitzgerald's employment by giving him a ninety-day appointment in the Customs Bureau. A few days later, Morgenthau ran into Joe at the White House, and he told him of the ninety-day extension.

Thanking him, Joe said, "I can't help it that I married into an SOB of a family." Then he shocked Morgenthau by adding, "Perhaps the old man won't live longer than ninety days, and then we won't have to worry about him anymore."

Morgenthau even went over the issue with Roosevelt, who agreed that Fitzgerald should not be rehired, if only because Fitzgerald had lied about his age when hired originally. When Morgenthau told him of Joe's remark that the man might die in the interim, Roosevelt said, "No one can tell what an Irishman will do," meaning Joe was unpredictable.

Joe had to strike a balance between reforming Wall Street and encouraging investment. Joe and Landis tended to make compromises, while Pecora and Healy wanted tighter regulation. For example, Joe took little interest in developing strict accounting standards. As a result, Healy found that his push to regulate accounting firms got little support. Pecora became so frustrated that he began missing meetings. After six months, he resigned to accept a seat on the New York Supreme Court.

Corcoran, like the others, had been skeptical about Joe's appointment. When Moley told him the news, he exploded. When Corcoran calmed down, he said, "Oh, well, we have four out of five." What did he mean? Moley asked. "What I mean is that four are for us and one is for business," said Corcoran, who had helped draft the SEC legislation.

But in the end, Corcoran thought Joe struck the right balance and got the job done, restoring confidence in the investment community. He became impressed by Joe's purposefulness, the fact he was "in tune with the times," and the way he took control at the SEC. "He was a handsome vital guy—the girls were crazy about him," Corcoran recalled. "He had a great capacity for getting people to join him," he said. And Joe enlisted to his side "the two most brilliant guys over there"—Douglas and Landis. "It was a testimony to his magnetic instinct," Corcoran said. "He had the capacity to pull them around." Joe had "sheer animal vitality." He was not only a glamorous personality, he had the showman in him. "It comes from the beginning, from the movies," Corcoran said. "Joe took good care of himself," he said. He always looked twenty to thirty years younger than he was. He didn't drink alcohol. He slept well and exercised. "He squeezed the last percent out of his physical energy."

The fact that Joe seemed to have a close relationship with Roosevelt bolstered his power. "The president enjoyed Joe," Landis recalled. "He used to go down to Joe's house and watch movies. Joe would get films before they were released, and the president used to kid him about this."

But Joe's biggest asset was the way he handled the press. One reason, recalled Walter Trohan, who became chief Washington correspondent of the *Chicago Tribune*, was Joe's friendships with the major publishers. Joe and Colonel Robert R. McCormick, publisher of the *Tribune*, were neighbors in Palm Beach. Joe fed McCormick inside tips on Washington. "Joe was an angle-shooter," Trohan said. "He'd cultivate the hell out of anybody who could be useful to him."

Trohan recalled that Joe regularly gave cases of Haig & Haig Pinch Bottle Scotch and A. Sulka ties from London to the eight reporters—including Trohan—who regularly covered Roosevelt. Since Roosevelt often talked with the reporters off the record, they knew more about what was going on and what the president was planning than anyone else. "Joe worked on us and got chummy with us," Trohan said. "Then he would ask what Roosevelt had said. I didn't realize at the time he wasn't in love with us. It was to help him." Trohan came to realize from others who worked for Joe that Joe was likely using the information to make a killing on the stock market.

In turn, Joe never failed to let the press know about any

contact he had with the president. To highlight his own importance and his chummy relationship with Roosevelt, Joe wrote a long, dramatic memo, which he leaked to the press, recounting the events of February 18, 1935. On that day, the Supreme Court was expected to announce a decision on a lawsuit brought by a group of bondholders who were unhappy that the United States had gone off the gold standard in June 1933. Formerly, the government had been required to redeem all paper currency in gold at a fixed ratio. Because increases in the money supply were tied to the amount of gold held in national coffers, the gold standard created inflexibility in exchange rates, which had little reference to economic conditions. Congress went along with Roosevelt and abandoned the gold standard to stop a decline in prices for goods and lay the basis for an expansion of the economy.

The bondholders sued, demanding that their obligations be paid in their full gold value, as promised by the bonds they had purchased. If the Supreme Court sided with them, total government debt would increase by $70 billion. Since the Supreme Court was still dominated by men who had not been appointed by Roosevelt, many assumed that the Court would rule against the government. In anticipation of that, stock prices had been fluctuating wildly.

On the day of the expected decision, Joe arrived at his SEC office and called a meeting to see if the other commissioners thought the exchanges should be closed. Since the Court's ruling was not yet known, they decided against it. At 10:30 A.M., Joe called Colonel Marvin McIntyre, one of Roosevelt's assistants, at the White House. The president's aide said the president was shaving. At 11:55 A.M., Missy LeHand, Roosevelt's personal secretary, called Joe. In a serious tone, she told him that since it was a beautiful day, the president had decided to "take a nice, long automobile ride," according to Joe's memo.

At 12:07 P.M., John Burns, the SEC's chief counsel, notified Joe that the Court had decided in favor of the government. Joe called Roosevelt and informed him. The stock market began to rise rapidly, but it soon calmed down. The next day, Roosevelt sent Joe a memo suggesting that in view of his "shrunken face, sunken eyes, falling hair, and fallen arches," the president commanded him to proceed to Palm Beach and "return to Washington six hours after he gets there."

Besides financing Roosevelt's campaigns, Joe served Roosevelt's purposes by giving speeches praising his New Deal policies. Robber baron or not, he talked the language of businessmen, and they respected him. Like everyone else, Roosevelt was taken by Joe's charm: To those he wanted to cultivate, he was fun to be with.

As a member of the Washington establishment, Joe no longer felt the sting of social rejection. On the recommendation of Roosevelt aide Colonel McIntyre, the exclusive Burning Tree Golf Club accepted him. Besides Burning Tree, he could list in his Harvard class report the Metropolitan and National Press Clubs in Washington; Harvard in New York; Siwanoy in Bronxville; Oyster Harbors in Osterville near Hyannis Port; and Bath and Tennis, Gulf Stream, and Seminole in Palm Beach.

Yet for all their camaraderie, Roosevelt had come to consider Joe a pain. On April 13, 1935, Morgenthau met with Roosevelt for an hour and a half. The price of gold had been fluctuating, and Roosevelt was worried that the problem could affect the economy and his chances for reelection. When Missy LeHand disturbed them to take some motion pictures, he waved her away.

Morgenthau then said he had a suggestion for a man to head the Allotment Board, a new agency that would buy gold on the open market to stabilize gold prices.

"I have a man also," Roosevelt cut in.

"Should I give you mine first?" Morgenthau said.

"Yes."

"My man is Joe Kennedy," Morgenthau said.

"Mine is Frank Walker," said Roosevelt, referring to Frank C. Walker, who had been treasurer of FDR's 1932 campaign.

Having first introduced him to Roosevelt, Morgenthau still thought highly of Joe. He argued that Joe had an "outstanding record" and could handle people. "He is popular on the Hill and with newspapermen," he said. But Morgenthau could see that Roosevelt was not buying.

"What is the matter?" Morgenthau asked.

"The trouble with Kennedy is you always have to hold his hand," the president said. At irregular intervals, Joe "calls up and says he is hurt because I have not seen him." In Roosevelt's view, Joe was "too temperamental," Morgenthau recorded in his diary two days later.

A week later, Roosevelt offered the job to Joe anyway, but he turned it down. Joe did not get along with Harold Ickes, who was interior secretary and would have to work with the Allotment Board. Joe said he could not take the job unless the president fired Ickes. Joe knew Roosevelt would not do that.

Temperamental or not, Roosevelt often accepted Joe's hospitality. On June 29, 1935, Joe invited Krock to spend the weekend at Marwood. It was then that Roosevelt decided to take Joe up on his open invitation to come over for dinner, and Joe did not want to tell Roosevelt that Krock was already there. Joe told Krock to stay out of sight, and the newsman later recorded what happened.

"At 7 p.m., I saw two White House cars coming up the drive and [I] fled upstairs," he wrote. He became an "involuntary eavesdropper."

Roosevelt had several mint juleps, and then they watched the movie *Ginger*. Corcoran, another guest, played the accordion, and Roosevelt sang. Roosevelt asked Corcoran to play "Tim Toolan," a ballad about an Irish lad who makes good in politics.

The "favorite jest" of the evening revolved around the Yankee pronunciation of "boat." Roosevelt pronounced it "bhutt." From that time on, Krock recorded, whenever Roosevelt said "boat," "float," or similar words, Missy LeHand, a tall woman with large blue eyes, would chime in with "bhutt" or "flutt."

The singing and drinking went on well after midnight, when Krock fell asleep.

On July 1, 1935, Joe was reelected chairman of the SEC. Yet as James Fayne observed, Joe liked challenges but became bored quickly. On September 4, 1935, Joe sent Roosevelt clippings showing that the SEC had moved against a fraudulent enterprise in Nashville. Called National Educators' Mutual Association, it was about to sell $750,000 in bonds for $750 each. The company claimed they would be redeemable in ten years for $1,000, but a statement in much smaller type specified the payment would consist of $750 in cash and stock then worth only 50 cents.

Two days later, Joe reminded Roosevelt that he had accepted the appointment at the SEC on the understanding he would not be able to remain in the position much longer than a year. For "personal reasons," he said he would have to resign as of September 23, 1935. Yet he still considered himself an "unofficial" part of Roosevelt's administration.

Joe's last act was to vote for Landis as his successor. While committed to the SEC's basic objectives, Landis was indecisive and not as aggressive on cracking down on fraud as Joe had been. As it turned out, Landis had a drinking problem that would eventually contribute to his suicide after he became dean of Harvard Law School and eventually began working for Joe. Landis drank only Scotch. "He had it figured out to the last inch what the liver would take," said Corcoran.

When Joe's resignation was announced on September 12, the news depressed stocks on Wall Street. As *Newsweek* reported, Joe's administration of the SEC had won respect from friend and foe alike.

John T. Flynn of *The New Republic*, previously a critic of Joe's appointment, said he turned out to be the "most useful member" of the commission, helping not only business but national recovery.

Corcoran thought Joe's greatest contribution was the administrative system he set up. "Joe is the kind of man who has organizing ability," he said. Referring to Oliver Wendell Holmes Jr., the former Supreme Court chief justice, Corcoran said, "Holmes said that the first duty of an organized man is to organize himself out of a job. Joe picked good men to put in, and he won people over, and he organized himself out of a job."

10

PROFITEERING

I am now through with public life forever," Joe told journalists after quitting the SEC. But Roosevelt was not about to let him go so quickly. Having made a national name for himself, Joe was now an even more valuable commodity. With an election coming up, Roosevelt wanted to make sure Joe was in his camp. Immediately after his resignation, the president asked him to visit Europe to report on monetary and economic conditions. "When I lie awake at night, as I often do, I worry about the condition of Europe. . . ." the president told Joe. "I wish you would do a trouble-shooting job and find out for me just what the threat to peace amounts to."

With presidential letters of introduction to the leaders of governments and opposition parties in Great Britain, France, Italy, Switzerland, and the Netherlands, Joe embarked on the trip with Rose on September 25, 1935. In London, they saw Jack, who had just enrolled at the London School of

Economics and Political Science. Because of an attack of jaundice, Jack soon had to withdraw. He entered Princeton University, but a recurrence of the illness forced him to leave at the end of the first semester.

At Bernard Baruch's suggestion, Joe met with Winston S. Churchill. Then a member of Parliament, Churchill had served in the British government as chancellor of the exchequer and was about to become first lord of the admiralty, overseeing the British navy during the country's entry into World War II.

At a luncheon for Joe and Rose at his home in Chartwell, Churchill suggested that the two countries begin to build stronger navies to defend themselves against Nazism. By now, Hitler had proclaimed himself führer or supreme leader and chancellor of Germany. In defiance of the Versailles treaty, he had reinstituted military conscription. He had evicted Jews from trade and industry.

Churchill saw the Nazi threat for what it was. In the November 1935 issue of *The Strand*, Churchill warned of the German menace, noting that German soil was "pock marked" with concentration camps. Here, masses of Germans, from "world famous scientists" to "wretched little Jewish children," were being persecuted. Churchill cited Hitler's statement in his 1925 book *Mein Kampf* [My Battle], that Jews were a "foul and odious race." Churchill had adopted the position that the truth would always be the opposite of what Hitler said. He cited Hitler's statement in *Mein Kampf*: "The great masses of the people . . . will more easily fall victim to a great lie than a small one."

But Joe saw no threat. Rather, when he returned to Washington on November 14 and stayed overnight at the White House with Rose, he gave Roosevelt a confused report. Vaguely, he talked of the "tensions and hypocrisies I witnessed." In his confident, booming voice, he said Europe was "unsettled and confused" with an "Alice-in-Wonderland" quality.

Of more interest to the president, Joe advised him on

deflecting domestic political attacks from the right. He urged Roosevelt to continue wooing William Randolph Hearst and Father Charles Coughlin, the Detroit demagogue and anti-Semite who preached his fascistic views to millions of Americans on his Sunday afternoon radio show. Joe periodically met with Coughlin in an effort to temper his criticisms. As Coughlin's friend and a leading Catholic layman, Joe was perfect for that assignment. Coughlin blamed the nation's problems on Roosevelt, Jews, Communists, and "godless capitalists." He would later urge his audiences to "kill the Jews." He had formed the National Union for Social Justice Party and fielded William Lemke as a candidate in the presidential election. Yet Coughlin was a fan of Joe's, later naming him "Man of the Week" in his pro-Nazi magazine *Social Justice*.

"Joe was fascinated by Coughlin's talent on the radio," James Roosevelt observed. "He recognized it as demagoguery but revelled in what the priest could accomplish. He was intrigued by Coughlin's use of power."

If Coughlin was despicable, he was not as powerful as Hearst. Hearst supported Coughlin in his newspapers and opposed most of Roosevelt's initiatives, including his effort to bring the United States into the League of Nations' Permanent Court of International Justice, known as the World Court. Referring to him as "that bastard," Roosevelt told Joe that in his opinion "no man in the United States is as vicious an influence as Hearst." Joe promised to keep in touch with Hearst and try to contain him.

Having returned to private life, Joe was even more in demand for his financial advice. On May 1, 1936, Paramount Pictures announced it had retained Joe as an adviser. He was to survey the studio's operations and make a report. When issued two and a half months later, the report tore the company apart for its wasteful extravagance. As a result, Paramount's president, in office only a year, was fired. For his efforts, Joe got a fee of $50,000.

Joe also began consulting for his friend Hearst and for Joseph M. Patterson, publisher of the *New York Daily News*.

Hearst's publishing empire was in financial trouble. Joe worked out a reorganization plan that included Joe acquiring some of Hearst's choicest assets at bargain prices. For $8 million, Joe said he would take Hearst's magazines off his hands. Armand Hammer, who learned of Hearst's difficulties when he bought art from him, considered Joe's offer to "help" Hearst self-serving. He asserted $8 million was only a fraction of what the properties were worth.

◆ ◆ ◆

In Hyannis Port, Joe's schedule was inflexible. "Rise prior to 7 A.M., ride the horses at 8, breakfast and business calls until 10:30," said Edward Gallagher, a friend who worked for James Roosevelt's insurance business. "He'd go to the outdoor gym in Yarmouth a couple of times a week, have a sauna and massage by Henry Askelei, formerly at the Harvard Club in Boston. Back home for lunch, nap for half an hour each day. . . ." At 3 P.M. Joe would play golf. If the water was warm enough, he would return home for a swim in the ocean. After dinner, he would often watch a first-run movie in the projection room in the basement at 8:30 P.M. Then he would read and go to sleep by 10:15 P.M.

But having tasted power, Joe was loath to relinquish it. To help Roosevelt's campaign, Joe decided to produce a book called *I'm for Roosevelt*, a defense of the New Deal. Besides further ingratiating himself with Roosevelt (he had just sent him two trunks of Haig & Haig for Christmas), Joe decided to write the book because he had gotten wind of a possible government investigation of him for income tax evasion, according to Roosevelt adviser Jim Farley. One of Joe's favorite practices, as his friend Morton Downey told his son Morton Jr., was to give huge contributions to the Vatican, deduct the full amount as a charitable contribution, then obtain half the money back.

Joe would give "$1 million to the Vatican," Downey said.

"It was totally tax deductible. The Vatican, in turn, would give $500,000 back."

Later, Joe used the church to launder money for payoffs during Jack's presidential campaign, with additional tax implications, according to what one of the couriers told author Peter Maas.

Farley confided to Walter Trohan, the *Chicago Tribune* bureau chief in Washington, that Joe was about to be investigated. "I was a great friend of Farley," Trohan said. "Farley told me he [Joe] wrote the book because he was on the hook [over an impending investigation]," Trohan said. "Kennedy cleared himself with Roosevelt by writing that book."

While *I'm for Roosevelt* was purportedly written by Joe, Kennedy offered Arthur Krock $1,000 a week for five weeks to write most of it. Krock responded that he would do it for free. Krock recalled that he gave Joe the title and "wrote a good deal of the book and edited the rest." Joe "signed his name at least," Krock said.

"I have no political ambitions for myself or my children," Joe wrote in the book, which was published by Reynal and Hitchcock on August 12, 1936. When Joe later asked Roosevelt to autograph his copy, the president put it off. Finally Missy LeHand wrote "you must do this" on a note attached to Joe's letter. Roosevelt complied, signing it, "Dear Joe: I'm for Kennedy. The book is grand."

In fact, the book was a shallow, cheerleader's defense of Roosevelt's policies. A few weeks before it came out, *Time* ran a cover story on Joe in its July 23, 1936, issue. Citing his work at the SEC, the magazine said of Joe, "He makes it easy for the honest." Taking advantage of the publicity, Joe wrote to Harvard's dean of freshmen asking the college to admit Jack. Jack began Harvard on September 28.

Joe organized seven or eight "Businessmen for Roosevelt" dinners and began funneling more money into Roosevelt's campaign. But he got even more bang for the buck by supporting Roosevelt's son Jimmy, who was willing to do almost anything for him in return. Joe was on the phone constantly with Jimmy or playing golf with him, Eddie Gallagher recalled. Joe underwrote speeches Jimmy gave in Massachusetts on behalf of his father. On September 18, Jimmy noted that Joe's aide Paul E. Murphy had advanced him $1,000 toward a trip he planned.

"I am not being boastful when I say that I think it is the only chance we have of carrying the state," Jimmy told Joe. Asking for more, Jimmy said he had deposited the money Joe had advanced him at Columbia Trust Company. Joe later sold the bank to National Shawmut Bank for $557,400.

On October 5, in a Columbia Broadcasting System radio address, Joe urged Roosevelt's reelection. Even though Joe had resigned from the SEC, Roosevelt still thought of him as part of the administration. On October 9, Roosevelt discussed with Harold Ickes his complaints about "prima donnas" in his administration. Besides Raymond Moley, he singled out Joe. Roosevelt complained, as he had before, that he had to "send for Joe every few days and hold his hand."

On November 3, 1936, Roosevelt was reelected by another landslide, carrying all but two states and achieving the largest presidential plurality in history. Two days later, at his home in Hyde Park, Roosevelt held a previously scheduled luncheon that Joe had arranged for Eugenio Cardinal Pacelli, the Vatican secretary of state. Roosevelt wanted him to silence Father Coughlin.

Then a Boston bishop, Francis Joseph Spellman, who attended the luncheon, noted in his diary that he had advised Joe to have the president issue the invitation directly. While Roosevelt had approved the idea of the luncheon before the election, he waited until after the election to meet with the papal representative.

Joe provided a special train to bring him from New York to Hyde Park. After the luncheon, he invited Cardinal Pacelli to his home in Bronxville for tea. By arranging the meeting with Pacelli, Joe had not only helped Roosevelt but ingratiated himself with the church official whom he believed—correctly—was next in line to be pope. When Pope Pius XI died in February 1939, Cardinal Pacelli became Pope Pius XII. Joe was also cementing his ties with Spellman, who would become archbishop of New York two and a half years later.

Born in Whitman, Massachusetts, Francis Joseph Spellman had come to know Joe when Spellman was a bishop in Massachusetts. When he was assigned to the Vatican in 1927, he became close to Pacelli and to Pacelli's friend and adviser, Count Enrico Galeazzi. Galeazzi had become friends with the Kennedys as well, when Rose traveled with James Roosevelt and his wife for a private audience with Pope Pius XI.

At the count's suggestion, Joe helped persuade Roosevelt to appoint Myron Taylor as the president's personal representative to the Holy See. This was a first step toward accommodating the Vatican's desire to establish diplomatic relations with the United States. Whether Roosevelt succeeded in persuading the Vatican to silence Coughlin is not known. But at about the same time Roosevelt sent an emissary to Rome, Coughlin left the airwaves.

◆ ◆ ◆

While Joe was happy making money in the stock market, he still wanted to be treasury secretary. To bolster his influence, he kept Roosevelt and his coterie supplied with gifts—trunks of Haig & Haig Pinch Bottle, stone crabs flown in from Florida, orchids for Eleanor Roosevelt. He helped arrange jobs for people who wanted to leave the administration. He brought in Wall Street powers for secret meetings with Roosevelt. Most important, he made sure James Roosevelt was indebted to him. To Jimmy, Joe was the Sun King, a man of fabulous wealth to be courted and obeyed.

Jimmy was always strapped for money, and Joe played him like a fish on a hook, giving him a consulting fee here, a free meal there. During the winter, Joe turned his Palm Beach home into a luxury resort for Jimmy and his family. Just three weeks after he had arranged the luncheon in Hyde Park with Pacelli, Joe and Spellman had dinner at Joe's Palm

Beach home with Missy LeHand, James Roosevelt's wife, Betsey, Arthur Krock, and Eddie Moore. The next day, December 1, 1936, they listened on the radio to Roosevelt's speech in Buenos Aires and sent him a telegram of congratulations.

"All greatly enjoyed your treat . . ." Jimmy wired Joe after receiving a shipment of stone crabs packed in dry ice. "Missy, Father, Bets [Jimmy's wife] join in sending you love and thanks."

While Roosevelt was not willing to replace Morgenthau at the Treasury Department, he recognized that Joe's success at the SEC had been due to his ability to sell business on the need for regulation. As a president whose agenda included forming dozens of new regulatory agencies, Roosevelt needed Joe's special talent in this area. At the same time, Roosevelt saw Joe as a possible rival. Including him in the administration would keep him under control. After being inaugurated for a second term on January 20, 1937, the president asked Joe to become chairman of a newly formed five-member Maritime Commission, replacing the moribund U.S. Shipping Board.

When Roosevelt called him to Washington to discuss the job in February, Joe expressed reluctance. "If it's all the same to you, let some other patriot take it on the chin," Joe said. "There's a lot of money to be made in the market. I'd like to skim off my share of profits." But Roosevelt's charm was equal to Joe's, and now he turned it on. For his part, Joe missed the thrill of being at the center of power. On the basis of Roosevelt's personal appeal, he agreed to head the new commission.

After Roosevelt nominated Joe on March 24, 1937, the Justice Department reviewed his background to make sure he had no conflicts of interest. Justice decided Joe's $20,000 mortgage on his brother-in-law's oil carrier would not be a problem. His ownership of 300 shares of the stock of Union Pacific Railroad, which owned 1,100 shares in a company that repaired ocean vessels, also was not a serious conflict.

What did bother the department was Joe's ownership of 1,100 shares in Todd Shipyards Inc., which repaired ships. The Merchant Marine Act of 1936, which had set up the commission, prohibited any commissioner from having any interest within three years of his appointment in any shipping company. Nor could a commissioner have a "substantial interest" in any company associated with ships or shipping.

The question was whether Joe's interest—valued at $60,500—was "substantial." Ultimately, the Justice Department decided that if Joe disposed of the stock, it would not pose a problem. Using his Wall Street pal Elisha Walker as a trustee, Joe sold the stock over the next sixty days.

Meanwhile, Joe told James Roosevelt, now that the president had named him to the Maritime Commission, he would cancel $17,000 of a total of $54,000 owed to him by the Democratic National Committee. Thus he used the loans he had given Roosevelt's campaign as a lever to extract jobs for himself. Eventually, he would cancel the entire amount.

After confirmation by the Senate, Joe was sworn in on April 16, 1937. Once again, Joe brought in his own coterie of assistants—Eddie Moore at $1 a year and John Burns, who had been chief counsel of the SEC, as a special adviser. He again rented Marwood. Like any government worker, he arrived at his office on the fourth floor of the Commerce Department Building by nine each morning.

America's commercial ship industry—known as the merchant marine—was in distress, with strikes, an aging fleet, and declining shipbuilding. Shipping, Joe said, was a "very sick industry."

World War I had underscored the importance of a strong merchant marine. The belligerent countries refused to ship cargo between America and foreign ports. Since the merchant marine was needed in time of war, the government subsidized it in peacetime through fat mail delivery contracts. But the government and the ship owners were constantly in disputes over the size of the contracts.

The new law abolished the mail delivery contracts. Under the terms of the new act, shippers and shipbuilders were to receive outright subsidies to stimulate American shipbuilding efforts. In return, the commission was to approve routes, salaries, and profits.

The commission also had to approve a settlement of the old mail contracts, which had been abrogated. This became Joe's first task. Joe loved to negotiate. "First came his personal comfort and happiness," said a confidant. "Then he liked negotiations, business, horse racing, and women."

But as Joe put it, he liked to negotiate from strength. In this negotiation, the cards were stacked against the shipping industry. To Roosevelt's satisfaction, Joe withheld money due under the old contracts and settled the shippers' claims of $73 million for just $750,000.

Joe employed the same ruthlessness when the crew of the American-owned SS *Algic* staged a sitdown strike in Montevideo, Uruguay. The American crew objected to the fact that nonunion longshoremen had been brought in to load cargo, and had done it haphazardly, after the local longshoremen's union had gone on strike. Joe recommended that the union leaders be brought back "in irons." When Roosevelt suggested an alternate course, Joe, in characteristic language, told the president this would land them both in the "shit house." Eventually, Joe came up with a compromise that would not send union members to jail.

Soon, Joe had the commission members, the press, and the public eating out of his hand. At one of the first meetings of the commission, Joe brought up the criticism that he knew nothing about shipping. "Well, they criticized Roosevelt for appointing me to head the SEC because I knew too much about the stock market to be trusted with its regulation," he said. "Now, they say I know too little about shipping to be trusted with its regulation."

Joe used the same directness to win friends in the press. He would call reporters by their first names, give them tips on machinations within the administration, and send them bottles of Haig & Haig. Joe enjoyed the sensation his comments caused. It was a way of asserting control. At the same time, reporters mistook his bluntness for genuine candor.

Joe was a "genius at public relations," said Harvey Klemmer, an aide whom Joe hired to write speeches. "He had the whole country waiting" for a survey of the shipping industry. "He'd built up the suspense until you'd think it was the second coming of Christ, maybe."

In a feature on Joe, Eddy Gilmore of the Associated Press wrote that he "breezed through a sea of press conference questions with the grace of a clipper ship." Gilmore described Joe as dressing "as nattily as a yacht captain in soft, double-breasted business suits and rakishly cut stiff sport collars."

"When he walked into a room, he filled it up," said Janet Des Rosiers. "His back was straight, his smile was on, his joviality was there. He enjoyed a joke and a laugh."

Joe attacked both labor and management for the plight of the merchant marine. At a speech on May 22 at the Propeller Club in New York, he said the merchant marine was going bust and needed to be replaced without "profiteering."

While only one new ship was built during Joe's short tenure, "He was responsible, directly or indirectly, for a program that built fifty ships a year at an estimated cost of $1.2 billion," said Admiral Emery Scott Land, who was a member of the commission with Joe and succeeded him as chairman. With other commission members, Joe "spanked" U.S. shipbuilders into building ships at more reasonable prices. Meanwhile, the commission's staff increased to five hundred.

Near the end of his tenure, Joe had Burns and other aides prepare a forty-thousand-word report. Pinpointing the shortcomings of the industry and the legislation, it urged that federal mediation be imposed in labor disputes. The *New York Times* called the report "one of the finest of its kind ever submitted."

◆ ◆ ◆

In the early summer of 1937, Joe showed up at his twenty-fifth Harvard reunion. This was the first he had attended since the tenth in 1922. Ever since graduating Joe had had a love-hate relationship with the college. A year earlier, Joe had lobbied to be nominated to the Harvard Board of Overseers. The review committee, headed by Charles Francis Adams, rejected him. Adams had served with Joe on the board of Massachusetts Electric. Presumably, he knew all about Joe's stock manipulations. But Joe attributed the rejection to anti-Catholic bias.

For his twenty-fifth reunion, Joe contributed $10,000 to the university. He arrived in a chauffeur-driven Rolls-Royce and brought all nine children plus a governess, requiring special permission of the reunion committee.

On the first night of the four-day reunion, Joe's classmates put on a musical called *Oscar in Wonderland*. It included a skit that spoofed Joe, played by Edward Gallagher, who was treasurer of the Boston and Maine Railroad. Before he came onstage, a secretary briskly answered a battery of telephones: "No, Mr. President, it isn't nine o'clock, because Mr. Kennedy hasn't come in yet," she said. When Eleanor Roosevelt called, the secretary told her the same thing. Then Gallagher, wearing a high hat and cutaway coat, walked onto the stage, at Rindge Technical High School auditorium in Cambridge. "Get me Frank," he said. After a pause, Gallagher took the phone. "Frank, this is Joe," Gallagher said. "I'm here; it's nine o'clock. Start the country."

For the twenty-fifth anniversary report, Joe wrote that his office was at 30 Rockefeller Plaza and that he was proud to be a Democrat. He said he "became active" in party affairs on behalf of "our fellow alumnus" Roosevelt. Now, he said, "I prefer to have my activities referred to not as political but rather an interest in public affairs."

This was a formulation the family would always follow. Jack, Bobby, and Ted would all describe their pursuits not as "politics," with all its foul connotations, but rather as "public affairs" or "public service."

If Joe thought his presence at the reunion would soften

Harvard's attitude toward him, he was mistaken. When Joe was named ambassador to London the following year, he lobbied for an honorary degree. Again, Harvard rejected him. An official primly noted that Harvard did not give such honors simply because one had been named to a government post; one had to demonstrate that one had carried out his duties properly. Deeply hurt, Joe leaked stories to the press claiming *he* had rejected the offer of an honorary degree.

The last straw in Joe's fraying relations with the college came when Joe's son Joe Jr. "was not called into play during the closing minutes of a Harvard-Yale game," recalled Joe's Harvard classmate Ralph Lowell. "Indeed, Joe cussed all the way down from his seat to the field and bawled the coach out."

After that, Lowell, an active alumnus and former class treasurer, found that when phoning Joe, he had to begin the conversation by telling him he was not calling to raise funds. If he forgot to preface his conversation in that way, "Joe might hang up," Lowell said.

Joe had better luck with *Fortune* magazine. Launched in 1930 by Henry R. Luce, the founder of *Time* and *Life*, the magazine had prepared a hard-hitting profile of Joe. Written by Earle Looker, it described him as a greedy profiteer and philanderer. The magazine had agreed to let Joe take a look at the article before publication—a common practice in those days. Infuriated, Joe wrote to Russell Davenport, the managing editor.

"Generally, my comment on this article is that it is permeated with distrust of my character, dislike of my occupations, and social prejudice against my origin," he told Davenport. Pointing out what he claimed were fifty-four inaccuracies, Joe went on in a follow-up letter: "I have no trouble in trusting you. The trouble is with Looker, whose presentation of me is so cheap and tawdry that a rereading of the script sickened me. There are so many deliberate misrepresentations that I believe that either Looker has an ingrained hatred of the Irish or a resentment against me personally."

Correcting the alleged errors was not enough; Joe wanted the article killed. Incredibly, that is what he got. Joe threatened Luce with financial extinction if the story ran. "In that piece, they mentioned that he was running around in Hollywood with Gloria Swanson," said Dimitri Kessel, a former *Fortune* and *Life* photographer, who heard what had happened from friends in Luce's office. "So he read it and called Luce to ask him to lunch. He said, 'You print that story, and I'll put you out of business, take over Time Inc.' So they changed it, they eliminated it, and then they became close friends."

On Luce's orders, Davenport assigned a new writer, Robert Cantwell, to the piece. Cantwell had orders to ignore Davenport's work and rereport it. After weeks of exhaustive research, Cantwell wrote an article that portrayed Joe in the glowing light to which he had become accustomed. Authoritative in tone, the February 1937 profile became the foundation for many of the stories that appeared on Joe throughout his life.

11

REWARD

After just a few months as chairman of the Maritime Commission, Joe was bored. "He became chairman of the Maritime Commission and was first chairman of the SEC, but he wanted something bigger and better," James Roosevelt recalled. Joe made it clear he "deserved a reward." He hinted broadly that "the reward he had in mind was secretary of the treasury," Jimmy said. In his columns, Arthur Krock had already begun touting Joe for the job.

James Roosevelt knew that it was out of the question. His father would not replace Morgenthau. Moreover, as Roosevelt told James Farley, Joe would want to run the Treasury Department in his own way rather than according to the president's wishes. So Joe decided ambassador to the Court of St. James's would do just fine. James Roosevelt was already in Joe's pocket, and now Joe expected him to deliver.

Joe could not have found a more effective fixer. Upon the death of Louis Howe, Roosevelt had called in Jimmy and said he needed someone he could trust. Jimmy became one of his father's top aides. His job was to act as liaison with the independent agencies, but in reality his purview was unlimited.

Moreover, Jimmy's services were for sale. Under an arrangement with William O. Schwartz, a lobbyist, James Roosevelt had approached William Douglas, who had replaced Landis as chairman of the SEC. Jimmy baldly proposed what amounted to an open bribe: Public utility holding companies whose securities were regulated by the SEC would each pay Schwartz $10,000 a year. Schwartz would split the money with Jimmy and others and solve the companies' problems with the SEC.

Douglas was horrified, but Jimmy was insistent. He explained that it would be foolish for the Democrats not to make money now that they were in power. "What chance do we have when the Republicans take over?" Jimmy asked.

Douglas wrote to the holding companies that "neither Mr. Schwartz nor any other person is the intermediary between the commission and the utility companies." Saying that he seemed to be standing in the way of ambitious people, Douglas then went to the White House and offered his resignation. Roosevelt literally cried when Douglas told him of his son's proposal. "Jimmy! What a problem he is. Thanks for telling me. Now get back to your desk," he commanded. "Of course you're not going to resign."

Having failed to enrich himself with this clumsy approach, James Roosevelt now turned to Joe's request. "I'd like to be ambassador to England," Joe told him. He said the idea of being the first Irishman to be ambassador to London intrigued him: It would give him the prestige he craved all his life. Yet Jimmy was surprised. Joe was a "crusty old cuss," Jimmy Roosevelt recalled. He could not picture him as an ambassador.

When Jimmy went to see Joe about his request, the ubiquitous Arthur Krock was staying at Marwood. After Jimmy left, Joe told Krock indignantly, "He tried to get me to take secretary of commerce, and I knew it was only an attempt to shut me off from London, but London is where I want to go, and it is the only place I intend to go, and I told Jimmy so, and that's that."

When Jimmy suggested the idea to Roosevelt, his father "laughed so hard he almost fell from his wheelchair." But the president had a playful, almost mischievous side to him. A gifted manipulator, he still needed Joe's money and still feared him as a possible rival. The president later called Jimmy and said that the idea of "twisting the lion's tail a little, so to speak" appealed to him. Roosevelt asked Joe to see him.

When Jimmy took Joe into the president's office, Roosevelt asked if Joe would mind stepping back so he could get a good look at him. "Joe, would you mind taking your pants down?"

Joe asked if Roosevelt had said what he thought he had heard him say. Roosevelt said he had, and Joe complied.

"I guess it was the power of the presidency, because Joe stood there in his shorts, looking silly and embarrassed," James Roosevelt recalled.

Roosevelt said he had been told that Joe was bowlegged, and now he could see that it was true. "Don't you know the ambassador to the Court of St. James's has to go through an induction ceremony in which he wears knee breeches and silk stockings?" Roosevelt asked. "Can you imagine how you'll look? When photos of our new ambassador appear all over the world, we'll be a laughing stock. You're just not right for the job, Joe."

"Mr. President," Joe said, "if I can get permission of his majesty's government to wear a cutaway coat and striped pants to the ceremony, would you agree to appoint me?"

By Jimmy's account, Roosevelt said he doubted the British would agree, and he needed to appoint a new ambassador soon. Robert Worth Bingham, the publisher of the *Louisville Courier-Journal*, who held the post, was seriously ill with malaria at Johns Hopkins University Hospital and was about to resign.

"Will you give me two weeks?" Joe asked.

Chuckling, Roosevelt agreed. Within two weeks, Joe came back with a letter granting him the exemption.

"He'd called father's bluff, and father laughed and agreed to name him ambassador to England," James Roosevelt said.

In fact, it did not happen quite that way. Joe did obtain permission from the British to dispense with wearing knee breeches, but only after he was named ambassador. To make a good story, Jimmy had embellished upon the events.

Nor was getting Joe appointed quite as simple as Jimmy made it seem. Other Roosevelt advisers pushed the president to give the London post to Joe, but not because they thought he was qualified. Tommy Corcoran did "everything he could" to get Joe the position because "he wanted to get Joe out of Washington," according to what he told Harold Ickes. Corcoran was concerned because Joe and James Roosevelt were "very close." Indeed, it was with "Kennedy's help that Jimmy built up his insurance business that he had in Boston and amassed in a short time a fortune estimated to be not less than a quarter of a million dollars," Corcoran said. Now it seemed that Joe was "pouring his conservative ideas in the sympathetic ears of Jimmy, who relays them to the president." Jimmy "has his father's ear at all times," Corcoran said. Whenever the president is "tired or discouraged, Jimmy is at hand to say what may be influential."

Ickes shared Corcoran's concerns. No one was closer to Roosevelt than Jimmy. "Even Miss LeHand cannot counter-act his influence," Ickes wrote in his diary. In coming battles, it would be important to have liberal allies. Jimmy's ambition was to be governor of Massachusetts. To achieve that, Jimmy was willing "to sacrifice the whole New Deal," Ickes thought.

Why would Joe want the job? Corcoran quoted Joe as saying it was largely to please Rose. "You don't understand the Irish," Corcoran told Ickes. "London has always been a closed door to them. As ambassador of the United States, Kennedy will have all the doors open to him."

Nor did Roosevelt have any illusions about Joe. In fact,

for all the show of camaraderie, he considered Joe a viper. In a replay of the utility companies' earlier offer to James Roosevelt, Roosevelt told Morgenthau on December 8, 1937, that he had been told by three independent sources that Floyd Odlum, a utilities executive, had offered Joe $1 million to represent the utility companies in Washington. Joe had agreed to split the money with certain parties—presumably government officials who could help the utilities. When confronted with the story, Joe had denied it. But Roosevelt said he considered Joe "a very dangerous man."

When Morgenthau asked why he was planning to appoint Joe ambassador, Roosevelt said he was going to send him to England with the understanding that the appointment would be good for only six months. In doing so, the president made it clear he was discharging any obligation to him.

"Well, Mr. President, England is a most important post, and there have been so many people over there talking against the New Deal," Morgenthau said. "Don't you think you are taking considerable risks by sending Kennedy, who has talked so freely and so critically against your administration?"

"I have made arrangements," Roosevelt replied, "to have Joe Kennedy watched hourly, and the first time he opens his mouth and criticizes me, I'll fire him." Roosevelt repeated, "Kennedy is too dangerous to have around here."

Morgenthau was not sure what Roosevelt meant when he said he would have Joe watched. In fact, Roosevelt apparently was inventing stories to please Morgenthau when he said Joe had the job on the understanding he would be in London only six months. The president told Farley that he did not think Joe would want to stay more than a year in the job.

In any case, Morgenthau was relieved to have Kennedy out of the capital. "I take it that is the way the president feels" as well, he wrote in his diary. William H. Seward, Abraham Lincoln's secretary of state, had said that "some persons are sent abroad because they are needed, and some are sent because they're *not* wanted at home." So it was with Joe.

After receiving permission from Jimmy, Krock broke the story of Joe's appointment. When it ran on December 9, Roosevelt confirmed the story. Apparently not aware that his son had given Krock approval to run with it, Roosevelt later lambasted Krock for the "premature" disclosure. He said it may have "hastened" Ambassador Bingham's death after a major stomach operation. He was sure that Krock was getting even with Bingham for promoting another editor above him at the *Louisville Courier-Journal*.

If Joe was being ejected from Washington, one would never know it from reading the papers. The newspapers were filled with glowing stories about the first Irish Catholic ambassador to the Court of St. James's and his famous predecessors. They included five ambassadors who had become president—John Adams, James Monroe, John Quincy Adams, Martin Van Buren, and James Buchanan.

"Kennedy has probably a better press right now than any other member of the administration," Ickes wrote. "He is a grand hand at cultivating the correspondents. He is a very rich man who is always doing favors for newspapermen. For instance, when he is to be away from his large and luxurious Washington house, he will turn it over to some newspaperman who can entertain lavishly, leaving all the bills to Kennedy when he returns."

At the time, Joe's fortune was estimated at $9 million, equal to $92 million today.

At a dinner at the White House attended by Dorothy Schiff, publisher of the *New York Post*, someone—perhaps Eleanor—complained about appointing "that awful Joe Kennedy" to London. Roosevelt threw back his head and laughed. Appointing an Irishman to the London post was a "great joke," he said, "the greatest joke in the world." No one else laughed.

Besides enriching him by referring business to his insurance company, it is likely Joe paid James Roosevelt to get him the ambassadorship, just as he had offered to supplement Roosevelt aide Raymond Moley's salary. Just after his formal nomination as ambassador, James Roosevelt telegraphed Joe about some other unspecified request, "It is almost done. I haven't failed you yet." The tone was that of a subordinate reporting to his boss.

◆ ◆ ◆

When Roosevelt told Joe he planned to announce his nomination as ambassador, Joe protested that the eight correspondents who covered the White House were coming to dinner. They would kid him about being an Irishman at the Court of St. James's.

"That's your problem," Roosevelt told him. To soften the expected ribbing, Joe stationed a waiter behind each chair with orders to keep filling the champagne glasses of the reporters and their wives.

"An Irishman being ambassador to England was funny in the first place," Walter Trohan, one of the eight at the dinner, explained. "He would say he was busy and had to make a phone call, to get away from it. We ribbed him unmercifully."

When the Senate confirmed him on January 13, 1938, Joe wired Roosevelt from Montana. Prophetically, he said, "I don't know what kind of a diplomat I shall be, probably rotten, but I promise to get done for you those things that you want done."

Along with his congratulations, James Roosevelt sent Joe a ditty to be sung to the tune of "Sweet Adeline": "Joe's wearing tights/And meeting knights/And dukes and earls/And duchess girls/Bostonian he/He'll dump their tea/And he'll surely spill the beans/Across the sea."

Five days later, Secretary of State Cordell Hull, a tall, stately former senator from Tennessee, wrote the forty-nine-year-old ambassador to give him his commission and issue him Diplomatic Passport Number 1751. After having served ten months, Joe resigned as chairman of the Maritime Commission on February 17. The next day, Associate Supreme Court Justice Stanley Reed swore him in as ambassador. Joe began receiving a salary of $17,500 a year, an increase from his $12,000 annual salary as chairman of the Maritime Commission.

Joe demanded that the State Department ship his 3,600-pound black Chrysler and two other cars to London, and he insisted on taking Rose's Airedale and French poodle. Since the dogs belonged to an ambassador, Joe claimed the British government would waive its requirement that newly arrived animals be quarantined for six months. But the federal Despatch Agency, as it was called, informed Joe that such regulations were never waived. "If the king himself brought in a dog, it would have to spend the usual six months on quarantine."

The Kennedy family came in waves. First Joe arrived in Plymouth on the SS *Manhattan* on the morning of March 1. Only two people accompanied him: Harvey Klemmer, Joe's speechwriter from the Maritime Commission, and Harold B. Hinton, a former *New York Times* Washington correspondent whom Joe had hired as a public relations man. In a welcoming speech on the rain-spattered docks, the lord mayor of Plymouth reminded Joe of England's ties with the United States.

Two weeks later, Rose arrived on the SS *Washington* with five of their children—Ted, Jean, Robert, Patricia, and Kathleen. Then Eunice, a student at the Convent of the Sacred Heart in Darien, Connecticut, and Rosemary, a student at Marymount Convent in Tarrytown, New York, followed on April 20. Jack and Joe Jr. were left behind at Harvard. The children came with cooks, governesses, and fourteen huge trunks. "Only seven in the first installment, so as not to complicate the housing problem," Joe told the British press.

The family moved into the thirty-six-room ambassador's residence at 14 Prince's Gate. Rose was delighted. The home, with its great double doors, sweeping private drive, and huge round foyer, had been given to the United States in 1921 by J.P. Morgan. Rose supervised twenty-three house servants, three chauffeurs, and twenty part-time employees. She quickly added such touches as windowboxes in the upper rooms for red geraniums, white daisies, and blue forget-me-nots.

Besides Eddie Moore, Joe added three other chums: Arthur Houghton, whose salary was supplemented by the Motion Picture Producers' Association; Jack Kennedy, a rough-looking former RKO employee who was known as "Ding Dong Jack" to distinguish him from Joe's son; and James Seymour, another Hollywood friend. Joe supplemented their government salaries from his personal funds.

A few days after his arrival, Joe and Houghton shot a round of golf at the famous Stoke Poges golf course. On the short second hole, Joe's drive rolled onto the green and into the cup for a hole in one. The next day, the British papers trumpeted his triumph as a good omen. Joe wrote to Landis, "I couldn't have done anything better to make a hit in England if I had had 25 years to discover the best answer."

On March 4, after a brief ride through the streets of London on horseback, Joe made an official call on Prime Minister Neville Chamberlain at 10 Downing Street. The aging Birmingham industrialist had become prime minister in May. Telford Taylor, the historian, described the Conservative leader as "highly competent but grim and graceless." Hitler had just annexed Austria, carrying out the Nazi idea of *Anschluss* or union. While Britain had protested, Chamberlain enunciated a policy of appeasement, meaning reconciliation and accommodation. Like Joe, Chamberlain looked at war as chiefly an economic catastrophe.

Joe explained to Chamberlain that the American people were "completely anti-war and because Great Britain seemed to be the natural ally in the event of a possible war, America was most wary of entangling alliances." Chamberlain said he already knew this but appreciated having it said "rather coldly without any preliminaries." Chamberlain was convinced "concrete concessions must be made to Germany and Italy." He was "prepared to make them to avert a war."

Based on this one-hour meeting, Joe decided that Chamberlain was a "very strong character; one that could easily dominate a situation" and that he had a "realistic, practical mind." But Joe wired the State Department that England was in dire straits and "has used up practically all of its aces."

Joe saw Sir G. Sidney Clive, marshal of the diplomatic corps, at Buckingham Palace. Apparently Clive had not been told that the British had already granted Joe permission to dispense with wearing knee breeches. Joe "straightened out with him the fact that I do not have to wear knee breeches— praise be to Allah," Joe told James Roosevelt. But Joe told Roosevelt's son, "I am afraid I shocked him very much when I told him I didn't want to present any American debutantes" because the existing selection process was "undemocratic." For years, American ambassadors had presented the daughters of American society to the king and queen. Only about twenty were selected from a list of more than two thousand applicants. But Joe's motives for stopping the tradition were likely more personal. He did not want to detract from his own daughters' presentation to London society. The British official was "quite stunned" by Joe's request. He asked for a "little time to talk it over with Lord Chamberlain."

Ten days later, Clive wrote Joe to inform him that the king "has been graciously pleased to grant Your Excellency's request to be permitted to wear ordinary evening dress at Court Functions, instead of knee breeches."

Joe had a spacious office on the second floor of the red-brick embassy at 1 Grosvenor Square. But he asked Jimmy to pass along to his father that he had a "beautiful blue silk room, and all I need to make it perfect is a Mother Hubbard dress and a wreath to make me Queen of the May. If a fairy didn't design this room, I never saw one in my life." He added that the designer was not only a "fairy" but "probably the most inefficient architect I have ever seen." Joe closed by asking Jimmy to tell the "boss" that "there are two things I am for: the USA and FDR."

In his unpublished memoirs about his days in London, Joe described his study as including a portrait of Joseph H. Choate, who was the American ambassador from 1899 to

1905. Joe wrote that Choate "watched me daily as I began and closed my work. At times it seemed to me that I could hear him say, 'You are a cad, sir!'"

Was Joe unconsciously conveying what he thought of himself? Or was he projecting what he thought WASPs thought of the Irish? More likely, it was the former, since Joe presumably would have used a derogatory expression about the Irish rather than "cad" if he thought Choate was looking down his nose at him because of his origin. In any case, Joe thought better of the reference and later crossed it out.

Four days after he saw Chamberlain, Joe officially presented his credentials to King George VI at Buckingham Palace. His title—ambassador to the Court of St. James's—stemmed from the fact that the royal court was once at St. James's Palace, a Tudor structure built by Henry VIII.

An ornate British state carriage attended by footmen and outriders in traditional scarlet cloaks picked up Joe at his residence and drove him to Buckingham Palace. Wearing white tie and tail coat, Joe was passed on to the master of the household, who ushered him into the grand hall. For fifteen minutes, Joe chatted with the king, who was resplendent in the uniform of an admiral of the fleet.

"The ceremony was very simple, especially since no speeches were made," Joe told Hull. "I was shown into a room in which the king was standing and handed to him the letter of credence. The Foreign Secretary [Lord Edward W. Halifax] remained during the audience. We talked for about 15 minutes on various subjects ranging from unemployment in the United States and Great Britain to my hole-in-one of last Saturday. . . ."

On May 11, Joe, Rose, Rosemary, and Kathleen were presented at court. Rose, who wore a Molyneaux gown, had carefully studied the State Department's notes on dress. "The ladies may . . . be reminded that trains should hang from the shoulders. Feathers, veils and long white gloves extending above the elbow must be worn. Flowers and fans are optional, but it is customary for debutantes only to carry flowers, and for others to carry fans if they desire to carry anything. A handbag should not be carried, although there is no objection to a very small vanity case which can be concealed under flowers or fan. . . ."

Winston Churchill's son Randolph remarked in his column in the *Evening Standard* that the "only trousers at last night's court were those worn by himself [Kennedy] and some of the less important waiters."

As in the United States, the British press crooned over Joe. Joe was seen as Roosevelt's right-hand man, a major political figure, someone who could help England with such issues as the World War I debt and trade pacts. He was accessible to the press, giving off-the-record interviews with his feet up on his desk. After he had made particularly pungent remarks, his aides would take reporters aside and say, "Of course, you won't publish anything the ambassador said."

The fact was that many American ambassadors before Joe had disregarded the English tradition of wearing knee breeches at court. Only Joe had made an issue of it, using it to win attention. After Joe presented his credentials to the king, he gave an interview about it to the *Daily Telegraph*. Since the court considered such meetings to be personal, the interview raised eyebrows among the blue bloods. Protocol forbade quoting what the king had said. But through these gestures, Joe created the impression that he was as jolly as Santa Claus.

Dubbing him the "Nine-Child Envoy," the newspapers ran photos of Joe with his toothy grin. They remarked that he looked like a "schoolboy." Normally, photographs of ambassadors' families, if taken at all, were staged. Joe allowed his daughters to be photographed in unposed positions, as when a secretary hitched up Kathleen's frock just before she was to be presented at court. Joe's children were photogenic, all with identical horse teeth. Kathleen, in particular, won the hearts of the British. She was brash, direct, informal, and funny. At weekend parties in country houses, she would quickly join in conversations and kick off her shoes.

Joe courted reporters with lavishly catered sit-down dinners complete with champagne, followed by first-run movies. The papers reported on his fondness for Beethoven's Fifth Symphony, chocolate layer cake, rugby, horseback riding, and golf. A cartoon in the *Evening News* pictured a large bus outside the American embassy. "Mr. Kennedy takes his family to the theater," the caption said.

Soon, the Kennedys were the weekend guests of King George VI and Queen Elizabeth at Windsor Castle. Joe went riding on Rotten Row, received honorary degrees, and was bestowed membership in the Royal Thames Yacht Club. Having refused to see him earlier, J.P. Morgan visited Joe and confided he was "very depressed" about financial conditions and was even considering "giving up his business."

Joe's reception in England impressed Roosevelt. In an ebullient mood, the president told Joe, "When you feel that British accent creeping up on you and your trousers riding up to the knee, take the first steamer home for a couple of weeks' holiday."

"Well, Rose, this is a helluva long way from East Boston, isn't it?" Joe remarked to his wife, who often wore a diamond tiara at functions.

◆ ◆ ◆

With Harold Hinton, Joe labored over a speech he was to give to the Pilgrims Club, which was dedicated to improving American-British relations. Since Germany had just devoured Austria, this would be the first American response to the threatening development.

Hull was appalled when Joe submitted a draft of the speech. Hull informed Roosevelt that the draft was "entirely too isolationist," and he ordered his aides to have the speech revised. Instead of saying "the average American has little interest in foreign affairs," Hull's subordinates inserted "the details of foreign affairs." Joe's statement that "the great bulk of the American people is not now convinced that any common interest exists between them and any other country" was excised. Joe's statement that the United States "has no plans to seek or offer assistance in the event of war" was struck as well.

The task of telling Joe about the changes fell to Jay Pierrepont Moffat, chief of the State Department's European Affairs Division. Before leaving for London, Joe had met with Moffat and told him that his theater managers had checked on opinions of patrons. They had found that nearly everyone opposed an aggressive foreign policy while the country was in a recession. Moffat felt Joe had a "realistic approach" that was a "breath of fresh air." But now that Hitler had annexed Austria, it was all too clear that he would not stop there. Moffat's task was to draft a telegram to Kennedy "pointing out as tactfully as possible" that Hull did not agree with him.

While Joe acquiesced to the changes to his speech, he also demonstrated his power by writing directly to Roosevelt or by writing letters to James Roosevelt and sending copies of them to Hull. He plied Roosevelt with gifts, sending him live lobsters at his retreat in Warm Springs, Georgia. "This is the first time live lobsters ever flew to Pine Mountain," Roosevelt said in a thank-you telegram. "We are informing Smithsonian." Joe sent James Roosevelt a horse, advising him, "Sell him or give him away if he is any expense."

While Hull found Joe's actions annoying, he was grateful that Roosevelt never overruled him when he countermanded Joe. He always let him know what Joe was saying. Roosevelt realized that, having just fought World War I, Americans were not yet ready to commit to another war. At the same time, declaring that the United States had no interest in helping its allies would only encourage Hitler. Joe's position not only gave the German dictator free reign, it made little sense. After receiving Hull's revisions, Joe wrote to Roosevelt directly that Hitler and Benito Mussolini, the Italian Fascist dictator allied with Hitler, "having done so well for themselves by bluffing," were not going to stop bluffing "until somebody very sharply calls their bluff."

In other words, only a strong front would deter German aggression. But then Joe added that he and "the heads of the British government" are convinced that the United States would be "very foolish to try to mix in."

Joe sounded the same theme with Bernard Baruch. He told his friend that "nobody is prepared to talk turkey to Messrs. Hitler and Mussolini, and nobody is prepared to face the risk of war by calling their bluffs." Yet to Joe, the solution was not military intervention but rather an improvement in the economic situation in Germany. "An unemployed man with a hungry family is the same fellow, whether the swastika or some other flag floats above his head."

In fact, Joe told Baruch, "much as I dislike saying it," the truth was that "Germany is really entitled to what she is asking for." He called the Treaty of Versailles—which Hitler had already abrogated—an act of "vengeance." Yet Joe's stay in London so far was both pleasant and profitable, based on "the latest quotations from Broad and Wall."

Joe gave his speech to the Pilgrims Club on March 18, 1938, at Claridge's Hotel. What was needed, he said, was "realism," which he defined as "peace." One cannot "run down a customer with a bayonet."

Back in Washington, Corcoran confided to Ickes, his secretary of the interior, that Joe had been "taken in hand by Lady Astor and the Cliveden set." Lady Nancy Astor, a member of Parliament and noted political hostess at the stately Astor house at Cliveden, often entertained Joe and Rose. In 1936, the influential left-wing newsletter *The Week* had coined the term the "Cliveden Set"—with the first "i" pronounced as in "living"—to refer to Astor and her circle of friends. A dreary-looking lady, she espoused appeasement and was known for her anti-Semitic remarks and sympathy with Germany's aims. Astor had said to a member of Parliament, "You must be a Jew to say something like that." Churchill had responded, "I have never heard before such an insult to a member of Parliament as the words just used by that bitch."

Morgenthau wondered how "the English [the Cliveden set] could take into camp a red-headed Irishman."

It was at Lady Astor's home on May 5, 1938, that Joe met Charles A. Lindbergh, who would soon become a leader of the Keep America Out of War movement. The other guests were George Bernard Shaw and his wife, an editor from the *London Times*, and William C. Bullitt, an independently wealthy Philadelphian who had been the first American ambassador to Moscow and was now ambassador in Paris. In his diary, Lindbergh recorded that Joe was "not the usual type of politician or diplomat." His views on the European situation were "intelligent and interesting."

Lindbergh soon became one of Joe's favorite advisers. A Minnesota farm boy turned pilot, Lindbergh on May 20, 1927, completed the first nonstop solo flight from New York to Paris. His thirty-month-old son later was kidnapped and killed. At Hitler's invitation, Lindbergh had toured Germany and reviewed its air force. Lindbergh concluded that the *Luftwaffe* was the strongest air force in the world. In Germany, he found "a sense of decency and values which in many ways is far ahead of our own." Hitler was a "great man" who had "done much for the German people," Lindbergh was quoted as saying. It was American Jews who were "among the principal war agitators," he said.

For his comments, Hitler awarded Lindbergh the Service Cross of the Order of the German Eagle with the Star, the second highest of all German decorations. When Nazi documents were released after the war, they showed that Lindbergh's prewar evaluation of Nazi air strength was wrong, William Manchester wrote. Lindbergh's British friend Harold Nicolson said Lindbergh "believes in the Nazi theology" and hated "democracy as represented by the free press and the American public." Roosevelt told an aide he considered Lindbergh a Nazi.

12

THE JEWISH QUESTION

For an hour on June 13, 1938, at the German embassy in London, Joe met with Herbert von Dirksen, the German ambassador. The two got along famously, and Dirksen later reported on the conversation in great detail to Baron Ernst von Weizsäcker, the German state secretary.

Joe told the German ambassador that Chamberlain was anxious to have some sort of settlement with Germany. By saying this, he undercut Great Britain's negotiating position with Hitler. He said Roosevelt was not anti-German and wanted friendly relations with Hitler. However, no European leader spoke well of the Germans because most of them were "afraid of the Jews" and did not "dare to say anything good about Germany."

Echoing what Lindbergh and Joe Jr. had told him, Joe said Hitler's government had done "great things" for the country. The Germans were "satisfied" and enjoyed "good living conditions." A report that said the limited food in Germany was being reserved for the army could not be true, Joe told the ambassador. After all, Joe said, the professor who had made the report "was a Jew."

Turning to "the Jewish question," Dirksen told the German secretary of state, in Joe's view, "it was not so much that [the Germans] wanted to get rid of the Jews that was so harmful to us, but rather the loud clamor with which we accompanied this purpose." Dirksen reported that Joe said he "understood our Jewish policy completely; he was from Boston and there, in one golf club, and in other clubs, no Jews had been admitted for the past fifty years."

Neglecting to mention that Joe's Catholic father-in-law had been mayor of Boston, Joe claimed to Dirksen that his own father had been unable to win election as mayor because he was a Catholic. While such prejudice is common in America, Joe said, Catholics avoided "making so much outward fuss about it."

"The average American took a very simple view of problems of foreign policy," Joe told Dirksen. The United States had only "3.5 million Jews," and the overwhelming majority of them "lived on the East Coast," he said. Most other Americans have no anti-German feeling. However, the press on the East Coast was "predominant in the formation of public opinion in America" and was "strongly influenced by the Jews."

In a formulation Joe would later adopt in his own speeches, Dirksen replied that countries with authoritarian governments could maintain friendly relations with democratic states. Agreeing wholeheartedly, Joe said he did not see much difference between the two approaches. After all, he said, "during the first years of the Roosevelt administration, the United States had been governed in an authoritarian manner."

At the end of their conversation, Dirksen suggested that

Joe visit Hitler to see for himself what he was doing with the country. Joe was amenable.

Later, Dirksen wondered about the motives behind Joe's fawning declarations. In May 1938, *Liberty*, a popular magazine, had started a presidential boomlet for Joe. "Will Kennedy Run for President?" the article by Ernest K. Lindley asked. Lindley touted Joe's "brains, personality, driving power, and the habit of success." He described him as having "an athlete's figure, a clean-cut head, sandy hair, clear straight-shooting eyes, a flashingly infectious smile, and faultless taste in dress." Other papers soon ran with the story.

Were Joe's political ambitions behind his criticism of Roosevelt? Since Dirksen came away with a "very good impression" of Joe, Dirksen told the German secretary of state that he tended to believe Joe was sincere.

Upon reading Dirksen's cables, Hans Dieckhoff, the German ambassador in Washington, dismissed Joe's comments. He wired back that Joe was undoubtedly following his own idea of policy rather than the State Department's. Such "trivia" as a visit to Germany by Joe would be of no significance. Unlike Dirksen, Dieckhoff thought Joe was spouting off to further his own political career.

Based on what his father had told him, Morton Downey Jr. said, "I think if Joe had had his way, Hitler would have succeeded in his annihilation of the Jews . . . He always found great favor in Hitler. He would have loved to see him succeed."

Yet Joe continued to count such Jews as Arthur Krock and Bernard Baruch his friends. On the recommendation of James Roosevelt, Joe had hired as an assistant Page Huidekoper, who came from a wealthy Virginia family and was a regular at White House parties. Huidekoper recalled that on the one hand, Joe often referred to Jews as "kikes." On the other hand, Joe made a point of promoting Alan Steyne, a Jew who was in the consular service, into his inner office at the London embassy.

◆ ◆ ◆

Having been in London only three and a half months, Joe asked Hull to let him return home. Referring to Joe Jr., he wrote, "On the 23rd of June my eldest son graduates from Harvard. He is chairman of the Class Day committee. I would like to see him graduate." As an afterthought, he said, "I would also like to discuss with you and the department my very definite impressions about the situation here [and] consult with the president. . . ."

On June 15, 1938, Joe took the SS *Queen Mary*, which had gone into service the previous year, to New York. On June 20, James Roosevelt rode out with newspapermen on a coast guard cutter to greet him in New York Harbor. Later, Joe told James Roosevelt it would be a "complete breach of faith with President Roosevelt" if he had his eye on the presidency, according to what Jimmy told biographer Michael R. Beschloss. Joe told Jimmy he was worried that "fascism might very well sweep the world" and "we would have to prepare ourselves."

The next day, Joe met with Roosevelt at Hyde Park. Per custom, the two agreed on language to describe their meeting to the press. According to that script, the president asked Joe to give Chamberlain a message that was purposely vague: If Chamberlain had difficulty keeping the peace, Roosevelt would use the moral power of his office on the side of peace.

In fact, the meeting had been chilly. Ever the practical jokester, Roosevelt could not however take kidding about aspirants for his job. He quickly took steps to squelch Joe's presidential ambitions. He had his press secretary Stephen Early call in Walter Trohan of the *Chicago Tribune*.

"He said, 'You're a friend of Joe Kennedy,'" Trohan recalled. "I said, 'Yes.' He said, 'You know Joe wants to be president.' I said, 'Yes. He has as much chance as I do.' He said, 'Would you take him over the coals if it were justified?' I said, 'Any time I can get a New Dealer, I'm delighted.'"

Early told Trohan that Roosevelt was angry with Joe over his thinly disguised presidential bid. It appeared Joe was using the position Roosevelt had given him to try to unseat him. Roosevelt knew that Joe had enlisted a "prominent Washington correspondent" to direct the presidential boom from Washington. "Joe Kennedy never did anything without thinking of Joe Kennedy," Early said.

The piece ran on page one of the June 23, 1938, edition of the *Tribune*. "Kennedy's 1940 Ambitions Open Roosevelt Rift," the headline said. Attributed to "unimpeachable sources," the story began, "The chilling shadow of 1940 has fallen across the friendship of President Roosevelt and his two-fisted trouble-shooter. . . ." Early's quote about Joe's selfishness was attributed to a "high administration official." While he was not named, the "prominent Washington correspondent" orchestrating the campaign for Joe was Arthur Krock.

When Trohan next saw Joe, Kennedy "drew his hand across his throat," meaning he was about to cut his throat. "He went to my boss, Colonel McCormick," Trohan recalled. He "asked McCormick to fire me. . . . Of course, McCormick told him he was running his paper his way. He thought he had me captured and in his corner. I was out for news. If I had news, I was going to print it."

Trohan told Eddie Moore, "He knows where I got that story. It could only have come from one place, the White House."

Joe took Trohan off the list to receive Sulka ties and cases of Haig & Haig. But when Trohan was next in London, Joe invited him to the embassy and served him thirty-five-year-old Scotch. "He knew Roosevelt was behind it," Trohan said. "He didn't want to blame Roosevelt."

Meanwhile, for an article C.L. Sulzberger was writing for the *Ladies Home Journal*, Joe "confessed" that he "never thought about an ambassadorship, and this offer [to be ambassador] came as a complete surprise." Joe made the same bogus claim in his unpublished memoirs, telling James

Landis to write, "To this day I do not know whether the offer initiated with the president himself or with one of his advisors." Kennedy told Sulzberger that he had heard of suggestions that he run for president but would not do so because he loved his family. "I've never given the presidency a serious thought," he said.

Sulzberger was unconvinced and made it clear in the article that Joe was seriously considering a run—later confirmed by Arthur Krock. Joe saw the article and demanded a revision. When Sulzberger refused, Joe warned that the publisher of the magazine was a close friend: "I'll see to it that your piece is never published." When the article was published, Sulzberger found it so changed that "it almost seemed as if the ambassador had written it himself."

Joe had no such problems with Krock. The columnist continued merrily to turn out paeans of praise to the man who put him up in Florida and sent him cases of Scotch and other goodies. On the same day that Trohan's *Chicago Tribune* story appeared reporting that Roosevelt had little use for Joe, Krock reassured the readers of the *New York Times* that in the American political community, Joe remained "trusted and popular." Krock attributed that to Joe's "forthright methods" and his "unusual gift of naturalness, plus wit and wisdom and a sound philosophy." According to Krock, Joe could spot a "high-hat" a mile off, and he "never wanted to wear one." Joe had ordered people out of his office in Washington when they "said things he considered derogatory to the dignity of a government official." But Krock knew that Joe routinely called Roosevelt a "son-of-a-bitch" behind his back. The columnist presumably did not consider the president to be a government official.

On June 26, Ickes and his wife, Jane, had dinner with Roosevelt at the White House. They had just visited Joe in London, where he entertained them lavishly. He put a chauffeured limousine at their disposal and invited them to dinners with such luminaries as Lady Astor, John D. Rockefeller Jr., Winston Churchill, Viscount and Viscountess Astor,

Sir Alexander Cadogan, Prime Minister Chamberlain, *New York Times* publisher Arthur Hays Sulzberger, and the Duke and Duchess of Kent.

During the visit, Joe confided to Ickes that "the State Department did not know what was going on in Europe" and "nothing got to the president unless he sent it to the president direct." Ickes realized that Roosevelt saw through Joe's bluster. Roosevelt told Ickes he did not expect Joe to last more than two years in the job. Joe was the "kind of man who liked to go from one job to another and stop it just when the going became heavy."

Both men chuckled over a newspaper item claiming Joe had turned down an honorary degree from Harvard. Over his lifetime, Joe would collect ten honorary degrees, none from Harvard. Ickes encouraged his wife to recount what John Cudahy, the American ambassador to Dublin, had told her. Cudahy had said that Joe was so intent on collecting honorary degrees that during negotiations over the settlement of claims between England and Ireland, Joe had pressed him to persuade the ancient and prestigious Trinity College of Dublin to give him an honorary degree. As he often did, Joe claimed he wanted the honor not for himself but "for the sake of his children," Jane Ickes said. Even that self-serving statement had not gotten him the degree. Roosevelt burst out laughing when told this morsel.

Turning serious, Roosevelt said Joe had "remonstrated with him for criticizing fascism in his speeches," Ickes recalled. "He wants him to attack Nazism but not fascism. The president asked him why, and he said very frankly that he thought we would have to have some form of fascism here," Ickes said. "The president thinks that Joe Kennedy, if he were in power, would give us a fascist form of government. He would organize a small powerful committee under himself as chairman, and this committee would run the country without much reference to Congress."

Roosevelt said he knew Joe wanted to be the first Catholic president. In May, a public opinion poll had found Joe would come in fifth among potential Democratic candidates if Roosevelt did not run. Roosevelt did not think a Catholic could get elected, and he later termed the idea of a presidential run by Joe "absurd." But to head off threats by Vice President John Nance Garner, a conservative Texan, Roosevelt said he might be forced to turn to Joe as his running mate in 1940.

Roosevelt asked Ickes if he knew that the isolationist circle around Eleanor M. "Cissy" Patterson, publisher of the conservative *Washington Times-Herald*, was boosting Joe for the presidency. With contempt, the president compared her elitist "cell" of party goers to the Cliveden Set.

Ickes noted that Krock was ready to take time off to "devote himself to spreading the Kennedy-for-President gospel." Krock was hoping to become "editor of the *New York Times*." Joe was boosting him for the job and was "ready to support Krock financially if necessary" to help him get it. Ickes said Kennedy had lots of money and was "willing to spend it freely."

Arthur Sulzberger had just told Joe in London that he hesitated to promote Krock. If he did, he might eventually run the paper. But Sulzberger felt it would not look good if a Jewish publisher chose a Jew as his top editor, according to a letter from Joe to Krock. While that may have been true, the fact that Krock's conservative views and criticism of the New Deal did not accord with Sulzberger's would have been enough to take him out of the running.

At the end of June, the *Saturday Evening Post* exposed James Roosevelt's profiteering. Among other things, it cited Jimmy's help in getting Joe the ambassadorship and the exclusive rights to Haig & Haig distribution in the United States. "Jimmy has helped Kennedy to reach the two great positions he now holds—that of ambassador to London and that of premier Scotch whisky salesman in America."

Joe had tried to suppress the article. When it came out, James Roosevelt asked Corcoran how he should respond. Corcoran advised him to check into a hospital and not issue any statement. Sure enough, Jimmy checked into the Mayo Clinic.

While boarding the SS *Normandie* for England, Joe told reporters, "I admit I am the ambassador, but I deny I am the premier Scotch whisky salesman in the country. I do like to be the best in everything." He added, "I suffered by knowing James Roosevelt. If the rest of the *Saturday Evening Post* article is no truer than the part about my connection with James Roosevelt, it's all a lie."

To the *Boston Traveler*, Joe later admitted that Jimmy Roosevelt had had a "lot to do" with both successes. Then in a letter to the editor, he said he had been misquoted and had never said whether Jimmy did or did not help him.

◆ ◆ ◆

Three weeks after arriving back in England on July 4, 1938, Joe reported to Herbert von Dirksen, the German ambassador, that Washington had not taken kindly to his suggestion that he visit Germany. Based on his discussions at the State Department, Joe said he did not think he could obtain approval to visit Germany unless he were going on some other mission besides discussing relations with the United States. He could then have "short tours."

Joe exulted when Dirksen told him that Hitler was willing to negotiate over arms limitations—the same sorts of limitations Hitler had renounced in tearing up the Treaty of Versailles. "This morning his manner was a revelation to me," Joe told Hull. "What was particularly made clear to me was that Dirksen thought that it was now the time for Britain to make a proposition to the Germans; that Hitler was very much in the mood to make an [armaments] agreement. . . ."

Hull was amazed at how gullible Joe seemed, but not when it came to money. Just before Joe left for Washington, the *London Daily Express*, owned by Joe's friend Lord Max Beaverbrook, had said that after three months as ambassador,

Joe "wants to quit his job with a blaze of glory, and for that reason he is arranging a settlement of the British debt to the United States." Another version of the story, carried two weeks later by Reuters, said Joe had worked out a devaluation agreement that was already causing "a sharp expansion of hoarding" of gold, raising its price.

Morgenthau called Hull and asked him if he knew anything about the rumors. Hull said no. In fact, he had just been asked at a press conference earlier in the day about the reports. He had told the reporters the same thing.

Even though Joe denied the stories, the rumors had already sent the prices of silver and gold soaring. Morgenthau would later determine that Joe floated such rumors so he could make a killing on the market. Today, such practices would be considered violations of criminal law.

Now that Joe was back in London, Hull and Morgenthau commiserated with each other about their problems with him.

"Why, when he was here, he doesn't let me know, and he comes in one morning and says he has got to see me right away," Hull told Morgenthau. "Then, when he gets ready to go away, I have a meeting on with 12 people, and he sends in word, 'Can't you step out and say good bye . . .' " Further, he would claim to have put through the trade treaty, when in fact he "does not even know the first thing about it."

◆ ◆ ◆

Having just returned from the United States, Joe decided it was time for a vacation. "With your approval, I am hoping to go away . . . next week to join my family in Cannes," Joe wrote Hull. "I have arranged to be able to fly back in five hours if something arises that makes it necessary for me to be in London. . . ."

On August 3, Joe flew to the south of France. From there, he gave an exclusive interview to Hearst's *Boston Evening American* urging Americans "not to lose our heads" over the

German threat. Roosevelt was incensed. "Frankly, I think that Joe Kennedy's attention should be called to this," he told Hull. "If all of our 55 ambassadors and ministers were to send exclusive stories to specially chosen newspapers in the United States, your department might just as well close shop."

Gently, Hull suggested to Joe that the practice of giving such exclusives would be regarded as "unfair" by other news agencies. If other ambassadors pursued the same course, Hull said, "great confusion" would result.

For some time, Hitler had been urging Czechoslovakia's minority of 3 million German-speaking citizens who lived in the Sudetenland to demand greater autonomy. Now, as Hitler prepared to take over Czechoslovakia, Joe asked Hull for approval to give a speech that included the statement, "for the life of me, I cannot see anything involved which would be remotely considered worth shedding blood for." When Roosevelt saw the draft, he parodied what Joe had said: "I can't for the life of me understand why anyone would want to go to war to save the Czechs." To Morgenthau, he said, "The young man needs his wrists slapped rather hard."

Instead, Roosevelt simply asked Hull to request Joe to drop the offending language. In response to one of Joe's letters, Roosevelt wrote, "I know what difficult days you are going through, and I can assure you that it is not much easier at this end."

For all the smooth talk, Roosevelt continued to express his dissatisfaction with Joe through the press. Citing "the highest authority," columnists Joseph Alsop and Robert Kintner reported that the Cliveden Set had adopted Joe. "While Kennedy is loved in London," they wrote, "he is no longer popular at the White House. The president knows of his private talk, resents it, and rebukes it when he can."

After the column ran, Arthur Krock confronted Alsop and demanded, "What do you mean by telling lies about Joe Kennedy?"

◆ ◆ ◆

The London air was misty and filled with coal smoke as Joe had lunch at the embassy with Lindbergh and his wife, Anne, on September 21. After lunch, Joe and Lindbergh discussed the European situation.

In an inflammatory speech, Hitler had just called for "justice" for the Sudetenland. At Chamberlain's request, Hitler had met with him at Berchtesgaden on September 15. Chamberlain proposed ceding to Germany those parts of Czechoslovakia where more than half the population favored it. After meeting him, Chamberlain decided that Hitler was "completely ruthless" and was "cruel, overbearing, and has a hard look," Joe reported after Chamberlain had briefed him on the visit.

Even though the English were "not prepared," Joe told Lindbergh they were ready to fight. He quoted Chamberlain as saying Hitler would risk a world war if necessary to achieve his aims.

"Without doubt," Lindbergh told Joe, "the German air fleet is now stronger than that of any country in the world." Lindbergh said Germany now had the means of destroying London, Paris, and Prague "if she wishes to do so."

So impressed was Joe by Lindbergh's "acute" analysis that he asked him to put it in writing so he could give it to the British. But the analysis received a "cursory rejection" by State. Joe attributed the rejection to unfounded accusations that, because of his "acceptance in an unguarded moment" of a decoration from Hermann W. Goering, Lindbergh was a Nazi propagandist.

With events turning more ominous, Joe decided to send Rose and the family back to the United States. The Associated Press had calculated that Joe's children had gotten ten times more publicity than he had. But as his increasingly isolationist views became more well known, the favorable press Joe had enjoyed began to evaporate.

"We have a rich man, untrained in diplomacy, unlearned

in history and politics, who is a great publicity seeker and who apparently is ambitious to be the first Catholic president of the U.S.," Josiah Wedgwood, a liberal member of Parliament opposed to Chamberlain's foreign policy, said of Joe.

After Rose had gone, Joe called Barbara Hutton, heir to the F.W. Woolworth fortune, whom he and Rose had known socially in London. The embassy had begun sending out warning letters to American residents suggesting that they leave England. But Joe decided to deliver the message personally to the glamorous woman.

Joe told Hutton he had called her in because of the urgent political situation. While she was no longer an American citizen, he reassured her that he had conferred with the State Department, which agreed that she could reenter on her Danish passport.

As they talked, Joe became more playful. He offered her a drink, but she declined. Hutton wanted to leave, but Joe was becoming more aggressive, even threatening. Within minutes, he was propositioning her, offering to make her his mistress, and chasing her around the desk.

Hutton was aghast and subsequently related the incident to Lady Diana Cooper, whose husband, Alfred Duff Cooper, would later become ambassador to France. In turn, Lady Cooper wrote about the incident to Conrad Russell, a cousin to the Duke of Bedford. "Kennedy was eager to help, but the help was to consist mainly of setting Barbara up as his mistress," she wrote. "I gather some pouncing accompanied the proposition." She added that "poor Barbara feels she can never look Kennedy in the face again."

◆ ◆ ◆

As the British cabinet debated what to do about Czechoslovakia, Joe continued to insist that the United States was neutral. Hull again reproved Joe, telling him to not interfere with Washington's carefully crafted statements.

Meanwhile, Roosevelt asked Sir Ronald Lindsay, the British ambassador in Washington, to meet with him at the White House. Lindsay came away with the impression the president would not approve of compromising with Hitler, who was now demanding all of the Sudetenland.

Roosevelt said while he appreciated the difficulties faced by the British, he could not countenance a sellout of the Czechs. Yet Roosevelt could not publicly reject a compromise, because that might encourage the Czechs: If they resisted, they would be slaughtered. Unless Britain were invaded, Roosevelt doubted he could justify sending troops.

Once again, on September 29, 1938, Chamberlain appeased Hitler. Acting for England and France, Chamberlain signed an agreement at Munich that ceded to Germany the entire Sudetenland, a sixteen-thousand-square-mile territory, nearly a third of Czechoslovakia. In return, Hitler gave him a vaguely worded friendship agreement. With this piece of paper, Chamberlain returned home.

"I believe it is peace for our time," Chamberlain declared. "Peace with honor."

It was but one more bluff by Hitler, and while the British momentarily rejoiced, they quickly realized that Hitler's signature on the agreement was worthless. Joe, on the other hand, appeared to assume that Hitler was a rational person who could be trusted. Joe would later argue that the agreement had bought "precious time" for the allies to fortify their armaments. But the agreement also bought time for the Germans. In a totalitarian society, rearming could be done in secrecy.

If Joe's naïveté seemed out of character, that was because it was a facade. In his private statements, Joe made it clear that he thought Hitler would prevail, even to conquering the United States. But Joe did not see that as such a bad thing. As he said many times, the United States already had an authoritarian form of government and might one day require a fascist one. Moreover, Joe had neither the courage nor the will to fight. Like most bullies, he had little inner strength. When confronted with might, he caved. Asserting control and maintaining his own luxurious lifestyle came before anything else.

"Isn't it wonderful?" Joe said to Jan Masaryk, the Czech ambassador in London, after Chamberlain returned. "Now I can get to Palm Beach after all!"

Just after Munich, Joe demonstrated his posture of neutrality when he told the annual Trafalgar Day Dinner given by the British Navy League in London that it was "unproductive" for democracies and dictatorships "to widen the division now existing between them by emphasizing their differences," which are "self-apparent." Instead, he proposed that they work toward "solving their common problems." After all, he said, we "have to live together in the same world whether we like it or not."

Almost word for word, Joe had adopted the propaganda Dirksen had foisted on him a few months earlier. According to that formulation, the issue at hand was not armed aggression, the survival of democracy, morality, justice, or decency, but rather ideological differences over political systems. Already, the British were preparing for a German invasion. Joe reported seeing antiaircraft guns being placed in Hyde Park and "hundreds of men" digging ditches. But he persisted in casting the threat in terms of a debate between two equally valid political systems.

Joe's speech caused consternation in diplomatic circles. Many countries inquired unofficially whether Joe's speech meant a change in United States policy. The Canadian ambassador to the United States expressed annoyance and said he could not understand the basis for Joe's views.

The White House was besieged by critical telegrams. The State Department had approved the speech in advance only on the understanding that the comments would be presented as Joe's personal views. That point had gotten lost in the shuffle. Hull was so upset that at any mention of the speech, "He loses his amiability and wishes that all ambassadors would forgo all speeches," Moffat reported.

Felix Frankfurter, an adviser to Roosevelt who was about

to be appointed to the Supreme Court, complained bitterly to the president. "I wonder if Joe Kennedy understands the implications of public talk by an American ambassador," he said. "Such public approval of dictatorships, in part even, plays into their hands."

American press reaction was equally negative. The *New York Post* characterized the proposal as tantamount to suggesting that "the United States make a friend of the man who boasts that he is out to destroy democracy and religion." The paper called the idea shocking to "free Americans." Writing in the *Wall Street Journal*, Frank Kent agreed with a proposal Heywood Broun had made—that upon his return to the United States, Joe be dropped in Boston Harbor. If he were dunked in "alien tea," Joe's Americanism might be restored.

Many of the columns contained references to Roosevelt's lack of faith in Kennedy, who told friends he thought he had been stabbed in the back.

"I am so God damned mad I can't see," Joe wrote to his friend Senator James F. Byrnes, a conservative New Dealer from South Carolina. He described himself as sick of "all the insidious lying" he had read in recent columns about him.

From Harvard, Jack wrote to his father that while the speech "seemed to be unpopular with the Jews, etc." it was "considered to be very good by everyone who wasn't bitterly anti-fascist. . . ."

13

THE KENNEDY PLAN

After the adverse publicity from his Trafalgar Day speech, Joe suddenly began working with Chamberlain on a plan calling for huge financial contributions from governments and individuals so that Jews could be evacuated from Germany. The plan was almost exactly what Washington lawyer George Rublee had been working on for months. Rublee headed the Intergovernmental Committee on Refugees, which had evolved from the Evian Conference, a meeting of ambassadors from thirty-two countries who had met on July 6, 1938, in the French resort town of Evian-les-Bains.

Polls showed that while an overwhelming majority of Americans feared and hated Hitler, 83 percent favored barring more immigrants to the United States. Rublee hoped to ship German Jews to Africa or South America. But Joe "did not seem interested, and never gave me any real support or assistance," Rublee said.

Now Joe told journalists that he was working with Chamberlain on what became known as the "Kennedy Plan." The plan seemed to exist mainly in the press, which got daily reports from Joe about the latest developments.

"There seems to be no doubt that Mr. Kennedy is negotiating on his own with the British government, but he has never so much as reported a word to the president, the secretary, or Mr. Rublee," the State Department's Jay Pierrepont Moffat noted in his diary. Moffat never ceased to be amazed by Joe's publicity seeking. In another diary entry, he said, "We are still in the dark as to what Mr. Kennedy is doing in London on refugees."

If Joe's plan was a publicity stunt, it had the desired effect. Henry Luce's *Life* suggested that if the plan succeeded, "it will add new lustre to a reputation which may well carry Joseph Patrick Kennedy into the White House."

When nothing came of Joe's plan, Rublee continued on his own and finally worked out an agreement with the Germans in January 1939. Then Joe "called me up, and in an entirely new tone, expressed great surprise," Rublee recalled. " 'How could it have happened? Why hadn't they [the Germans] done something like this before if they were willing to do such things?' "

In fact, German interest in the plan was nothing more than propaganda, intended to conceal persecution of the Jews—persecution that was becoming increasingly difficult to hide. On the evening of November 9, 1938, the Nazis rampaged against Jews on *Kristallnacht*—Crystal Night, or the Night of Broken Glass—in Germany. The excuse for the attack was the shooting of a German diplomat in Paris by a seventeen-year-old German Jewish refugee whose father had been among ten thousand Jews deported in boxcars to Poland. At least two hundred synagogues were razed by fire or wrecked. Almost a thousand Jewish shops and homes were destroyed. More than twenty thousand Jews were arrested and placed in concentration camps. At least 236 Jews, including women and children, were killed. Another six hundred were maimed. Two days after the attacks, Nazi edicts required that all Jewish businesses be liquidated. For a 10 percent reimbursement in German marks, Jews were required to turn in all stocks, bonds, and precious metals. For their "abominable crimes," as Goering put it, German Jews were ordered to pay a $400 million "atonement fine" to the German government equivalent to the amount insurance companies owed them for damage to their own property. Three months later, Hitler announced that in the new world dominated by Nazis, the Jews in Europe would be destroyed.

No longer were the stories of Nazi attacks against the Jews buried inside newspapers. The November 15, 1938, issue of the *New York Times* carried a story at the top of page one reporting that Hitler had decreed that Jews would be expelled from all high schools and colleges and forbidden to sell their stocks. Jewish children in grade schools had already been forbidden to attend.

With the outbreak of war, Rublee's plan would die. When Joe's aide Harvey Klemmer reported to Joe on the treatment of Jews in Germany, Joe dismissed the atrocities by saying, "They brought it on themselves."

A month after Roosevelt had condemned the Nazis for the *Kristallnacht* attacks on Jews, Joe finally chimed in. When a reporter asked him what he thought of it, he called persecution of Jews in Germany "the most horrible thing I have ever heard of." It would be his only publicly recorded criticism of Hitler or his policies.

Nor did Joe display any interest in British restrictions on the number of Jews who could emigrate to what was then known as Palestine. Later, after Jack was elected to Congress and favored creation of the state of Israel, Joe fumed that only the Jews were interested. "The Jews are kicking up a lot of fuss about the British attitude in Palestine, but it is all coming from the Jews," he wrote to his friend Beaverbrook. "The rest of the country is very little concerned about it."

If efforts to save the Jews did not interest Joe, playing censor did. In a newsreel on the Czech crisis, Paramount had included comments by A.J. Cummings and Wickham Steed, two influential journalists who opposed Chamberlain's appeasement policies. Claiming that such comments would undermine its position with Hitler, the British government asked Joe if something could be done. Censoring American films on behalf of the British government was not part of Joe's portfolio as ambassador. But he quickly agreed to speak with his friend Will Hays of the Motion Picture Producers and Distributors of America. Hays got Paramount to remove the clip.

After the offending section had been cut, Ickes wrote in his diary that Joe had suppressed the film even though "there was no allegation that the section of the film which was cut misrepresented the facts in any way." When the incident became public in November 1938, the *Chicago Tribune* editorialized, "Our ambassadors in London should be discouraged from playing the role of office boy of empire."

Having succeeded as censor, Joe turned his attention to an impending visit to the United States by King George VI and Queen Elizabeth. Joe had suggested the visit, but when he tried to get involved in the State Department arrangements, Hull rebuffed him. "I have been requested by the president to let you know that he has taken up the arrangements to be made for the visit to the United States of the king and queen through the British Embassy in Washington," Hull wrote. If Roosevelt were visiting England, those arrangements would be made by Joe, Hull pointed out.

Joe could never accept that. He continued to fume about his embarrassment at having first suggested the trip to the king and queen, then being denied the pleasure of making the arrangements.

◆ ◆ ◆

Having just taken a month-long vacation on the Riviera, Joe now decided to take another vacation in Palm Beach. Before leaving, he told the Plymouth Chamber of Commerce in London that we "must not forget that the surest road to defeat is resignation to defeat." If that conflicted with his own defeatist speeches, Joe never seemed aware of it. So long as he said what he had to say with authority, and the press picked it up, he did not much care what the content was. As Lindbergh observed of him, "He does not seem to like the press, yet seems fascinated by it. . . . I am not sure whether he enjoys being in the spotlight of publicity or whether he simply considers it a necessity in present conditions."

By now, the State Department was going around Joe, and Roosevelt had almost lost patience with him. Discussing the president's attitude with James Farley, Morgenthau said Roosevelt was "peeved" with Kennedy.

"Terribly," Farley interjected. "He's got good reason to be."

"Yes, of course he has," Farley replied. When Joe came back, it would "probably be the beginning of the end."

Farley felt Joe was "like a spoiled child," as he wrote in his diary. "I think he is hurt if he is not consulted at all times," Farley said. "You have to 'hold his hand' now and then to make him feel alright."

On December 10, Joe left for the United States on the SS *Queen Mary*. Boake Carter, an isolationist right-wing columnist who enjoyed Joe's hospitality at Palm Beach, predicted a massive confrontation with Roosevelt. "The White House has on its hands a fighting Irishman with blazing eyes and a determination to strip the bandages of deceit, innuendo, and misrepresentation bound around the eyes of American citizens," he wrote.

Newspapermen met Joe at the pier in New York. "What did you think of Hitler?" a reporter asked. "Come and see me the day I resign," Joe said. "Did he consider himself part of the Cliveden Set?" "I don't know what it is." There were only two choices: "chaos or war." If there was any other way, it would be worth trying, he said.

Joe met with Roosevelt for two hours on December 16. Full of self-pity, he complained about the State Department's failure to consult him. He offered to resign. Roosevelt discounted the rumors and insisted he remain on the job. Joe would be a far greater threat to the president outside his camp than inside. Moreover, as a conservative, Joe could deflect right-wing critics who claimed Roosevelt was a Communist.

At the State Department, Moffat remained sympathetic to Joe. Joe confided in him that while the United States government supported his position, American public opinion was "hostile" to him: "He attributes this largely to the Jews who dominate our press."

Ironically, Arthur Krock, a Jew who was probably the most influential journalist in Washington, supported Joe's position. The attacks on him in recent months had been motivated by "jealousy," Krock wrote in a letter to Joe.

Krock never disclosed in his columns the emoluments he received from Joe. The *New York Times* man had just spent a week at Joe's Palm Beach home, all expenses paid. "It's a shame to have that beautiful place going to waste," Joe had written to him. He had instructed the caretaker to "take very good care" of Krock. Nor did he publicly disclose his real opinion of the man. He would later say that Joe was "amoral." Only a Roman Catholic could be "amoral and still be religious," he said. "That is, you can carry an insurance policy with the Deity and at the same time do all these other things, with this cover to save you at the end by penitence." He also said he was aware of Joe's many affairs, but they never bothered him. "Rose acted as if they didn't exist, and that was her business, not mine," he said later.

Felix Frankfurter, who knew Joe from his days as a Harvard Law School professor, told Ickes that he had heard Joe say that he was "supporting that fellow," referring to Krock.

"Perhaps, after all, there is something to Tom Corcoran's belief that Krock is on Kennedy's payroll," Ickes wrote in his diary.

Years later, Krock recalled that Joe had offered him a bribe. Perturbed with an item he had written, Joe had called him and said, "I don't want to hear any nonsense from you. You look out the window Christmas morning, and you'll see an automobile."

"I will see nothing of the kind," Krock replied. "I'll have it towed away if it's there." That was the kind of "coarse bribe" Joe would engage in, Krock said. "That's the way his mind worked."

But if Krock was not susceptible to coarse bribes, he was perfectly willing to succumb to more refined ones. For more than two decades, he would mythologize Joe in his columns while enjoying Florida vacations and cases of Haig & Haig.

◆ ◆ ◆

While Rose and eight of the children skied at St. Moritz, Joe spent Christmas in Palm Beach with Jack. Jack had just been granted a leave of absence from Harvard for the spring semester and planned to work for Joe in London. Joe's son Joe Jr. was already working for him as an attaché.

In Palm Beach, Joe sat by the pool calling Colonel McCormick of the *Chicago Tribune*, Father Coughlin, who had by now given up his radio show, and Tom Corcoran, who feared Arthur Krock was "running a campaign to put Joe Kennedy over for president." Besides Boake Carter, Joe had as his guest the influential gossip columnist Walter Winchell.

After Christmas, Joe visited Boston and had his annual checkup at the Lahey Clinic. He had Dr. Sara M. Jordan write to Roosevelt to say he had experienced a flare-up of gastritis, which he had had for "some years." She recommended a two-month vacation in Florida so he could rest.

Since his appointment to London nearly a year earlier, Joe had managed to spend four months—one third of his time—back home. As Europe marched toward war, Joe was trying to extend a two-month vacation in Florida into a three-month stay. Finally, Moffat had to tell Joe on February 9 that Roosevelt wanted him to return to his post. Joe had planned on returning February 23.

The next day, however, Roosevelt was careful to write and

thank Joe for his Christmas present—"the most luxurious dressing gown I have ever owned."

◆ ◆ ◆

By January 1939, Roosevelt had become convinced of the bankruptcy of appeasement. He asked Congress for a substantial increase in defense spending. Even Chamberlain was beginning to revise his thinking. He abandoned his earlier position that England should address Germany's economic grievances. He told his cabinet that Hitler's attitude "made it impossible to continue to negotiate on the old basis with the Nazi regime."

Joe continued to seesaw between buoyancy and gloom. "What now? What's to be done next?" Joe asked Foreign Minister Halifax. He told Roosevelt, "People here are a good deal more optimistic than when I left, but there is still plenty of trouble on the horizon."

Again, Joe flip-flopped, telling the president in a memo that America needed to build a mighty arsenal. Demonstrating his monumental lack of faith in the American people or democracy, Joe said that the heavy sacrifices required to fund such a project might produce rebellion and would "inevitably mean the destruction of the American form of government. . . ." In Joe's view, "To fight totalitarianism, we would have to adopt totalitarian methods." His memo was met with silence.

In February 1939, Pope Pius XI died. As Joe had predicted, Eugenio Cardinal Pacelli, the Vatican secretary of state, was named to succeed him. In a telephone call on March 5, Joe asked Roosevelt to let him represent him at the ceremony. "By all means, do," Roosevelt said. Some in the State Department had reservations, saying a Protestant should attend. But Sumner Welles, the undersecretary of state, called Joe to confirm that he would be the president's special representative to the event.

On Saturday, March 11, 1939, Joe, Rose, and eight of

their children arrived for the coronation of Pope Pius XII. (Joe Jr. was in Spain gathering information for his father on the Spanish Civil War.) On March 12, Joe and his family were among the people crowded into the church to hear the pope celebrate mass. In his memoirs, Joe called the beauty of the experience that day "beyond belief."

The following morning, the new pope interrupted his morning conference to receive Joe and his family in a private audience. The children brought along rosaries and other holy items to be blessed. The new pope was especially pleased to see seven-year-old Ted. The pope later named Rose a papal countess and bestowed on Joe the Order of Pius IX, a decoration generally reserved for heads of state and high-ranking government officials.

Joe kept Spellman, still an auxiliary bishop in Boston, informed on the new pope's attitude toward him. Referring to Count Galeazzi, the pope's confidant, Joe told Spellman, "Enrico is in there fighting for you all the time." Soon, Spellman received a special delivery letter saying he was appointed archbishop of New York.

♦ ♦ ♦

On March 15, Hitler dispelled all doubts about whether he had meant what he said to Chamberlain: Nazi tanks were rolling into Prague. The Czechs, with their best fortifications already in Hitler's hands, put up little resistance. Joe had to return from Italy five days early.

At first, Chamberlain tried to deny what had just happened, saying that Hitler had not reneged on the Munich Pact because the country whose independence had been guaranteed no longer existed. Britons reacted with anger to this obvious subterfuge, and two days later, Chamberlain reproached Hitler for breach of faith. Even to Chamberlain, it was apparent that his own policy of appeasement had failed.

Joe remained one of the few diplomats who continued to

believe in appeasement. On April 29, Joe talked with Hull about the possibility of paying off Hitler to switch to peaceful pursuits. Joe had found that almost everyone was susceptible to bribes. Why not Hitler?

"He has no money, and he can't change all these people who are engaged in wartime activities into peacetime activities without having a terrific problem," Joe told Hull.

Humoring him, Hull said, "I wish you would send us anything that occurs to you. . . ."

A new round of stories began appearing in the press reporting that Roosevelt wanted Joe out as ambassador. Joe himself told William Phillips, the American ambassador to Italy, that ambassadors were "mere messenger boys," and he planned to resign by July. He later complained to Roosevelt that in "this day and age," an ambassador may be "hardly more than a glorified errand boy." He said he got discouraged because he had "worked harder and longer on this job than any other"—a theme he sounded each time he left a job. Yet, he said, three quarters of his efforts were wasted because of the "terrific" number of things he had to do bearing no relation to the real job at hand.

In a conversation with Ickes on March 29, Roosevelt said that Joe appeared to have no intention of leaving London. While it was true that Joe usually tired of a job in a year, that did not take into account that Joe was "mixed up socially with duchesses and princesses and what-not. . . ." Ickes noted that Joe was "having the time of his life."

Indeed, just before King George and Queen Elizabeth left for the United States, Joe threw a dinner party for them at the American embassy. For the May 4 affair, Joe ordered that the menus be printed in English rather than the traditional French. He served American favorites—Baltimore shad roe, Virginia ham, Georgia pickled peaches, and strawberry shortcake. Besides all nine of his children, Joe invited the Duke and Duchess of Beaufort, the Duke and Duchess of Devonshire, the Earl of Eldon, the Countess of Airlie, and Viscount and Viscountess Astor.

Joe never failed to be dazzled by the pomp and circumstance that attended royalty. "Promptly at 8:30 the king and queen arrived," Joe recalled. "I went to the foot of the steps to greet their majesties in accordance with the tradition that governs their honoring a house by visiting it. My wife's maid stepped forward to take the queen's coat, a prerogative belonging to the personal maid of the hostess. Upstairs the guests had already assembled, and after their majesties had shaken hands with all of them, including the children, cocktails were served," Joe said. "The king and queen declined them, the queen remarking that they never lifted her but instead made her sleepy when she wanted to be awake, or else stimulated her when she wanted to be sleepy." After dinner, Joe showed *Goodbye, Mr. Chips*, a movie filmed in England about a shy schoolmaster who devotes his life to "his boys."

"I remember clearly as the lights went up after the performance that the queen, like some of the other ladies present, was dabbing at her eyes with a handkerchief to brush away the tears," Joe said.

◆　◆　◆

For some months, James D. Mooney, president of General Motors Overseas, which ran the automaker's foreign operations, had been trying to broker a deal to buy off Hitler. An engineer, Mooney feared economic disruption in the event of war. His company had a heavy investment in Germany. He was already close to Hitler's regime, having received the German Order of Merit of the Eagle in 1938. Like Joe, Mooney assumed that Hitler was rational.

On April 25, 1939, Mooney met with Joe at the embassy and told him of discussions he had been having with Emil Puhl, a director of the Reichsbank, and Helmuth Wohlthat, minister-director on Field Marshal Hermann Goering's staff. In Mooney's view, the entire problem between Washington and Berlin was a "lack of understanding" because neither side had "conscientiously discussed" the issues in contention between them. Joe was interested in Mooney's ideas and said he would like to talk with Hitler's representatives "quietly and privately." He suggested he could meet with them in Paris "ostensibly for a weekend visit."

Wohlthat, described later by Joe as "Goering's right-hand man," readily agreed to the meeting. It was in Germany's interests to diminish fears of Hitler, giving the country more time to rearm while stalling Allied mobilization. After the other side had agreed, it occurred to Joe that perhaps he should obtain permission to pursue the negotiations. After Joe proposed the visit to Hull, Sumner Welles cabled back that they both felt it would be "almost impossible to prevent your trip to Paris and the names of the persons you will see from being given a great deal of publicity." Joe then appealed to Roosevelt, who also refused permission.

"This turn of events was most embarrassing to me," Mooney would later write. Still, he persisted. On May 5, Mooney gave Joe his notes on a proposed peace plan. It would require the United States and England to give Germany a gold loan of $500 million to $1 billion, to lift trade embargoes against Germany, and to allow it to acquire colonies previously prohibited under the Treaty of Versailles. In return, Germany would sign nonaggression pacts, limit its rearmament, and be allowed to trade with the United States and England without barriers. When Mooney showed him the plan, Joe said, "What a wonderful speech could be built up from these points back home."

Joe promised Mooney he would try again to persuade Roosevelt. The next day, Joe told Mooney gloomily that he "had been up half the night" trying to get through to the president. When he finally talked with him, Roosevelt had refused permission a second time.

Since Roosevelt had vetoed a Paris meeting, Mooney proposed that Joe meet with Wohlthat in London, this time without asking for permission. Joe agreed to this obvious subterfuge. Joe met with Wohlthat on May 9, 1939, at the Berkeley Hotel, where Wohlthat and Mooney were staying.

The talks went on for two hours. "Each man made an excellent impression upon the other," Mooney recalled. "They both talked freely and frankly."

Joe might have better spent the time reading *Mein Kampf,* in which Hitler had spelled out his intention to look for *Lebensraum*—breathing space or elbow room for Germany.

Two days later, the *Daily Mail* ran a story headlined "Goering's Mystery Man Here." The story said Wohlthat had arrived on a "special mission," possibly to discuss trade. The German embassy denied the story.

Mooney later met with Roosevelt and then Hitler. The Germans resolved to listen to him "politely," recognizing that he "proceeded from an erroneous assumption—that Roosevelt was more sympathetic toward Germany than believed."

Joe's cousin Joe Kane said Chamberlain and Joe at one point presented the king with a similar plan. Joe would go to Germany and allow it to expand if Germany would stay on the continent. "They took the idea to King George, who had Roosevelt on the transatlantic phone inside of minutes," Kane said. Then Roosevelt called Joe, telling him to forget it.

"I'm coming home," Joe responded petulantly. "You stay there," Roosevelt said. Joe replied, "God damn you, no one is going to tell me what to do."

Joe's friend Oscar Haussermann said Joe looked at Britain's situation in terms of "cold, hard cash." With Britain's reserves dwindling, Joe "thought the country would be finished when the pounds ran out," he said. "He's a supreme realist, who wants the facts, not his own or somebody else's feelings, to shape his decisions. But this can cause a blind spot on intangibles."

◆ ◆ ◆

Joe's blindness to the larger picture was causing consternation on both sides of the Atlantic. At a dinner at his home in Georgetown, Frankfurter told Ickes that Joe was a "bounder"

who believed that "anything in the world can be bought."
He said Joe was certain that he would be the "compromise
candidate for president on the Democratic ticket" the following year. Frankfurter would later say of Joe, "I never liked
Joe Sr. Does anybody like Joe Sr.? Have you ever met anybody, except his family?"

Frankfurter's wife, Marian, mimicked the way Joe tried to
ingratiate himself with Chamberlain, frequently and explo-
sively calling him "Neville." Chamberlain's Adam's apple
would work up and down convulsively three or four times,
and then he would emit a loud "Joe!"

In London, Churchill was making it clear that he had no
use for Joe either. In June 1939, Churchill attended a dinner
party given by Harold Nicolson, a member of Parliament, and
his wife, Vita Sackville-West. Columnist Walter Lippmann,
another guest, had met that afternoon with Joe. Lippmann
reported his impressions to the guests: that Joe was pro-Nazi,
anti-Semitic, and convinced that war was inevitable and that
Britain would be defeated.

"He thinks that Hitler has every reason to go to war and
is able to win," Lippmann recorded in his diary. In Joe's
opinion, the British fleet was "valueless" and Russia's help
would be "useless." Even America was doomed. "I am also
a bear on democracy," Lippmann quoted Joe as saying. "It's
gone already." Indeed, Joe told Lippmann, "All the English
in their hearts *know* this to be true, but a small group of
brilliant people has created a public feeling which makes it
impossible for the government to take a sensible course."

Lippmann's disclosure—which never appeared in his columns—prompted what Nicolson called "a magnificent oration" from Churchill. As Nicolson described Churchill, "He
sits hunched there, waving his whisky and soda to mark his
periods, stubbing his cigar with the other hand." Churchill
assured Lippmann that these trials would "steel the resolution
of the British people and enhance our will for victory."
Churchill did not "for one moment suppose" that Joe was
right. But if Joe were, Churchill vowed he would "willingly

lay down my life in combat, rather than, in fear of defeat, surrender to the menaces of these most sinister men."

In contrast to Joe's claim that the British knew they would be defeated, Edward R. Murrow, in his *This Is London* broadcasts, told his American listeners that the English expected war and discussed the prospects with a casual "Bad show." Murrow said he had found no one who said, as they might have a year earlier, that they hoped Chamberlain would "find a way out."

The British government started keeping a secret file on Joe's more offensive remarks. According to one item in the file, Joe "with some relish" had expressed the opinion at a dinner party that the British were about to be thoroughly "trashed."

On May 4, Arthur Krock wrote in the *New York Times* that Joe's "standing in the [State] department has never been higher" and that his sources were "the best informed in Europe." Krock had to know that the State Department held Joe in contempt. Joe himself recognized that his stay in London was likely coming to an end soon. He wrote to Helen Ogden Reid, publisher of the *New York Herald Tribune*, that he could not yet tell if he would be back in the United States by October to attend a forum on international issues. "I have arrived at the point where I dare not make appointments for more than a week ahead," he said. By October, he said, "perhaps . . . I will be an ordinary citizen."

Through a friend, Roosevelt received a copy of *National Zeitung*, a Swiss newspaper, reporting that Joe was making defeatist and anti-Roosevelt comments to what was considered the pro-German circle behind the London *Times*. Joe often suggested that the "democratic policy of the United States is only a Jewish matter" and Roosevelt "will disappear by 1940." Similarly, the May 17, 1939, issue of the British newsletter *The Week* reported that Joe was making anti-Roosevelt remarks, telling his Cliveden Set friends that "the democratic policy of the United States is a Jewish production" and "Roosevelt will fall in 1940."

Ickes and Roosevelt discussed the items, which were reprinted in the *New York Post*. When Roosevelt read that Joe had said "the Jews were running the United States," Roosevelt said facetiously, "It is true."

Joe's comments prompted Jack D. Snow, president of the American Jewish League, to write Hull in protest. Jews were accustomed to such statements from "bigots and anti-Americans," he wrote, "but we hope the time is not yet here when high officials of our government can make such statements without accounting for same."

On July 3, Ickes had lunch with John Cudahy, the American ambassador to Dublin, who confided that Joe was making highly critical, coarse comments about Roosevelt in front of his English servants. When Cudahy cautioned him one day about it, "Joe said that he didn't give a damn." If Joe could not be loyal to Roosevelt, "he should resign," the ambassador said.

When Ickes told Roosevelt what Cudahy had said, the president said he knew Joe was not loyal, but he was as good as anyone in reporting carefully what was happening in England. Yet Roosevelt clearly did not believe that. A few moments later, he began derisively chuckling over a note Joe had sent reporting favorably on Hitler's latest claim that he had no intention of harming England and merely wanted what Germany lost in Europe during World War I.

In fact, Joe tended to report selectively. After a meeting with Halifax on September 10, 1938, he wired the State Department that when Halifax asked what America's reaction would be to a German invasion of Czechoslovakia, Joe had told him that he did not "have the slightest idea, except that we want to keep out of war." But Halifax wired Lindsay, the British ambassador in Washington, a detailed account of what Kennedy had said. According to that account, Joe had responded that the immediate American reaction would be a "desire to keep out of" war, but that if London were bombed, the United States probably would enter the war.

Joe's naïveté knew no bounds. Somehow, he had gotten

permission from the State Department to meet again with Wohlthat. Later, Joe told Hull that Wohlthat had assured him that Hitler "has definitely decided in his own mind that his ultimate victory will be made possible by the mistakes the British are making. . . ." Joe cited the inability of the British and the Soviets to mount a united front against Hitler.

"Wohlthat thinks that because Hitler believes his position is being improved by the tactics of the British every day, he is not disposed to strike quickly," Joe told Hull. "I realize, of course that, after all, while Wohlthat is high in Goering's confidence, nobody knows Hitler's mind, and that the idea is one that cannot be dismissed of getting propaganda over to me. . . ."

Trying to claim credit for his incisive reporting, Joe said he "received the important impression from him that Hitler is not disposed to hurry or to worry about economics, nor to make any conciliatory moves as he feels his position is improving so much politically by the bad tactics of the British . . ."

Meanwhile, on August 23, 1939, Germany and the Soviet Union had signed their ten-year nonaggression pact. A secret protocol provided for the division of Poland and the Baltic states between the two countries. It meant that Hitler would not have to fight a war on two fronts, because Josef Stalin, the Soviet dictator, would not object to a move against Poland.

Just before Hitler attacked Poland, Joe cabled Roosevelt, passing on, without a hint of skepticism, the dictator's claim to having only limited ambitions in Poland. Once these were achieved, Hitler would "make a deal with England that would guarantee the British empire forever." He would then "go back to peaceful pursuits and become an artist, which is what he wanted to be," Joe wrote to Washington.

While Joe took what Hitler said at face value and never condemned him, he attacked Roosevelt mercilessly. Roosevelt was not fooled. Enclosing one of the articles quoting Joe's critical remarks about him, Roosevelt let Joe know in a letter that he was aware of what he was saying yet discounted the item as "silly." When Arthur Krock wrote a column claiming that Joe really was loyal to Roosevelt, the president wrote to Joe tongue-in-cheek, saying that Krock had done Joe a disservice by calling attention to the rumors that he was disloyal. Roosevelt referred to Krock in his letter as "a social parasite" whose surface support could be "won by entertainment and flattery."

"Of course, the purpose of the president was to hit Krock over Kennedy's shoulders, knowing full well that Kennedy would lose no time in getting this letter, or the substance of it, back to Krock," Ickes noted.

Now Joe began sounding a new theme—that Britain must remain strong by staying out of war. He wrote Roosevelt to warn of the makings of "the worst economic condition the world has ever seen." The solution, he said, was for the United States to insist that for at least a year England stay out of war.

Seeking to humor him, Roosevelt wrote that the big question was what the United States could do to keep its financial position strong.

Both two-faced, both temporizing, Joe and Roosevelt continued to use each other for their own ends. For Roosevelt, the paramount concern was keeping Joe in London where he would have difficulty mounting a presidential bid. For Joe, remaining ambassador meant not only prestige but riches. Besides depressing the stock market, a war would impinge on Joe's substantial income from liquor importation. Because of the threat of war, England had begun using its merchant marine for military shipments. The amount of goods that could be shipped overseas was restricted. Joe instructed Harvey Klemmer, the aide Joe had brought over from the Maritime Commission, to use his position as ambassador to obtain precious space on cargo ships destined for the United States.

Klemmer "resented the fact that Joe was using the position for helping Joe with his liquor business," recalled Huidekoper, Joe's aide in London. "I think he felt he was doing coolie labor by shipping his liquor back for him." Yet Klemmer complained to Huidekoper that Joe would not even pay for his Christmas present. "For Christmas, he [Klemmer] got Sulka ties from Joe," Huidekoper said. "He didn't like them and exchanged them. But it turned out Rose had bought them for him. Harvey thought it was chintzy."

Aside from his liquor business, Joe continued to use his position to gain inside information and manipulate the markets. From London sources, Ickes learned that "Joe Kennedy was speculating in the stock market very heavily, but under cover, through London agents."

14

THE PARTY IS ON

Having just learned that German battalions had thrust into Poland, Joe called first Roosevelt, then Hull, in the early morning hours of September 1, 1939. His voice breaking, Joe kept repeating, "It's all over. The party is on."

As young children were evacuated from London and a quarter of a million hospital beds prepared, Chamberlain desperately looked for some other way out. But his cabinet and Parliament had had enough of abject passivity. For the sake of its own dignity and survival, Great Britain needed to honor its treaty commitment to Poland.

On September 3, the British prime minister showed Joe the speech he planned to give that day. Great Britain was about to declare war on Germany. With tears in his eyes, Joe read Chamberlain's admission of failure: "Everything that I have worked for, everything that I have hoped for . . . has crashed into ruins."

Joe made his way back to the embassy and called Roosevelt.

The president could barely recognize his voice. He predicted a new Dark Age would descend on Europe. "It's the end of the world, the end of everything," Joe said. The president tried to comfort him.

That same day, New Zealand, Australia, and France followed Great Britain in declaring war on Germany, officially starting World War II. Off the northwest coast of Ireland, Germany responded that evening by torpedoing the British liner *Athenia*, bound for Canada. One hundred twelve people, including twenty-eight American citizens, were killed. On September 5, the Royal Air Force Bomber Command attacked German warships.

Joe was sure that what Brooks Adams had written about England was right. The nation was past its peak, about to go bankrupt, and not worth saving. He blamed the U.S. failure to accommodate Hitler on the "growing Jewish influence in the press and in Washington," along with the Democrats' belief that they would stay in power if the war continued.

Joe was used to getting his own way, and he arranged a morning meeting with King George to present his views. After the meeting, Alexander Cadogan, the permanent undersecretary in the British Foreign Office, found the king "depressed." The king thought that Joe spoke a "different language" and saw "everything from the angle of his own investments."

Just to make sure Joe understood his position, the king wrote to him after their meeting. "As I see it, the U.S.A., France, and the British Empire are the three really free peoples in the world, and two of these great democracies are fighting against all that we three countries hate and detest, Hitler and his Nazi regime, and all that it stands for." He added, "The British empire's mind is made up."

The appeal to decency and democratic principles sailed over Joe's head. A day after meeting with the king, Joe wrote to Roosevelt. The fact that Great Britain and France were fighting for their survival made no difference. The United States should be "on our guard to protect our own interest," he said in the September 10 message. Continuation of the war would mean "complete economic, financial, and social collapse, and nothing will be saved after the war is over." Above all, he said, the United States must "be able to maintain the right kind of trade and to maintain the strength of our financial system." Joe suggested that if Roosevelt negotiated with Hitler, he would be in a position to "save the world."

"I want to tell you something and don't pass it on to a living soul," Roosevelt told Farley after receiving Joe's telegram. Roosevelt said Joe had sent "the silliest message to me I have ever received. It urged me to do this, that, and the other thing in a frantic sort of way."

To Morgenthau, Roosevelt complained that his London ambassador was a pain. "Joe has been an appeaser and will always be an appeaser," he said. "If Germany and Italy made a good peace offer tomorrow, Joe would start working on the king and his friend the queen and from there on down to get everybody to accept it, and he's just a pain in the neck to me."

Like King George, Roosevelt wanted to make it unmistakably clear that Joe's defeatist views would not be tolerated. The truth was, Roosevelt had not entirely ruled out some kind of compromise. On August 24, he had cabled Germany, Poland, and Italy, urging arbitration to avoid war. In a fireside chat, Roosevelt had declared neutrality in the war. A few weeks later, he went before Congress to urge repeal of the arms embargo provisions of the Neutrality Act of 1937. Roosevelt did not want to give up any option. But whatever course he chose, Roosevelt did not want Joe involved.

Roosevelt directed Hull to send Joe a resoundingly negative response. In strictest confidence, Hull passed on to Joe Roosevelt's message that the United States government saw "no occasion nor opportunity for the American president to initiate any peace move." Any alternative that "would make possible a survival or a consolidation of a regime of force and of aggression would not be supported by the American people."

Joe's impassioned efforts to accept a settlement were beginning to circulate in London diplomatic and journalistic circles. British officials worried that they would strengthen Hitler's resolve and dissuade neutral countries from entering the war on the British side. Over and over, officials in the British Foreign Office concluded that Joe was a "coward" who thought only of his own wallet. One official called his efforts a "propaganda campaign against us." Tales of Joe's defeatist comments began piling up in a file referred to as "Kennediana."

Meanwhile, Joe barraged the State Department with messages complaining about delays in getting aid to survivors of the *Athenia*. Jack was meeting with them in Glasgow. Some had spent twelve hours adrift in lifeboats. Privately, State Department officials fumed that Joe had had plenty of warning that such an attack might occur. Yet he had failed to mobilize his staff. "Kennedy has been condemning everybody and criticizing everyone, and has antagonized most of the people in the administration," Breckinridge Long of the State Department's European Division wrote in his diary.

With the German threat mounting, Joe concerned himself with the interests of the film industry, which exported $35 million in movies to the English. To conserve dollars needed for armaments, the English government proposed cutting film imports to $5 million. Joe mounted a private campaign to avoid the cutback. With characteristic overstatement, he told Hull that the reductions would mean the demise of the motion picture industry "in its present setup."

Joe's aide Arthur Houghton was already receiving a supplemental salary from Will Hays' motion picture trade association. Given the fact that Joe paid little attention to trade problems of other American industries, it is possible he was receiving a stipend from Hays as well. But it was more likely that Joe saw the motion picture industry as one of his few areas of expertise. He enjoyed the opportunity of playing the expert.

In view of the British need for American support during the war, Joe's lobbying on behalf of the film industry amounted to extortion. As might have been expected, the British agreed to a reduced cutback, allowing $30 million in annual trade.

Joe also injected himself into how and when the British would sell off American securities in order to purchase armaments. The British estimated they would need to sell $7 to $8 billion of their American gold, securities, and real estate holdings. If the investments were sold too quickly, the American stock market could be affected. Joe insistently asked Washington what the American policy would be on the timing of the sales. Roosevelt was sure Joe wanted the information to benefit his own investments. Sumner Welles, the undersecretary of state, told Treasury Secretary Morgenthau that Roosevelt had ordered him not to answer Joe's questions. Roosevelt said he was trying to "protect Joe against himself."

By now, it was widely assumed that Joe was using his position to enhance his own wealth. Baron Erik Palmstierna, a former Swedish minister to London, told a Foreign Office official that there were "funny stories" about Joe and his stock market dealings. The inference, wrote the Foreign Office official, was that Joe's activities were both unscrupulous and antithetical to British interests. Another Foreign Office official said the questions Joe asked him lent support to a widespread feeling that Joe was thinking "all the time about (1) his own financial position and (2) his political future."

Yet Joe's publishing friends had not abandoned him. For the second time, *Time* placed Joe on its cover, which was Henry Luce's inspiration. Luce was aware of Joe's three-year affair with Gloria Swanson, but the glowing September 18, 1939, story made no mention of it. The story called the "London Legman" a "stiletto-shrewd" businessman whose attitude was, "Where do we get off?"

◆ ◆ ◆

After a month under attack, Poland fell on September 27. Germany joined with Italy and Japan in a ten-year military pact. Joe used the occasion to step up his campaign to accommodate Germany. As he told Roosevelt, he had talked with military experts, who gave Great Britain no more than a "Chinaman's chance" of survival. The country was merely fighting for "possessions and a place in the sun, just as she has in the past." The Brits would continue to fight even though "confused about what they want and what they'll get after they win."

When Chamberlain acknowledged that appeasement would not work, Joe became his critic. Because of his knowledge of the movie industry, Joe knew that people who did not say that things were "great" without enough emphasis really meant they were "lousy." Thus when Chamberlain said everything was "great" without just the right punch, it meant Britain was really unprepared for war.

On September 30, 1939, Joe wrote to Roosevelt to compare World War II to World War I. "Regardless of the God-awful behavior of the Nazis, surely the fact is that the English people are not fighting Hitler; they are fighting the German people," he said, "just as they fought them 25 years ago. . . ." In an allusion to Brooks Adams' theories, he said he could not conceive of the results of the war running "counter to the evolutionary process. England passed her peak as a world power some years ago and has been steadily on the decline. Regardless of the outcome, war will only hasten the process."

Joe's comment about the Nazis suggested they were rowdy fraternity brothers who had gotten out of hand at a party— a nuisance but no threat. To Joe, there was little difference between the Nazis and the allies, between totalitarianism and democracy. As he told Roosevelt, ". . . democracy as we now conceive it in the United States will not exist in France and England after the war, regardless of which side wins or loses. France is ruled by a dictatorship . . . and England, which has always had a concentration of power in the so-called governing class, will certainly not be a democracy in our sense of the word. . . ." The United States, he said, must therefore curb its "sentimentality" and guard its "vital interests," which lay in the Western Hemisphere.

Joe's philosophy had always been that might makes right. What mattered in life was power and winning. He seemed now no more interested in fighting for Great Britain than he had been in fighting for the United States during World War I. Leaving America's allies in the lurch seemingly meant nothing to him.

Joe fretted that Roosevelt never replied to his letter suggesting that the United States cast Great Britain adrift. If Washington was not listening, neither was Germany. In mid-October 1939, Joe met with Herbert von Dirksen, the German ambassador in London. As if nothing had changed, he again discussed the possibility of visiting the "institutions of the new Germany." He told the ambassador that the average American had more liking for the average German than for the average Englishman. In summarizing the conversations, Dirksen wrote that Joe again mentioned "the very strong anti-Semitic tendencies" that existed in the United States. He said a "large portion of the population had an understanding of the German attitude toward the Jews."

As before, Hans Dieckhoff, Germany's ambassador in Washington, wrote off Joe's comments. He pointed out that Joe had wrongly sized up his own country. It would be hardly possible to express a "more negative and hostile attitude toward Germany than is now being shown almost daily by the president and many members of the Cabinet, as well as by the entire press, radio and film industry," the ambassador cabled home.

When Dirksen's cables were later disclosed (on July 16, 1949), Joe called the account of his conversations "pure poppycock." But the comments Dirksen attributed to him mirrored what Joe said directly to American officials. When Ickes showed Roosevelt a story in *The Week* reporting that Germany hoped to continue to maintain contacts with England through Joe, Roosevelt said, "There is a lot of truth to that."

◆　◆　◆

Now that Churchill was in the British cabinet, in charge of the navy, Roosevelt initiated a secret correspondence with him about the war. Churchill and Roosevelt had known each other since World War I, when both had served in top naval positions. Accordingly, on October 4, 1939, Joe sent this message to FDR via Hull: "Yesterday, I received your letter in the pouch, and it was delivered to the gentleman. I was asked by him to send you this reply: 'The Naval Person [Churchill] will not fail to avail himself of the invitation and he is honored by the message. He is writing immediately.'"

Churchill's messages were hand-carried to the American embassy code room for transmittal to the State Department for delivery to the White House. While the correspondence was highly irregular and circumvented both Joe and Chamberlain, Roosevelt let Joe know about it. Often, Joe saw the correspondence before it was sent. However, since Churchill usually had the letters delivered late at night, Joe sometimes did not see them.

The messages were encoded using the Gray Code, a fast commercial code that was easily deciphered. A day after Joe sent the first message from Churchill, Tyler Gatewood Kent, a snooty-looking man who had been assigned to the American embassy in Moscow, reported for duty at the embassy in London as a code clerk. Like Joe, Kent never had a good word to say about the British and sympathized with the Germans. He was sure that Churchill and Roosevelt were intent on dragging America into a fruitless war. Almost immediately, he began passing along to the Nazis the statesmen's messages to each other. At the same time, MI5, the British counterintelligence agency, became aware of Kent's espionage activities. Eight months later, they arrested him. It then became clear that the British had been intercepting communications to and from the American embassy in London all along.

Robert T. Crowley, a former high-ranking Central Intelligence Agency official who learned of the operation when he later worked with the British intelligence service, said the British intercepted both cable traffic and telephone calls to and from the embassy to find out what Joe was doing. "Joe was prospectively dangerous," Crowley said. "Joe had become an expert on the fact the British were failing."

♦ ♦ ♦

With British ships under attack by the Germans, Joe again decided to play movie censor. This time, the offending film was *Mr. Smith Goes to Washington*. In the film, James Stewart plays a young idealist who encounters corruption in the United States Senate. To Columbia Pictures, which released the film, Joe wrote that the picture portrayed a "governor, senators, the press and radio" all "taking orders from crooks." Joe told Will Hays the film was "one of the most disgraceful things I have ever seen done to this country." It was "criminal" that the film was being shown in Europe. The motion picture industry should consider the "impression" it created in foreign capitals and the portrayal of "morals" in the United States. Joe suggested that the picture of decay might create opposition to Chamberlain, and he sent a copy of his letter to Hays to Roosevelt.

♦ ♦ ♦

Shortly after the war started, Joe found a home in the country so that he could avoid the possibility of being bombed during night raids. Called St. Leonard's, the seventy-room house was owned by Horace Dodge, who broke with Henry Ford in 1913 and began building Dodge motorcars with his brother. The mansion came complete with a nine-hole golf course and required a staff of twenty-five. Neither the king and queen nor the prime minister had moved out of London, even after the royal residence was hit by bombs. Nor did most other ambassadors flee to the country.

Later, Joe obtained the palatial residence of George K.

Weeks, a Wall Street and London based attorney, at Headley Park near Epsom, Surrey. The twenty-two-room house was twenty-two miles from London on the main road to Portsmouth. Yet, as he later wrote, "There was only one thing I really wanted to do, and that was to have at least two weeks in Palm Beach. Then I would not have to be on guard. I could read detective stories and sleep and swim and sleep again."

Joe's request for home leave in the middle of a war did not go over well in Washington. On November 18, Hull told Joe that Roosevelt had decided that because of the "present conditions," his stay in the United States should be "as short as possible." Since Roosevelt believed it would not look good for chiefs of mission in Europe to return to the United States for vacations then, Joe would receive a note instructing him to return for "consultation."

Joe left on November 29 after dictating another doom-and-gloom message to Roosevelt. This time, he insisted that the British people would pressure their own government to admit defeat and end the war. While he acknowledged that "everyone hates Hitler," the British and the French still did not want to be "finished economically, financially, politically, and socially."

Newspapermen greeted Joe in New York and asked if he would run against Roosevelt in 1940. "I can't go against the guy," Joe said. "He's done more for me than my own kind. If he wants it [a third term], I'll be with him."

Joe took the night train to Washington. Weary and unshaven, he arrived on December 8 and told the press outside the White House that he supported Roosevelt for a third term. It was now official. Inside the mansion, Joe met with the president in his bedroom. Roosevelt dispensed with Joe's report on the war by asking if he was still a "bear." Joe averred he was. Joe then told Roosevelt what he had just told the press. Roosevelt feigned a lack of interest in a third term.

"Joe, I can't," Roosevelt said. "I'm tired. I can't take it."

Roosevelt later told Corcoran that Joe had suggested that

the United States let Hitler take over Europe because "we could not possibly do business with the Russians but could always assassinate Hitler." Roosevelt expressed horror at Joe's remarks.

At the Navy Department, in a talk laced with expletives, Joe insisted that no one in Germany wanted to fight. He accused the navy of wishing for war and said the army was asking for "absurdly large and quite unnecessary" expenditures. The only contribution the United States should make was in having a "strong economy" after the war.

Three days after seeing Roosevelt, Joe spoke in East Boston at a dinner dance given by the Church of the Assumption, where he had once been an altar boy and had gone to parochial school. If the United States were to enter the war, he told his fellow Catholics, it would mean its demise.

Joe then went to Palm Beach, where he entertained Arthur Krock and William Douglas, who had just been named to the Supreme Court. When stories began to appear in the press about Joe "basking in the sun," the State Department decided to require him to seek a ninety-day leave of absence without pay. But as he had done before, Joe got a doctor to say he was sick, and he put in for sick leave. On January 3, 1940, Roosevelt thanked Joe for a fishing rod he had sent him. He hoped Joe was getting a "complete rest." Two weeks later, Joe wrote to Roosevelt to tell him he was sick again and planned to enter a Washington hospital.

There is no evidence that he did. Nor did Joe's "illness" prevent him from raising trial balloons about his own presidential ambitions. "Kennedy May Be Candidate," proclaimed a headline on page one of the February 12, 1940, *Boston Post*. The story said Joe had "refused a definite answer" on whether he would run. On February 14, the *New York Times* quoted Joe as saying he was declining entreaties from "his supporters" that he run for president. "I cannot forget that I now occupy a most important government post which at this particular time involves matters so precious to the American people that no consideration should permit my energies or interests to be diverted."

Krock would later confirm that Joe "hoped to be nominated in 1940, without any question." He had tested the waters through people like his friend Father John J. Cavanaugh, president of Notre Dame University. "He found out that his reputation had not been cleansed completely by his very impeccable service as head of the SEC."

Without missing a beat, Joe turned to his eldest son, Joe Jr., to fulfill his own aspirations. "From the time I was seven, I heard he [Joe] wanted Joe Jr. to be president," recalled Mary Lou McCarthy.

Two days after the *Times* said Joe would not run, Joe Jr. filed nomination papers as a candidate for delegate to the Democratic National Convention from the ninth congressional district.

◆ ◆ ◆

In February, just before leaving for Europe, Joe dropped by the State Department. As Ickes recorded in his diary, Joseph Patterson, publisher of the *New York Daily News*, and Doris Fleeson, his Washington correspondent, were interviewing Bill Bullitt, the ambassador to France. Unexpectedly, Joe came into the office and sat down. Cheerfully, Joe entered into the conversation. Before long, he was saying that "Germany will win, everything in France and England will go to hell, and his one interest was in saving his money for his children," Ickes recalled.

Joe began to "criticize the president very sharply," whereupon Bullitt attacked him. The two began arguing violently, and the news people excused themselves. "As Joe continued to berate Roosevelt, Bullitt called Joe disloyal and said he had no right to speak as he did in front of Patterson and Fleeson," Ickes wrote. "Joe said that he would say what he goddamned pleased before whom he goddamned pleased. . . ." Bullitt told him he was "abysmally ignorant on foreign affairs and had no basis for saying what he was saying." They parted in anger. Bullitt commented he doubted whether he would ever speak to Joe again.

After almost three months away from his post, Joe sailed for Europe on February 23, 1940. A hostile press met him. Harold Nicolson, a member of Parliament, wrote in *The Spectator* that Joe would be welcomed back by an "embarrassing" variety of people, including former members of now-banned Nazi organizations and "native or unhyphenated rich, who hope that he may bring with him a little raft of appeasement on which they can float for a year or so longer before they are finally submerged."

As Joe had done with the British, he now attributed his own views to the Americans. He told the press that Americans "understood the war less and less as they go along." An angry letter-writer responded to the *New York Times* that Joe was full of "cockeyed nonsense." Americans understood the war very well; however, they had been "misrepresented by our spokesman in England."

The Germans used Joe's comments in their propaganda. The German News Agency released a report that Joe had sent a defeatist cable to Washington. According to the alleged cable, the Western powers had no chance of winning the war, and German arms manufacturers were far superior to French or British manufacturers. Joe issued a statement denying the German report, calling it "the best fairy tale I've read since *Snow White*." But the comments were vintage Joe Kennedy— the same line he had been consistently giving for the past year.

Then the Nazi government published a *German White Paper* containing what were said to be excerpts of documents captured from the Polish archives. The aim of the white paper was to show that the British, French, and Americans had pushed Poland into war with Germany. The excerpts quoted Joe as telling the Polish ambassador in London during the

previous summer that he would urge the British to aid the
Polish leaders with cash. While the State Department claimed
the documents were fabrications, Breckinridge Long, who
was now an assistant secretary of state, admitted privately
that "there is just a sneaking suspicion in our minds that
there is more truth than fiction in some of the reported conversations." What was upsetting to him and to Hull was the
fact that, once again, Joe had defied State Department policy
guidelines by making promises that the American government
had not approved and did not support. For once, Joe was
silent, refusing to comment on the reports. In his unpublished
memoirs, Joe said the documents "were not forgeries."

By now, Chamberlain was cutting Joe out of confidential
exchanges of information, and Joe's embassy staff was disgusted with him. General Raymond E. Lee, an air attaché
based in the embassy, characterized Joe as having "the speculator's smartness but also his . . . insensitivity to the greater
forces which are now playing like heat lightning over the
map of the world." Aware that he was becoming an outcast,
Joe cast himself as a prophet and man of honor—a "candid
man beset by hypocrites," as Ralph F. de Bedts wrote.

Joe relied more and more on Carmel Offie, Bullitt's assistant and third secretary at the American embassy in Paris.
According to a report Bullitt made to State, Joe would call
Offie as many as four times a day "whenever he considers a
question of sufficient importance for Offie to decide. . . ."
When Joe visited the embassy, he would snoop around in
the cables section, Bullitt said, and often stayed at Offie's
home.

"I wish you could add the salary of the counselor of
embassy in London to Offie," Bullitt wrote. "For the past
year, Ambassador Kennedy has used Offie as acting counselor
of embassy in London." If, he added, "the embassy in London
has not made more messes than it has made, the thanks are
due to Offie."

If Joe was under attack from all sides, he had not lost his
sense of humor. On March 13, 1940, Joe, along with Moffat

and Welles, who were visiting from Washington, went to a small stag dinner given by Chamberlain at 10 Downing Street. Near the end of the evening, the talk turned to the pending threats. Churchill, who was present, said no one understood better than he the mentality of the ordinary Britisher. "Take the workman, for instance," he said. "His back is up. He will stand for no pulling of punches against Germany. He's tough."

"Well," Joe said, "if you can show me one Englishman that's tougher than you are, Winston, I'll eat my hat." The guests broke into laughter.

Nor was Joe's libido impaired. For some months, Joe had been carrying on an affair with Clare Boothe Luce, the wife of Henry Luce. With blonde hair and big baby blue eyes, Clare Luce was not only sexy but bright. She was then writing *Margin for Error*, a Broadway play that became a film directed by Otto Preminger. She later served two terms as a congresswoman from Connecticut and was ambassador to Italy. In her diary, Clare Luce confessed that she had by then stopped having sex with her husband. Facetiously, she wrote, "What went wrong [twenty years ago] with me and Harry was that he often came home, and after we'd had dinner, I'd 'go to bed' and start to write a play. Obviously, I didn't know what a BED was FOR!"

Before returning to London, Joe had sailed from the United States on the SS *Manhattan* to Genoa, Italy, with Clare. In his unpublished memoirs, Joe said the trip was marked by "inclement weather and poor food. Happily, Clare Luce was on hand. She had an assignment from *Life* to do a running commentary on the European scene, and her gay conversation was a contrast to the greyness of the sea and sky."

But Clare provided Joe with more than conversation. After returning to London, Joe traveled to Paris to see Clare. To conceal the purpose of his trip to Paris, Joe issued a statement claiming he had to visit Eddie Moore, his personal secretary, who was said to be "ill." The story appeared in the April 3, 1940, edition of the *New York Times*.

In her diary entry for April 2, 1940, Clare Luce recorded

her activities at the Ritz Hotel in Paris. She said that Joe was "in bedroom all morning." Meanwhile, Clare signed her telegrams to Joe "love," and Joe—in sending her a $1,000 check for one of her charities—referred to her as "my beautiful one."

Clare was always careful to write warm notes to Rose. But in her diary, she described an Irish Catholic Madonna figure who sounded suspiciously like Joe's wife: "We are all familiar with the overly pious—pietistic—Irish Catholic immigrant of the lace curtain era who referred everything—the most trivial incident—to God—or rather to her interpretation of God's will—who crossed herself if the cat jumped, who interminably mumbled prayers, sought indulgences, hounded her parish priest, passed judgments on everyone else's sobriety and state of grace, and who never stopped talking about salvation and damnation."

For his part, Henry Luce became heavily involved in an affair with Lady Jean Campbell, a voluptuous brunette who was the granddaughter of Joe's friend Lord Max Beaverbrook, publisher of the *London Daily Express.* Henry Luce told Campbell that he and Clare Luce had stopped having sex six months after they were married. Clare had persuaded him that she was not interested in sex. Luce also complained to Campbell that Clare had laughed at a draft of a speech he had written and had shown her.

Through Beaverbrook, a noted ladies' man himself, Campbell had learned about Clare's affair with Joe. She did not pass the information on to Luce. She also learned about Joe's other London affairs. Joe was "nonstop" and "grabbed everybody attractive," she said. When Joe visited Beaverbrook at his country home, "He would go to bed with one of [his] researchers, give her presents, and then she would mail Joe a weekly report on everything happening in the household," Campbell told author Ralph G. Martin. "But grandfather's secretary would steam open the letters before she could post them, copy the contents, and give them to grandfather."

15

DEMOCRACY IS ALL DONE

Henry Morgenthau Jr., Roosevelt's treasury secretary, had a 10:15 A.M. meeting with his top aides on April 29, 1940, to discuss what he called Joe's latest "typical asinine" letter to Roosevelt. Ten days earlier, Germany had invaded Norway and Denmark, but Joe's concern was more with his own pocketbook. Interjecting himself into Morgenthau's jurisdiction, he was urging Roosevelt to propose legislation to prohibit the government from purchasing gold. Morgenthau said there was no need for such legislation.

"I can't understand it," Morgenthau said. "Here is this fellow over there" who has "done an about face" on the issue. When a Treasury official asked why Joe was taking such an "absurd" position, Morgenthau replied, "The only thing that has explained Joe Kennedy to me for the last couple of years is that he has been consistently short in the market." Morgenthau said he had made inquiries and learned that Ben Smith, a notorious bear who was Joe's partner in previous stock pool deals, constantly traveled to London to see him. "Every move he makes is to bear down on our market," he said. "It is the only explanation I can get. Every single move he has made is to depress our securities and our commodities."

It was a damning commentary on Joe, suggesting that his constant predictions of doom were calculated to force down stock market prices so that he could make a killing. Today, such activity would bring prosecution for violation of securities laws.

Morgenthau drafted a reply for Roosevelt to sign. The reply dismissed Joe's latest attempt to meddle.

On May 10, Joe wired Welles in Washington that the Germans were advancing on The Hague. He promised to keep him informed. "Please do, Joe, because you are the only means of communication we have," Welles said. "We can't even reach Paris."

But Adolf Berle in the State Department said that when he called Joe, he found he was "innocent as a babe unborn" of the German movement. "His mind is as blank as an uninked paper," he later remarked.

On May 20, Joe informed Hull that the British had just told him that Tyler Kent, the new clerk at the embassy, was "closely associated with a gang of spies working in the interests of Germany and Russia." Armed with search warrants, officers from MI5 and Scotland Yard had that morning knocked on the door to Kent's apartment at 47 Gloucester Place. "Don't come in," Kent said twice. The officers from Scotland Yard broke down the door and found Kent with his scantily dressed mistress, a Russian woman married to a British subject. Searching the flat, the officers found the deciphered text of 1,500 embassy cables, many labeled top secret. Included were the coded messages between Naval Person and Roosevelt, most of which had been in Hitler's hands within days of transmission. Also found were copies of gummed labels prepared by Anna Wolkoff, Kent's accomplice, declaring, "This is a Jewish War." Both were later convicted of communicating confidential documents that might help the enemy. Kent was sentenced to seven years in prison.

By now, Neville Chamberlain had resigned, having failed to muster enough support in the House of Commons. On May 10, Churchill succeeded him. In his first speech after becoming prime minister, Churchill told the House of Commons the objective was quite simple: "Victory: Victory at all costs. Victory in spite of all terror. Victory however long and hard the road may be: for without victory there is no survival." In a radio broadcast, he told the British people, "I have nothing to offer you but blood, toil, tears, and sweat."

Churchill mistrusted Joe, whom he regarded as a prominent member of the appeasement clique. For his part, Joe resented the respect that Churchill commanded. His eloquence, inner strength, and steadfastness were in sharp contrast to Joe's inarticulateness and chameleon-like vacillation. Joe whispered about Churchill's daily liquor intake, which usually began at breakfast. Ultimately, Churchill's rise would hasten Joe's decline.

By May 15, 1940, Germany had swept through the Netherlands, putting an end to what some called the "phony war," a six-month lull in fighting after Germany had conquered Poland. During that time, Hitler had been preoccupied with strategic planning. Joe told Hull that "only a miracle can save the British expeditionary force from being wiped out, or as I said yesterday, surrender." He said the Germans would still be willing to make peace with England and France on terms that "would be a great deal better" than if the war continued. The British, he said, "really do not realize how bad" the situation is.

By May 28, King Leopold of Belgium had ordered his troops to surrender to Hitler, winning accolades from Joe, who saw it as a sensible way to avoid destruction. Churchill denounced the Belgian king's decision as an act of treason, which exposed the Allied flank. Later James Landis, the former SEC chairman who was now on Joe's payroll, wrote a sixty-page accolade to the king, which the Joseph P. Kennedy Jr. Foundation printed in 1950 as a pamphlet under the title *The Surrender of King Leopold.*

Five days of frenzied efforts to evacuate British and French soldiers from Dunkirk in France could not prevent German soldiers from capturing the remaining French soldiers there on June 4. This prompted Churchill's most famous wartime speech. "We go on to the end . . . we shall defend our island, whatever the cost may be, we shall fight on the beaches, we shall fight on the landing-grounds, we shall fight in the hills; we shall never surrender," he told the House of Commons.

Joe paid a visit to Ivan M. Maisky, the Soviet ambassador in London, at the Soviet embassy. "Kennedy at the time was almost in a panic," Maisky recalled. "He was of the opinion that England was almost powerless in relation to Germany, that it had hopelessly lost the war and had to make peace with Hitler, the sooner the better."

Joe expressed surprise when Maisky disagreed, saying "nothing had been lost for England" and it had "great opportunities to successfully resist and fight the German danger if it only showed courage and the willingness to fight." Maisky told Joe the British were steadfast in their desire to fight. He said only the members of the Cliveden Set, who had adopted Joe as their hero, felt otherwise. In Maisky's opinion, the members of the Cliveden Set believed neither "in themselves or in the future of their country." Joe shrugged and exclaimed, "You are an optimist. I have not even heard such a view from the British!"

The Germans had no intention of negotiating a peace settlement. On June 30, Baron von Weizsäcker, the German state secretary, issued a memo stating that he would be telling the directors of the Foreign Ministry departments on July 1: "Germany is not considering peace. She is concerned exclusively with preparation for the destruction of England."

But the Germans used Joe's statements to their advantage. Professing to have obtained the information from the State

Department code room in Washington, Hans Thomsen, a counselor in the German embassy in Washington, reported to the German Foreign Ministry that in classified State Department messages, Joe had claimed that Churchill did not represent the views of the British people.

Inevitably, Joe's statements against war appeared in speeches by isolationist members of Congress. Gleefully, Thomsen boasted to the German Foreign Ministry that he was orchestrating a "propaganda" campaign by encouraging each member of Congress who was an isolationist to send his speeches to a million Americans, using the free postage provided to members of Congress. Thomsen told the ministry that Joe's position on Germany had made the American public "more hopeful."

By June 14, Paris had fallen to German forces, and on June 22, France was defeated. For Hitler, the Nazi-Soviet pact had been a temporary arrangement to be abandoned eventually. After the defeat of France, he began planning an invasion of the Soviet Union. Called Operation Barbarossa, the invasion took place on June 22, 1941.

Joe insisted the British would cave in as soon as the going got tough. "Saw Joe Kennedy who says everyone in the U.S.A. thinks we shall be beaten before the end of the month," Chamberlain wrote in his diary on July 1. Back in Hollywood, Joe had kept a sign on his desk at 780 Gower Street. It said, "Don't kid yourself." The message was that Joe wanted to be given the truth, not what people thought he wanted to hear. But Joe's own fact-gathering was seriously flawed. More often than not, when he said "everyone" believed a particular point, it meant he believed it.

Clare Boothe Luce tried to talk sense into Joe, cabling him that if he thought "we are going to be let off" the "evil course" without supporting our allies, "you are crazy." Fruitlessly, she wrote to him that democracy and Christianity "cannot survive in a nazified world." In her diary, she noted, "I was amazed that he seemed to feel that we were arming too fast and too ferociously."

To Hull, Joe said, "My own opinion is that if the Germans come over here and successfully bomb in a major manner any objectives in spite of the British Air Force, the strong feeling of fighting 'till [sic] death will stop then and there. . . ." Indeed, Joe's timetable for England's defeat was shorter than Hitler's. He predicted to Chamberlain that England would be gone by the end of July 1940.

Sir William Stephenson, the Canadian-born head of the British MI6, which collects foreign intelligence, urged Roosevelt to obtain an impartial evaluation of British strength. Roosevelt gave the job to their mutual friend, William J. "Wild Bill" Donovan, a New York attorney with an outstanding record in World War I. Roosevelt would later appoint Donovan to head the Office of Strategic Services (OSS), the precursor to the Central Intelligence Agency.

As a cover story, Hull told Joe in July 1940 that the United States military was sending Donovan to do a "brief survey" on "certain aspects of the British defense situation."

Peevishly, Joe cabled back, "I will render any service I can to Colonel Donovan whom I know and like. It is impossible to make any arrangements or preparations in advance because I do not know the nature of his mission." He added that British government departments "much prefer to deal with permanent attachés, and have frequently declined to furnish information to anyone else." To send "a new man" from Washington "is to me the height of nonsense and a definite blow to good organization."

When Donovan returned to Washington in August, he praised the British spirit and preparations for war. The military attachés were filing reports that differed radically from Joe's pessimistic outlook, he said. Donovan was convinced Britain would hold up.

Even as Donovan was making his report, Joe wired that only a "miracle" could save the British, who "realize they haven't a chance in the long run."

◆ ◆ ◆

Despite the demands on his time, Joe wrote long letters to each of his children and savored each detail he learned of their sailing races, social lives, and school courses. Writing to eight-year-old Ted, Joe said, "I am sure, of course, you wouldn't be scared, but if you heard all these guns firing every night and the bombs bursting, you might get a little fidgety." He sympathized with the poor who were seeing their homes destroyed. "I hope when you grow up you will dedicate your life to trying to work out plans to make people happy instead of making them miserable, as war does today."

For all the good lessons he taught them, Joe's impact on the children was so overpowering that they rarely came up with their own thoughts. Only Kathleen had the gumption to take on her father. In May 1940, she told him in a letter that she strongly disagreed with his gloomy view of the British. "I still keep telling everyone that the British lose the battles but they win the wars," she wrote.

James A. Rousmanière, Jack's Harvard friend, recalled that Jack was so controlled by Joe that he "attended Harvard instead of his first choice Princeton because his father insisted on it. . . . We searched—my wife and I—in vain for some sign Jack might be rebelling or striking out on his own emotionally or intellectually."

For his course in international government at Harvard, Jack had written a thesis entitled "Appeasement at Munich." Both the subject and the conclusions were suggested by his father. Joe "influenced his son on his choice of his thesis and then devoted considerable time to shaping Jack's ideas and the final product," Rousmanière said.

After writing a draft, Jack sent the 150-page thesis to his father, saying it represented more work than he had ever done in his life. Joe thought it was a "swell" job and sent him a letter with some suggestions. Jack then changed the conclusions to conform with his father's opinions, adopting large portions of the letter almost verbatim. The thesis was an apology for appeasement. It proposed that criticism of the Munich pact was misdirected, that the real problem was "the state of British opinion and the condition of Britain's armaments, which made surrender inevitable." Ironically, before Joe had injected his opinion, Jack had gone even further in blaming the "British public," rather than Chamberlain, for the Munich fiasco.

Joe asked Harvey Klemmer, his speechwriter in London, to rewrite the thesis for publication. "He [Joe] told me that Jack, who had been visiting him in London, had written as his senior thesis a work that he considered superior, and what could we do about it? Could we get a publisher?" Klemmer recalled that the paper was "terribly written and disorganized." In fact, "the sentences were ungrammatical, and even the spelling was bad. I had to rewrite the whole thing, including the final sum-up paragraph."

Once Klemmer had finished with it, Joe sent the manuscript to Arthur Krock, who thought it "amateurish in many respects," but not as bad as some student theses. Nevertheless, Krock obtained an agent for Jack and edited Klemmer's draft. As Krock later put it, "We worked it over." Krock gave him the title—*Why England Slept*, a variation on the title of Churchill's book *While England Slept*. He was "an editor, yes, an advisor, and I may have supplied some of the material as far as prose was concerned."

After Joe solicited Henry Luce to write a foreword, Wilfred Funk published the 252-page book on August 1, 1940. Having just graduated *cum laude* from Harvard on June 20, Jack was now a published author. While the book was said to have sold eighty thousand copies, tens of thousands were purchased by Joe and his employees. For years, extra copies were stored in the attic of Joe's Hyannis Port home and in a storage warehouse in Manhattan.

"There were boxes of *Why England Slept* in the warehouse in New York," said Gertrude Ball, Joe's former New York secretary.

After the book had been out a few weeks, Joe sent a copy to Harold Laski of the London School of Economics. Even though Laski had a reputation as a socialist, Joe had sent Joe

Jr., and later Jack, to study with him. On August 21, 1940, Laski wrote to Joe to say that it would have been easy to repeat the "eulogies" that Luce and Krock had showered on Jack's book. But Laski had to tell Joe the truth. Even after the book had been worked over by Klemmer and Krock, Laski said, he regretted that Joe had let him publish it. "For while it is the book of a lad with brains, it is very immature, it has no real structure, and it dwells almost wholly on the surface of things," Laski wrote. In a good university, he went on, "half a hundred seniors do books like this as part of their normal work in the final year." But they don't get them published. "I don't honestly think that any publisher would have looked at that book of Jack's if he had not been your son, and if you had not been ambassador." Thinking, Laski said, is a "hard business." One had to pay the price of admission. By giving him his true thoughts, Laski said, he was engaging in an act of real friendship, in contrast to "yes men" like Krock.

Joe never forgave Laski. In a note to Missy LeHand, Felix Frankfurter would later recount that Joe had made a disparaging remark about Laski because of his criticism of Jack's book.

Charles Spalding, who became a close friend of Jack's, recalled that the first time he met him, Jack was signing copies of *Why England Slept* at the Hyannis Port home. "Here's this young guy seated on the floor with his brother [Joe Jr.]," Spalding said. "He just had a towel on. He was signing books. I saw a stack of them and I said, 'How's it going?' He grinned and said, 'Great. Dad's seeing to that.'"

Spalding later became friends with Joe as well, often playing golf with him at the Oyster Harbors Club in Osterville. In one of their first sessions, Joe confessed to Spalding that he would like to take out his wife. "We were playing golf, and he had a terrible reputation for making passes even at friends of his kids or their wives," Spalding said. "My wife, Betty Cox, was a very good golfer. As we got to the eighteenth hole, he said, 'You know, Chuck, it's been a wonderful afternoon. But I find myself being drawn closely to your wife.' So I said, 'Really? I hope you can get over that between now and dinnertime, because if you can't we're on our way.' After that, I had a good relationship. He quit." Joe had a "really tough exterior," Spalding said, "but if you really challenged him, he backed down."

◆ ◆ ◆

In August 1940, the German Luftwaffe began an all-out attack on British ports, airfields, and industrial centers and, finally, on London. The goal was to crush British morale and wipe out the Royal Air Force in preparation for Operation Sea Lion, an invasion of England. The Battle of Britain was the first great air battle in history, dwarfing the legendary World War I dogfights between German Fokkers and Allied open-cockpit fighters. For fifty-seven nights, London was attacked by an average force of 160 bombers. The outnumbered RAF, employing the effective Spitfire fighter and aided by radar, destroyed 1,733 aircraft while losing 915 fighters. German air power could not continue sustaining such heavy losses. In October, Operation Sea Lion was postponed indefinitely.

Whenever air raid sirens wailed, two officers were to go to the roof of the American embassy. Equipped with gas masks, binoculars, and helmets, they were to watch for anything approaching the building and to sound a buzzer if they saw bombs dropping. A klaxon was then sounded to signal the staff to proceed to the air raid shelter in the basement of 1 Grosvenor Square. There, Joe had a special cache of twenty-four bottles of spring water. For the rest of the staff, there were forty-eight half-gallon bottles of London water. The shelter also stocked six tins of beef and ham roll, twelve tins of lambs' tongues, six tins of cheddar cheese, 144 bars of chocolate, and twenty-four tins of Spam.

As bombs fell, Harvey Klemmer and Joe walked through St. James's Park. "I'll bet you five to one—any sum—that

Hitler will be in Buckingham Palace in two weeks," Joe told Klemmer. Joe threatened to return to the United States and "tell the American people that that son-of-a-bitch in the White House is going to kill their sons off in a war." Besides spending inordinate amounts of government time securing precious cargo space for Joe's whisky shipments, Klemmer later complained that he had to help provide Joe with young women. One was a former French model known as Foxy.

In a lengthy report to Roosevelt and Hull on September 11, Joe said a delayed time bomb exploded fifty yards from his car. "Boy, this is the life," he said. Joe insisted that because of British censorship, "there is no question but what the English people are completely ignorant of what the real dangers to Great Britain are. They don't regard the attack by the Germans as a serious menace as they heard about their air force smashing the German planes almost to bits in daytime attacks. . . . For the United States to come into this war and sign a blank check for the difficulties that are faced here is a responsibility that only God could shoulder."

Two weeks later, Joe followed up with a telegram reporting his "complete lack of confidence in the entire conduct of this war. . . ." Joe said he was "delighted to see Roosevelt say he was not going to enter the war because it would be a complete misapprehension to imagine for one minute that the British have anything to offer in the line of productive capacity in industry or of leadership that could be of the slightest value to us. . . ." In another cable monitored by the Germans, Joe said that England was "finished" and the United States would have to "pay the bill" if it entered the war.

But Joe was not going to wait for that. With bombs dropping all around, he decided he had had enough. On October 1, less than a month after the bombing started, Joe wrote to Clare Boothe Luce that it would take a long time for him to get used to sleeping without "gunfire nine or ten hours a night" in his ears. "There is a popular song called 'There'll Always Be an England.' There always will be, but you'll hardly recognize it; and I know damn well I'll not be around to be in it!'"

◆ ◆ ◆

At all costs, Roosevelt wanted to keep Joe in London until after the election. Joe had been plotting with Clare and Henry Luce to support Wendell Willkie, Roosevelt's Republican opponent. In a wire to Luce, he declared he would endorse Willkie and generate "25 million Catholic votes . . . to throw Roosevelt out." But the British had been tapping Joe's wires, learned about the plot, and tipped off the White House. Roosevelt feared that if Joe came home, he would use his influence against him.

Joe asked for home leave, and when no reply was forthcoming, he cabled on October 16, 1940, that he was coming home regardless.

Joe visited King George VI and Queen Elizabeth at Windsor Castle on October 20. From the way he said his good-byes, it was clear he was leaving for good. As T. North Whitehead of the Foreign Office noted, "It rather looks as though he was thoroughly frightened when in London and has gone to pieces as a result."

"It is doubted that he will return as ambassador," the *New York Times* said. "He has made it no secret among intimate circles that he feels he has done his bit and that he is entitled to a long, peaceful holiday and to pick up his life with his family after a long separation."

On a plane provided by the British government, Joe left London for Lisbon on October 22. When he arrived, he was given a letter from Roosevelt asking him not to make any public statement until he saw him at the White House. In Lisbon, Joe took a plane for the United States. Three days later, a secretary handed Missy LeHand a note saying that Arthur Goldsmith, a close personal friend of Joe's, had called to suggest that Roosevelt send Joe a note on his arrival and that "someone important" from the State Department meet him. Still trying to contain Joe until after the election, Roosevelt responded by asking Joe and Rose to stay at the White House on October 27.

That day, Roosevelt had lunch with Lyndon Johnson, then a Texas congressman. During the lunch, Roosevelt took a call from Joe at the table. "Ah, Joe, old friend, it is so good to hear your voice," Roosevelt said. "Please come over to the White House tonight for a little family dinner. I am dying to talk to you. You have been doing a wonderful job." Johnson said that Roosevelt hung up, looked at Johnson, and then "drew his forefinger across his throat like a razor."

Roosevelt asked then-Senator James Byrnes and Missy LeHand to sit in on his conversation with Joe. Joe blew up about the State Department, saying he had been treated "horribly." He said he had been left in London to cool his heels while presidential messages swirled around him. And he insisted he had never said anything about Roosevelt that he had not said to his face.

Roosevelt kept nodding his head and saying, "Yes, yes." That encouraged Joe even more. Then Roosevelt took a turn railing about the State Department, which he said was populated by officious "desk men."

"As the president went on," Byrnes later wrote, "I thought Kennedy was even beginning to feel a touch of sympathy for the State Department. In any event, once his complaint had been made and approved, Kennedy became more cordial, and the President asked him to make a radio speech advocating his reelection. The moment Kennedy agreed, Miss LeHand telephoned the National Committee and arranged for radio time. . . ."

Joe gave the radio address over CBS on October 29. "My wife and I have given nine hostages to fortune," Joe said. "Our children and your children are more important than anything else in the world. The kind of America that they and their children will inherit is of grave concern to us all. In the light of these considerations, I believe that Franklin

D. Roosevelt should be reelected president of the United States."

Roosevelt was delighted. "I have just listened to a great speech. Congratulations," he wired. Years later, Clare Boothe Luce asked Joe why he had done it. Joe told her, "We agreed that if I endorsed him for president in 1940, then he would support my son Joe for governor of Massachusetts in 1942."

Just before the address, Lindbergh met with Joe at the Waldorf Towers. "He feels, as we do, that the British position is hopeless and that the best thing for them would be a negotiated peace in the near future," Lindbergh wrote. Indeed, Joe said that the "war would stop if it were not for Churchill and the hope in England that America will come in."

Roosevelt won reelection for a third term on November 5, 1940. On November 6, in a meeting that lasted five minutes—from 12:55 P.M. to 1 P.M.—Joe resigned. But Roosevelt said he could not accept it until he found a replacement. Roosevelt asked Joe to retain the title of ambassador until he found a successor. But according to Elliott Roosevelt, Roosevelt's second son, his father had asked for Joe's resignation.

◆ ◆ ◆

On the morning of Friday, November 8, 1940, Lawrence Winship, managing editor of the *Boston Globe*, left a note on reporter Louis Lyons' desk. "We ought to get a Sunday piece on Kennedy," he said.

With the help of Honey Fitz Fitzgerald, Lyons managed to horn in on an interview with Joe that had already been set up for the next day with Charles K. Edmonson and Ralph Coghlan, two editorial writers from the *St. Louis Post-Dispatch*. Joe was staying at Boston's Ritz-Carlton, his favorite haunt. Owned by Edward N. Wyner, a Boston real estate developer, the Ritz-Carlton was operated like a private club for the very wealthy. Guests had to be recommended by other guests or listed in *Who's Who in America* or the social register before they could lodge there. If their letterheads requesting rooms were not of high enough quality, Wyner rejected their requests. The hotel, the oldest Ritz-Carlton in continuous operation, maintained its own upholstery and print shops and retained a full-time craftsman who painted the gold stripes on the hotel's furniture. Joe loved to sit on the Ritz Roof and listen to Benny Goodman or Tommy Dorsey.

"The owner, Edward Wyner, told me, 'Don't tangle with Joe Kennedy. He is the most powerful man in the U.S.,'" said Bobby Young, the concierge. "I would give him a big, 'Hi, Ambassador.' He loved it."

Joe told the three newspapermen what he had been saying in cables and in off-the-record talks almost since becoming ambassador. The difference was that this time he did not take the precaution of setting the ground rules. He merely assumed that the reporters would consider his remarks to be off the record. In the case of the two St. Louis writers, his assumption was correct. Neither wrote a story quoting his comments. But unlike many reporters of the day, Lyons, who was also curator of Harvard's Nieman journalism fellowships, did not consider protecting politicians from themselves to be his responsibility.

Still, the story that ran on page one of the Sunday, November 10, 1940, *Boston Globe* backed into the real news. It began by describing Joe sitting in shirtsleeves, munching on apple pie and American cheese. "Pinch Coming in United States Trade Loss," the headline said. Not until the sixth paragraph did the story hint of what was to come. "I'm willing to spend all I've got to keep us out of war," the story quoted him as saying. "There's no sense in our getting in. We'd just be holding the bag." Finally, the story quoted Joe as saying, "People call me a pessimist. I say, 'What is there to be gay about? Democracy is all done.'" Later, Lyons quoted him as being even more specific. "Democracy is finished in England. It may be here. Because it comes to a question of feeding people. It's all an economic question."

Joe went on, "Now, I tell you when this thing is finally

settled, and it comes to a question of saying what's left for England, it will be the queen and not any of the politicians that will do it." What Joe apparently still did not appreciate was that it was the politicians, not the king or queen, who made political decisions in England.

Joe said England was not fighting for democracy. "That's the bunk. She's fighting for self-preservation, just as we will if it comes to us." Joe proclaimed that he was about to go to the West Coast to meet with Hearst about organizing newspapers against the war. "I know more about the European situation than anybody else, and it's up to me that the country gets it," the story quoted him as saying.

Joe minimized Eleanor Roosevelt, describing her as a person who is "always sending me a note to have some little Suzie Glotz to tea at the embassy." Joe's reference to "Glotz" was taken to mean that she wanted him to meet with Jews.

The story ended with Joe's ironic parting words: "Well, I'm afraid you didn't get much of a story."

When the paper came off the presses, the Associated Press quickly moved the story, using Joe's quote about democracy in the lead paragraph. Ralph Coghlan, the chief editorial writer of the St. Louis paper, checked with Joe, who said Coghlan was right to assume that the remarks had been off the record. Using circular reasoning, Coghlan later said that he found it impossible to believe that an ambassador "could be so stupid as to talk like that if there were any danger that he would be quoted."

Coghlan called his paper to ask if they wanted him to write the story that he had ignored. He was told to forget it. Instead, the paper used the AP story. "Democracy All Done in England," the headline said.

Coghlan later conceded to Krock that "Kennedy said most of the things Lyons quotes him as saying," but the total effect was to "create a false impression." Kennedy was "talking in shirtsleeves and should have been protected." Kennedy was talking "privately" to publishers like Hearst, and he had "wanted his views to get out that way." Indeed, Joseph Pulitzer, publisher of the St. Louis paper, later chimed in that he felt "disgust" that the *Boston Globe* had published the story, even though his own *Post-Dispatch* ran an Associated Press report on the *Globe* story.

As might have been expected, Krock thought Coghlan used "good judgment" in not publishing the remarks. He felt that Lyons had betrayed Joe, who had been candid with him. Krock later wrote Joe to offer to do anything he could to dispel "the ill effect of that unfortunate interview." Krock knew full well that Lyons' story accurately portrayed Joe's views. Seven months earlier, Joe had written Krock to reiterate his opinion that "if England stayed out of the war, it would be better for the United States. . . ." For that reason, he said, "I was a great believer in appeasement. I felt that if war came, that was the beginning of the end for everybody, provided it lasted for two or three years. I see no reason for changing my mind yet."

Nonetheless, Joe issued a denial to the *New York Times* and other papers. Joe called "nonsense" the idea that he held anti-British views or that he did not expect Britain to win the war. He said he "never made anti-British statements or said—on or off the record—that I do not expect Britain to win the war."

Then Joe denounced Lyons for allegedly breaking the rules of journalism, claiming both that the interview had not been on the record and that he had not said what was attributed to him. Finally, he indefinitely withdrew substantial liquor advertising from the *Boston Globe*. "When Mr. Lyons came to me in Boston, I made it clear to him in the presence of Mr. Coghlan and Mr. [Charles K.] Edmonson of the *St. Louis Post-Dispatch* that I should be very happy to give them my thoughts off the record, but I would make no statements that should be printed at this time," Joe said.

In private, Joe said he was impressed that Lyons had given such an accurate account of his comments without taking notes.

Joe's publicized comments produced a slew of disparaging

cartoons. One, in the *Chicago Tribune*, pointed up Joe's inconsistency. It showed him lecturing, "Democracy is finished in England. It may be here. I'm willing to spend all we've got left to keep us out of war. There's no sense in our getting in. We'd just be holding the bag. Help Britain but avoid war."

It was difficult to believe that any American, much less an ambassador, would have so little faith in democracy that he would say, on such flimsy evidence, that it was about to be extinguished. Still, Joe's effort to distance himself from the story fooled no one. Ickes noted that Joe had been "very indiscreet," then "complainingly declared that he thought he was talking off the record." Ickes hoped it spoiled any chance of his remaining in the government in any position.

Nor was Roosevelt fooled. Ickes wrote that Roosevelt told him he believed the quotes were authentic. He said that Ben Smith, Joe's friend, was working to acclimate the French government established by Hitler at Vichy toward Hitler and totalitarianism. Roosevelt fully believed that Joe thought Germany would win the war and that "the end of the world is just down the road."

Roosevelt's belief that Joe's *Boston Globe* interview was genuine was confirmed when he received a disturbing letter from Douglas Fairbanks Jr., a producer and son of film star Douglas Fairbanks. Fairbanks told the president that Joe had spoken for three hours at a Hollywood studio. Although his talk was off the record, his remarks soon leaked out. From four different people who were at the meeting, Fairbanks learned that Joe said the Lindbergh appeasement groups were not far off the mark when they said that the country could "reconcile itself to whomever wins the war" and "adjust our trade and lives accordingly." Fairbanks noted that Joe "apparently threw the fear of God into many of our producers and executives by telling them that the Jews were on the spot, and that they should stop making anti-Nazi pictures or using the film medium to promote or show sympathy to the cause of the democracies versus the dictators." Further, even as

Hitler was about to sign Directive 21 calling for the "final solution" to the Jews, Joe said anti-Semitism was growing in Britain. For the Jews, he declared, were "being blamed for the war."

Apparently, Fairbanks wrote, Joe thought that a dictator's word could be trusted, and that the United States was in "no peril whatsoever." The truth was that when the bombing started, "The ambassador was the most frightened man in the realm."

Roosevelt immediately showed Fairbanks' letter to Cordell Hull. The president wrote back to Fairbanks to thank him for sending it, saying that it "fits in with the general picture."

But Roosevelt, always temporizing, decided just before Thanksgiving to invite Joe to his home in Hyde Park to "see what he has to say." Roosevelt sent Eleanor to meet Joe at the train station. Now that the election was over, the president could take the gloves off. Just what transpired is a matter of conjecture. But Eleanor recalled that ten minutes after she had brought Joe in to see her husband, Roosevelt called her back. He asked Joe to step out of his study while he talked with Eleanor, who had rarely seen him so angry.

"I never want to see that son-of-a-bitch as long as I live," Roosevelt declared. "Take his resignation and get him out of here."

Eleanor reminded Roosevelt that he had invited Joe for the weekend, and the train did not leave until later that afternoon. "Then you drive him around Hyde Park, give him a sandwich, and put him on that train!" he said. Eleanor later reported that Roosevelt could not stand to hear Joe's name.

A few days later, Joe wrote to his friend Hearst, who could always be counted on to support his views. In the mid-1930s, Hearst convinced Hitler that he could improve his image in the United States by subscribing to Hearst's International News Service. The German government then agreed to a higher contract price than that paid by other subscribers. Under his own byline, Hearst told his readers that Hitler had "restored character and courage. Hitler gave hope and confidence. He established order and unity of purpose."

Without revealing that he had already resigned, Joe told Hearst that he felt himself to be in a "confused state of mind." On the one hand, he explained, he would hate to be away from England if a "serious break in the situation" occurred. On the other hand, if England were to sue for peace, he would hate not being there because the United States position could be influenced by the British attitude toward peace arrangements.

Joe had no more insight into how he was viewed in England than into the reasons the British resisted Hitler. He went so far as to venture to Hearst that if he did go back, "I am sure the British people would respond very happily." Indeed, his return "would probably be good for the morale of the American people." Hearst agreed, writing back that it would be "a serious thing for the American people" if Joe did not return to London. Hearst hailed his views as "patriotic" and "courageous."

Finally, Joe announced his resignation as ambassador and wrote a letter of resignation dated December 1, 1940. He dated his formal letter of resignation December 2, effective November 30. In January, Roosevelt announced the nomination of John Gilbert Winant as his successor.

A sigh of relief greeted Joe's resignation. In England, columnist A.J. Cummings wrote in the *News Chronicle*, "While he was here, his suave monotonous smile, his nine over-photographed children, and his hail-fellow-well-met manner concealed a hard-boiled businessman's eagerness to do a profitable business deal with the dictators, and he deceived many decent English people." George Murray of the *Daily Mail* said, "We can forgive wrongheadedness, but not bad faith." More in sorrow than in anger, he rebuked Joe: "How little you know us, after all. Your three years as ambassador have not given you insight into the character and traditions of the British people."

A poem circulated in England made fun of Joe: "When

hell was popping/And bombs were dropping/All over London town/Said Joe, Joe/'I've got to go/The British have let me down.'" The poem ended, "In this fateful hour/We should give no power/To our Army and Navy Chief/Just sit on our tails/Emitting wails/And similar sounds of grief."

The attacks prompted Joe to issue a statement saying he was disappointed in the British. "If an interview, which was repudiated by me, and a story in a gossip column are going to be sufficient to wipe out . . . my two years and nine months in London," he said, "then I begin to wonder if I ever had much standing in London."

The *New York Herald Tribune* said the termination of Joe's "unfortunate" career as ambassador meant Americans could "breathe more easily." The *Chicago Daily News* was pleased at his departure. But the *New York Daily News*, whose publisher, Joseph Patterson, had hired Joe as a consultant, said the United States had lost a "fine and effective ambassador." And the Hearst papers defended his "record."

Looking back many years later, Joe insisted that his effort to seek "some *modus vivendi* between us and the dictator nations" had purposely been distorted by those who "willingly contemplated a course leading to war, and even hoped that it might occur." Chief among these were "a number of Jewish publishers and writers." Patronizingly, he said they should not be criticized for their position. "After all, the lives and futures of their compatriots were being destroyed by Hitler. Compromise could hardly cure that situation; only the destruction of Nazism could do so. To that end they therefore bent their energies, and Munich, increasing as it did the misfortunes of their fellows, offered no hope to Jewry."

Thus, in one fell swoop, Joe ignored German and Japanese aggression, including the Japanese attack on American naval forces at Pearl Harbor, Hitler's broken promises to limit his territorial ambitions, and the fact that Hitler had conquered much of Europe. Instead, Joe attributed World War II, with its loss of 292,000 American military personnel, to Jewish opinion makers who wanted to save their brethren in Germany.

Ickes thought Joe's appointment an example of Roosevelt's management at its worst. "Despite the fact that Kennedy was nothing but a stock market gambler, with no political background and no social outlook, the president brought him here to make him chairman of the SEC," Ickes wrote. "There he did everything he could for the Wall Street gamblers. Kennedy made a stiff fight to become secretary of the treasury, and Morgenthau blocked him there. Against a less stubborn man than Morgenthau, or one not as close to the president, he might have won. As a consolation prize, the president sent him to the Court of St. James's. There he served the cause of appeasement. He worked hand in glove with Chamberlain, but he never got along with the Churchill government. Now he is back here undertaking to sabotage the president's foreign policy."

From Roosevelt, there was no "Dear Joe" letter praising his accomplishments, as there had been when he resigned from the SEC. Joe's parting shot in the *Boston Globe* was a final embarrassment in a blundering career. Like most of Joe's relationships, this one had ended in disaster and bitterness.

Yet Roosevelt was not through with Joe. On December 17, 1940, Roosevelt revealed his plans at a press conference to provide billions of dollars in war supplies to Great Britain. He wanted Joe to help him overcome the objections of isolationists to get his Lend-Lease legislation passed. Since the summer, Roosevelt had been preparing for war. He had begun to purge his cabinet of any remaining isolationists. To give his administration a bipartisan cast, he had replaced some of them with Republicans. He won enactment of a peacetime draft, and he proposed the Alien Registration Act aimed at curbing subversive activities. The Lend-Lease Act would allow the president to ship vital armaments to nations— primarily Great Britain—whose defense he considered to be necessary for U.S. security. Eventually, the United States would supply England with $13 billion in this way.

Already, in a letter to Congressman Louis Ludlow, who had introduced a bill to require a national referendum before war could be declared, Joe had criticized the Lend-Lease proposal. On the House floor, Ludlow read Joe's statement. "While our own defenses are weak," Joe said, "we are limited as to what we can do for Britain, even though we want to." Ludlow exclaimed, "Thank God for Joseph Kennedy."

Calling them foes of Roosevelt's foreign policy, *Life* prominently displayed a photo of Joe with Lindbergh, the Fascist Lawrence Dennis, and other America Firsters, as they were called.

Roosevelt invited Joe to the White House for a talk on January 16, 1941. As usual, Roosevelt schmoozed with him in his bedroom, allowing him to pour out his frustrations about the "boys in the State Department" and the president's "hatchet men," who had leaked nasty stories about him to the press. Dryly, Roosevelt remarked that he himself had suffered worse. The president recalled the good times they had had together and said it would be unfortunate if their relationship ended bitterly. Disarmed after ninety minutes of ego massage, Joe agreed to do what he could to support the president and tone down his criticisms.

Two days later, Joe spoke on the NBC radio network. Listeners were expecting a denunciation of the Lend-Lease program. Instead, Joe claimed he had been the subject of a "smear" campaign. He denied he was a "defeatist" or even an "isolationist." Much like any politician who promises both tax cuts and new spending programs, Joe had something to say on both sides of every issue. On the one hand, he said England should arm itself because a quick defeat would imperil America. "In order to get things done, you have got to have power in one hand—and to that extent, I am 100 percent for granting it," he said, referring to aid to Britain. But having said that aid should be extended to protect the United States, he flip-flopped. "For the life of me, I cannot understand why the tale of a great military machine three thousand miles away should make us fear for our security."

By the same token, he said, "Just as I regard it impossible for a foreign power to invade this country, so do I regard it impossible for us to invade Europe. . . ."

But then he flip-flopped once again, predicting defeat should Germany decide to invade the United States: "Some use the argument," he said, that should Germany and its allies prevail, they would "inevitably impose on America a totalitarian regime. They, therefore, argue that we should go to war to prevent this. But have they considered that by becoming involved in a war, they may lose the very thing for which they are fighting? How long could a democracy last while trying to fight a long drawn-out war?"

The evening before he was to testify on the Lend-Lease bill, Joe sat up with Walter Trohan, Joseph Patterson, and John O'Donnell of the *New York Daily News* and told them the proposal was wrong and would involve the United States in war. His listeners were sure he would testify against the bill. However, when he testified before the House Committee on Foreign Affairs on January 21, he advocated a program of supplying aid to England. He said the United States should not enter the war, but, at the same time, he said the country should rearm.

Commenting on the discrepancy between what Joe said on Roosevelt's behalf and what he actually believed, Trohan said, "There ain't a gut in Joe's body. He's like a trooper when he got into a jam, but in a showdown he'd cut and run."

Columnist Raymond Clapper called Joe "almost as good a witness for the administration as for the opposition." In fact, leaders of both sides seized on aspects of the testimony to support their views.

A few days after the testimony, John Boettiger, the husband of Roosevelt's daughter Anna, wrote to Joe to praise what he saw in Joe's comments as support for Roosevelt. Joe wrote a self-pitying note back, and Boettiger sent it to Roosevelt. The president then penned a response to his son-in-law that no doubt expressed his true feelings about Joe. Roosevelt said it was "a little pathetic" that Joe was worried about becoming, along with his family members, "social outcasts." Joe "ought to realize, of course, that he has only himself to blame for the country's opinion as to his testimony before the committees. Most people and most papers got the feeling that he was blowing hot and cold at the same time—trying to carry water on both shoulders."

Roosevelt averred that the "truth of the matter" was that "Joe is and always has been a temperamental Irish boy, terrifically spoiled at an early age by huge financial success; thoroughly patriotic, thoroughly selfish, and thoroughly obsessed with the idea that he must leave each of his nine children with a million dollars apiece when he died (he has told me that often). He has a positive horror of any change in the present methods of life in America." In Joe's view the "future of a small capitalist class" was "safer under a Hitler than under a Churchill," according to Roosevelt. "This is subconscious on his part, and he does not admit it."

Interestingly, Roosevelt missed the contradiction between his evaluation of Joe, on the one hand, as "patriotic," and his judgment, on the other hand, that if given a choice, Joe would choose domination by Hitler over democracy. Hitler, in fact, had just ordered that Jews be exterminated through gassing. Joe's repeatedly and vociferously proclaiming himself a patriotic American who was "for the U.S.A." convinced many people that he was. Like the Virgin birth, it was an object of faith. Similarly, despite his demonstrated cowardice, the *Oxford Dictionary of Quotations* attributes to Joe the phrase "When the going gets tough, the tough get going."

Over the next year, Roosevelt would receive other reports that more than justified his harsh opinion of Joe. On May 3, 1941, for example, J. Edgar Hoover, the FBI director, informed Roosevelt that a source had said Joe and Ben Smith had met with Goering in Vichy, France, and had donated a considerable sum of money to Germany. The same source said the Duke of Windsor, who had abdicated the throne in 1936 to his brother because of his determination to marry a divorced woman, had agreed with Goering that after Hitler conquered England, Goering would overthrow Hitler and install the duke as king.

While that report was not substantiated, others were. Even as he was preparing to entertain Joe for lunch at the White House on January 16, Roosevelt was ordering Harry Hopkins to investigate a report from Alfred Bergman, a West Point graduate, that just before Czechoslovakia fell, Joe sold Czech securities short, making a profit of £20,000. If the story could be substantiated, it would "utterly ruin him [Joe] in public estimation," Ickes noted gleefully. Hopkins had previously been the recipient of transcripts of some of Joe's bugged conversations while ambassador, according to Randolph Churchill, Churchill's son. The elder Churchill sent the material to warn Roosevelt of what his ambassador was doing, his son said.

After visiting London, Hopkins reported that Joe had indeed sold Czech securities short in that country's time of need. Joe's profit was said to be either $500,000 or £500,000.

16

LOBOTOMY

As Joe looked at his life, it seemed nearly perfect. He was about to sell his Bronxville home and change his legal residence to Florida, which had no income or inheritance taxes. In Palm Beach, he could bask in the sun, keep in touch with his New York office by phone, and watch his investments grow. He did not have to report to anyone, and he had plenty of opportunity to bed as many young women as he pleased.

Occasionally, he made contradictory pronouncements about the darkening situation in Europe, where German forces had overrun Greece and Yugoslavia. On April 29, 1941, he said that the United States should not aid Great Britain with arms or food because the sinking of one American ship could propel the United States into war. On May 25, he said in Atlanta that Germany could not defeat the United States, which was now preparing for war.

For all his apocalyptic predictions, Joe only worried about war as it would affect his pocketbook. He told Henry L.

Stimson, the secretary of war, that a few years earlier he thought he had made enough money to provide for his children, but now he lay awake nights because he feared it would all be gone. While anyone might have such concerns, it was hardly appropriate to express them as war loomed. Aside from that, he did have one more serious problem: his daughter Rosemary. Rosemary had always been slower than the other children. As she grew older, her sweet disposition turned sour, and she often flew into uncontrolled and violent rages.

Rose Kennedy dedicated her 1974 book *Times to Remember* to "my daughter Rosemary and others like her—retarded in mind but blessed in spirit." She wrote that, as a baby, Rosemary said her first words late and had trouble managing a baby spoon. As she grew older, she had trouble steering her sled, had difficulty reading, wrote from right to left, and could not keep up with schoolwork in first grade. But she said it took her some time to realize that "Rosemary was born a retarded child," meaning she had subnormal intellectual development because of congenital defects, brain injury, or disease.

After the family returned from England, Rose noted, "Not only was there noticeable retrogression in the mental skills she [Rosemary] had worked so hard to attain, but her customary good nature gave way increasingly to tension and irritability. . . . She was upset easily and unpredictably. Some of these upsets became tantrums or rages, during which she broke things or hit out at people. Since she was quite strong, her blows were hard. Also, there were convulsive episodes."

Joe could not tolerate losers, any more than he could tolerate crying. He banned Rosemary from the house. Before his assignment to London, his aide Edward Moore and his wife, Mary, took care of her. "She stayed for many years with the Moores," said Ann Gargan, Joe's niece from Rose's side of the family. "Eddie and Mary Moore took care of her." In London, Joe sent her to a special boarding school. After his return to the United States, he sent her to convents in Boston and Washington. At twenty-two, she took to going out alone in the middle of the night, walking the streets. While slightly overweight, she was well endowed and, after Kathleen, the prettiest of the Kennedy daughters. Joe and Rose worried that she would be molested. Rose said she and Joe consulted experts, who felt "a certain form of neurosurgery" was needed.

Just how accurately Rose described her daughter's condition is open to question. She tended to mirror whatever Joe's line was at the moment. Indeed, while implying in her book that she and Joe had agreed on the neurosurgery, Rose would later say she knew nothing about it until after the surgery had been performed.

What is corroborated is that Joe consulted two surgeons in Washington who had become the leading proponents of prefrontal lobotomies. Newspapers had carried stories about their work, but Joe most likely learned about it through his daughter Kathleen.

Page Huidekoper, Joe's assistant in London, had become through Arthur Krock a research assistant at the isolationist *Washington Times-Herald*. Then on New York Avenue at 13th Street NW, the paper had the biggest circulation in Washington. Joe had told Kick it was time for her to earn her own living, and Huidekoper arranged for Frank Waldrop, the associate editor of the paper, to interview her in August 1941. Waldrop had known Joe for some time. Even though they held similar views on the war in Europe, Waldrop had little respect for Joe. He thought of him as "cold-blooded and calculating." Joe would do "whatever his self-interest suggested he do," he said. Moreover, he considered him highly anti-Semitic, as he constantly referred to "the goddamn Jews."

If Waldrop had reservations about Joe, he liked Kick. After he hired her, Joe took him to lunch. "He said, 'I'm entrusting my little daughter to no one else but you,'" Waldrop recalled. Kathleen "couldn't spell 'cat,' but she had beautiful manners," Waldrop said. "When I would say, 'I'm busy, tell him to go to hell,' she would say, 'Mr. Waldrop is so sorry, but he can't see you today.'"

Kick began dating John White, the paper's star feature writer. White was more enamored with Kick than she with him. He would have to beg for kisses. Kick—no one knows how she got the name—claimed that none of the Kennedys was capable of deep attachment, but Huidekoper said that may have been her way of fending White off. "I don't think she wanted to have a love affair with him. He was very smart and funny, but he had no sex appeal," Huidekoper said.

After they began dating, Kathleen made a sly reference to North Carolina. White wondered how she knew where he had grown up. Finally, he asked her. Her reply left him dumbfounded.

"Every time one of us goes out with somebody new, we have to call our father," she said. Joe would then have a background check conducted.

"Has he done a background check on me?" White asked.

"You bet he has," she said.

"Then how on earth can he let you go out with me?"

"Oh, he considers you frivolous but harmless," she replied.

While Kick seemed resigned to Joe's penchant for control, she became visibly upset when she overheard a remark at a party at the Mayflower Hotel about her father's swordsmanship, according to White, who was with her at the time. Later, at a dinner party in London, someone made a disparaging remark about a man having an extramarital affair. "That's what all men do," she replied, with a tone of authority. "You know that women can never trust them."

White was doing research for a series on mental illness, and Kick seemed fascinated by the subject. She snapped up any information she could from him. One day, they were walking through a park. In a small voice, she confided to White what seemed to be a shameful secret: Her sister Rosemary had a problem. As Lynne McTaggart described it in her book *Kathleen Kennedy*, Rosemary was being taken care of by St. Coletta's School in Jefferson, Wisconsin. If she had learning problems, that was not what concerned Joe. Rather, it was the "mood changes" that the doctors there attributed to a "new neurological disturbance." White told McTaggart that the family considered Rosemary "a disgrace and failure."

Joe decided the solution was a lobotomy. The lobotomy era had begun in the early 1930s when a pair of neurological scientists severed the frontal lobes of chimpanzees' brains, rendering them docile and relaxed. They presented their findings to a conference in London in 1935, where Portuguese scientist Egas Moniz decided that what seemed to work for apes might work for humans. He returned to Lisbon and drilled holes in the skulls of twenty hopelessly ill mental patients. He reported that most of them "recovered" or "improved."

Dr. Walter J. Freeman, who had an appointment to St. Elizabeths Hospital in Washington and was a professor of neurology at George Washington University School of Medicine, read his reports and became an evangelist for the procedure. As a partner, he enlisted his associate, Dr. James W. Watts. In 1935, Freeman had invited Dr. Watts to join the neurology department. Born in Lynchburg, Virginia, Watts had obtained a medical degree from the University of Virginia and received training in neurosurgery at Massachusetts General Hospital in Boston. He eventually became chief of neurosurgery at George Washington University Hospital. He was also a consultant in neurological surgery at St. Elizabeths Hospital, Washington's city-owned mental hospital. Highly regarded in medical circles, Dr. Watts became the ninety-first president of the Medical Society of the District of Columbia.

Both doctors sincerely believed in what they were doing. At the time, no drugs were available to treat mental illness. Those with severe symptoms were confined to mental hospitals, often for the rest of their lives. As described in a published paper by Drs. Freeman and Watts, lobotomies relieved "certain patients of mental symptoms by a destructive operation carried out upon their frontal lobes," which are responsible for the brain's higher intellectual functions. The operation entailed "cutting the matter of each frontal lobe." The doctors claimed that the procedure "bleaches the affective component connected with the consciousness of the self" in those "whose preoccupation is fixed and unyielding. . . ." This "allows the personality to appear in purer form," with only minor changes in "energy and intelligence."

Evaluating their own work, the doctors rated the results "good" in more than half the cases. Their article showed pictures of people who looked depressed before the operations; afterward, they appeared to be smiling but were glassy-eyed. The doctors admitted that some patients "remain somewhat indolent, lacking in the imaginative capacity to see for themselves what needs doing." At least three patients died on the operating table. Yet they said others were freed from "the restraints imposed by timidity, sensitiveness, or embarrassment."

In fact, in most cases, the operations substituted one set of disturbing symptoms for another. Instead of being disruptive and irrational, the patients essentially became zombies because of brain damage. At the time Joe asked the doctors for their help, they had performed only sixty-six prefrontal lobotomies, nearly all the lobotomies performed at that time.

While Dr. Freeman supervised, Dr. Watts did the surgery. In the only interview he ever gave on the subject, Dr. Watts described to the author how he performed the lobotomy in the fall of 1941. After Rosemary was mildly sedated, "We went through the top of the head," Dr. Watts recalled. "I think she was awake. She had a mild tranquilizer. I made a surgical incision in the brain through the skull. It was near the front. It was on both sides. We just made a small incision, no more than an inch."

The instrument Dr. Watts used looked like a butter knife. He swung it up and down to cut brain tissue. "We put an instrument inside," he said. As Dr. Watts cut, Dr. Freeman asked Rosemary questions. For example, he would ask her to recite the Lord's Prayer or sing "God Bless America" or count backward. Her pulse became more rapid, and her blood pressure rose.

"We made an estimate on how far to cut based on how she responded," Dr. Watts said. When she began to become incoherent, they stopped. "I would make the incisions, and Dr. Freeman would estimate how much to cut as she talked. He talked to her. He would say that's enough."

Beginning in 1946, Freeman and Watts refined their methods. Instead of cutting holes in patients' skulls, they inserted a device that looked like an ice pick through the eye cavity. Freeman, who has since died, later estimated that between 1936 and the late 1950s, he performed or supervised four thousand of the forty thousand to fifty thousand lobotomies performed in the United States. By the late 1950s, the lobotomy era had ended. Tranquilizers replaced the procedure.

Dr. Watts told the author that, in his opinion, Rosemary had suffered not from mental retardation but rather from a form of depression. At the age of ninety, he could not recall with certainty what kind of depression she had. Then as now, the terminology of psychiatric illness was constantly changing.

"It may have been agitated depression," Dr. Watts said, using a term then used to describe patients who seem overwrought or agitated. "You're agitated, you're shaky. You talk in an agitated way. All kinds of things go on in the eyes."*

A review of all of the papers written by the two doctors confirmed Dr. Watt's declaration. All of the patients the two doctors lobotomized were diagnosed as having some form of mental disorder. As described in one of the papers reporting on their first fifty-four cases, Freeman and Watts listed these disorders as agitated depression, involutional depression, "obsessive compulsive, ruminative states," tension with depression, schizophrenias, psychoneurosis, conversion hys-

---

*Dr. Watts died of cancer a few weeks after being interviewed. His interviews were tape-recorded, and he signed a statement that Rosemary Kennedy had a mental illness and was not mentally retarded.

teria, chronic alcoholism, and manic-depressive depression. None of the papers listed any of the patients as being mentally retarded, or being imbeciles, feeble-minded, or morons, as the condition was then called. In a later paper after Rosemary's operation, the doctors listed the diagnoses for their 136 cases to date. Again, mental retardation was not among them. Even in the relatively unregulated atmosphere of the 1940s, mental retardation was not grounds for performing a lobotomy. According to a review in the *American Journal of Psychiatry* of all reports of lobotomies ever done, the procedure was only used for psychiatric illness.

Many of the symptoms described by Rose and Kathleen Kennedy conform with a diagnosis of depression. As now defined, depression includes irritable mood or persistent anger, changes in weight, pacing, waking up during the night, and retardation of speech or thinking. While major depressive illness may begin at any age, it begins most commonly in the mid-twenties, about when Rosemary's symptoms became more troublesome.

In fact, Rose noted in her book that a "neurological disturbance or disease of some sort seemingly had overtaken her, and it was becoming progressively worse." The "disease," according to Dr. Watts, was mental illness.

Dr. Watts did not recall what happened to Rosemary immediately after the operation. Typically, patients are disoriented, have flattened voices, and vomit. They cannot complete whole sentences and "thumb the pages of newspapers or magazines, but are unable to recall what they have read," the doctors reported. Patients may also fumble with their genitalia or exhibit signs of euphoria.

Subsequent independent evaluations of lobotomies were devastating. A 1962 report on more than two hundred lobotomies done in western Pennsylvania pointed out that there was "little relationship" between "discharge and recovery." The report said that four of seventeen patients who were discharged from one hospital "seem to feel happier, are able to work more consistently, and are certainly less destructive," but the remaining thirteen showed "a variety of symptoms ranging from psychosis and vegetable existence to persistence and exacerbation of functional complaints and obsessional ruminations." A 1970 Missouri Institute of Psychiatry report said that although many patients benefited from lobotomies, the side effects "often proved more disabling than the psychiatric illness itself." The authors described "post-lobotomy syndrome," which included a high incidence of "confusion, urinary incontinence, unequal pupils, facial asymmetry, convulsions. . . ."

In Rosemary's case, it became immediately clear the operation had not succeeded. In fact, it made her condition far worse. Rose said that while the operation stopped Rosemary's violent behavior, it also "had the effect of leaving Rosemary permanently incapacitated." She "lost everything that had been gained" by teaching her, and she now needed "custodial" care.

"They knew right away that it wasn't successful," Ann Gargan said. "You could see by looking at her that something was wrong, for her head was tilted and her capacity to speak was almost gone. There was no question now that she could no longer take care of herself and that the only answer was an institution."

Before, Rosemary was able to write endearing letters, dance, and do arithmetic. At the age of nine, Rosemary neatly and correctly multiplied and divided: $428 \times 32 = 13696$, for example, $693 \times 65 = 45045$, and $3924 \div 6 = 654$. "A very nice paper," her tutor wrote at the top of one paper.

At the age of sixteen, Rosemary wrote to her father, "I would do anything to make you so happy. I hate to disapoint [sic] you in anyway [sic]." At the age of six or seven, she wrote, "dear Santa Claus, i am writing to you i want a doll, and doll carriage and some paper doll block boad [sic] little set of dishes. Your friend Rose Kennedy 31 Naple rd." The fact that her spelling and grammar were poor was of no significance. Even after having graduated from Harvard, Jack's spelling was atrocious. At age twenty, Kathleen wrote to her father of a vote taken in her class, "I and other girl were the two yeses."

It was Richard Cardinal Cushing, before he became archbishop, who recommended to Joe that he send Rosemary to St. Coletta's in Wisconsin. Within the family that posed as being so loyal, Rosemary had ceased to exist. Rose's letters did not refer to her, and Eunice later said she had no idea where she was.

"Rosemary's name was never mentioned in the house," recalled Janet Des Rosiers. "I knew she existed because I saw the family photographs in the attic. But her name was never mentioned. I think Mrs. Kennedy went every year to see her. I heard she did. As far as I know, Joe didn't see her."

Like the friends and partners who had helped Joe over the years, Rosemary now was a nonperson. "If you were in his disfavor, you no longer existed," Des Rosiers said. "As long as you were in favor, you were in. . . . Sad isn't it, very sad, because your love shouldn't stop just because someone isn't perfect."

"The operation erases any active thinking, and I think Mr. Kennedy decided it would be better for Rosemary not to be exposed any longer to the general public in case she ran away," said Luella Hennessey, the children's nurse. "It would be better to almost 'close the case.'"

"Mrs. Kennedy told me twenty years ago that it was pretty sad when she found out about the lobotomy, because nobody had ever told her," said Nancy Tenney Coleman, the childhood friend of the Kennedy children. Rose told Doris Kearns Goodwin the same thing. Given Joe's authoritarian way of handling family matters, that was probably true. Nellie McGrail, a Kennedy family cook, said, "The old man took her and didn't tell anyone. Mrs. Kennedy didn't know. He said, 'We'll have her home one day, but she has to get well.' She went along with that."

Joe orchestrated an elaborate cover-up. When asked about her, he would tell writers who were given access to the Kennedys that Rosemary taught retarded children, as Joe McCarthy wrote in his book *The Remarkable Kennedys*. Or James Mac-

Gregor Burns was told that Rosemary "helped care for mentally retarded children," as he wrote in his book *John Kennedy: A Political Profile*. Before it was published, Burns had submitted his book for review by the family.

(In the same way, Joe covered up the fact that Jack had been born with an unstable spine. Instead, Burns and others blamed his bad back on a football injury.)

The first mention of anything wrong with Rosemary was in the July 11, 1960, issue of *Time*. It quoted Joe as saying that Rosemary was a childhood victim of spinal meningitis and was a patient in a nursing home in Wisconsin. "I used to think it was something to hide," Joe was quoted as saying, "but then I learned that almost everyone I know has a relative or a good friend who has the problem. I think it's best to bring these things out in the open."

Actually, Joe had told George Bookman, the *Time* reporter who interviewed him for the story, that the "problem" Rosemary had was mental retardation. In his report on the June 30, 1960, interview, Bookman quoted Joe as saying he had never before told a reporter about it.

Inexplicably, the *Time* editors cut short Joe's quote to exclude the term "mental retardation." Instead, they referred to the malady as "spinal meningitis," an inflammation of the meninges of the brain and spinal cord characterized by fever, vomiting, intense headache, and stiff neck. Since spinal meningitis is not a widespread problem, it does not conform with Joe's quote. Yet in a footnote to the story, *Time* said Rosemary's misfortune had led the Kennedy family to contribute to causes to help the mentally retarded. Did Joe have second thoughts about his disclosure and ask the editors to change "mentally retarded" to "spinal meningitis"? In their rush to make the change, did the editors neglect to delete the footnote? While this would seem a likely explanation, neither Bookman nor Otto Fuerbringer, then *Time*'s managing editor, could recall what actually happened.

Of course, whether *Time* called Rosemary's problem spinal meningitis or mental retardation is beside the point. Rosemary's real problem was mental illness. Clearly, Joe felt it would be less embarrassing to portray Rosemary as mentally retarded. No one in the press picked up on the story, and it was not until after Jack was elected president that Eunice felt comfortable talking about Rosemary publicly. Writing in the *Saturday Evening Post*, she said that Rosemary "was not making progress but seemed to be going backwards." She was becoming "increasingly irritable and difficult. Her memory and concentration and judgment were declining. . . ." Skipping over the lobotomy, she said, "My mother found an excellent institution that specialized in the care of retarded children and adults. . . ." Rose discussed what she said was Rosemary's retardation for the first time in an October 31, 1963, *New York Times* article.

Contrary to what Joe had said himself, Ted insisted in a letter to *Newsweek* that his father was not "ashamed" of Rosemary's condition, nor "did he hide the fact from any who inquired." Ted said, "Just four years after" Rosemary's condition was "fully diagnosed," his father "established the first major foundation to help in the prevention and treatment of retardation. . . ."

This was another rewrite of history. Established on May 14, 1945, the Joseph P. Kennedy Jr. Foundation, now with assets of $22 million, was begun because Cardinal Cushing pushed Joe to donate more to charity. "Cardinal Cushing asked for a donation and for a while Joe said no," said Mary Lou McCarthy, the daughter of Joe's sister Loretta. "Then he came around."

In its first ten years, the foundation gave money to a range of charities such as St. Mary's Infant Asylum, the Joseph P. Kennedy Jr. Memorial Hospital, St. Coletta's, and the Convent of Notre Dame. The foundation's first grant, made on August 12, 1946, was to the Franciscan Missionaries of Mary for the Joseph P. Kennedy Jr. Convalescent Home for Poor Families. Not until 1957, when Eunice Shriver took control of the foundation, did it begin to focus on mental retardation.

The donations not only helped the retarded, they created

good will for family members who constantly ran for office. The headlines told the story: "Kennedys Give $17 Million for Retarded" (November 25, 1962, *Boston Globe*); "Kennedys to Spend $10 Million on Centers to Assist Retarded" (July 31, 1959, *Boston Globe*); "Stanford Given Kennedy Grant: Retardation Study Gift Is $1.1 Million" (March 11, 1962, *Boston Herald*); "Kennedy $2M for Retarded" (April 8, 1964, *Boston Herald*). In making the first grant, Joe had Jack present the $600,000 check to Cardinal Cushing.

In a typical year, the foundation gives $1.4 million in grants. A smaller Kennedy foundation, the Park Foundation, gives out a sixth of that for projects not related to mental retardation.

Only a few doctors who worked for the Kennedys knew the truth about Rosemary's condition, as did the FBI. At the request of the White House, J. Edgar Hoover ordered the FBI on February 6, 1956, to begin a background check on Joe because President Eisenhower was about to appoint him to the Presidential Board of Consultants on Foreign Intelligence Activities. In establishing Rosemary's whereabouts, the bureau interviewed Joe's Boston attorney, apparently Bartholemew A. Brickley. For "many years," he told the FBI flatly, Rosemary had suffered from "mental illness."

By focusing attention on mental retardation rather than mental illness, Joe diverted support from the far more prevalent but also more embarrassing problem. During any given year, psychiatric disorders affect 40.7 million Americans, compared with the 7.5 million Americans who are mentally retarded. About 89 percent of those 7.5 million are mildly retarded and often indistinguishable from those without retardation.

In 1968, Eunice Kennedy Shriver founded Special Olympics International Inc., which promotes sports training and athletic competition for the mentally retarded and has assets of $19.2 million. Because of her work, the Clinton administration in 1995 coined a commemorative silver dollar honoring her. Thus an entire industry was founded on Joe's prevarication.

One of the doctors who knew the truth was Dr. Bertram S. Brown. A former director of the National Institute of Mental Health, Dr. Brown has unique qualifications to comment on Rosemary's condition. As a special assistant to President Kennedy, he was executive director of the President's Panel on Mental Retardation. In that capacity, he learned from other doctors retained by the Kennedy family that Rosemary had been "mentally ill" and was "not retarded." In dealing with Eunice and other family members, he also learned about the family's attitudes toward mental retardation and mental illness in general.

According to Dr. Brown, the fact that Rosemary could do arithmetic meant that her IQ was well above 75, the cutoff used by most states for purposes of classification in schools to define mental retardation. "If she did division and multiplication, she was over an IQ of 75. She was not mentally retarded," said Dr. Brown, who is the author of a book and ten papers dealing with mental retardation. "It could be she had an IQ of 90 in a family where everyone was 130, so it looked like retardation, but she did not fall into IQ 75 and below, which is the definition of mental retardation," he said. "There is no way I can picture her at less than a 90 IQ, but in that family, 90 would be considered retarded."

Dr. Rene S. Parmar, associate professor of special education at the State University of New York at Buffalo, confirmed that the types of arithmetic problems done by Rosemary indicated she was not retarded. While a few retarded children may be able to multiply or divide with single-digit numbers, "In my experience, I haven't seen them do double-digit arithmetic problems," she said. Similarly, Dr. Melvyn I. Semmel, professor emeritus of special education at the University of California at Santa Barbara, said anyone who could perform double-digit arithmetic at the age of nine was not retarded.

"I've seen an awful lot of families where everyone is bright, and you get a kid who is sort of average," Dr. Brown said. "They then begin to internalize that they are dopes, that they're retarded," he said. "The intense competitiveness of the Kennedy family—who is brightest, who is faster with touch football—means that if someone is on the other end of the curve, it affects them, and they start to internalize that they are stupid."

Confirming Dr. Brown's analysis, Luella Hennessey, the children's nurse, said, "Maybe you would notice a difference because the others were so smart."

Dr. Brown, who was director of NIMH from 1970 to 1978, said that from his dealings with Eunice and other family members, he came to realize that the family's effort to deny that Rosemary was mentally ill affected their attitude about psychiatry and helping the mentally ill. In his role in the Kennedy White House, Dr. Brown constantly had to try to overcome the family's antipathy toward psychiatry. Because of their attitude, he said he had to fight harder for budget allocations for mental health programs and research. "There was a basic attempt to deny that the sister had any mental illness, meaning crazy. There was hatred of psychiatry, because mental retardation was more acceptable to them. It's pretty clear that if someone has mental illness in their family, how does he become president? Mental illness is a stigma," Dr. Brown said. "You could not afford to have a mentally ill member of the family."

In Dr. Brown's opinion, the family's treatment of Rosemary led to her mental illness. "I think it's likely she was somewhat slower than the others. Then she was treated as if she was retarded. Then it becomes reactive depression, including rages and loss of control. That is mental illness. Agitated depression means they feel life is hopeless, but they are agitated, they pace back and forth. The reason she got depressed was that she reacted to being treated as a lesser member of the family." While the children tried to include her in their activities, "Given the highly competitive environment of the Kennedy family, they could not help but communicate to her that she was not up to their standards," he said. The fact that Joe banished Rosemary to live with his aide Eddie Moore demonstrated his rejection of her.

Joe's later cover-up "focused attention on mental retardation for the wrong reason, in order to hide that it really was mental illness," Dr. Brown said. "The stigma of mental illness in those days was like tuberculosis or cancer or worse. Mental retardation is more benignly not your fault. . . . Even in [Dr. Watts's] day, performing a lobotomy on someone who was mentally retarded would have been medical malpractice."

Dr. Brown called the suppression of the truth "the biggest mental health cover-up in history." Since the "public story" is still that Rosemary was retarded, the "lack of support for mental illness is part of a total lifelong family denial of what was really so." He added, "Some of us knew the secret and kept it secret because we felt it would be too devastating for them to know. . . . I knew the truth, but didn't want to confront them with it." Yet Dr. Brown also said, "It's my sense that they knew."

That is supported by the way Kathleen related Rosemary's story to her boyfriend John White. According to what White told Lynne McTaggart, Kick did not mention mental retardation. Rather, she said doctors attributed Rosemary's "mood changes" to a "new neurological disturbance." Presumably, Joe's other children had the same details.

When asked for comment, Melody Miller, Ted's spokesperson, vehemently denied that Rosemary was mentally ill. "If it was mental illness, they would not have established a foundation to combat mental retardation," she said. "Anybody who says that [that Rosemary was lobotomized after being diagnosed as mentally ill, and that she was not mentally retarded] is a liar and is bringing unnecessary hurt upon the Kennedys."

But Miller said she had not yet asked the Kennedys about the issue. She said she would bring it to Ted Kennedy's attention. She also suggested going over the new information with Eunice Kennedy Shriver. But letters to both Ted Kennedy and Eunice Kennedy Shriver produced no response.

Suddenly, after it became clear that the truth about Rosemary would come out, the Kennedy family moved to minimize her importance. After all, if she was not retarded, the family's efforts over the years to help the retarded would appear to be founded on a fabrication. So, for a story on the Special Olympics, which the Joseph P. Kennedy Jr. Foundation created, Eunice Shriver told the *New York Times* that Rosemary's condition had very little to do with the establishment of the Special Olympics. Indeed, the June 23, 1995, story gave the impression that it was a mere coincidence that the family had devoted itself to the retarded. The story pointed out that the Kennedy Foundation had been named for Joe Jr., not for Rosemary. It said Rosemary had never competed in the Special Olympics. And the story said that Eunice "dismissed out of hand" the idea that the Special Olympics "existed because of Rosemary."

While it was true that the foundation had not been started to help the retarded, its focus shifted to them in 1957, when Eunice took over its direction. By then, Rosemary could not have competed in any athletic events. Because of the lobotomy, she was not capable of playing board games, let alone taking part in athletics.

Contrary to what Eunice told the *Times*, Joe himself flatly told a *Time* reporter in a June 30, 1960, interview that the "reason [for the family's interest in helping the retarded] is that eldest daughter Rosemary is mentally retarded herself," according to the reporter's paraphrase. And in her memoirs, Rose quoted Eunice as saying of the family's philanthropic interest in helping the retarded, "My dad decided immediately to enter this field. He was particularly enthusiastic because my sister Rosemary was retarded. . . ."

Yet the Kennedys had succeeded in damage control. When the evidence came out as expected that Rosemary had not been retarded, the Kennedys could always point to a *New*

York Times story suggesting that it made no difference because Rosemary had had nothing to do with the family's decision to help the retarded. If the incident illustrated how willing the Kennedy family was to bend the truth, it also showed how accomplished the family was at it.

Today, Rosemary lives in a separate house on the grounds of St. Coletta's. She has the development of a two-year-old. She cannot wash or dress herself, cannot put her shoes on, and must be supervised at all times. After interviewing the nuns who take care of her, Laurence Leamer wrote that she knows her Hail Marys. Several times a year, Rosemary visits the family at Hyannis Port, Palm Beach, or New York.

"She is very quiet," said Nellie McGrail. "She fools around with cards. She is like a baby. . . . She is like someone with a stroke who knows what you are saying and would like to let you know that she knows but she can't."

Rose was devastated; she considered it the first of the Kennedy family tragedies. "Rose told me one day in tears, 'I'm deeply hurt by what happened to my boys [who were assassinated], but I feel more heartbroken about what happened to Rosemary,'" Nellie McGrail said. "She tried to blame herself. The assassinations hurt, but it was a different kind of hurt."

"I think Rose thought about her all the time," said Dr. Robert Watt, Rose's physician. "It was a very upsetting experience for Rose."

While Joe was deeply shaken by the later deaths of Kathleen and Joe Jr., he never expressed any remorse about Rosemary.

"There was this extraordinary demanding drive and hardness," said Charles Spalding of Joe. "There was a savagery about him."

Joe had sought to control Rosemary, and he had succeeded: His rapacious ambition for his own children had wound up consuming one of them.

17

BINGO

Arthur Krock had an eye for pretty women, and when he saw Inga Arvad at Columbia University's School of Journalism he was dazzled. Blonde and blue-eyed, the five-foot, four-inch twenty-eight-year-old student was stunningly beautiful. At the age of seventeen, at a contest in southern France, she had been crowned Beauty Queen of Denmark. She could speak and write in four languages.

After a meeting of the Pulitzer Prize Board at the school, Krock made a point of asking her who she was. She asked if he could help her find a newspaper job. "I was so stupefied by the beauty of this creature that I said I would," Krock said.

"That procurer," as Frank Waldrop called Krock, recommended Arvad to him. Waldrop hired her to write the *Washington Times-Herald*'s "Did You Happen to See . . ." column. The column presented superficial interviews with Washington personalities.

Again at Krock's suggestion, Arvad moved in temporarily with Huidekoper. "Inga was extremely attractive, with a lovely sort of soft purring laugh," Huidekoper recalled. "She was part child, part seductress. She was lovely fun."

Kick introduced Inga to her brother Jack, and Inga did a column on him. On June 24, 1941, Jack had joined the United States Naval Reserve as a seaman second class. Jack told his friend Red Fay that Joe's influence was "instrumental" in getting him into the navy despite his poor health. Joe got his friend Captain Alan Goodrich Kirk to arrange to have a medical friend give Jack a second physical, which he passed. Kirk also got Jack assigned to a cushy job. On October 6, he was appointed an ensign and assigned to work on the *Daily Digest* in the office of the chief of naval operations in Washington. The publication summarized local and world events.

In a memoir, Arvad recalled how she first learned about Jack. Kathleen was at Huidekoper's Georgetown house and was "curled up like a kitten, her long tawny hair fell over her face as she read a letter; then she jumped up. . . ." Her "Irish-blue eyes flashed with excitement as she leaped onto the floor and began a whirling dance like some delightful dervish." She said, "He's coming to Washington. I'm going to give a party at the F Street Club, you will just love him!"

"Who?" Arvad asked.

"Jack," Kick said. "He's in the Navy and is going to be stationed in Washington. Super, super."

Arvad decided Kick had not exaggerated. "He had the charm that makes birds come out of their trees," she wrote. "He looked like her twin, the same thick mop of hair, the same blue eyes, natural, engaging, ambitious, warm, and when he walked into a room, you knew he was there, not pushing, not domineering, but exuding animal magnetism. . . ."

Jack's book *Why England Slept* had just been published, and Cissy Patterson, publisher of the paper, suggested she do a column on Jack.

"An old Scandinavian proverb says the apple doesn't fall far from the tree," Arvad wrote in the November 27, 1941, issue. "No better American proof can be found than in John F. Kennedy. If former Ambassador Joe Kennedy has a brilliant mind (not even his political enemies will deny the fact), charm galore, and a certain way of walking into the hearts of people with wooden shoes on, then son No. 2 has inherited more than his due." He is "the best listener I have come across."

Soon, Jack and Arvad, who was married, were having a torrid affair. Jack called Arvad "Bingo" or "Inga Binga." He introduced her to his friend Charles Spalding, who was impressed. Spalding said Arvad was "blonde and well-dressed, always with bright colors and looking great. But the thing about her, her conversation was miles and miles ahead of anybody's."

Arvad confided to John White that she liked Jack, who was then twenty-four, because he was "so single-minded and simple to deal with. He knows what he wants. He's not confused about motives and those things." But she said she wouldn't trust him as a long-term companion. He is "very honest about that. He doesn't pretend this is forever. So, he's got a lot to learn, and I'll be happy to teach him."

White recalled Arvad as being "better than perfect." She was "very smart" but also "extremely loving." What had so enchanted Jack? "Oh, sex. She was adorable, just adorable," he said. "She looked adorable and was. She was totally woman. She wasn't handsome, she was gorgeous. Luscious, luscious is the word. Like a lot of icing on the cake."

Jack knew nothing of her past. But the FBI already had begun an investigation of her. Born on October 6, 1913, in Copenhagen, Inga Marie Arvad married Kemal Abdel Nabi, an Egyptian diplomat, when she was seventeen. In 1935, she was having lunch at the Danish embassy when someone said Hermann Goering was going to marry a well-known Berlin actress. Arvad called the actress and pretended to represent a Danish paper, even though she did not. The actress agreed to the interview and then invited Arvad to their wedding. Adolf Hitler was best man. At the wedding, Goering struck up a conversation with Arvad. He asked if he could do anything for her, and she said he could arrange an interview with Hitler.

By her account, Arvad interviewed Hitler twice and had lunch with him. Hitler called her the "perfect Nordic beauty." While in Berlin, she stayed with her uncle, a "chief of police" in the city. She later told her son Ronald T. McCoy that she rejected efforts by the SS to get her to report what she heard at parties in Paris. She took a part in a Danish movie and, divorcing her first husband before she was twenty, married Paul Fejos, a Hungarian who was the director. Having moved to the United States in September 1940, she entered Columbia Journalism School and attended it until June 1941.

If Jack did not know about Arvad's background, he did know that she was anti-Semitic and pro-Hitler. "She made no secret of her views. She was very pro-Nazi," said Pat Munroe, a classmate at Columbia. "She used to object to the fact that we had several Jewish members in the class. She called them 'Chews.' Those goddamned 'Chews.' That was her accent."

Indeed, it was Arvad's expressed admiration for Hitler that had prompted someone from the journalism school to write to the FBI about her, touching off the bureau's investigation. By then, Hitler had required all Jews to wear a yellow star, and the first killing of Jews by poison gas had occurred at Auschwitz. Soon, stories appeared in the *New York Post* and *New York Times* reporting that Paul Culbertson, assistant chief of the State Department's European Affairs Division, had received "eye witness accounts of returning Hungarian officers" that "between 7,500 and 15,000 Jews had been killed" in the Ukraine, their corpses floating in the Dniester River.

◆ ◆ ◆

On December 7, 1941, the Japanese attacked the United States naval base at Pearl Harbor, Hawaii, provoking a U.S. declaration of war on Japan the following day. On December 11, Germany and Italy declared war on the United States. The European war now merged with the Pacific war into one global conflict.

Joe sent a telegram to Roosevelt from Palm Beach. "In this great crisis, all Americans are with you," he wrote on December 7. "Name the battle post. I'm yours to command." Joe got only a form reply from Stephen Early, Roosevelt's press secretary.

Five days later, Page Huidekoper told Kathleen that she would not be surprised if Inga Arvad were a spy for a foreign power. She said she had seen a photo in some old papers of Inga with Hitler at the Olympic Games in Berlin. Distributed by International News Photos, it described her in the caption as a Danish beauty who had been made chief of Nazi propaganda in Denmark. Kathleen told Arvad and White what Huidekoper had said. Insisting that she wanted an investigation to clear her name, Arvad informed Cissy Patterson of her past. The paper was in a vulnerable position. Having editorialized against war and published secret defense plans, the paper's patriotism was suspect. To protect herself, Patterson instructed Waldrop to bring both Arvad and Huidekoper in to see the FBI.

"I went to the FBI field office and said I wanted to see the agent in charge," Waldrop recalled. "I said, 'This young lady says this young lady is a German spy. Good afternoon.' And I left them there."

Arvad described the FBI agent who took her statement as a "frightened mouse." When Arvad demanded that Hoover issue a "certificate" clearing her, the agent said that would not be possible. Instead, while the FBI had already been probing Arvad's activities because of the letter it had received the previous June, the bureau now intensified its investigation. Through interviews, the FBI established that Arvad openly expressed pro-Hitler views. She referred to the "damn dirty

Jews" and the necessity of persecuting them to further Hitler's program. Yet there was nothing illegal about expressing such opinions. They were not that different from what Joe often said about the Jews. In her effort to demonstrate her innocence, Arvad tried to see Hoover himself on December 17. She had interviewed Hoover's deputy, Clyde Tolson, and thought the connection would give her access to the director. But Hoover would not see her.

When the bureau learned on January 17, 1942, from the Office of Naval Intelligence, that Arvad was carrying on an affair with Jack, it became more concerned. Jack had a security clearance and access to information classified top secret about American war plans. Moreover, Arvad's husband, Fejos, participated in scientific expeditions funded by Axel Wenner-Gren, the founder and chief stockholder of a Swedish gun manufacturing company who was close to various Nazis. Hoover concluded that his expeditions to the Amazon were probably a Nazi "front for an ulterior purpose." Could Arvad be picking up information vital to the Germans through pillow talk?

The FBI began watching Arvad's apartment, which was Suite 505 at 1600 16th Street NW. Several times, the agents saw Jack leave the building early in the morning. On January 24, Jack reported to the Sixth Naval District to work on defense plans at the District Security Office in Charleston, South Carolina. Jack met Arvad at the Francis Marion Hotel there. The FBI planted bugging devices in the hotel and in Arvad's apartment. The bureau also intercepted Arvad's telephone calls and conducted a search of her apartment. There, agents found evidence that she had received $5,000 from Wenner-Gren in the fall of 1941 and other smaller payments prior to that.

After Jack had had intercourse with Arvad one evening at the hotel, Jack discussed his father and his views. The FBI transcripts of the conversation show Jack was as misled about his father as anyone else. He said the trouble with Joe was that he had not talked enough about his views. If he had, he would not have been accused of being an appeaser. The reason he stopped talking was that he was afraid he might hurt his "two sons' "chances in politics. But then Jack went on to echo his father's views, saying British soldiers were "no goddamn good." Parroting his father, Jack said the British empire was "through," and Churchill knew it.

The FBI picked up extensive information on the couple's lovemaking. The transcripts usually noted that the two had engaged in intercourse on "numerous occasions." But not once did Arvad and Jack discuss his work for naval intelligence. She later told the FBI that the payments received from Wenner-Gren were advances on her husband's salary. If Arvad was a spy, she was not very good at it.

◆ ◆ ◆

On January 12, 1942, Walter Winchell's column, published in the *New York Mirror* and other papers, said, "One of Ex-Ambassador Kennedy's eligible sons is the target of a Washington gal columnist's affections. So much so she has consulted her barrister about divorcing her exploring groom. Pa Kennedy no like."

When Arvad walked into the office that day, a friend asked if she had seen the column, which had also appeared in the *Times-Herald*. "No," she said and grabbed the paper. "My name wasn't mentioned," she later recalled, "but at that time I was the only blonde columnist in Washington with an explorer husband, and Washington is a very small rat hole when it comes to gossip."

The column was yanked from the second edition of the *Washington Times-Herald*, but it went to hundreds of other newspapers. Patterson later determined that Hoover himself had leaked the item to Winchell.

"No sooner in office than he became embroiled in the great case of the ambassador's son and the beautiful blonde spy," John White wrote in his diary.

"Well, here it is, your first break in the greatest institution of newspaper writing in the U.S.," Arvad's husband, Fejos, wired her sarcastically. "You made Winchell's column."

Almost immediately, Hoover was on the phone to Joe, suggesting that he get Jack to break up with Arvad, according to what Jack later told William Sutton, one of his campaign workers and aides. "One day the FBI had their room bugged, and the next day Joe got a call from J. Edgar Hoover," Sutton said. "Hoover told him Jack was in big trouble and he should get him out of Washington immediately."

In the opinion of Lawrence J. Heim, a former FBI official who worked for Hoover, part of the FBI director's motive was to protect Joe. The two men used each other: Joe constantly praised Hoover as the finest public servant in the land, while Hoover helped Joe with information about his enemies.

Swiftly, Jack did as he was told. Within days of his father's call to him, he let Inga know that they were through. On January 19, Arvad wrote to Jack, "I am not going to try to make you change. It would be without result anyway because Big Joe has a stronger hand than I." A week later, she wrote to Jack that she noticed that while Kick had gotten a letter from him, she had not. "Distrust is a funny thing, isn't it?" she said. "There was a peculiar feeling at the realization that the person I love most in the world is afraid of me. Not of me directly but of the actions I might take some day. I know who prompted you to believe or rather disbelieve in me, but still I dislike it." On March 11, she wrote, "Jack dear, from your Binga. There is one thing I don't want to do and that is to harm you. You belong so wholeheartedly to the Kennedy clan, and I don't ever want you to get into an argument with your father on account of me." If she were eighteen, she said, she would "fight like a tigress over her young" to keep him. "Today I am wiser," she wrote. "Nevertheless, I may as well admit that since that famous Sunday evening, I have been totally dead inside."

In the view of many of Jack's friends, Arvad was one of

Jack's few true loves. "Inga Arvad was a great girl," Spalding said. "She was a sensational girl. She really loved him. She was one of the few girls he really fell for. She was fabulous."

Arvad later confided to Arthur Krock that Jack was a poor lover—a "boy, not a man, who was intent upon ejaculation and not a woman's pleasure."

To make sure Jack did not see Arvad, Joe got his friend James V. Forrestal, then undersecretary of the navy, to reassign him. Jack told Arvad that Joe had called Forrestal personally and gotten him moved. Jack had become bored with desk work anyway and wanted to see action. He was transferred to the South Pacific.

If Arvad had been engaging in adultery, Jack had committed a mortal sin. But that was not what bothered Joe, who made a pass at Arvad himself. She told her son Ron McCoy that when she and Jack spent a weekend at Hyannis Port, Joe had tried to get her in bed. "She thought it was just a totally amoral situation," McCoy said. "She said it [the pass] was after dinner one night, and he [Joe] said, 'I'm not going to let my son marry you, but . . .'"

As far as Joe was concerned, Arvad posed a threat to Jack's political future. For the same reason that he checked the backgrounds of his children's dates and later hired private detectives to watch them, Joe did not want Jack's reputation sullied by a possible German spy. Anyone who married Jack would have to be a political asset, not a liability.

Arvad thought Jack was afraid of his father. He was, in her view, a hard, mean man who was "very charming when she and Jack were with him, but if she left the room, he'd come down on Jack about her and if Jack left the room, he'd try to hop in the sack with her," McCoy said. In her memoirs, she described Joe as a "typical slick politician, a good handshaker with a flashy smile but cold eyes, sly, intelligent, and too sure of himself."

Arvad could not understand how the family put up with so much control by Joe. She thought "they had to want the money" and had been raised in an atmosphere where "there was no questioning." Quoting his mother, McCoy said, "He was in control. . . . The family environment impressed her as tribal or patriarchal to an unhealthy degree. The kids did pretty much what he wanted them to do. . . . He liked being classified as tough. He was a bully, is the way she felt."

To Arvad, the entire family was weird. "The way she thought of it," McCoy said, "the old man would push Joe, Joe would push Jack, Jack would push Bobby, Bobby would push Teddy, and Teddy would fall on his ass."

The FBI turned off its bugging devices when agents overheard Arvad say that the FBI had a Dictaphone in her apartment. But on May 4, Roosevelt sent Hoover a note. In view of Arvad's connection with Wenner-Gren, who was banned from entering the country, and in view of "certain other circumstances which have been brought to my attention," Roosevelt thought it would be "just as well" to have her "watched specially."

Now the FBI redoubled its efforts, conducting physical surveillance on her twenty-four hours a day. Still, the agents saw nothing suspicious. On July 27, 1942, Arvad resigned from the paper. Cissy Patterson sent her flowers, and Kathleen got her column. Arvad divorced Fejos, who had become jealous of Jack. She planned to marry Nils Blok, a Danish writer living in New York. She had been having an affair with him while seeing Jack Kennedy. Occasionally, Jack called Arvad or wrote to her.

Having found nothing to implicate Arvad in spying, the FBI closed the case the next month. In 1947, Arvad married cowboy film star Tim McCoy. She died in California at the age of sixty, confiding to her son that she still loved Jack.

18

MERCHANDISE MART

With the nation at war, Joe was on the outside looking in. He yearned to be part of the action again.

On March 4, 1942, Joe wrote to Roosevelt. He had tried to call him, he said, but was told the president was unavailable. When he left a message, the call was not returned. Then Joe heard from his friend John W. McCormack, a Massachusetts congressman and Democratic majority leader, that Roosevelt was surprised he had not heard from Joe after the attack on Pearl Harbor. In his subsequent letter to Roosevelt, Joe enclosed a copy of the telegram he had sent at the time, along with a reply he'd gotten from press secretary Stephen Early.

"I don't want to appear in the role of a man looking for a job for the sake of getting an appointment, but Joe and Jack are in the service, and I feel that my experience in these critical times might be worth something in some position," he said. "If you want me, I am yours to command at any time."

Almost certainly, Roosevelt had been informed originally of Joe's telegram. Now with the nation at war, Joe offered his services. Most likely, Joe had sent McCormack in to Roosevelt, and the president had invented the story that he had never seen his telegram.

In his reply to Joe, Roosevelt apologetically noted that "thousands" of letters and telegrams had poured in after Pearl Harbor. Would Joe accept a job helping the country accelerate its shipbuilding program? Roosevelt had in mind naming Joe to head a War Shipping Administration.

On hearing the idea, other members of the administration were aghast. "We know, or think we do, that Kennedy is an appeaser," Bullitt, now ambassador at large, pointed out to Ickes. He said Joe continued to "speak ill" of the president, calling him "that son of a bitch" or worse.

"I know that the president hates Kennedy," Ickes wrote in his diary. "Bill's explanation of how it came about that the president made this offer is that it was the result of importunities by Jimmy Roosevelt. Of course, Jimmy has no sense of the proprieties or even any sense of decency." If it would help James Roosevelt financially, he would do "anything." Ickes speculated that Joe had "loaned him money" or that Joe had agreed to give Jimmy "a considerable sum."

Such speculation received added weight when J. Edgar Hoover wrote to Roosevelt on April 20, 1942, that a source of "unknown reliability" had stated that Joe Kennedy and James Roosevelt were paying off James Farley, who had left the administration, to get Roosevelt to lower tariffs and other taxes on liquor imports, which would benefit Joe's company. The fact that these and other allegations Hoover passed along to Roosevelt remained unproven did not mean they were false. A master politician, Hoover made it a practice never officially to investigate public officials for the purpose of indicting them. Instead, he made sure that those in power knew that he was aware of possible indiscretions. Through this not-so-subtle form of blackmail, he maintained power, retaining his position as FBI director for some forty-eight years, despite ordering illegal wiretapping and break-ins.

Indeed, a year after passing along to Roosevelt the tip about Joe, Hoover made Joe a "special service contact," meaning that he was supposed to pass along leads on issues that might be of interest to the FBI. For example, the bureau might ask him about issues in shipping or the movie business. Each FBI field office had three or four such contacts. The contacts were Hoover's way of ingratiating himself with the powerful. Many of the contacts did nothing but write fawning articles about the bureau, as did Joe. In an article in the *Commercial and Financial Chronicle*, Joe praised Hoover and his men as "tops in administration and service."

◆ ◆ ◆

Not long after Roosevelt offered Joe a job boosting the war effort, administration officials leaked his plans to the press. The outrage expressed far exceeded the reaction Roosevelt got when considering appointing Joe to the SEC. On April 21, 1942, Ralph Ingersoll, editor of New York's *PM*, ran an "open letter" to "friends" of Roosevelt who might be boosting Joe for the shipbuilding assignment. Ingersoll said that Joe talked off the record the way Charles Coughlin, the Detroit radio priest, talked publicly.

Zeroing in on Joe's well-crafted image as a tough, frank public official, Ingersoll wrote, "So Joe Kennedy is tough, is he? On what is your opinion based? The fact that he uses profanity and vile language? I was in London when Joe Kennedy was there, and the bombs were falling, and they had a different definition of the word *tough*. It did not include Joe Kennedy's anxiety to get out of town when the bombs fell."

In times of war, personal loyalty was especially in demand, Ingersoll said. Yet "Kennedy's brand of personal loyalty was to turn on his chief and always to end his insincere public flattery with personal attacks on Roosevelt. . . . There is no need to tell you what he told me, that this was a phony war, that the president of the U.S. did not know what he was talking about or doing. . . . He was always loud-mouthed, indiscreet, and good for a good laugh. But talk like that isn't funny any longer in wartime."

"The longer he talked of his honor, the faster we counted our spoons," the poet Ralph Waldo Emerson said. So it was with Joe. For all his self-proclaimed patriotism, Joe was interested in helping the nation during the war only on his terms. Over the next year, the president suggested several other appointments, including naming Joe chief of the Smaller War Plants Corporation or giving him a position on the War Production Board. Joe told Clare Boothe Luce, who was by then a Connecticut congresswoman, that he had no intention of taking any of the jobs to help the war effort. Sounding a familiar theme, he said, "Of course, they'd like to have me back" to take the heat. The jobs may sound attractive, he said, but "there isn't any solution as long as the Army and Navy concern themselves with winning the war as quickly as possible and not with our economic process."

As he put it to his friend, columnist Frank Kent, Joe told Roosevelt to "stick it." Despite his earlier vow to the president that he was "yours to command," Joe said the idea of giving him a job to help the war effort was "merely an excuse for putting me under cover." As far as Joe was concerned, he was still "in the leper colony."

Clearly, if Roosevelt had offered him a more prestigious job, such as treasury secretary, Joe gladly would have accepted. But Joe was not interested in the gritty work of helping the nation win a war. Joe saw Roosevelt's offers as rejection, further evidence that the Democratic administration had closed him out. To conserve food and supplies for the military, the government had started rationing such items as shoes, cheese, flour, fish, canned goods, and meat. But Joe couldn't bring himself to roll up his sleeves. Now that he was no longer in the inner circle, he decided the Democrats were not worth bothering with anyway. "It is my well-considered opinion that, short of a miracle, the New Deal is finished," he wrote to his publisher friend Max Beaverbrook.

◆ ◆ ◆

Now that his father had pried him loose from Inga Arvad, Jack was about to become commanding officer of a patrol torpedo (PT) boat, a light, maneuverable craft that launches torpedoes against enemy craft at sea. Yet Jack continued to be under Joe's thumb.

"One day Jack was home on leave before going out to the Pacific in the navy in World War II," Henry James Jr., a friend of Jack's, recalled. "He wanted to see someone in Florida. Jack said, 'Come along and ride with me.' He was seldom without someone with him, groups of people in fact."

Soldiers were stationed along bridges to Palm Beach, stopping young men who were not in uniform. Anyone who was in the military was required to wear a uniform at all times. Jack was not in uniform and James, who had been exempted from being drafted because of bad knees, also was in civilian clothes. The soldiers motioned for Jack to stop. Jack got out of the car and explained why James was not in the service. When Jack's explanation did not satisfy the soldiers, they asked James to step out of the car.

When a corporal asked James how old he was, he gave the wrong age. "I got the year mixed up. I have a dislike of thinking about my birthday," he said. When James displayed his draft card, the soldier noted that James had given him an incorrect age.

When the two arrived late for lunch at his Palm Beach home, Joe berated Jack. "For God's sake, Jack, why are you late again?" he said. "I like to start lunch on time. It's a simple idea. We're all here and waiting."

The two would have been late for lunch anyway, and the fact that they had been stopped was as much Jack's fault as his friend's. Yet Jack replied to his father, "Well, Henry got us in trouble." In James' view, the fact that Jack felt he had to place the blame on his friend showed that Jack "was really somewhat afraid" of his father.

Jack clearly admired his father, particularly his success with women. But James felt that Jack also empathized with his mother and her plight. "I saw the hurt in Jack's face, I saw it in his eyes, when he told me about Rose going away to get away from the scandals of the father," James said.

Nor did Jack have any reservations about his father's methods. Smugly, Jack told James that his father had called the White House to get soldiers bumped from a flight so he could take it. "During the war, transportation was hard to get, especially planes," James recalled. "They were being sent to the front. Jack got some time off from the navy and called his father, who said, 'Come on down to Palm Beach. The sun will do you good.' Jack was in Newport. Jack told me that it turned out that his father, who was in Washington, wanted to get on the same plane with Jack. Jack, being in the navy, could wangle it quite well. But his father called up, and the airline said, 'Sorry, that plane is overbooked. There is just no room for you on that flight. You'll have to go the next day.' Kennedy blew up. He said, 'I'm not going to tolerate that.' They said, 'I'm sorry, but it's wartime, and naval personnel are taking that flight. We can't impede the war effort.' Do you know what Kennedy did? He called Roosevelt."

Either directly through the president or more likely through his secretary, Missy LeHand, Joe bumped a soldier to make room for himself. Jack seemed proud that his father had so much power.

◆ ◆ ◆

Within months of rejecting Roosevelt's offers, Joe started a new career as real estate investor. Through Cardinal Spellman, Joe had met John J. Reynolds, a shrewd commercial real estate broker from the Bronx. As the broker for the New

York archdiocese, Reynolds was well connected politically and socially. Moreover, the square-jawed Reynolds was a good judge of real estate values. From his office on Park Avenue, he had negotiated scores of major real estate deals in Manhattan.

Yet Joe was actively involved in his own investment decisions. James Landis, who became one of Joe's advisers, recalled that Joe had a knack for analyzing investments by breaking them down into components, and he absorbed details well. At the same time, it was often difficult to determine how Joe came up with his conclusions, and his conversation "jumped around," Landis said.

Years later, Harold E. Clancy, who worked briefly for Joe, was similarly impressed. Clancy, a former *Boston Traveler* managing editor who later became publisher of the *Boston-Herald Traveler*, said that after he had investigated a possible investment, he would say to Joe, "I have twenty-four points to go over," at which point Joe began naming them for him. More importantly, said Tommy Corcoran, "Joe ha[d] a great capacity to analyze what a guy wants most. If he gets this, what will he give up?"

"Always remember that Joe is Irish," Corcoran said. "He has a hot heart and a cold head. That's what makes him interesting—the steam in him."

Joe eschewed operating businesses and foreign investment. At one point, Landis wanted Joe to invest in properties in Caracas, but Joe would not "take risks in places I don't know anything about." About another proposed investment, Landis wrote to Corcoran that Joe had decided to drop "the Puerto Rico business" because he "fundamentally hates to go outside the United States."

Operating responsibility was "of no interest to him," Landis said. He did not want to invest in companies that might produce labor problems or other difficulties. He kept liquid and could write a check for $5 million "right off the bat," Landis said.

Promoters of Charles "Tex" Thornton's Electro Dynamics Inc., which made microwave tubes for the navy and later became Litton Industries Inc., came to see Joe at his 230 Park Avenue office with a proposition. For $250,000, Joe could buy control of the company. After Litton went public in 1954, the price would prove to be a bargain.

"We had it right in our hands," said James Fayne, who had been with Joe at the SEC. But Joe, with an eye to Jack's political career, "wanted no part of a company that did 90 percent of its business with the government."

Thornton later claimed he was glad Joe didn't bite. Even if Joe had had a small interest, Thornton felt, he would have dominated the company.

Joe took full advantage of his credit line. He might buy a building for $2 million, and "if you are Joe Kennedy," he could borrow up to $1.8 million at interest of 4 percent a year, Landis said. The building might return 6 percent a year on the investment, which meant Kennedy made a net profit each year of $48,000 on his investment of only $200,000— a profit of 24 percent. In another example of the profits to be made, with a down payment of $200,000 Joe purchased a building at 616 Sixth Avenue for $1 million in 1943. Three years later, he sold the building for $1.5 million.

While Joe leveraged his deals, "The only financial advice he gave was to keep liquid. In other words, keep cash," recalled his friend Igor Cassini.

Once Joe bought an office building or apartment house, he immediately hiked the rents. During an investigation of rent gouging by the New York City Council in September 1944, attorney Harry J. Halperin cited a typical example. After buying a building at 45 West 18th Street, Joe boosted the rent paid by Goodstein Brothers, a clothing manufacturer, from $42,500 a year to $73,000 a year—an increase of 72 percent. Joe then offered the company a five-year lease allowing himself, but not the tenant, to cancel after two years. Over a barrel, the company signed. Asked for comment by a *New York Times* reporter, Joe said the leases were held by a trust for his children. Thus, he said, he had "nothing to do with the building."

That was but another subterfuge. Since the trustees of Joe's trusts were his lawyers or friends, he had complete control over the trusts and their investments.

At Reynolds' suggestion, Joe bought nine thousand shares in Hialeah racetrack from the estate of Colonel Edward "Cal" Riley Bradley. Joe's ownership interest in the track gave him extra cachet in his chief avocation—young women. "I used to go to races at Hialeah, and he always had Joseph Timilty, the Boston police commissioner, and he was Joe's man Friday, if you know what I mean," said Fred Good Jr., the son of Rose's obstetrician. "Joe would always have a gal with him but would always attempt to give the impression she was with Timilty." Rose was usually away. "If he was in Europe she would be here, and if he was in New York, she would be in Palm Beach. If he was in Palm Beach, she would be in New York."

Janet Des Rosiers, Joe's mistress, said Joe would use her to impress everyone with the size of his bets at the track. "Joe would give me a $1,000 bill, and he would tell me to go into the business office to change it to small bills, and then he would bet $2," she said. "I placed the bets for everyone. . . . He knew the fallacy of betting, letting the others lose their shirts. The $1,000 was to impress people."

Margot Prendergast, one of Reynolds' daughters, recalled that her father often complained that Joe would try to reduce his commissions and would call him at all hours of the night. "Joe Kennedy just thought that anyone who worked for him was a slave," she said. "He thought nothing about calling at midnight, 3 A.M., 5 A.M. [from overseas or California] with no respect."

Reynolds is generally credited with finding Joe's most lucrative and important investment—Chicago's Merchandise Mart. A limestone hulk on the north bank of the Chicago River, the mart was built by Marshall Field & Company for $35 million in 1930. Complete with a twenty-five-story tower, the mart originally had 4 million square feet of floor space, making it the world's largest building at the time.

Field president Hughston M. McBain had decided the company should get out of the real estate business and concentrate on retailing. Low-paying government agencies occupied more than a third of the space, and the building was not needed for the company's operations. On the books of Marshall Field, the building was valued at only $21 million.

Joe bought the building in July 1945 for just $12,956,516. To cover most of the purchase price, he borrowed $12.5 million from Equitable Life Assurance Society of the United States. Four years later, Joe took a new loan for $17 million from Prudential Insurance Company of America, allowing him to invest the excess in other projects. The Joseph P. Kennedy Jr. Foundation bought a quarter interest in the property.

Joe installed Wallace Ollman, a tall, amiable accountant, as manager of the building. Joe told him he had "never been identified with a loser," and he didn't intend to start. Ollman thought Joe had a tremendous grasp of the mart's potential.

On one of Joe's trips to Chicago, Ollman mentioned that the rates the government was paying were "submarginal, and they could cancel on 30 days' notice." Ollman thought he could dislodge the government, and Joe gave him the go-ahead. Three years later, the government agencies had largely moved out.

"Kennedy could see that the trick was to get the government out and some high rent tenants in," Corcoran said.

With Joe, Ollman shaped the mart into a home furnishings marketplace where the industry offered its latest lines to buyers looking for next year's stock. Joe also agreed to install air conditioning, a luxury in those days, and decided to recoup the cost by assessing each tenant.

To oversee Ollman, Joe hired R. Sargent Shriver, who was then an assistant editor at *Newsweek*. Through mutual friends, Shriver had met Eunice, and Joe invited him to breakfast on the thirty-fifth floor of the Waldorf Towers. Joe asked Shriver his opinion on some of Joe Jr.'s unpublished diaries. Could they be compiled into a magazine article?

"They were sort of outdated, had no insights about prominent figures, and there was no color . . ." Shriver recalled. "I suggested he have them privately printed, for the family." Joe followed the suggestion, printing *As We Remember Joe*, a collection of his material along with recollections of friends and family.

Joe told Shriver he had just bought the Merchandise Mart. Would Shriver like to work for him? Shriver agreed to be Joe's "personal representative." He later married Eunice.

Over the years, the Kennedys added to the project and renovated it. In late 1961, Stephen Smith, who had married Joe's daughter Jean, approached André Meyer, the legendary financier at Lazard Frères, to obtain advice on the family's investments. By then, the mart was valued at $150 million and accounted for the majority of the Kennedy family's assets. Meyer advised the family to expand the mart to compete with the plan of some Chicago real estate interests to lure apparel company tenants into another building. He suggested constructing the Chicago Apparel Center, which cost $70 million.

"It became such a success that it is one of the main assets of the family," said Nellie McGrail, who later became a cook for the Kennedys. "Joe said usually the Jews take up all these things. This is one thing they didn't get."

It was "simply a case of my dad having a better idea of the value of the property than Marshall Field," said Michael Reynolds, Reynolds' son.

But as usual, there was more to the story. While Reynolds enthusiastically endorsed the idea of buying the mart, it was Joe who had learned that the property was about to be offered for sale. James T. Lee, a friend who was a tough and successful real estate investor, had mentioned to Joe that he was planning to buy the mart. Joe then bought it himself, earning Lee's eternal enmity.

As it happened, Lee was the maternal grandfather of Jacqueline Lee Bouvier. Having been double-crossed by Joe, Lee was outraged when, eight years later, he was told that his granddaughter planned to marry Joe's son Jack. Before the wedding, "Everyone was nervous about whether James would come, and how he would act," said Jackie's half brother, James L. Auchincloss, who was one of Lee's grandsons. "He had to be persuaded to come. And once there, would he make some sort of a scene?"

◆ ◆ ◆

In May 1944, Joe gave an interview to Joseph Dinneen Sr. of the *Boston Globe* and Lawrence Spivak, then editor of *American Mercury*, a popular magazine, at the Ritz-Carlton Hotel in Boston. This time, there would be no question about what Joe had said. Accomplished at shorthand, Dinneen prepared a verbatim transcript.

"They say you're a Jew hater and a Jew baiter," Spivak began.

"Who says it? And where do they get the idea?" Kennedy impatiently responded. "It is true that I have a low opinion of some Jews in public office and in private life. That does not mean that I hate all Jews, that I believe they should be wiped off the face of the earth, or that I favor pogroms or persecutions. I don't," he said. "It was inevitable that I should find myself in conflict at times with Jews. I do, and I have done business with them. I can give you the names of Jews on my own books, Jews whom I have carried for years. They're all right. They're good businessmen."

But Joe said many Jews "actually promote anti-Semitism in their very efforts to combat it. I'm sorry to say that there are, in my opinion, Jews who actually exploit anti-Semitism. . . ."

By 1944, the fact that Germany was exterminating Jews was well known. As early as December 5, 1941, the *New York Herald Tribune* had editorialized that "the fate reserved for the Jews by the Nazis is worse than a status of serfdom—it is nothing less than systematic extermination." On June 25, 1942, the *London Daily Telegraph* said Jews were being exterminated with poison gas. "More than 700,000 Polish Jews have been slaughtered by the Germans in the greatest massacres in the world's history," the paper said. A second report was headlined, "More than 1,000,000 Jews killed in Europe." On June 30, the *New York Times* picked up the *London Daily Telegraph* reports. In fact, by January 1, 1943, according to a contemporaneous SS report, 2.5 million Jews had been killed.

But Joe said the Jews had brought it on themselves. "If the Jews themselves would pay less attention to advertising their racial problem, and more attention to solving it, the whole thing would recede into its proper perspective," he said during the interview. "It's entirely out of focus now, and that is chiefly their fault." In fact, some Jews took advantage of their persecution. "If a Jew enters public life, he becomes a target for public criticism," Joe said. "That's the normal, American way. Too often, if he is criticized, he ascribes it to anti-Semitism, when the bald fact is that the person is being criticized and not the race. It is no secret that I have not a high regard for a number of Jews in high places, but that doesn't mean that I condemn all Jews because of my personal feelings for some."

Despite the fact that the interview clearly established Joe's anti-Semitism, the *Boston Globe* never published the story. A *Globe* editor, saying that Kennedy "protesteth his anti-Semitism too much," failed to see the news value in that. Why Spivak did not write a piece is not known.

If the *Globe* did not appreciate the significance of the interview, Jack did. Joe cooperated with Dinneen when he wrote *The Kennedy Family*, and Dinneen included three paragraphs from the interview in the manuscript. As a courtesy, Dinneen gave Jack the galley proofs one night in 1959. A week or two later, Jack called Dinneen.

"You've got to take out those paragraphs about my father's

anti-Semitism," he said. Dinneen said the plates for the book had already been cast, and the book was ready to roll off the press. "I don't give a damn," Dinneen quoted Jack as saying. "I want those paragraphs out of there."

Dinneen argued but finally capitulated. Little, Brown and Company deducted half the cost of the changes from Dinneen's royalties. Three years later, Joe's remarks appeared for the first time in Richard J. Whalen's *The Founding Father*.

♦ ♦ ♦

When he read a column in the *New York Journal-American* by Igor Cassini, a Hearst columnist who used the pen name Cholly Knickerbocker, Joe was livid. Cassini, the brother of fashion designer Oleg Cassini, had reported that Joe's daughter Kathleen was about to marry a Protestant and was considering changing her religion. In a rage, Joe immediately called Hearst to demand that he fire the influential columnist.

As it turned out, the column was half correct. As predicted, on May 6, 1944, Kathleen, twenty-four, married William John Robert Cavendish, the Marquess of Hartington. Known as Billy, he was the heir of the Duke of Devonshire, one of the richest members of the British landed aristocracy. But while Billy was Protestant, Kick did not change her religion. Nonetheless, the impending marriage traumatized Rose. Joe tried to get some sort of dispensation for the union of a Catholic and Protestant from Cardinal Spellman. Spellman's efforts failed, but the cardinal told Joe not to worry about it.

"Kick marrying outside the church was very devastating for Rose especially," Mary Lou McCarthy said. "Joe even tried to work through the Vatican. In those days you had to promise the children would be raised Catholic. Joe said she would bring the children to church, but they would not be raised Catholic. It was bargaining with the Holy See."

Just before the wedding, Rose checked herself into New England Baptist Hospital. As she left the hospital, the press asked for her opinion of the marriage. She said she was "physically unfit" to comment. Neither she nor Joe attended the wedding.

◆ ◆ ◆

After Joe demanded that Hearst fire Cassini, the publisher summoned Cassini to his estate in San Simeon near San Francisco. Every night for a week, Cassini had dinner with Hearst and Hearst's mistress, Marion Davies. Russian by birth, Cassini castigated rich people in Hollywood and New York who were pro-Stalin. Hearst approved of Cassini's position. Moreover, Cassini, coiner of the term "jet set," was one of the most powerful and widely read columnists of his day. Not only did Hearst not fire Cassini, he wound up giving Cassini a raise.

A few months later, Joe saw Cassini while he was putting at Seminole Golf Course in Palm Beach. "He said, 'Are you Igor Cassini?'" Cassini recalled. "I said yes. He said, 'I'm Joe Kennedy.' He said, 'I'd like to meet you.' I said, 'I'm glad, because I didn't think you liked me.' He said, 'No, you're doing a good job.' He said, 'Why don't we have lunch sometime?' If he couldn't beat you, he became your friend," Cassini said.

Cassini associated that trait with being a good politician. But it was also characteristic of a bully. The few people who had the courage to face Joe down found that he quickly caved.

Besides playing golf—Joe had a 14 handicap—Joe and Cassini had lunch or dinner together once or twice a week, usually at Le Pavillon in New York. Le Pavillon was up to Joe's exacting standards. *Guide Michelin*'s Pierre Lamalle judged it to be equal to any of Paris' five best restaurants. It was the shrine of *haute cuisine* in the United States.

According to Joe's confidant Frank Morrissey, with Joe's financial help, Henri Soulé opened the restaurant in October

1941 on East 55th Street. He had previously managed a French restaurant at the 1939 World's Fair in New York.

Soulé was normally "aloof as a cardinal," as Craig Claiborne put it, but he called Joe "Excellence." He always gave Joe Table 7 in an area of seven tables to the right as one walked in. Joe continued to frequent the restaurant when it moved to the Ritz Tower Hotel at 111 East 57th Street.

Cassini was happy to get tips from Joe. In turn, being with Cassini opened up new opportunities for Joe. Dashing and powerful, Cassini was always surrounded by beautiful women. "He was always interested in going with lovely women," Cassini said. "I seldom brought somebody for him," he said. Once at a restaurant, while Igor was in the men's room, Joe made a pass at his date, Hjordis Tersmeden, a beautiful Swedish model who would later marry David Niven.

"When we left [the restaurant], she said he offered to move her to a beautiful apartment if she had any trouble with me ever. He came on strong," Cassini said.

Igor had no illusions about Joe. "The Kennedys would sacrifice anyone for their own power," he said. Cassini found Joe's relationship with Rose particularly curious. For photographers, they posed holding hands and smiling. Yet even when Joe and Rose were in the same city, they stayed in separate hotels.

"When he stayed in different hotels, it was so he could take a girl out if he wanted to," Cassini said. "Their marriage was a marriage of conversation. They would have children together by Catholic custom. That is how their children grew up. Jack, Bobby, and Ted were all philanderers. . . . The sons grabbed everything that was introduced to them," Cassini said. Joe "could do anything at all as long as appearances were maintained."

19

PAPPY'S EYES

At about 2 A.M. on Sunday, August 2, 1943, the Japanese destroyer *Amagiri* rammed *PT-109*, which Jack commanded, as it patrolled the dark waters of Blackett Strait west of New Georgia in the Solomon Islands. The torpedo boat was sliced in half.

After the fire of burning gasoline died out, Jack and five crew members crawled aboard a piece of the hull. In the darkness, Jack called out, and five of seven missing crew members shouted back. But two others were gone.

Patrick H. McMahon, the boat's engineer, cried out that he was badly burned. Jack jumped into the sea after him. Because of the currents, it took an hour for Jack to rescue him. While other crew members rescued some of the other men, Jack swam to two others in the water. After three hours, the eleven survivors made it back to the rest of the broken hull of *PT-109*.

As the sun came up, it became apparent that the broken

hull was taking on water. The survivors had little choice but to make their way to land. The Japanese occupied many of the nearby islands, so the crew members picked an island four miles away that they believed to be safe. Dressed only in underwear, Jack towed McMahon, who could neither swim nor tread water. Once they arrived on the island, Jack decided to try to signal passing boats. Carrying a lantern, he swam to a small island half a mile to the southeast. A strong current drove him back, and he tried again. But his trip was unsuccessful, and he was exhausted.

With Jack believed dead, the Navy Department sent a telegram to Joe reporting Jack as missing in action. He later told the *Boston Post* he did not tell Rose because he still believed his son was alive.

By August 4, the survivors' supply of meat and coconut milk was almost gone. Jack decided they must swim for another island. There, they found some natives who helped them meet up with American PT boats on August 7.

When Joe got word his son was not missing and had been involved in heroics, he seized on Jack's bravery to market it, just as Joe used his own Irish heritage to win sympathy and gain attention. The war had seen tens of thousands of American heroes. What would make Jack different was that his father had the savvy, drive, and connections to use his actions during the war for political advantage.

While there were lingering questions about why Jack's patrol boat was in a position to be torpedoed in the first place, "I talked to everyone in his crew, and those men would do anything for Kennedy," said Robert Donovan, who wrote a book on the subject. "There is no question that Kennedy was brave and that he saved [a] crewman's life."

Jack's friend Red Fay recalled that Joe decided that Jack should get a medal. "He was going for the Congressional Medal of Honor and had the Navy Cross in mind as a fallback position," he said. Jack wound up receiving the Navy and Marine Corps Medal.

On June 17, 1944, *The New Yorker* published a detailed

account of Jack's heroics by John Hersey, an author who was married to Frances A. Cannon, a former girlfriend of Jack's. Arthur Krock, who had just spent a week at Joe's Palm Beach home, introduced Joe to Paul Palmer, a *Reader's Digest* editor. Joe convinced Palmer to condense Hersey's article, "Survival," for the August 1944 issue of the magazine. In this way, Jack gained national attention.

Later, during Jack's first run for Congress, Joe would distribute reprints of the *Reader's Digest* article. "It was the ambassador who got the reprints of the *Reader's Digest*. He got around 150,000 copies printed," Joe's confidant Frank Morrissey said.

After Jack returned from the South Pacific, he was hospitalized at Chelsea Naval Hospital with back injuries. When Joe visited Jack at the hospital, Jack told him that his car, which Jack had been driving, had been stolen. "The ambassador was about to turn the state upside down, but Jack persuaded him to let nature take its course," said Joe Kane, Joe's nephew and political adviser. Jack calmed him down, saying, "When whoever took it learns that it belongs to a vet, he'll return it." When Joe left the room, Jack confided to Kane that he had sneaked out of the hospital the night before with a nurse and had left the keys in the car while they were out together. When they returned and looked for the car, it was gone.

Kane asked Jack if he wanted to enter politics. "No, that's Joe's department," he said, referring to his brother Joe Jr. "I want to go into the news business."

But on August 12, 1944, Joe Jr. was killed in a PB-24 Liberator, a new plane that was designed to be loaded with high explosives and directed to its target remotely after the pilot and co-pilot had bailed out. Before Joe flew the mission, Lieutenant Earl Olsen, an electronics officer, warned him that the remotely controlled electronic device that was to detonate the explosives on the plane was faulty. Because of that, almost anything—radio static, a jamming device, or excessive turbulence—could trigger an explosion before the pilot and co-pilot bailed out. Olsen urged Joe to abort the mission. Joe ignored the warning and flew anyway.

The plane exploded at 6:20 P.M. over England. Military investigators later determined that Olsen had been right; the device was faulty. In ignoring Olsen's warning, Joe Jr. had endangered not only himself but his co-pilot, Lieutenant Wilford J. Willy, who also died on the mission.

Two navy officers delivered the somber news to Joe and Rose at Hyannis Port.

"I was there when they showed up to tell him that his son had been killed," Rose's nephew Joe Gargan said. "It was after lunch. They came to the door and asked to see Mr. Kennedy. He said to come up to his room. He came down to the sun room and told the children. Rose was there, and he told her, of course. He probably told her upstairs. They were both distressed, but Jack said, 'Joe would not want us to stay around here crying, so let's go sailing.' The children went sailing."

Joe went to his bedroom and locked the door. For weeks, Rose consoled herself by saying the rosary.

Krock was convinced that the reason Joe Jr. had volunteered for such a dangerous mission was to compensate for his father's reputation as a coward. "Harry Hopkins came back from London and told Roosevelt that the reason that Joe Kennedy had taken a house in Ascot where he slept was because he was afraid," Krock said. ". . . Roosevelt told many people that Kennedy was yellow. And Joe, when he volunteered on this final mission, which was beyond his duty, [wanted to prove] that the Kennedys were not yellow, and that's what killed the boy. And his father realized it. He never admitted it, but he realized it."

While Krock's theory has a certain logic to it, based on Joe Jr.'s character, it is much more likely that he ignored the warnings out of recklessness, stupidity, or both. Like most of the rest of the family, Joe Jr. could be foolhardy. In contrast to Jack, he was not very bright.

Joe "never thought Jack would do anything," Jack's friend Chuck Spalding said. "He didn't realize that by all odds, Jack was the most gifted. He thought Joe Jr. was."

"Joe's death has shocked me beyond belief," his father wrote to James Forrestal, then the secretary of the navy. "All of my children are equally dear to me, but there is something about the first born that sets him a little apart—he is always a bit of a miracle and never quite cut off from his mother's heart. He represents our youth, its joys, and problems."

Then on September 10, 1944, a second tragedy struck. Kathleen's husband, Lord Hartington, a captain in Britain's Coldstream Guards, was killed in action in Belgium, just four months after marrying Kathleen.

Joe had reconciled himself to the marriage, and now it was over. The more he'd heard about Hartington, Joe said, the more he realized "what a fine boy he was." Because of the religion problem, they "braved a great deal to have one another," he said. Joe felt their marriage was a "real love match."

Joe saw the losses as a vindication of his appeasement position. "For a fellow who didn't want this war to touch your country or mine, I have had a rather bad dose," Joe wrote to his friend Max Beaverbrook. "Joe dead, Billy Hartington dead, my son Jack in the Naval Hospital. I have had brought home to me very personally what I saw for all the mothers and fathers of the world."

Perhaps to console himself, Joe sent word to Roosevelt, who was running with Harry S. Truman for an unprecedented fourth term, that he would like to see him. He then told the press that Roosevelt had sent for him. After their meeting on October 26, Roosevelt remarked that he had "a bad taste" in his mouth.

Joe told Krock afterward that he told the president he had "great affection" for him, but men like Harry Hopkins had surrounded him with "Jews and Communists and alienated Catholics."

To Truman, Joe unleashed an even more bitter tirade. Truman and Joe knew each other from Washington. Joe had invited Truman, then a senator, to Marwood. While campaigning in Massachusetts, Truman asked Joe to meet with him at the Ritz-Carlton Hotel in Boston. In the candidate's suite, Joe said to Truman, "Harry, what are you doing campaigning for that crippled son of a bitch who killed my son?" Truman later said he kept quiet as long as he could. He then told Joe, "If you say another word about Roosevelt, I'll throw you out that window."

Robert Hannegan, the Democratic national chairman, took Truman aside and reminded him how important Joe's money was. "I'm going to get $10,000 out of that old son of a bitch for the Democratic Party," he said. Hannegan extracted from Joe at least half that amount.

◆ ◆ ◆

"He had lived through the Boston Brahmins, and it was sheer hypocrisy," Tommy Corcoran said of Joe. "He had lived through European aristocracy, and it was sheer hypocrisy. Power is the only end, and if you don't like the code of the game, what is it then?" Having tried and failed, Joe knew he could never become president, but his sons could. He quenched his thirst for power through them.

In Palm Beach during Christmas of 1944, Joe gave Jack his orders: He was to take Joe Jr.'s place and enter politics. More than a decade later, for an International News Service series in May 1957, Jack told reporter Bob Considine: "It was like being drafted. My father wanted his eldest son in politics. 'Wanted' isn't the right word. He *demanded* it. You know my father. . . ."

"I got Jack into politics. I was the one," Joe told *McCall's* in a burst of genuine candor for its August 1957 issue. "I told him Joe Jr. was deceased and that it was therefore his responsibility to run for Congress. He didn't want to. He felt he didn't have the ability, and he still feels that way. But I told him he had to."

In making the statement, Joe was going against his own advice: Always, he told Jack, refer to his career as "public service." A friend recalled of Jack, "He wouldn't say 'politics' to save his life."

To Krock, it was clear that Joe had ordained that Jack fill the shoes of his dead brother. "It was almost a physical event: 'Now it's your turn,'" Krock said.

Later, when Jack ran for the presidency, Joe successfully covered up his role in orchestrating Jack's political career. He told columnist Marguerite Higgins then that it was "nonsense" to suggest that he urged Jack to run for president. But Jack's friend Red Fay recalled Jack's having said that Christmas, "I can feel Pappy's eyes on the back of my neck."

Nor was the ultimate goal ever in doubt. Just six months after Joe commanded Jack to enter politics, "We were at Hyannis Port for the weekend," recalled James A. Reed, a friend of Jack's from the war. "Mr. Krock was there, Red Fay, Jack, Honey Fitz, and others. It was July 1945. We were having a drink. Mr. Kennedy never drank much. But we were having a drink before dinner. Honey Fitz proposed a toast to Jack, to the future president of the U.S. He looked right at Jack."

Fitzgerald never saw his grandson enter the White House. He died on October 2, 1950, at the age of eighty-seven of coronary thrombosis. Rose was in Paris and did not attend the funeral. Perhaps because he resented Joe and knew Rose did not need the money, Honey Fitz cut Rose out of his will, saying he had purposely omitted her "for reasons best known to myself." Similarly, when his wife, Mary Fitzgerald, died in 1964, she left money for her two sons, a daughter-in-law, and two granddaughters but none to Rose. Paralleling her husband's, the will stated, "I intentionally omit to make provision for any other children or relatives of mine for reasons best known to myself."

◆ ◆ ◆

Fortuitously, Jack began his run for Congress just as World War II ended. On May 7, 1945, Germany surrendered unconditionally. A month before that, Roosevelt had died of a cerebral hemorrhage while on vacation in Warm Springs, Georgia. Later that evening, Harry S. Truman, the vice president, was sworn in as president. Four months later, on August 6, Truman ordered the United States to drop the first atomic bomb on Hiroshima, killing 78,000 Japanese and nearly destroying the city.

Joe saw this as senseless injustice. He and Henry Luce called on Cardinal Spellman to ask him to persuade Truman to give the Japanese five or six days to surrender. But before Spellman reacted, Truman, on August 9, 1945, ordered a second atomic bomb dropped, this time on Nagasaki, killing 40,000 Japanese. On August 14, Truman announced that Japan had surrendered unconditionally.

Deliriously relieved that the war was over, Americans were ready to embrace any returning war hero. The man who had been so identified with appeasing Hitler now told Jack that his wartime record would be the centerpiece of his campaign. On April 15, 1946, Joe told the Seaman's Club in Boston that veterans should assist each other in their return to civilian life. "The whole theme was the veterans are coming home, and they're ready to take over the country," Kane Simonian said. What was Joe running for? Simonian asked his friend Joe Kane. Kane had asked Joe the same question, and Joe had responded, "I have a youth ready."

To highlight Jack's war record, Joe arranged for him to become commander of a new Joseph P. Kennedy Jr. Veterans of Foreign Wars post, based at Boston's Parker House Hotel. Ironically, Jack might never have had the opportunity to see active duty if he had not been dating a Nazi sympathizer and had not been ordered by his father to leave town. Nor did Joe ever give up his view that the war was pointless. "I still can't see what the war has accomplished for us all," he wrote to Max Beaverbrook in 1946.

Two years later, Joe recalled how strongly he had opposed

"getting in the war" and his predictions about "what I thought it would do to civilization." In retrospect, he said, he had been absolutely right. Anyone "who used for an excuse, as one of our friends did, that we were fighting for an ideal has certainly demonstrated that it is complete poppy-cock," he said. The fighting had accomplished nothing, and socialism had become a threat, a "way station on the road to dire destruction." Joe was sympathetic to revisionist historians like Charles A. Beard, who said America had been "tricked" into belligerency.

As for his benefactor Roosevelt, for whom he had professed "great affection," his death was "a great thing for the country," Joe told his daughter Kathleen. Roosevelt had stirred up such hatred that "no matter whether he proposed anything good or bad, half the country would be against it."

Maurice J. Tobin, the Massachusetts governor, wanted Jack to run with him for lieutenant governor, but Joe insisted he run for Congress. "My judgment to the ambassador was he [Tobin] couldn't be reelected, and I thought we could win the Congress seat," Frank Morrissey, Joe's confidant, said.

Joe Kane, in a March 7, 1946, letter, gave Joe similar advice. Kane would be called a political consultant today. He was a colorful character with white hair, a ruddy complexion, a rather large nose, and false teeth that got in the way when he tried to talk as fast as he thought. He had fashioned a sort of headquarters for himself out of Walton's restaurant, a cafeteria near City Hall in downtown Boston. It was Kane who came up with the winning slogan for the campaign: "The new generation offers a leader."

"Give the kid a break!" Kane said in his letter to Joe. Not only might Tobin be "licked," but Jack's lack of a "public record" would make him "vulnerable" to "Republican Party and press attacks if he ran for lieutenant governor." On the other hand, if he sought the congressional seat in a district where the Republicans and press could not hurt him, he only would have to "overcome opposition of the opponents." As a congressman, Kane said, Jack would be in "demand as a public speaker," while as lieutenant governor, he would merely be a "silenced political priest."

In reply to Kane, Joe said he would still like to see Jack as lieutenant governor, but he agreed with Kane that Jack would have an "easier chance" in Congress. Therefore, he said, "I am inclining more toward that idea."

As it turned out, the advice Joe received was right: Tobin lost.

Joe and his advisers decided that the eleventh congressional district, with its concentration of Irish Catholic voters, would be the perfect launching pad. The district included East Boston, the North and West End, Charlestown, and part of Somerville. There was one problem: James Michael Curley, the former mayor of Boston and governor of Massachusetts, occupied the seat. But Curley, the prototype for Edwin O'Connor's fictitious Frank Skeffington in *The Last Hurrah*, was in danger of being indicted for mail fraud. Joe decided that what the man needed most was some money.

"Curley knew that he was in trouble with the feds over the mail fraud rap," recalled Joe Kane. "The ambassador paid him to get out of his congressional seat. . . . Curley figured that he might need the money." Joe paid Curley $12,000 through his bag man Joe Timilty. He promised additional campaign help if Curley chose to run again for mayor of Boston in the 1946 election, which Curley did. After being elected, Curley was sent to prison for mail fraud. He continued to serve from prison.

To Joe, this was standard operating procedure, recalled Kane, who claimed credit for spotting the potential opening. ". . . Everything [he] got," Kane said, "he bought and paid for. And politics is like war. It takes three things to win. The first is money and the second is money and the third is money."

On April 25, 1946, Jack announced his candidacy for the Democratic nomination to Congress. The next month, Joe founded the Joseph P. Kennedy Jr. Foundation. The timing was not coincidence. Soon, the foundation began furiously pumping money into Catholic institutions in Jack's adopted district. "The gifts from the foundation were critically important," said Joseph Casey, a Massachusetts congressman at the time. There were "gifts to hospitals in the Italian section [of Cambridge], to Catholic churches that were Italian, things of that sort. Perfectly legitimate, fine, laudatory gifts. However, they were also political currency."

In August 1945, Joe had accepted Tobin's invitation to head a commission to study the state's economic problems. Like the foundation, the move was calculated to win favorable publicity for the Kennedy family. Soon, the commission issued a report calling for establishment of a Massachusetts Department of Commerce to reverse a downward trend in state industrial activity.

Joe's main job now became running his son's campaign. To say that he was the de facto campaign manager would be to diminish his role. In effect, he *was* the candidate, devising campaign strategy and making every financial and policy decision. Joe approved campaign workers, doled out the money, and met with Jack at the Ritz-Carlton at the end of each day of campaigning to go over the next day's schedule. Jack was merely the vehicle for the campaign, the smiling, charismatic presence who devoted himself to climbing the stairs of three-deckers in Boston's Charlestown section to meet the voters. Jack did not even have a permanent address: His residence in Boston was Room 308 of the Bellevue Hotel next to the State House. To James Landis, who resigned as dean of Harvard Law School to work on the campaign for Joe, it seemed that Jack never really had wanted to run, but once he began campaigning, he liked it.

To conceal his own role and the extent of Jack's financing, Joe paid for everything clandestinely and in cash. David Powers, who ran Jack's Charlestown headquarters, recalled how Eddie Moore, Joe's aide, would hand over the rent to him.

"It was the strangest experience," Powers said. "I would meet Moore at the campaign's central headquarters at 18 Tremont Street, and he would then lead me into the men's room, where, putting a dime into the slot, he would take me into a closed toilet stall. Then, with no one able to watch us, he would hand me the cash, saying, 'You can never be too careful in politics about handing over money.' "

"Joe's people in New York controlled the finances," said William P. Sutton, who worked for Jack. "It was his money, and most everything had to be approved by him first before it could be carried out."

Joe arranged to have the Maine and New Hampshire Theatres Company, which he still owned, pay Jack a salary. Joe could deduct it as a business expense. The theater company in Boston sent the check to Paul Murphy in Joe's New York office. Murphy, in turn, deposited the check in Jack's account. In addition, two of Joe's employees at the theater company kept track of all expenses. If Jack needed a rental car, he simply charged it to Joe's theater company.

"I never thought too much of the boys," said William J. Mulcahy, who booked movies at the theater company. "They didn't seem to have any sense of responsibility whatsoever. They would rent a car and forget about it, and we would have to go and dig it out."

To insure that Jack won the primary campaign, Joe paid Joseph Russo, a janitor, to enter the race. This split the votes cast for Joe Russo, a legitimate politician who was already on the ballot, confusing voters. Russo the janitor recalled that Joe's friend Joseph Timilty and another man visited him one day and asked him to run. In return, Russo said, "They gave me favors. Whatever I wanted. I could of gone in the housing project if I wanted. If I wanted an apartment, I could of got the favor. You know?" In fact, he said, he wound up getting very little—occasional payments of $50 in cash.

Even the aunt of the real candidate voted for the janitor, recalled Joseph A. Russo, the real candidate's son. "They didn't leave anything unturned," he said. "My dad said others were put in in other areas to break up the Irish vote or some other vote. They played for keeps."

Jack won the Democratic primary for Congress on June

18, 1946, receiving 22,183 votes, or 40.5 percent of the total cast. That compared with 11,341 for Michael Neville and 5,661 votes and 799 votes, respectively, for the two Joseph Russos. The next month, Joe sold Somerset Importers Inc., freeing $8 million to help Jack in his campaign and insuring that his liquor holdings would not become an issue.

To promote Jack, Joe chose John C. Dowd, whose advertising company he used for Somerset Importers' liquor accounts. Dowd was a trim, dapper Irishman with a pencil mustache. He was impressed by Joe's decisiveness. Once he came to a decision, Joe acted quickly, surgically going to the heart of the matter, Dowd said. Paraphrasing a typical Kennedy command, Dowd said, "Do it quickly, and do it with every god-damned comma in place."

Dowd blanketed the state with billboard advertisements and wrote press releases and speeches. In general, Jack stressed his military record, avoiding making any specific promises. John T. Galvin, who ran public relations at Dowd's agency, recalled one campaign meeting at the Ritz with Joe and Mark Dalton, the titular campaign manager. "Joe said, 'Jack, I think you should attack the Jews,' " Galvin said. "He and Morton Downey referred to them as 'Canadian geese.' He had just been in Hollywood and had had a fight with them. It was a bitter battle. . . . Mark got up and walked out. I thought he was going to the men's room. But he didn't come back."

In contrast to Joe's anti-Semitism, Jack told guests at an awards ceremony in Boston's Faneuil Hall of an episode he had observed in the South Pacific. A Japanese prisoner pulled a hidden gun and shot a Jewish chaplain to death, just as the chaplain was giving the prisoner a glass of water.

"Every time an American voices expressions of anti-Semitism," Jack said on February 13, 1944, "he is fighting for our enemies."

As he had with the rent for Jack's campaign offices, Joe paid cash for Jack's advertising. "The money for advertising might have come from Eddie Moore in the Blue Hills at midnight in cash to David Powers," Galvin said. "It was handled so very few people knew. . . . There was a campaign law that limited campaign contributions. It didn't affect us very much."

Joe trusted no one—not even Jack. He had Morrissey report to him on his activities, and one of Joe's employees kept a log for Joe listing everyone who visited Jack at his campaign headquarters.

Peter J. Cloherty, a campaign aide, recalled that Joe would come into town and send for people individually to get reports from them at the Ritz. "He compared the stories of each one about the progress of the campaign," Cloherty said. "He was strictly business. He'd ask you how you thought the campaign was going and if you had any suggestions. . . . And then you were dismissed, that's all."

At night, Joe held court at Locke Ober, a venerable Boston restaurant, where Chico, the maître d', always gave him a table in a private dining room upstairs. Joe usually ordered fish chowder, oysters, and lobster.

Jack's friend Red Fay recalled walking down the street with Jack on Beacon Hill when an old friend of Joe's came up to him and gave him some money for the campaign. That night, Jack removed the money from his pocket. It was $1,000 in $100 bills. Yet Fay recalled how cheap Jack could be. When Fay was driving a construction truck, he lent Jack $20. At the time, the amount "meant a lot of money to me," he said. Jack did not pay him back, and Fay was "really irritated" with him. Later, Fay lost a bet with him and sent the money with a note: "See how fast you get it from me?"

Joe called in his chits with Hearst, who had a reporter from his *Boston American* check in at Jack's headquarters every day. No other candidate got such special attention. Joe also got Hearst to have his paper ignore Jack's opponent Michael Neville, the mayor of Cambridge, and the paper would not accept his advertising.

Joe also renewed his friendship with Henry Luce. Luce had been put off by what he called Joe's "outrageous" conduct as ambassador. The publisher had always been amused by Joe's approach. He considered him profane and inarticulate. He was given to "sweeping pessimism," always referring to things as "going to hell in a handbasket" as he swept up stocks or buildings at bargain prices. Yet Luce said Joe never lost sight of his main goal—making money and acquiring power. He considered him a shrewd capitalist who jumped in and out of business without taking operating responsibility.

Joe knew what money was for, and how to enjoy it, Luce thought. "You might say that Joe was in the movie business for a while, but I'm not sure whether he was in business or whether he saw this as a way of having fun and making pictures for Gloria Swanson and some of his other girl-friends," Luce said. "I don't know why I'm so dumb that I just sit here trying to run a business," Luce told Richard J. Whalen in a not-for-attribution interview. "Joe bought all those houses. He made all those movies. He played golf and what not. He understood about buying positions in government—London, for example. Most businessmen are pretty stupid about that. It doesn't cost very much to buy those jobs."

Moreover, Joe knew how to use money to push his children along, just as fast as they could be pushed, Luce said. "What was his secret with his children?" Luce mused. "That's the great mystery. How did he get them all set on the political line? . . . He told me once that he didn't think Jack would get very far, and he said he wasn't very bright. But he never believed in starting the kids at the bottom. If he had been in business, he never would have started them at the bottom."

Sure enough, as Jack began campaigning, Joe called Luce. "Harry, things are going to hell in a handbasket. . . . Look at the condition of the world today. It's terrible," Joe said, referring to the Soviet menace. "So I got hold of Roy Larsen [who would succeed Luce as president of Time Inc.], and one or two others, and we lunched with Joe at the Waldorf to talk about the state of the nation," Luce said. As always, such meetings provided Joe with the opportunity to promote Jack.

As campaign manager, Joe had enlisted Mark Dalton, a tall, polished Irishman with a brogue. It turned out Joe wanted Dalton, with his impeccable reputation for integrity, as a front man. Joe would call Dalton every three or four days and spend hours on the phone with him issuing a stream of instructions. Dalton thought this was the extent of Joe's involvement, until he noticed the old pols weren't against young Jack anymore.

"It turned out he had been talking to a great many people, and had been conducting an intensive behind-the-scenes operation," Dalton said. "The one thing about him was he was an administrative genius. There was no question he knew how to run a campaign. Every now and then I am called the campaign manager. But the essential manager of any campaign John Kennedy was in was Joseph P. Kennedy. He ran it. He was absolutely interested in every single detail of the campaign. He was on the phone wanting to know everything that was going on."

Joe spent $300,000 on Jack's first campaign, according to House Speaker Thomas P. "Tip" O'Neill, equivalent to $2.2 million today. O'Neill said the sum was six times what O'Neill himself spent in the same district during a tough race six years later. In O'Neill's view, Joe was the "real force" behind the Kennedys. He marveled that Joe "looked more like a Yankee than any other Irishman I've ever seen."

"I knew the money was coming from Joe's New York office," Dalton said. "John Kennedy never carried a cent with him. He would look to you to pay for a drink. There was never any doubt that Joe Kennedy was financing the campaign."

"Joe Kennedy was an ongoing factor in Massachusetts politics," O'Neill said. "Every time a Democrat ran for governor, he would go down to see Joe, who would always send him home with a briefcase full of cash. The word was that if Joe Kennedy liked you, he'd give you $50,000. If he really liked you, he'd give you $100,000."

On November 5, 1946, Jack was elected to Congress. He received 71.9 percent of the popular vote. Seven days later, he filed a report with the Massachusetts secretary of state certifying that no money had been collected for or spent on his campaign.

20

PHILANDERING

Now that Jack was in public office, he became even more attractive to young women, whom he shared with his father. An "almost incestuous atmosphere" pervaded the Kennedy household, according to Langdon Marvin, an aide to Jack who said he helped obtain women for him. "What I mean is that the Kennedy men passed their women around like community property, preyed off each other's dates, traded them like baseball cards."

Joe had never had any reservations about not hiding from his children his cheating on Rose. In fact, he shared his sexual proclivities with his sons. When Jack was going to Choate School, he told the headmaster, George St. John, that when he returned home from school, he found that his father had covered his bed at the Cape with sex magazines opened to display female anatomy. "I think it's Dad's idea of a joke," he commented.

If Jack sat next to a comely woman on an airplane, or

struck up a conversation with a stewardess, he would often bring her back to his hotel room if he could. "When he was finished with the girl, he usually gave her telephone number to his father or one of his brothers, and they did the same," Marvin said.

Susan Imhoff, one such flight attendant, recalled, "Because of his back, he preferred making love with the girl on top. He found it more stimulating to have the girl do all the work. I remember he didn't enjoy cuddling after making love, but he did like to talk, and he had a wonderful sense of humor— he loved to laugh."

"Jack had no respect for women, no respect at all," said Vic Francis, one of his Harvard friends. "He *needed* to make conquests for his own self-esteem—but he had no respect for women and would not put on any airs or pretensions for them."

Mark Dalton, Jack's campaign manager, was shocked by Jack's behavior. "The first thing he [Jack] did," another of Jack's aides recalled, was to get one of Dowd's staff members pregnant. The aide said he went into Jack's office one day and found him "humping this girl on one of the desks in his office. I said, 'Sorry,' and left. Later, the girl told my wife she was missing her period, then learned she was expecting. I told Jack." Jack's reaction was, "Oh, shit!" the aide said. "He said he didn't give a damn about the girl—it was just the inconvenience that bothered him. . . . In that sense, he was a pretty selfish guy."

"A couple of incidents occurred in my presence that showed he had these relationships," Dalton said. "I looked upon them as a leading Irish Catholic family in the country. If you had a bad thought, you were going to hell. That was why it was such a shock to me about John Kennedy and Joe Kennedy. Here was the pride of Irish Catholicism."

"Whenever he was at home," Lem Billings, Jack's friend, said, "there was always a girl around. Usually, it was a different girl each time. Almost without exception, every girl he showed any interest in became very fond of him. I think the reason for this was that he was not only attractive but also had tremendous interest in girls. They really liked him, and he was very, very successful. This was important to him, because he wanted to be successful in this area. He really enjoyed girls."

Yet Jack was a boy-man, still under the control of his father. Through a mutual friend in Georgetown, Jack met Mary Pitcairn, whom he invited to the movies in Washington and Hyannis. Pitcairn was amazed that Joe paid for the movies as if Jack were ten years old. "I can remember going up to Hyannis Port, and Mr. Kennedy would ask me if Jack owed me much money," Pitcairn said. "And I said, 'Yes, $10.' That was a lot of money in those days. And Mr. Kennedy would reach in his pocket and pay me."

One of Jack's girlfriends, Kay Stammers, a British tennis star who visited Jack at Hyannis Port, said she was amazed at how much control Joe had over Jack. "I mean, he was the boss," she said. "I remember one weekend at Hyannis Port we drank enormous quantities of Coke. I remember being out in the kitchen with Jack and seeing these cases of empty Coke bottles. Jack said, 'My God, my father is going to have a stroke.'"

Joe took Pitcairn to dinner at the Carlton Hotel in Washington and told her about Gloria Swanson. "I'll never forget it," Pitcairn said. "He told me how wonderful she was, and how he kept in touch with her. She was at the Plaza Hotel. He said, 'I'm going to call her up and make a date for tomorrow night . . . ' which he did."

Joe kept asking her personal questions, and she realized he had mentioned Swanson to show her that he was a successful swordsman.

"He did something that I heard he did to everyone," she said. "After dinner he would take you home and kiss you good night as though he were a young so-and-so. One night I was visiting Eunice, and he came into my bedroom to kiss me goodnight! I was in my nightgown ready for bed. Eunice was in her bedroom. We had an adjoining bath, and the doors were open. He said, 'I've come to say goodnight,' and [he] kissed me, really kissed me."

Pitcairn remembered thinking how embarrassing this was for Eunice, not to mention confusing for Jack. "He was a sensitive man, and I think it confused him, as to what kind of an object is a woman?" Pitcairn said. "To be treated as his father treated them. And his father's behavior that way was obvious. There was always a young, blonde, beautiful secretary around."

At parties, Joe would "lay hands" on women, said Larry Newman, a neighbor and friend. He "put his hands on their butts or would pat them on the ass as they walked by. He did it with married women, too."

Elizabeth "Cis" Drake, who was then a fiancée of Edward McLaughlin, a friend of Jack's who later became lieutenant governor of Massachusetts, recalled that Joe invited her to lunch at the Waldorf in New York. Joe asked her to meet him in his room, where he suggested they have room service. When the waiter arrived to take their order, Joe gave him two eggs with his name written on them in pen. He told the waiter to have the eggs boiled for two and a half minutes. When the eggs came back with his name still on them, he ate them along with seven pills.

"He asked me how much I thought Eddie would make when he returned to civilian life and started working," Drake recalled. "I said I didn't know, but that he hoped to be a lawyer. Mr. Kennedy said that he paid his butler more than Ed would ever make. He said I was wasting time with Ed. I was a nice looking girl, and I could do better than that."

Drake saw what was coming and got out of there as fast as she could, she said. She thought she would never hear from Joe again, but he called her soon after and asked her out for lunch. Foolishly, she said, she accepted twice more. "It was a challenge in a way," she said. "I thought I could handle this guy. Nothing was going to happen to me. But each time, he got rougher to fend off. The third time, I really had a rough time getting out of his apartment. I literally ran out. And then I'd see him down at the Cape, and he'd be perfectly charming."

Washington socialite Kay Halle was in a Washington restaurant when a waiter brought a note inviting her to join Jack and Bobby.

"When I joined them, the gist of the conversation from the boys was the fact that their father was going to be in Washington for a few days and needed female companionship," she said. "They wondered whom I would suggest, and they were absolutely serious."

In Hyannis Port, Joe would insist that Kathleen's friends sit next to him during movies in the basement, then proceeded to "pinch them during the feature," Kathleen's biographer learned. Joe outraged Kathleen's friend Charlotte McDonnell, whose sister Anne married Henry Ford II, by forcing her to join him in the bathroom to impress Will Hays, the United States film censor. She found Joe's behavior sick and said she would have "left home" if her father had played the same trick on her friends.

Rose was equally bizarre. Pitcairn recalled that Rose would come to the lunch table in Hyannis Port with scraps of paper pinned to her dress. On the scraps were questions to ask the children: "Who has taken your father's steamer trunk?" Even though Ethel Kennedy, who married Bobby in June 1950, lived a couple of hundred feet away, Rose would write notes to her as well, complaining that her children's bikes had been left outside.

"The only thing I remember Rose saying about her daughters' future was when she said to Kick, 'Katherine, come and arrange these flowers. It's very important when you are a hostess that you know how to arrange flowers,'" recalled Nancy Tenney Coleman, a childhood friend of the Kennedys.

"Joe ran the house in Hyannis Port just like the hostess would," said William Walton, who became friends with Jack in 1947. "He hired and fired the help. He seemed to plan the menus. He dominated the drinks. One thing he approved for all his children were daiquiris. Made the old-fashioned way, they are rather like a confection. One night, Jack came in and said, 'You don't have to have that stuff. Ghastly stuff.'"

Meanwhile, Rose maintained her puritanical stance. Much later, after Jack's assassination, Walton, an artist, recalled taking Rose around the Museum of Modern Art in New York. "By then, she had to have a wheelchair," he said. "It was a Cézanne show. When we came to the nudes, she looked away."

Rose never "saw things or acknowledged things she didn't want to," Pitcairn said. "I had the feeling that the children just totally ignored her. Daddy was it." In fact, Rose did not seem to want much interaction with the children. She was "always by herself," Pitcairn said. "You know that little house she had by the beach?" Pitcairn said to Joan and Clay Blair Jr., who wrote the groundbreaking book *The Search for JFK*. "She'd take her robe and her books down there. And when she went out to play golf, she'd go out by herself. She did everything by herself. I never saw her walking with one of the children on the beach. . . . She was sort of a non-person." Meanwhile, the children "were always quizzing you at meals. 'Which one of us is most popular?' 'Which one of us do you really think is the brightest?'"

This savage competitiveness was imposed by Joe, who even treated Jack in a competitive manner. Charles Spalding recalled that he and Jack were planning to go to the movies one night in Hyannis Port with Jack's date, Charlotte McDonnell. At the time, Jack looked somewhat gaunt because of the health problems that had plagued him since he was a child. Jack said, "Let's say good night to dad," Spalding recalled. "So we went up, and Mr. Kennedy was shaving. Jack opened the door and said, 'Dad, we're going to the movies, and we'll be quiet when we get home.' He turns to Charlotte and says, 'Why don't you get yourself a live one?'"

Not content with the young women around his children, Joe would pick up attractive females at the Stork Club, El Morocco, 21, and other watering holes of café society. He became friendly as well with Oleg Cassini, the designer, who always had beautiful fashion models at his table. As with Oleg's brother Igor, the two men "shared an intense appreciation of beautiful women," Oleg said. The two would dine at Le Pavillon or La Caravelle, opened by a disciple of Henri Soulé. Oleg would bring one or two stunning models along. The rest, as Cassini put it, was up to Joe.

"We met every Tuesday night at eight at La Caravelle," Oleg said. "I would usually bring some lady friends—top models or society girls." On some occasions, he said, Joe brought his own young women, who were "real beauties."

If Cassini planned to bring an extra girl for him, Joe wanted to know in advance who she was. He would then check the girl out. At dinner, Joe would let drop the name of the town where the girl grew up or the school she had attended. Without exception, the young women were flattered that he had put so much effort into meeting them.

"His manner was always very direct, very forceful, an outpouring of career advice and mild flirtation that was at once rather blunt and totally disarming," Cassini recalled. He would tell the young women they were not going to be models all their lives, and they should plan for their futures. They needed to make friends in the right places, people who could help them along. Then Joe would mention his ownership of the Merchandise Mart. He would claim that he had boosted the careers of many women through his connections in the fashion world.

"Girls were an ego trip that were necessary for a man with an enormous ego," Cassini said. "They were decorations and they continued the myth of power. The sexual part was secondary. He knew he could get anybody. The advantage was in getting a special girl."

One day, Cassini brought along Grace Kelly, whom he hoped to marry. Kelly, a Catholic, had misgivings, and Oleg, who was Russian Orthodox, asked Joe to persuade his co-religionist that religion should not be an obstacle. Instead, Cassini looked on in amazement as Joe said at lunch at La

Caravelle, "You know, Grace, I know this donkey. He's a pretty good buy, but you'd be making a terrible mistake to marry him."

Cassini tried to get Joe to shut up, but he persisted. Then Cassini noticed that Joe was stroking Grace's hand, trying to make a date with her. It was a replay of what Joe had done earlier with Igor and his date, Hjordis Tersmeden.

"We have to discuss this thing, you and I," Joe told Kelly. "You can count on me. I am at your disposal."

"There was no doubt he was interested in her," Cassini said later. "He said, 'I want to talk to you, we have to get together. . . . ' I said, 'What are you doing?' He said, 'I know what I'm doing.'"

It was telling that Cassini continued their friendship even after Joe tried to take away his love, who went on to marry Prince Rainier III of Monaco in 1956. "I thought his toughness and lack of remorse were kind of fun. I would not have found it so much fun if I had not had some control," Cassini said. Indeed, over dinner with two knockout young fashion models, Joe told Cassini, "I'm like Bobby. I'm a hater, not like Jack, who forgives all his enemies and courts them." Bobby, as Arthur Krock put it, was "cruel and ungrateful and driving." It was almost as if Joe believed, as the American epigrammist Minna Antrim said, "To be loved is to be fortunate, but to be hated is to achieve distinction."

Joe told Cassini that the way to make money was to make people think you have money, a variation on the maxim, "You have to think rich to become rich." Joe told Cassini that at one point Wall Street thought he was about to go under. "So I bought myself a new Rolls-Royce and had my chauffeur drive me around the financial district at all hours. People judge you by things of that kind."

Always, there was the wistful reminder of the loss of his first son, Joe Jr. "He was the best of the lot," Joe told Cassini. "He could have been president."

Later, when Jack entered the White House, Jackie, with her wide eyes, chestnut mane, and whispery voice, asked

Rose greets Joe
in New York in
December 1939 after
he arrives from Portugal.
(John F. Kennedy Library)

Joe bids farewell to
Winston Churchill as he
leaves London in October
1940. (AP/Wide World)

Joe's Hyannis Port home was his primary residence. (AP/Wide World)

Joe's Palm Beach home was his winter residence. (AP/Wide World)

Joe holds forth at his Palm Beach home with, from left, columnists Damon Runyon and Walter Winchell and radio commentator Ted Husing. (AP/Wide World)

Dr. James W. Watts, who performed a lobotomy on Rosemary Kennedy at Joe's request, said she had a mental illness and was not mentally retarded.

Joe had an aide pay Joseph Russo, a Boston janitor, to declare himself a candidate in Jack's first primary election, splitting the vote for another Joseph Russo. (Courtesy of Joseph LoPiccolo)

In 1953, Janet Des Rosiers, Joe's secretary and mistress for nine years, right, accompanies Joe and Rose to Hialeah racetrack, in which Joe owned an interest. (Courtesy of Janet Des Rosiers)

Janet Des Rosiers accompanied Joe to Èze-sur-Mer in southern France in 1954. Here the two had lunch with Gloria Swanson. (Courtesy of Janet Des Rosiers)

When Rose was away, Janet Des Rosiers, shown here posing outside Joe's Hyannis Port home in 1955, moved in. (Courtesy of Janet Des Rosiers)

Before going to a gala in Monte Carlo, Joe posed with Janet Des Rosiers in 1952 with, from left, former Boston police commissioner Joseph F. Timilty, Joe's lawyer Bartholemew A. Brickley, Rose and Joe's friend Arthur Houghton. (Courtesy of Janet Des Rosiers)

Janet Des Rosiers and Joe often had sex on Joe's yacht, the *Marlin*. (Courtesy of Janet Des Rosiers)

In 1952, Joe gave John Fox, publisher of the *Boston Post*, a $500,000 interest-free loan in return for his front-page endorsement of Jack for the Senate, making a critical difference in the race. (AP/Wide World)

After taking the Palm Beach
Biltmore Special from Palm
Beach, Joe and Rose had lunch
in 1954 at Hialeah racetrack with,
from left, Joe's sister Loretta,
Joe's mistress and secretary, Janet
Des Rosiers, and Joe's friend
Arthur Houghton.
(Photo Courtesy
of Janet Des Rosiers)

Joe and Jackie visit Jack at the
Hospital for Special Surgery in
New York after he underwent a
back operation there in 1954.
(UPI/Bettmann)

Joe told his friend Francis Cardinal Spellman that he paid Henry Luce $75,000 to place Jack on the December 2, 1957, cover of *Time*. (AP/Wide World)

The day after Jack was elected president, Joe posed with him along with Rose and Jackie in Hyannis Port. (UPI/Bettmann)

After Joe's stroke in 1961, Richard Cardinal Cushing visited Joe. At right is Ann Gargan, Joe's constant companion from 1957. (UPI/Bettmann)

Cassini to design her dresses. Joe told Cassini to send the bills to him.

◆ ◆ ◆

One day, Joe's friend Joseph Timilty called George A. Smathers, then an assistant United States attorney in Florida, and invited him to Hialeah. It turned out that Joe was behind the invitation. Joe "invited me three or four times," Smathers said. "I would always wind up sitting in the front row with two beautiful girls, one on either side. Joe would always sit in back. It never dawned on me until the fourth time that I was getting the credit for the girls. They were not my girls. They were Joe's."

One of the young women told Smathers that she would meet with Joe in Massachusetts, New York, or Chicago. "I know he was taking them to hotels," Smathers said. "I gathered he was giving them a lot of money, and they liked it. They were mostly brunettes but a few blondes. He had a stable of girls. He liked a lot of girls [two or three] at the same time. He would have three girls at the horse races. He always had a bunch."

Later, when Smathers became a senator from Florida, Joe asked him to familiarize himself with the details of Jack's trust funds so he could explain them to Jack. "I attempted to do what Joe Kennedy indicated he wanted me to do and talked it over with Jack, but I never met with much more success than his father did because every time I would talk about it, he wasn't too much interested."

In 1947, Joe spotted Carmen dell'Orefice, a Ford Agency model, on the cover of *Vogue*. Soon to become one of the great stars of the modeling world, dell'Orefice was only sixteen. But Joe decided she would be his mistress. He spotted her again at La Toque Blanche and arranged for a mutual friend whom she trusted to bring her to his apartment in New York. The friend left her in the lobby of the Park Avenue apartment and told her to ring Joe's bell. "I was in my knee socks with patches on," she said. "I had brown and white oxford shoes. I usually roller-skated everywhere.

"The door opened, and I had never seen wall-to-wall light beige or white carpeting," she said. "Under every painting was its own light. That singularly impressed me. I was looking around at everything. Mr. Kennedy said, 'Do you like this?' I said, 'It's beautiful.' He said, 'Well, do you think your mother would like to live here?' I said, 'Oh, yes.' He said, 'Well, go home and tell your mother that you think it is lovely and you would like her to live here. You have her call me.'"

She ran home and told her mother, Margaret, who was not impressed. Margaret said she told her daughter to "forget it." Looking back, her mother said, "I was sophisticated enough to know exactly what the situation was, and dealt with it."

Before a trip to California in 1955, Joe called the actress Joan Fontaine, whom he had met at a reception. The glamorous younger sister of Olivia de Havilland, Fontaine starred in *Rebecca* and *Suspicion*, two Alfred Hitchcock films. Fontaine told Joe that she was having a dinner party, and she invited him to her home. Before dessert was served, Joe got up and beckoned Fontaine, who was then between marriages, into the living room.

"I like it," he said. "I like your guests, your children, your house." Then he said, "Tell you what I'll do. I'll live here when I come to California. I'll invest your money for you . . . just as I did for Gloria Swanson."

Joe told Fontaine she could do what she liked when he was not in California. But "there's only one thing: I can't marry you," he said.

Fontaine was stunned. Joe had never even held her hand. "I simply laughed it off, chucked him under the chin, and returned to the table," she recalled.

Later, at a White House dinner in October 1962, Fontaine told Jack about the incident. He expressed no surprise. "Let's see . . . how old would he have been then? Sixty-five? Hope I'm the same way when I'm his age!" he said.

Joe had more luck with a twenty-five-year-old model whom he kept at his Palm Beach home. Slim Aarons, a society photographer for *Town & Country*, recalled that when Joe's friend Father John Cavanaugh, president of University of Notre Dame, visited, the knockout woman vanished. When he left, she reappeared. When Rose came, she disappeared again, then showed up when Rose had gone. Aarons said Joe liked to flaunt his women, and no one was off limits—"not your wife, your daughter, the girlfriends his sons brought home."

"Joe Kennedy represented the height of vulgarity," Doris Lilly, a vivacious columnist for the *New York Post*, said. "He was horny, that's all he was. He took me out one night for dinner at 21. It was the middle of the summer, and it was hot. Nobody had air conditioning in those days. I had all this wine with dinner, and I wasn't used to it."

After dinner Joe took her to El Morocco and gave her more to drink. Eventually, he took her back to her apartment building. "We were standing in the lobby, and he said, 'What's that over there?' 'Where?' I said. I turned my head and he clamped his mouth over mine, kissed me, and I ran upstairs and threw up."

◆ ◆ ◆

For all his philandering, Joe still found time for business. In March 1948, he visited the Merchandise Mart. Over steak and fresh asparagus, Joe told Illinois governor Dwight Green, Chicago mayor Martin H. Kennelly, and assorted journalists that he was setting up 50-cent public tours of the mart to publicize it. He told them the building was 100 percent rented by 1,000 tenants, and that some 400,000 buyers visited the mart each year.

When James Landis left the government in 1948, Joe invited him to work for the "Kennedy Enterprises." What were the Kennedy Enterprises? "Well, hell, I don't know, but come on down [to Palm Beach], and we'll figure it out," Joe told him.

Landis thought Joe was looking around for people to manage his money. "To him, the making of money is very easy, and he sees no reason why other people, assumedly smart, can't do the same thing. . . ." Landis said. Since Joe's family was not interested in business, Joe appeared to be looking for others to carry on, Landis thought. But Joe was not about to relinquish control of his investments, any more than he would loosen his grip on his children. But he did devote more time to recreation.

"When I was a young fellow, I busted my gut like the rest of you, working 24 hours a day and 400 days a year, and ended up at 35 under the doctor's care," Joe told Tommy Corcoran. The doctor told him he would "kick the bucket" early if he continued at that pace and advised him that he would make more money by resting six months a year. Sure enough, Joe found that if he devoted six months of the year to playing golf, he had the time to "think of the opportunities that [are] worth taking." As a result, he had made "10 times as much money as I ever made when my nose was so close to the grindstone that I couldn't see beyond the grindstone."

Joe had Landis and other professionals look into dozens of possible investments, but when they recommended that he buy, Joe rarely took their advice. For example, Corcoran suggested in July 1948 that since Cissy Patterson had died and left the *Washington Times-Herald* to seven heirs, Joe should buy it. "See what a principality Eugene Meyer built out of the *Post*—he turned it into the 49th state," Corcoran wrote. "Why don't you be the 50th and let me be part of the shadow." Joe told Corcoran, who was by then his lawyer, that in the past, he had made "several efforts" to buy the paper. Now "everybody in the country" wanted to buy it.

Joe toyed with the idea of buying newspapers like the *Boston Post* or the *New York Sun*, or even the Brooklyn Dodgers baseball team, but he never followed through.

What did concern Joe was the bite the government took in taxes, and he was always looking for ways to diminish his tax bill. In 1950, with the help of Raymond F. Kravis, he started dabbling in oil—drilling and exploration ventures. The idea was to take advantage of the oil depletion allowance. "It would have been criminal if a man of his wealth had not taken advantage of the tax laws," said James Fayne, one of Joe's aides.

Kravis, an oil investor from Tulsa, Oklahoma, told Joe none of the investments he was considering were worthwhile. Then he recommended Arctic Oil Company and began citing his reasons. Before Kravis could say a few sentences, Joe interrupted him. "I didn't understand a damn thing you're talking about," Joe said. He said Kravis was the "doctor" in this business, and if he recommended an investment, he would accept it.

In 1952, Joe formed Kenoil Corporation as an umbrella company to manage his oil investments. He formed Mokeen Oil Company of Corpus Christi, which got its name by combining the names of Kennedy and Jack Modesett, a well-known oil man. He also bought Sutton Producing Company of San Antonio, named for William Franklin "Bill" Sutton, who started the company.

Even as a bull market began, Joe was "extremely bearish" on the "trend of events as a whole," Landis wrote to Corcoran from the Breakers Hotel in Palm Beach on January 27, 1948. Indeed, Joe expected a mild recession within ninety days and saw it "gradually deepening." Joe was "almost wholly out of the market, and is even seriously concerned over metropolitan real estate values."

Joe's prediction was dead wrong. The bull market would continue into the mid-1960s, when the Dow Jones industrial average rose to nearly 1,000, compared with around 250, on an adjusted basis, when Joe made his prediction. Because of his bearishness, Joe missed out on exceptionally good investments. Nonetheless, by 1950, Joe's wealth was estimated at $400 million.

◆ ◆ ◆

Joe was at the George V Hotel in Paris when a *Boston Globe* reporter called at 6:30 A.M. on May 14, 1948, to tell him that his daughter Kathleen had been killed in a plane crash the previous evening.

After the death of her husband, Kick had begun dating Peter Fitzwilliam, a thirty-seven-year-old married British lord. With Peter's divorce pending, they decided to announce their engagement in mid-May. Meanwhile, they made plans to sneak away for a weekend in Cannes. They had rented a two-engine De Havilland Dove eight-seat plane in London for the trip. Fitzwilliam decided they should touch down at Le Bourget Airport in France so he could introduce some of his friends to Kick. Three hours later, Peter Townsend, the pilot, informed them that a thunderstorm was predicted. All commercial flights had been canceled, and the flight was too risky. But Fitzwilliam insisted they take off, and the pilot gave in. The plane went down in the Cevennes Mountains.

When the *Globe* reporter called, Joe Timilty answered the phone. When he put Joe on the line, he could not say anything. Devastated, Joe flew from Paris to Lyons, then traveled to the small village of Privas to identify her body. Joe still hoped there had been a mistake. But when an official opened Kick's coffin, Joe gasped and stared unbelievingly at the mangled remains of his twenty-eight-year-old daughter.

When Joe called home that evening, he said nothing about the horrible wounds he had seen. He told the family how "beautiful" Kathleen looked. She had been found on her back, with her shoes off, he said. "Wasn't that just like Kick, to walk around barefoot?" Meanwhile, to make their trip look better, Joe put out the word that Kathleen had been traveling with her boyfriend to France to obtain Joe's approval for marriage.

Now both Joe Jr. and Kathleen were gone. For all practical purposes, so was Rosemary. Joe Jr. "was Uncle Joe's favorite boy. Kick was his favorite daughter," said Mary Lou McCarthy, the daughter of Joe's sister Loretta. "Joe Jr. was like the summer sunshine. Kick was the only really blonde girl in the family. She adored the older brothers and was an outrageous tease."

The Cavendishes decided that as the widow of Billy, Kathleen should be buried in the family plot near Chatsworth, the family castle. Joe was the only Kennedy present for the Catholic mass in London. As a divorced Protestant, Fitzwilliam had been no more acceptable to Rose than Cavendish had been. She was perfectly willing to travel to Paris to see fashion shows and buy dresses, but now Rose found it inconvenient to attend her daughter's funeral. Joe left all the details to the Duke and Duchess of Devonshire. He also allowed them to choose the wording on Kick's tombstone: "Joy She Gave—Joy She Found."

21

———

JANET

With Jack safely elected to a second term in Congress on September 14, 1948, Joe decided he needed a new secretary. One by one, John Ford, Joe's man in Boston, brought forty young women to Joe to be interviewed in his suite at the Ritz-Carlton Hotel. Joe decided Janet Des Rosiers had exactly what he needed.

Certainly Des Rosiers, then twenty-four, had the requisite professional skills. A graduate of Leicester High School in Massachusetts, she had taken shorthand and typing. Then she had worked for a Worcester, Massachusetts, law firm; for the clerk of the Superior Court there; and for a Boston research firm. Des Rosiers had a quick mind. Although she had little experience outside of Massachusetts, her family circumstances had forced her into maturity early. Des Rosiers' father had died when she was twelve. As the oldest daughter in a family of five, she assumed responsibilities beyond her years.

Des Rosiers was savvy, intuitive, and funny, and she had good judgment. She had an upbeat outlook, a direct manner, and a way of flattering men without being cloying. But to top it all, she was good-looking. With an hourglass figure, she had a creamy complexion, green eyes, brown hair, and gorgeous legs. Des Rosiers never failed to get second glances. In retrospect, Des Rosiers decided, that was what Joe had been looking for in a secretary.

"He was very taken with me," Des Rosiers recalled in her alluring voice. "He made up his mind right then I would be his."

Joe told Des Rosiers to come to Hyannis Port the following weekend. He hired her then and rented an apartment for her in Hyannis. When he went out of town, he would call her just to chat. "You know, Janet," he told her, "you had the job the minute you walked in the room."

In December 1948, three months after he hired her, Joe seduced her. Their first encounter was in the two-bedroom house he rented for her in West Palm Beach, about ten minutes from the Kennedy home in Palm Beach. When Joe came to see her there around eight one evening, he began kissing and undressing her. She was not surprised. He had begun referring to her quarters as "our" home. Their affair would last for more than nine years, three times longer than Joe's affair with Gloria Swanson.

"It would be called sexual harassment now," Des Rosiers said. "He knew how to get what he wanted. He brought me into his life. I was his constant companion."

Des Rosiers talked about the affair for the first time in a series of interviews. She was hesitant at first and did not confirm that she had had a sexual affair with Joe until the third interview.

"Very few suspected that I was anything to him," she said. "I was not a sex bomb. I didn't wear sexy clothes. No one would suspect my other nature." But an associate of Joe's said it was widely assumed within his New York office that they were having an affair, since she was "always available," traveled with him, and was extremely attractive. A September 27, 1961, letter from Joe to Des Rosiers confirmed that Joe confided to her his distaste for Rose. "Mother [Rose] has gone to Rome for a while, but I guess she will be coming back around the middle of next month," Joe wrote to Des Rosiers. "But if she had the sense she was supposed to have, she would stay there until Christmas"—in other words, another three months.

When Joe seduced Des Rosiers, she was a virgin. "Joe was not surprised that I had not had sex," she said. "He taught me everything." In retrospect, she realized, "He was a professional at manipulating me with his charm, his warm and loving nature, and a softness that the rest of the world never saw. It was very easy for him to make me feel important in his life. It kind of stunned me. After all, I hadn't had an affair before. The whole thing took me unawares. I was young and ready for love."

Des Rosiers was so unsophisticated that she had never had a daiquiri before. Just after they began their affair, Joe took her to Havana, where they had daiquiris at a hotel bar. She thought they were to be sipped like fruit juice and was ill for two days of the three-day jaunt.

Des Rosiers understood that Joe could be ruthless, but she never saw that side of him. "He was fun, he was warm, he was thoughtful, never demanding, very considerate, and very gentle," she said. "It wasn't very difficult to fall in love with him. He was very charming. He overwhelmed me." He was also "well-endowed." Nor, according to Des Rosiers, was he bowlegged, as Roosevelt had claimed.

Joe and Des Rosiers would have assignations in her apartment in Hyannis, in the rented house in West Palm Beach, in Joe's apartment in New York or in Boston, or in Joe's villa when they traveled to the French Riviera for the summer. When Rose was away, as she often was, Joe would insist that Des Rosiers move into the Hyannis Port home and have sex with him in his bedroom. "Sometimes, I would just move in for a week or two," she said. "The servants assumed what was going on, but they all liked me. I think they were glad because they adored him, and anything that made him happy they approved of." If Des Rosiers were ill, Joe would have her move in with him and have the servants bring her meals in bed. "It was a very comfortable arrangement because nothing was obvious, nothing was flaunted," said the coquettish, dulcet-voiced woman.

Mathilda Heldal, the cook, would make rich dinners for both of them. "Mathilda could cook like you couldn't imagine," Des Rosiers said. "The vegetables floated in butter. There were steaks and chops every day. Rich desserts, crème brûlée, pies, ice cream." Joe was so taken with Heldal's cooking that, after she retired, he twice flew her to Palm Beach to make Christmas dinner.

Before Thursday, the cook's day off, Heldal would make lamb stew. "I would be in charge of that meal on Thursday," Des Rosiers said. "In Palm Beach, we ate in the butler's pantry. In Hyannis Port, we ate in the kitchen. Joe and I would do the dishes. He would wipe."

Joe paid for Des Rosiers' lodging, as he did for all his secretaries. He paid her a good salary but never gave her additional money or unusual presents. "I wasn't paid extra," she said. "I didn't do it for money. I was in love with him. Any girl in my circumstances would have done the same thing because he had a pretty good technique. He knew how to make me feel lovely and worthwhile and dear to him. I felt it was genuine."

For all their intimacy, Joe rarely slept overnight with Des Rosiers. Even when they traveled together and stayed in hotels, he rented a separate room for her. When they had sex together in his apartment in New York, she usually spent the night in a separate bedroom. Thus she was but another of Joe's compartments. He was not willing to reveal himself fully to anyone, as symbolized by the fact that since 1950 he had kept two apartments in New York. Both at 277 Park Avenue, one was for himself and the other for his family.

Joe wanted to be free to have others on the side. Long ago,

Joe had established a pattern. While constantly cruising for new conquests, he usually had one steady mistress. Doris Lilly, the former columnist for the *New York Post*, knew one of his earlier mistresses, a statuesque blonde he kept in an apartment on Beekman Place in New York. Lilly told C. David Heymann that a piece she wrote for the January 1963 *Cosmopolitan* about an unnamed mistress of a wealthy man was actually about one of Joe's many girlfriends. The mistress told Lilly, "Rose didn't care how many women Joe kept as long as she had her family," Lilly said. "The only thing Rose had sexual relations with her husband for was for the purpose of procreation. She was that devout a Catholic. . . . Many people talked about the 'long-suffering Rose.' It's not true. Rose didn't object to Joe's women as long as they didn't interfere with her personal life or with her family."

The unedited manuscript of Lilly's article said the woman met "John," as Joe was called in the piece, on the Riviera when he offered to help her cover a gambling debt. When she said she didn't have enough money to pay for her apartment in New York, he offered her the down payment for one. Whenever she needed extra cash, he gave it to her, usually $1,000 a month. In Palm Beach, "John" would play golf while she would "rest around in the sun at the Bath and Tennis Club or have lunch with friends.

"When he said cigarette smoking bothered him, I stopped smoking when we were together," Lilly quoted her as saying. "I never reproached him for not having telephoned, or having been away too long. I never spoke of other men who have admired me, nor bored him with what I had been doing unless he asked."

But as the affair approached the ten-year mark, she became more suspicious of other women. Finally, to force the issue, she made up a story that a man had proposed marriage.

"Did you accept?" "John" asked coolly. "Not yet," she replied, "but I think I will, since I feel I must make a more permanent life for myself somewhere and—"

"Well, then, I won't try to stop you if your mind is made up," "John" said.

Des Rosiers also suspected that Joe cheated on her, but she never saw any evidence of it. Just before their affair began, Joe had an attractive New York artist over for dinner in Palm Beach. Because of the way they treated each other, Des Rosiers suspected they were intimate. But after Des Rosiers and Joe began their affair, she never saw the other woman again.

Even though Joe was sixty when he and Des Rosiers began their affair, they made love as often as once a day. "The lovemaking went on for hours," she said. "There was joy and ecstasy and laughter and giggles, eating chocolate cake and drinking milk at midnight in the kitchen. He said sex should be fun, accompanied by laughter and light, which it was—afterwards."

Then as before, Joe's day followed an unchanging pattern. In Hyannis Port, he woke up by 6 A.M. and rode one of his two horses tended by a groom at Allen's Farm in Osterville. He had breakfast prepared by his cook, usually a poached egg on toast with coffee. He read the *New York Times*, the *Wall Street Journal*, and the Boston newspapers. By 9 A.M., Des Rosiers would arrive. He would embrace and kiss her, then begin dictating or having her place calls for him. He sat in an armchair in the living room overlooking the bay. Often, he held her hand as he talked on the phone. Around 4 P.M., they would go for a walk around Hyannis Port.

"Every night, he gathered in his living room with his houseguests and me and had one drink, Haig & Haig," she said. "His whole life was a ritual. He did the same thing over and over again. The routine was riding in the morning, working, playing golf, taking a nap, a drink before dinner. Dinner was served by the butler. Evenings he wore these exquisitely tailored soft wool or silk lounging suits made for him by Sulka in Paris. I would order them for him, as well as his ties and shirts. Then four times a week, movies were shown in his private basement movie theater. They were provided by John Ford in Boston."

Joe invited Des Rosiers and other friends to see the movies. After a movie, "He would walk me out to my car and kiss me good night tenderly. He was very gentle like that," she said.

In June 1952, Joe bought the *Marlin*, a fifty-six-foot, two-propeller yacht that could reach thirty-two knots. The greatest proportion of their lovemaking occurred there, as Frank Wirtanen piloted the boat and Rose busied herself going to church or writing notes to herself. "She went to mass every day," said her nephew Joe Gargan. "Sometimes in Florida, she went twice a day, at 7 A.M. and 9 A.M."

"We used to go out on the *Marlin* many afternoons," Des Rosiers recalled. "I'd take the work and Mathilda would pack a lunch." After Joe dictated a few letters, they would have a Dubonnet, then a gourmet lunch. They would repair to Joe's cabin. "The lower cabin was his, and the door would be shut," she said. After making love, they would take a nap together.

Sometimes they swam off a secluded beach on Nantucket or fished for bluefish. Rose hated the boat and went out on it only once, Des Rosiers recalled.

In Palm Beach, Joe would conduct business in the morning in what was known as the bullpen—a white, wood enclosure next to the diving board overlooking the pool. Des Rosiers would rub suntan lotion on him, and he would dictate, make calls, and see people.

On her own, Des Rosiers responded to letters asking for financial help. The pleas always seemed so real; they made her cry. Joe's answer was always the same: No. "If you asked him for anything, you never got a thing," she said. But Joe dispensed millions of dollars through the Kennedy Foundation.

Joe treated his servants with consideration, always going into the kitchen to praise the food and giving the help generous bonuses. On occasion, he let them go out on the *Marlin*.

Des Rosiers was Rose's secretary as well, but it was easy to conceal her dual role. "I didn't give any indication this was going on. I was the secretary of the house, and I acted like the secretary of the house." Usually, "Rose would wake up and have the maid bring her breakfast on a tray," Des Rosiers said. "I would spend an hour with her, and she would dictate to me. . . . It was very normal. I went into her bedroom in the morning with my dictation book. She would say, for example, 'I want to change the bedspread in Jack's room. Would you ask the decorator to send me samples?'

"When I started to work there, Mrs. Kennedy said, 'The servants will never be able to pronounce your name, so we'll just call you Miss Dee,'" Des Rosiers said. "So through the years, while servants came and went, I was Miss Dee."

Des Rosiers concluded that Rose was aware of Joe's affair with her and with others such as Gloria Swanson. She decided that Rose not only tolerated Joe's philandering but approved of it, since it took pressure off her. "She must have known I was around all the time and not unattractive," Des Rosiers said. "I used to massage Joe's scalp and neck with Rose in the living room. . . . I don't know what she thought her husband was made of. I feel she must have known. [But] she never uttered one word showing she suspected anything. . . . If Rose knew about it, she was grateful," Des Rosiers said. "It set her free. She never showed a sign of annoyance."

Playing her role well, Rose would talk of Gloria Swanson as if she idolized her. Des Rosiers recalled that midway through their affair Joe, Rose, and some of Joe's friends were having lunch in the dining room in Hyannis Port. Des Rosiers was in her office off the living room, but she could hear Rose's shrill voice. "I heard Mrs. Kennedy say, 'Men always fall in love with their secretaries.' She said it in a way so that I didn't feel any reference to me," Des Rosiers said. "She didn't say it with any malice. Then Joe got a very important telephone call. When he entered my office, I said jokingly, 'Oh, oh, the jig's up.' The man absolutely fell apart laughing. He roared out loud."

Again, Rose had performed flawlessly, giving no hint that she knew anything was amiss. Yet with Joe's luscious young secretary in the next room, Rose's comment about men falling in love with their secretaries could not have been innocent.

One balmy evening, Rose and Des Rosiers went for a walk in Palm Beach. "She said, 'If I had wanted to marry a shoe salesman, I would have.' She meant she married an important man, and she accepted [what went with it]. . . . When you marry a man of that caliber, you accept," Des Rosiers said. Perhaps more than anything, that summed up Rose's philosophy. Des Rosiers recalled that Rose's favorite saying was, "God does not give one more burdens than one can bear." Her life was one of acceptance, and she seemed happiest alone. Her one enjoyment seemed to be dressing herself— traveling to Paris to buy dresses for $5,000 to $10,000 each.

Joe called Rose "Mother." He never confided in Des Rosiers what he thought of their marriage. "I never heard him be impolite or raise his voice with her," Des Rosiers said. "There was no undercurrent of hostility. He seemed to respect her. They got along well, like friends. In that way, the household was amicable. It wasn't a normal husband-and-wife relationship. I think they had given that up a long time ago, including sex. I don't think he loved her." In fact, they rarely kissed, and then only on the cheek.

If Joe and Rose were friends, their friendship was superficial. It was to Des Rosiers that Joe confided his hopes and fears, and it was Des Rosiers who ran the household. After spending the day together, Joe and Des Rosiers would often talk for hours on the phone, simply chatting as friends. She saw no sign that Joe ever discussed his inner feelings with Rose.

Perhaps because of his Irish heritage, Joe had a fear of the wind. It brought to mind Irish folk tales about the banshees wailing. "The wind in Palm Beach drove him out of his mind," Des Rosiers said. But most of all, Joe feared becoming helpless. It was almost as if he had a premonition. "He told me many times he never wanted to be an invalid or be confined

to a bed where people would have to take care of him," she
said. " 'When I go, I just want to go,' he said. 'I don't want
a lingering sickness.' "

For all his posturing about being discriminated against in
Boston, Des Rosiers said Joe never talked about the Boston
Brahmins.

"The Irish versus the WASPs was a joke," said K. Dun
Gifford, who later worked for Ted Kennedy. "I've always
believed it was a cynical, manipulative ploy to make sure
your Irish electoral base is secure."

Joe often said, "What you are speaks so loudly I cannot
hear you when you tell me what you are." Yet Joe rarely
practiced what he preached. For example, he would tell Des
Rosiers that he avoided parties because guests always asked
for investment advice. "He said, 'Give a friend advice on
investments or loan him money, and you've lost a friend,' "
she said. Yet Joe loaned money to his friend Morton Downey
and invested Des Rosiers' salary for her.

In Des Rosiers' opinion, Joe was not aware of the conflicts
between what he said and did, between the image and the
reality. "He probably thought he took [his own] advice," she
said. "He was self-deluding. . . . He could convince himself
of anything to make it true, and then he believed it."

Des Rosiers dispensed money from two checkbooks, paid
the help, and dealt with the New York office, then in Suite
953 at 230 Park Avenue. She took inventory of the bottles
of wine in the cellar—about five hundred of the best that
money could buy, to be served on special occasions. One day
in Palm Beach, Des Rosiers told Joe that she believed a new
cook was stealing the meat shipped in barrels packed with
dry ice from Knickerbocker Meats in New York. The cook
was reselling the meat to a local butcher. "He got livid and
told the cook she had twenty minutes to clear out," she said.

"I did for him all the things that a wife should do," Des
Rosiers said. "I accompanied him on the boat, I ran the house
and the servants, I paid the bills, I helped him entertain."
Indeed, "He said, 'Sometime I would like to divorce Rose

and marry you instead,'" Des Rosiers said. "That was in the south of France, so it was in 1951 or 1952. I said that's not going to happen."

Much as she loved Joe, Des Rosiers did not want an older husband and was not prepared to face the uproar it would cause if she married someone almost four decades older than she. "Imagine how foolish that would be," she said. "I didn't follow up on it. Can you imagine the headlines? Ridiculous."

Des Rosiers was annoyed by Rose's habit of pinning notes to herself. When Rose bothered her servants, it upset her. "Mrs. Kennedy carried a little paper pinned to her chest, and she went from room to room looking for things that had to be done or improved upon," Des Rosiers recalled. For example, she would write that a cushion had to be re-covered or an old magazine had to be discarded. "She believed that every free moment of your life had to be occupied with learning or work," Des Rosiers said. "She would be having lunch with her grandchildren, and it was like a school. Rose didn't walk into a room to relax and enjoy the setting. It was to make a note of this or that that has to be done."

Rose had a penurious streak, which often found expression in how she treated the servants. "Did you pay her for that hour? She didn't work that hour," she would tell Des Rosiers, who was paymaster as well as secretary and mistress. "Rose was penny wise and pound foolish," she said. "She would spend millions on her dresses over time, and then get upset at me if a servant was paid for an hour he didn't work."

On a trip to France, Rose berated Des Rosiers because she had brought too many boxes of facial tissues and rolls of toilet paper to be used once they got there. "She would pick on the help," Des Rosiers said. "If you're a good Christian woman, you should be compassionate toward those who serve you night and day."

Given how much time she was away from home, Des Rosiers concluded that Rose did not like to be there. "She was at Palm Beach a lot in the winter," she said. "But she went to Paris a couple of times a year or to Vienna or Switzerland, always by herself. Then she went to see her mother in Boston."

The guests who came to the house were Joe's friends, not Rose's. The two rarely socialized together. "The only big party I saw in Palm Beach was when they entertained the Duke and Duchess of Windsor," Des Rosiers said. "The houses were his houses. They really weren't her houses. She changed the decor, but they were always filled with his friends. I never saw one friend of hers."

Most of all, Rose seemed concerned about her looks. She would often run around the house with a cosmetic mask on her face. One afternoon, Joe's chauffeur was driving Joe, Rose, and Des Rosiers in Joe's Rolls-Royce to Vence in the south of France. "We drove to Matisse's chapel," Des Rosiers said. "She put a black mask over her eyes so her face muscles could relax. This was really beautiful scenery, which she missed."

At the same time, Rose constantly practiced her French, using language records. Her accent remained dreadful.

In contrast to Rose, Joe seemed to feel vulnerable when not surrounded by his court. "He never wanted to be alone," she said. "He always had people around him. When I was there, he wanted me to be with him all the time." He had "an entourage of loyal friends who were not terribly illustrious or well known; they were his cronies," Des Rosiers said. "Arthur Houghton was one. He never left him. He practically lived with the Kennedys. Joe Timilty came down . . . Father John Cavanaugh, the president of Notre Dame, came."

Joe's friends served as court jesters. Joe would "love a joke. He loved to laugh. That's why he had all these guys around him who kept him amused. Like Jack had his Dave Powers."

But each served other purposes as well. Houghton, who knew of their affair, acted as a beard for Joe, pretending to be Des Rosiers' date when the situation called for it. When Hialeah racetrack opened for the season, Joe, Des Rosiers, Rose, and Joe's entourage would take the Palm Beach *Bilt-*

more Special from Palm Beach to Hialeah. An accomplished dancer, Timilty would escort Rose to dances on the Cape on Saturday nights, leaving Joe free to do as he pleased. Rose "had Timilty escort her to things," a confidant of Joe's said. "Joe rarely went out with her in later years. I think there was a certain amount of loneliness there." Said Des Rosiers, "Timilty was a bore. Such a bore. Not one ounce of originality."

In New York, Joe and Des Rosiers would dine at Le Pavillon and attend the theater or a show at Radio City Music Hall. He would "sit in the balcony so no one would recognize him," she said. "We would get there late and leave a couple of minutes early."

At one point, Gloria Swanson and a boyfriend came to visit Joe at Eze-sur-mer, a tiny village between Nice and Monte Carlo in southern France. Des Rosiers had lunch with them. In a reprise of her role a few years earlier in *Sunset Boulevard*, Swanson, then in her sixties, complained that Hollywood and its stars had gone to hell. "All she talked about was how inferior the actors and actresses of today were, and how none of them can act the way they did in her day," Des Rosiers said. "She berated Hollywood and criticized the quality of the performers."

Clare Boothe Luce also visited, staying three nights in Joe's villa. Des Rosiers did not know if they had sexual relations during the visit.

While Joe continued to be free to see others, he expected Des Rosiers to be faithful to him. Onc night, she was invited to a party on Cape Cod. Joe was distraught. Crying, he said, "Why did you leave me?" At another point, Des Rosiers had an innocent date with a man in Florida. "Joe found out about it. I think I told him. He almost killed me," she said. "He went into a rage. He said, 'Why did you do that? Don't you know better than that? You know I love you.' Clearly I was Joe's property, and nobody else was to have me."

Des Rosiers had to ward off passes from one of Joe's

married New York employees, who apparently was not aware that she was his boss' mistress, and from some of Joe's own friends. Justice William Douglas, for one, offered to let Des Rosiers stay in his cabin in the woods anytime she wanted. "I kind of figured that it meant he might be there, too. So I didn't take him up on that," she said.

When Des Rosiers began working for Joe, his son Joe Jr. and daughter Kathleen had just died. Despite his constant admonition "Kennedys don't cry," Joe often began to sob as he thought of his two lost children. "I heard Joe say, 'Kennedys don't cry' to his grandchildren," Des Rosiers said. "They were crying, and they really were told not to cry. [But] he cried in front of me, talking about Kathleen and Joe Jr. The tears would stream down his face."

Similarly, Rose "impressed on her children never to show their true feelings, because you just might get hurt," Des Rosiers said. "In other words, try not to be human, try not to be close to anyone. She suppressed everything." In Des Rosiers' opinion, "The Kennedys covered up their feelings with things that passed the time."

There was no question that Joe loved his children. In turn, "The children adored their father," she said. "They sort of tolerated the mother. Not that they didn't love her, but she wasn't the fun their father was, nor the intellectual stimulus." If Joe controlled them much more than most parents, they were used to it and never complained.

What was remarkable was the loyalty of the children toward each other. "The family pounced on the home every weekend," she said. "They played golf and tennis and swam together. They ate together. They completely enjoyed each other's company."

"Joe must have felt safe in this cocoon he built around himself," she said. "I think he lived vicariously through his children."

Contrary to the impression he so successfully conveyed, Joe was not at all religious. "He never went to church, I don't think. He never talked about it. . . . He did not go to confession. Oh God! If a priest heard his confession," said Des Rosiers, who is Catholic.

If any of the children suspected that Des Rosiers was having an affair with their father, they never let on. Joe Gargan, Rose's nephew, was always impressed that Joe seemed to be a family man who loved to stay at home. "He was not a fellow to go out at night or went away from the house. He was always there," Gargan said.

Gargan had no idea that Joe was living in sin.

◆ ◆ ◆

Like most of the Kennedys, Joe had what they all referred to as a "Kennedy stomach." Medically, no one was sure what that meant, but they often had pain in their stomachs. Even Rose had a Kennedy stomach.

"One time, Rose was talking to Kerry [McCarthy] about it, and Rose said, 'Of course, it's in the family,'" Mary Lou McCarthy said. "Kerry said Rose was a Fitzgerald. She stopped and looked at me and said, 'Well, then, it's proximity,' and walked away."

"All the Kennedys had a nervous stomach," Des Rosiers said. "Joe used to go to the Lahey Clinic in Boston. They gave all the Kennedys medicine known as No. 2. It was a green liquid that he took before meals. It was a religion with him."

To Des Rosiers, the explanation for the stomach pain was simple: "I don't know if the Kennedys ever had inner peace," she said. "Rose lived a life of acceptance, and sometimes that can gnaw at you, and you don't even know it." The rest of the family suppressed emotion, while Joe led a duplicitous life.

That judgment was confirmed by Dr. Robert D. Watt, a Hyannis general practitioner who became the family doctor in 1955. A brilliant diagnostician, Dr. Watt was first consulted by Ethel Kennedy. Her daughter, Kathleen, now lieutenant governor of Maryland, needed a routine checkup. Soon the rest of the family, including Rose, began using him. After Joe's stroke in 1961, Dr. Watt began treating him as well. He was thus privy to his entire medical history, both from records and from consultations with Joe's regular specialists and previous doctors.

"Mr. Kennedy had stomach problems from time to time, probably associated with tension," Dr. Watt said.

In a series of interviews, Dr. Watt for the first time candidly expressed his view of the Kennedys. To Dr. Watt, the family was an enigma. Their frenetic pace seemed to be an end in itself, and their mishaps often seemed to stem from an overarching recklessness. For example, Dr. Watt treated Bobby Jr., one of Ethel's children, when he jumped over a shed and severed a tendon. Bobby kept a falcon in his bedroom, and he kept rats in a cage outside so the falcon would be well fed. One of the rats bit Max, another of Bobby's children, and Dr. Watt had to give him a tetanus shot, then attempt to capture the rat to see if it was rabid (it wasn't).

Then there was the morning when Joe Kennedy II, now a United States congressman, turned on the gas in the oven at Hyannis Port so he could warm up some muffins.

"He turned on the gas, and some kid yelled out, 'There goes a bunny rabbit!' So they all go chasing after the rabbit," Dr. Watt said. "In the meantime, this gal from South Carolina looks in and lights a match. It blew her right across the room. She went from black to white. She had flash burns. So I checked her out at the hospital. I watched her for a week. She was fine."

One afternoon, Dr. Watt was seeing Rose at Hyannis Port and parked his Thunderbird in the Kennedy driveway. "One of the girls [Eunice], who had a big Lincoln Continental with three or four children in the back, had the car radio on full blast. She was shouting to us and got in the car. She started backing up. We were shouting at her. She went right into my Thunderbird with those fins," Dr. Watt said. "I don't think they have any fear."

Nancy Tenney Coleman, who lives directly across the street
from Ethel's Hyannis Port house, recalled that on the same
day photographers were taking pictures of Ethel for a mother-
of-the-year award, "Three of her kids were on the roof trying
to lasso the chimney. Nobody cared. I thought, 'Why don't
they turn the camera on that?'"

Because of her loud parties, Coleman said Ethel disturbed
her sleep at night, and she allowed her dogs to roam without
leashes. "I was attacked by one of Ethel's dogs," Coleman
said. "Cars, parties, everything is loud. You can call the police
ten times at 2 A.M., and nothing happens because it's the
Kennedys. . . . There is a leash law. She lets dogs roam, and
they nip. You are not supposed to bring dogs on the golf
course. She brings them and parks in the handicapped
spaces." Coleman said Ethel also objects when her guests
park their cars in front of Ethel's house. "She doesn't like
people parking on her side, but it's okay to park on my side,"
she said.

One day, Coleman was washing her Labrador. "Ethel said,
'What are you doing?' I said washing Keffi. She said, 'That's
cruel.' You're dealing with a different set of rules."

Jackie, on the other hand, was a devoted mother. "Jackie
did not like the running around and plain food," Dr. Watt
said. "Jackie was a very gracious lady. I was hospitalized,
and there were the flowers. When my wife died, there were
the flowers and a telephone call." He said that the other
Kennedys also treated him graciously at the time.

John F. Kennedy Jr., who was allergic to horses, had to
get allergy shots. "I gave them at home because it was a lot
easier to treat them at home than at the office. Can you
imagine what my office would be like if they came to the
office?" Dr. Watt said. "One time, Caroline fell from a pony
and broke her arm," Dr. Watt said. "I went over and was
seeing John. I was about to go out the door, and Jacqueline
said, 'Would you mind taking a look at Caroline?' I looked
at the arm, and it was broken. Both bones of the forearm

had been broken maybe weeks before. So we put her in a cast."

Rose's obsessively puritanical nature amused the doctor. When he told her he was planning a trip to Scotland, she asked to see him and his wife, Madeline. Rose mentioned how cold it could get there. Then, "Rose asked if I would leave the room," Dr. Watt said. "She had something she didn't want me to see."

Obediently, Dr. Watt disappeared. Then Rose felt it was safe to bring out what she was embarrassed for her own doctor to see. "It was some kind of the equivalent of winter underwear," Dr. Watt said. "She wanted Madeline to try them on, which she did. She wound up giving it to her."

22

PAYOFF

In June 1951, Harvard College expelled Ted for cheating. The story did not come out until the *Boston Globe* learned about it when Ted was running for the Senate in 1962. When Ted was expelled, Joe said to Janet Des Rosiers, "What a fool he was!" Whether Joe thought him a fool for cheating or a fool for getting caught, he didn't say.

The next month, Joe was sitting on the deck of the *Marlin*, finishing lunch, when he noticed a story in the *New York Times* reporting that nearly one hundred West Point cadets had been expelled for cheating. With him was his friend Father John Cavanaugh. Cavanaugh was one of Joe's courtiers, always looking for handouts. "Father Cavanaugh spent his time trying to get Joe to give Notre Dame enough money to start a graduate school," recalled Walter Trohan of the *Chicago Tribune*. "Joe never did."

At the same time, the priest's presence in Joe's entourage created the illusion that Joe was a devout Catholic. In April

1954, Cavanaugh officiated at the wedding of Patricia Kennedy and actor Peter Lawford at the Church of St. Thomas More in New York. Joe waited until June 1956, when Father Theodore M. Hesburgh became president of the university, to endow the Lord Beaverbrook chair in honor of his friend the London newspaper publisher.

Turning to Cavanaugh on the *Marlin*, Joe said, "What would it cost to send all these young fellows through Notre Dame?" When Cavanaugh told him, Joe said that's what he wanted to do. On Joe's instructions, Cavanaugh issued a public statement soliciting the expelled students to apply to Notre Dame. The university attributed the offer to an anonymous donor who was quoted as saying, "Because I feel with millions of Americans that in the American tradition, a man who makes a mistake should have a reasonable chance to rehabilitate himself, I make this offer. . . ." The donor said he would pay the "board, room and tuition of the young men, Catholic or non-Catholic . . . with the understanding that they meet Notre Dame standards and academic requirements, that they need such help, and that these young men will not participate in any form of varsity athletics."

"Actually, twenty-one of these young men applied for admission to Notre Dame, and thirteen finally came," Cavanaugh recalled.

Undoubtedly, given the way Joe conducted his life, he identified personally with the expelled students. But also by making the offer public, he suggested that anyone (like his son) who cheated on exams should be forgiven. When it came to building the images of his children, no sum was too large. Nor was Joe sincere when he said he wanted to remain anonymous. In September 1951, a month after he had made the offer, the *New York World-Telegram* broke the story that Joe had been the anonymous benefactor. Given his penchant for publicity, it was likely Joe had leaked the story.

"Joe always publicized his gifts," said Kane Simonian, a friend of Joe Kane, Joe's cousin. "He squeezed them for the last bit of publicity value."

Yet, like Joe's gifts through the Kennedy Foundation, Joe's support of the thirteen expelled students clearly was admirable. Donald Senich, one of the recipients of Joe's largesse, recalled that while attending Notre Dame, he sent a Christmas card each year to his benefactor through Notre Dame's financial office. Two years after Senich graduated in 1953, he sent a letter through the same channels outlining his latest activities. After some months had passed, he received a letter signed by Joe.

"It said, 'Rose and I are very pleased to hear about your activities. Godspeed. Joe,'" Senich recalled. "He gave me an education and a job," Senich said. "For that I am eternally grateful. I never would be where I am now otherwise. I am at the National Science Foundation. I coordinate activities in small high-technology firms. I would not be at the NSF if it had not been for Joe Kennedy. That man changed my life and the lives of everyone who went to Notre Dame from West Point."

◆ ◆ ◆

If Joe's reputation had been tarnished by his efforts to appease Hitler, he was still known as an efficient and successful businessman. Accordingly, on the recommendation of Herbert Hoover, Joe was appointed in July 1947 to the Commission on Reorganization of the Executive Branch of Government. Known as the Hoover Commission after its chairman. The commission's charter was to study ways to streamline the federal government.

Joe rarely attended the meetings. He took more interest in what was known as the second Hoover Commission, to which he was appointed in July 1953. That panel focused on policy and called for the abolishment of many New Deal agencies.

As his assistant on the first Hoover Commission, Joe chose Henry Luce III, Luce's son. "It was a useful opportunity for me to learn about government, which I did in spades," the younger Luce said. "I suppose it was also an opportunity to ingratiate himself with my father."

Later, Joe suggested to the elder Luce that he send his son to Congress from his home district in New Jersey. Luce recalled Joe's telling him, in effect, he should "buy him the seat, just as Joe did for his children."

On November 10, 1950, Joe spoke at a seminar given by Professor Arthur Holcombe at the Harvard Graduate School of Public Administration. He told the students he could see no reason why the United States was fighting in Korea, a conflict that had started five months earlier. At the same time, Joe said not enough had been done to get Communists out of government. He professed respect for Joseph R. McCarthy, the Wisconsin Republican senator who was beginning his witch hunt for Communists in government. Joe said he "knew Joe pretty well, and he may have something."

Joe's views on the international situation were as confused as ever. In a speech to the University of Virginia Law School Forum in Charlottesville on December 12, he warned that Communism was a force working to dominate Europe and Asia. The solution was to keep "ourselves strong." The way to do that was to maintain a high standard of living, one that inspired the downtrodden of the world. On the other hand, if Communism succeeded in dominating parts of Europe or Asia, the United States "cannot stop it," he said. In other words, he suggested the Communist system should be allowed to dominate other countries. Russia had planes of "high quality and great quantity," Joe warned. Its navy included a "powerful fleet of submarines." The country probably had the atomic bomb. The solution was to keep Russia, if it chose to march, on the other side of the Atlantic.

The first step, he said, was to get out of Korea. Referring to World War II, Joe said that billions had been "squandered" fighting in Europe, money that should have been spent "in this hemisphere." He said, "Had we the defenses in Iceland today . . . we could have purchased safety." The United States should "arm itself to the teeth" but choose its battles.

Joe's position conflicted with the Truman Doctrine, which Truman had enunciated in a message to Congress on March 12, 1947. Truman advocated supporting countries that were at risk of subjugation by outside forces, such as Communism, with economic and military aid. If Joe's views on Communist expansionism echoed his earlier views on Hitler, they also ignored the development of military planes and ships that could easily cross oceans and threaten the United States.

Commenting on his speech, the *Boston Traveler* said it was "almost unbelievable" that anyone would defend isolationism. The *Boston Herald* said the times "call for a lot of courage, vision, and perseverance. Not retrogression into the 17th century."

◆ ◆ ◆

Having been elected to Congress three times, Jack began a race for the Senate on April 24, 1952, seeking the seat held by Henry Cabot Lodge Jr.

"There was talk of his running for governor, and a few whispers that he might be able to take on the powerful and nationally known incumbent, Senator Henry Cabot Lodge Jr.," Eunice recalled. "There were, however, no whispers in our home about Lodge, only a mighty roar every time Jack came home." She quoted Joe as saying, "Jack, run for the Senate. You'll knock Lodge's block off."

Jack had discovered that women outnumbered men in Massachusetts. Joe found this fact important, according to Rose. "Joe said some way must be found to appeal directly to this big wad of women," Rose said. Eunice came up with the idea of holding teas. Joe thought it a "great idea," but he instructed the daughters to invite independents and Republicans as well as Democrats. "That's what Jack needs," he said. "Otherwise, this will be just another Democratic meeting."

The first tea was held on Saturday, June 15, at the Commander Hotel in Cambridge, where almost six thousand women heard Jack give a speech. In his only appearance on behalf of his son, Joe stood at the head of the receiving line.

The teas gave Jack a chance to woo women with his movie star good looks and his wit. In effect, the Kennedys had formed their own "high society." Everyone wanted to be invited. Lodge later blamed his defeat on "those damn teas."

Eventually, Joe forced Mark Dalton out as campaign manger, claiming he did not run things tightly enough. "They shouldn't have put me in the job in the first place. All of a sudden I was responsible for all phases of the campaign," Dalton said.

Bobby became the titular campaign manager. Yet Joe continued to run the show. Ralph Coghlan, who had won Joe's gratitude by treating the interview with Louis Lyons off the record, briefly became a speechwriter for Jack. He soon quit. "The old man hovered over the whole thing like a bird of prey," he recalled, "and Mark Dalton was the first casualty."

As in his business, Joe spread rumors to achieve his ends. "In 1952, during Jack's Senate campaign, Joe Alsop had been in Boston, and I met him at a bar on Third Avenue in New York," said William Dufty, Gloria Swanson's husband. Alsop said, "There's no stopping the Kennedys. That old fuck is so brilliant." According to what Alsop told Dufty, Joe used rumor to smear opponents.

At the same time, Joe was careful to write letters that gave the opposite impression of what he was doing. "Joe would write a letter that went in the files, and then do the reverse on the phone. But the Ph.D.'s are going to buy the letters," said Dufty.

When Joe's anti-Semitism became an issue, Jack defused it. At a closed meeting of three hundred prominent Boston Jews, Jack ticked off his votes on Jewish issues. "What more do you want?" he asked. "Remember, I'm running for the Senate, not my father."

The race was still a toss-up when Joe learned that John Fox, who had just bought the powerful *Boston Post* from the estate of Richard Grozier for about $4 million, needed money. In its day, the *Boston Post*, with a circulation just over 300,000, had been credited with helping to defeat James Michael Curley during his last campaign for mayor in 1949 and with being responsible for the success of Maurice Tobin, who rose from school committeeman to governor of Massachusetts.

The newspaper was located on Washington Street in what was then called Newspaper Row in downtown Boston. The *Boston Globe* was directly across the street. The *Boston Record-American* was a few minutes away in Winthrop Square. Finally, the *Boston Herald-Traveler* was a seven-minute walk away on Mason Street.

Fox had grown up in South Boston and went on to Harvard College and Harvard Law School. He had achieved remarkable success as a financier, operating out of an inconspicuous office at 89 State Street, when he decided to buy the *Boston Post* in June 1952. On September 4, a notice appeared on page one of the paper. "Mr. John Fox has assumed control of the *Boston Post* as sole owner," it said. The statement promised the paper would report the news impartially and in a "dignified manner." It also pledged that the paper would fight Communism. A supporter of Joe McCarthy, Fox was rabidly anti-Communist. By 1954, he would run editorials calling for a preemptive strike against the Soviet Union.

A paunchy man of medium height with prematurely gray hair, the new publisher immediately found himself unable to pay his bills. As a down payment, Fox had paid $2 million for the newspaper, but the IRS immediately took it for back payment of his own taxes. Even though the Massachusetts Supreme Judicial Court ordered him to do so in 1961, Fox never did pay any of the purchase price of $4 million. Nor did he pay the pensions owed to *Post* employees because, as Fox said, "I want to fight Communism."

So desperate was Fox for funds that, in an effort to bludgeon Sears, Roebuck into advertising in the paper, he had Jim Dobbins draw a cartoon holding Sears up to ridicule. "The cartoon depicted a tough, young Fox as the defender of the people and an opponent of Sears' efforts to get the necessary zoning changes to expand its operations in the Fenway area of the city," Dave Farrell later recalled in his *Boston Globe* column. Farrell called it a "brazen shakedown attempt."

"My father was always a wheeler-dealer and always needed seed money," said Michael G. Fox, his son.

Joe Kennedy was only too happy to help out. While traditionally a Democratic newspaper, the *Boston Post* under Fox favored Republicans. Just after Fox took over, the paper endorsed Dwight D. Eisenhower for president and was expected to endorse Lodge. Indeed, Fox's doctor, Dr. Julius Siegel, said Fox "hated JFK." But Robert L. Lee, a Massachusetts state senator from 1941 to 1946, recalled meeting with Joe at his apartment on Beacon Street two days before the election. After fifteen or twenty minutes, Joe received a call. He told Lee he had to leave to meet with Fox.

"The rumors were that the *Post* was with Lodge," Lee said. "About an hour afterwards, when Mr. Kennedy returned, he stated that the *Post* within two days would openly endorse Congressman Kennedy for United States Senate."

Lee called Fox's front-page endorsement of Jack the "turning point" in the campaign. Lodge had "neglected the campaign because of managing Eisenhower's fight for the presidency," Lee said. Lodge had assumed the paper would back him, and the paper's endorsement "would have been sufficient to put him back in the running."

The Republican *Boston Herald-Traveler* endorsed Lodge, while the *Boston Globe* carried on what was then its tradition of not endorsing candidates.

In June 1958, a House subcommittee held hearings on Sherman Adams, an assistant to President Eisenhower, and his intercession with federal agencies on behalf of New England textile manufacturer Bernard Goldfine, who had given Adams gifts. In response to a question, Fox, who had done business with Goldfine, admitted at the hearing that Joe had given him a $500,000 loan in late December 1952. He insisted he "repaid it with interest," and that it had nothing to do with his paper's endorsement of Jack. Fox said that just two weeks before the election, a friend had persuaded him to give up his previous support of Lodge.

Joe issued a statement saying the loan—the equivalent of $2.7 million today—was "purely a commercial transaction for 60 days only with full collateral, at full interest, and was fully repaid on time. . . ."

In interviews for this book, Raymond G. Faxon, Fox's friend and the financial vice president of John Fox & Co., the publisher's investment business, revealed the truth about the transaction for the first time. "It was part of the package to endorse Jack," Faxon said. "Please don't ask any more questions." Slowly, after many interviews, Faxon revealed more. He said that two days before the election, John Griffin, editor-in-chief of the *Boston Post*, informed Joe that the paper was about to endorse Lodge. He also told him that Fox was desperately in need of cash, having been turned down for a loan by local banks. Joe called Fox, who asked him to meet him at the 99 Club at 99 State Street, which Fox owned. In return for an endorsement of Jack, Joe offered Fox a loan that, contrary to what both men later said, carried no interest and was not fully collateralized.

"Fox needed the money, and he got it from Joe," Faxon said. "It was $500,000. Fox paid him back, but Fox took his time in paying him back. Joe had to threaten him." Faxon said it took four or five months for Fox to repay the loan.

Fox gave Joe collateral of shares in an unlisted stock worth $350,000. "There was collateral, but it was not worth $500,000," Faxon said. "The whole thing was a payoff."

Based on Faxon's recollection that a bank would have charged interest of about 5 percent at the time, the interest waived amounted to about $10,000, the equivalent of $54,000 today. Aside from that, making any loan to such a shaky financial operation without full collateral represented a bribe. "No bank would have made the loan," Faxon said. "The word 'payoff' was exactly what it was."

To this day, Faxon is afraid of some unspecified retribution. Faxon believed that, when crossed, Joe Kennedy was vicious. He recalled that Jack Kennedy himself had called from the White House to warn a friend of Faxon's of dire consequences if Faxon ever exposed what had happened.

Fox continued to try to put out the paper until 1956, when he filed for protection under the bankruptcy laws. After 125 years of publication, the paper came out with its last issue on October 24. Fox lost his yacht, his airplane, and his forty-seven-acre Connecticut estate. Always known for having a pint in his pocket, Fox began drinking even more heavily. In 1973, at the age of sixty-six, *Boston* magazine found him living in the Williams Book Store at 52 Province Street in downtown Boston. Still ranting that he would make a comeback, he blamed his troubles on the IRS. "I expect to make $5 million next year," he told the magazine.

Fox's last address was a red-brick Bowdoin Street boardinghouse, where a lady friend stopped in to care for him. He died in obscurity in 1985 at the age of seventy-eight in a Veterans Administration Hospital in Boston's Jamaica Plain section. No obituary marked his death. Perhaps that was the way he had wanted it. "He was a very brilliant man. The booze killed him," said Dr. Siegel.

Once Jack was in the White House, journalist Fletcher Knebel asked him about the loan to Fox. "Listen, that was an absolutely straight business transaction," Jack insisted. "I think you ought to get my father's side of the story," Jack said, and he offered to make Joe available. Then, as Knebel was leaving, Jack looked up and said he had to level with him.

"You know, we had to buy that paper," he said to Knebel, who later reported the remark to his wife, writer Laura Bergquist. "That remark, of course, Fletch never printed," she said.

Jack won the Senate race on November 4, 1952, polling 1,211,984 votes to Lodge's 1,141,247 votes. When Lodge called to concede defeat at 6 A.M., he reached Janet Des

Rosiers, whom Joe had placed in charge of the Beacon Street apartment where Joe stayed. She relayed the message to Jack that Lodge had conceded.

Jack reported expenses for the campaign of $349,646, probably not enough to pay for the billboard advertisements alone. It was widely assumed the true cost was several million dollars.

◆ ◆ ◆

In December 1952, Joe called Senator Joseph McCarthy, the Wisconsin Republican who had just become chairman of the Permanent Subcommittee on Investigations of the Senate Government Operations Committee. Joe had contributed to McCarthy's campaigns and invited him a number of times to Hyannis Port. There, while hanging on to a rope behind a sailboat, McCarthy had almost drowned. Besides McCarthy, the others on the boat were Joe Gargan, Jack, and Hearst. "We were dragging him with the boat, and he got his foot caught," Gargan said. "Jack dove overboard to try to pull him up. You can't stop a sailboat like a motorboat. I just reached back and untied the rope, and he came up."

Like Joe, McCarthy was a bully, adept at creating suspicion and circulating rumors to smear people as Communists. At first an undistinguished legislator, McCarthy captured national attention in February 1950 by arguing that the State Department was riddled with card-carrying members of the Communist Party. Shrewd at public relations and media manipulation, McCarthy cowed his opponents and evaded demands for tangible proof as he developed a large and loyal following. He accused the Roosevelt and Truman administrations of "twenty years of treason."

McCarthy's activities gave rise to the term McCarthyism, referring to the use of sensational and highly publicized personal attacks, usually based on unsubstantiated charges, as a means of discrediting people thought to be subversive.

Several times, Joe took McCarthy to Arthur Krock's

Georgetown home as a "valued friend," Krock recalled. McCarthy was also a guest when Eunice married R. Sargent Shriver Jr. on May 23, 1953, at St. Patrick's Cathedral in New York.

When Joe called McCarthy, the senator had already started his "jihad," as Arthur M. Schlesinger Jr. put it. But Joe admired his friend's stand. To Joe, Communism, not Nazism, posed the greatest threat. He was an old hand at spreading rumors himself.

Joe wanted McCarthy to give Bobby a job on the committee, preferably as chief counsel. McCarthy chose Roy Cohn for that job, but in January 1953 he named Bobby assistant counsel.

Bobby was blind to McCarthy's demagoguery. Joe McCarthy's "methods may be a little rough," he told reporters. "But, after all, his goal is to expose Communists in government, and that's a worthy goal. So why are you reporters so critical of his methods?"

McCarthy's failure to substantiate his claims of Communist penetration of the army in the nationally televised army-McCarthy hearings finally discredited him. On December 2, 1954, the Senate voted to condemn him, 67 to 22. Jack had been admitted to the Hospital for Special Surgery–Cornell University Medical Center in Manhattan, where he had had a double-fusion operation on his back. Infection had set in, and he had been placed on the hospital's critical list. Thus Jack was in the hospital and did not vote. Yet, under the Senate rules, Jack could have put himself on record by pairing his vote with that of another absent senator who opposed the censure. He did not give instructions either way. Thus he was the only Democrat who neither voted against nor paired against McCarthy. The family allegiance to McCarthy was demonstrated again when Bobby attended McCarthy's funeral in Appleton, Wisconsin, in May 1957.

Pat Gardner Jackson, who later worked on Jack's second senatorial campaign, recalled that when McCarthy was still powerful, he was determined to get Jack to renounce McCarthy. "I prepared a newspaper ad that quoted 99 men on the faculty of Notre Dame who issued a statement: 'Communism and McCarthy: Both wrong,'" Jackson said. "Jack agreed to sign it if [Congressman] John McCormack would co-sign it. McCormack agreed. So I took it up to Jack's apartment the next morning. Jack had on his coat and went dashing out as I arrived. Sitting at a card table in the center of the living room were Joe Kennedy and three speech writers, including Jim Landis."

Jackson read the ad aloud. After he had read two sentences, Joe "jumped to his feet with such force that he tilted the card table against the others, and he stood there shouting at me, one thing after another."

"You're trying to ruin Jack," he said over and over, "you and your sheeny friends." Joe included liberals and union leaders, as well as Jews, as part of the plot.

The next day, Jackson asked him what made his father act that way about his children.

"My father's one motive that you can understand, Pat, is love of family," he said. Then he paused and added quietly, "Although sometimes I think it's really pride."

♦ ♦ ♦

Now that Joe had gotten Jack elected to the Senate, he told him to find a wife. In May 1952, journalist Charles Bartlett had introduced Jack to Jacqueline Lee Bouvier at his home. "She took to Jack right away," Bartlett said.

"I leaned over the asparagus and asked her for a date," Jack said. Jackie smiled when later told of his comment. "There was no asparagus," she said.

Jackie had "all the social ingredients that Joe Kennedy thought would help Jack achieve the presidency," C. David Heymann wrote in *A Woman Named Jackie*. "Miss Porter's, Vassar, the Sorbonne, Debutante of the Year, the Prix de Paris, Merrywood and Hammersmith Farm. If nothing else, she gave the impression of great wealth, dispelling the notion that she might possibly be a gold digger. Her wealth was largely an illusion because in reality Jackie was almost penniless. But nobody knew that until after the marriage."

When Jack brought Jackie to Hyannis Port, Joe decided she would be Jack's wife. When she arrived, a *Life* photographer was waiting. She thought she and Jack would go sailing alone; instead, the photographer trailed after them. "*Life* Goes Courting with a United States Senator," was the headline.

Jackie cultivated Joe; she knew where the money and the power were. She wasn't afraid of him, as many others were, and she would tease him and fawn over him.

As usual, Jack did what his father told him to do. On June 24, 1953, Hugh and Janet Bouvier Auchincloss announced the engagement. Jackie had recently quit her job at the *Washington Times-Herald*. On September 12, they were married by Boston archbishop Richard Cushing in St. Mary's Church, Newport's oldest Catholic church. Nearly three hundred guests, including James Lee, Jackie's maternal grandfather, attended. Despite his hatred of Joe, Lee behaved like a gentleman.

"Joe Kennedy not only condoned the marriage, he ordained it," Jack's friend Lem Billings said. "A politician has to have a wife," Billings quoted Joe as saying, "and a Catholic politician has to have a Catholic wife. She should have class. Jackie probably has more class than any girl we've seen around here."

Lem Billings said that Jack and Jackie "were both actors, and I think they appreciated each other's performances."

Emulating his father, Jack kept his options open, dating other women. "Obviously, Jack was influenced by Joe as far as women go," Spalding said. "I think the fact the old man was so obvious with women must have made Jack come to different conclusions about them. . . . I think Joe made this distinction between marriage and man's quest for women. He thought there was an excuse for it [philandering]."

Later, Spalding and Jack were swimming at Camp David.

"I was getting a divorce," Spalding said. "Jack said, 'Why do that? Try it my way.' In other words, nab girls while you're married. Everybody was fair game to go to bed with. I said, 'You don't understand. I fall in love. You don't.' He said, 'That's been said.'"

Jack's sisters made fun of Jackie, just as they later belittled Virginia Joan Bennett, who married Ted in 1958. They referred to Jackie as "The Deb" and noted that her preferred pronunciation of her name—"Jack-LEAN"—rhymed with "queen." For her part, Jackie ridiculed the sisters' frantic lifestyle and their need to win every game instead of enjoying sports. She called the Kennedy daughters the "rah-rah" girls. When they pulled her into a touch football game, she looked desperately at Ted Sorensen, Jack's speechwriter, and said, "Tell me one thing. Which way do I run?"

Rose and Jackie merely tolerated each other. Jackie called Rose "scatterbrained" and made fun of Rose's habit of pinning notes to herself. Rose was amused by Jackie's habit of running water in the bathroom to drown out the sounds of her going to the toilet.

Yet they were more alike than not. Like Rose, Jackie had a fetish about expensive clothes and little interest in sex. Photographers at the *Washington Times-Herald* thought of Jackie as a "boy." Gore Vidal, a stepson of Jackie's stepfather, said she was "ultra-fastidious." As a result, he said, she "never particularly concerned herself with sex. She finds it untidy." Close friends said her reaction to her first sexual experience was, "Oh! Is that all there is to it?"

Nonetheless, when Jackie found a man she wanted, she became a lighthouse, charming everyone in sight. "She zeroes in on you with those wide-set eyes and listens to you with a shining, breathless intensity," Vidal said.

Married or not, Jack's appetite for sex with different women continued unabated. He would pick up women at parties and leave Jackie stranded. He rented an apartment at the Carroll Arms, where he participated in "groups" with two young secretaries at a time, according to his friend George

Smathers. "He used to go to the Carroll Arms with [a friend], and they would have some girls over there from time to time," Smathers said.

In contrast to Rose's stony attitude, Jackie was clearly upset by Jack's philandering. "Jack kept assuring us that she didn't suspect, when it was obvious that she knew exactly what was happening," Jack's friend James Reed said. "He was so disciplined in so many ways. Discipline was, after all, the secret of his success. But when it came to women, he was a different person. It was Jekyll and Hyde."

23

COMPARTMENTS WITHIN COMPARTMENTS

One of Gertrude Ball's earliest assignments as Joe's New York secretary was to type the research reports that Joe's employees had written and which became chapters in Jack's book, *Profiles in Courage*.

"Mr. [James] Fayne did some of the research on it, and [James] Landis did some of the research on it while Jack was in the hospital in New York City with a bad back," Ball said. "I typed up their reports, their notes, to give to him. I typed up some work from Jack after he got their notes and put some of it together. It might not have been the final form. The Daniel Webster chapter Landis did most of the research on. Mr. Fayne did research on some of the other chapters." Ball said she understood Ted Sorensen, the bespectacled, lean, intense, and completely devoted lawyer who became Jack's speechwriter, wrote final drafts.

Harper & Row published *Profiles in Courage* on January 2, 1956. A compendium of prosaic vignettes of men like John

Quincy Adams and Daniel Webster, the book was a bestseller and gained Jack national attention. A year after its publication, the book won Jack the Pulitzer Prize.

Joe Kane, Joe's cousin and political adviser, later said that Joe had employees buy huge quantities of the book at critical bookstores to generate enough sales to place *Profiles in Courage* on bestseller lists, just as he had done with Jack's previous book.

Joe then persuaded Arthur Krock to lobby the Pulitzer Prize Board on behalf of *Profiles in Courage*. Krock said Joe "came to me for that," Krock recalled. While Krock was no longer a member of the advisory board, he was able to "logroll" its members, writing letters to most of them.

To be sure, Jack had suggested people to profile and had collated the material others produced for him. Janet Des Rosiers recalled seeing Jack working on the book. "I saw Jack write *Profiles in Courage* in Palm Beach after his back operation," she said. "His bedroom was piled high with reference books. He would sit in bed and write in longhand."

But Jack was a poor writer and had little patience for tedious research. Mark Dalton, who wrote speeches for Jack during his first campaigns, recalled that Jack would contribute ideas and concepts. "He could write," Dalton said. "What he needed was a good editor. It might be incoherent and not quite fit together."

For his 1980 book on Jack, author Herbert S. Parmet compared Jack's handwritten version of the book with the finished product and found there was little resemblance between the two. He described Jack's writing as a "disorganized, somewhat incoherent mélange from secondary sources." He found "very rough passages without paragraphing, without any shape, largely ideas jotted down as possible sections, obviously necessitating editing."

"Jack told me Joe got people to help him with Jack's writing," his friend Henry James Jr. said. "Jack told me they did a rewrite job."

This was hardly the way Pulitzer Prize winning books are

supposed to be written. In disclosing that she had typed research reports that formed the basis of *Profiles in Courage*, Ball revealed for the first time that not only the writing but most of the research for the book was not Jack's. But at the time, Ball was not about to go to the newspapers and say that Jack's father had, in effect, written his book for him.

On Monday morning, December 9, 1957, Jack asked Washington lawyer Clark Clifford to come to his office in the Senate. By now, Jack was a member of the prestigious Senate Foreign Relations Committee. Joe had called Senate Majority Leader Lyndon B. Johnson, the Democratic whip in the Senate, and "pleaded with him to get his boy on the Senate Foreign Relations Committee," former senator George Smathers, a friend of Jack's, said. Johnson complied.

But that Monday, Jack had more pressing things on his mind. He was disturbed about columnist Drew Pearson's appearance on ABC's *Mike Wallace Interviews*. In the interview, Pearson charged that Jack had won a Pulitzer Prize the previous May for a ghostwritten book.

"Jack Kennedy . . . is the only man in history that I know who won a Pulitzer Prize on a book which was ghostwritten for him, which indicates the kind of public relations setup he's had," Pearson said.

Jack called the report "a direct attack on my integrity and honesty." He wanted Clifford to sue ABC, Wallace, and Pearson.

It soon became clear that Jack was only carrying out his father's commands. As the two talked, Joe phoned. Clifford could hear Joe screaming at Jack. Joe then asked to speak with Clifford. Before Clifford could say hello, Joe said, "I want you to sue the bastards for $50 million. Get it started right away. It's dishonest, and they know it. My boy wrote the book. This is a plot against us."

"Mr. Ambassador," Clifford said, "I am preparing at this moment to go to New York and sit down with the people at ABC."

"Sit down with them, hell!" Joe screamed. "Sue them, that is what you have to do, sue them!"

"Well," Clifford said, "we may have to do that, but first we want to try to see if there isn't some solution."

Joe continued to demand that Clifford sue, but Jack seemed to understand that the issue could be handled less contentiously. Clifford met with ABC officials, who had asked Pearson who the ghostwriter was. He had said it was Sorensen. Jack pointed out that he had identified Sorensen in the acknowledgments as his research associate. He said he paid him $6,000.

Meanwhile, Sorensen had begun assembling affidavits from people who said they had seen Jack writing the book. In return for Jack's promise to drop all claims against the network, ABC agreed to air a retraction at the beginning of Wallace's show on Saturday evening, December 14, 1957. Oliver Trayz, an ABC vice president, said in the statement that ABC had inquired into the charge and had determined that it was "unfounded." Abjectly, the ABC official continued: "We deeply regret this error and feel it does a great injustice to a distinguished public servant and author and to the excellent book he wrote. We extend our sincere apologies to Senator Kennedy, his publishers, and the Pulitzer Prize Committee."

Wallace disassociated himself from the apology. Later, he called it a "craven gesture and an insult to Pearson." He said ABC should have had "the fortitude to call [Kennedy's] bluff."

A year after the incident, Clifford suggested to Jack that he meet with Pearson. Jack dazzled Pearson with his wit and charm, and later Pearson wrote in his diary that Jack had showed him his original notes. "I'm still dubious as to whether he wrote much of the final draft himself," Pearson wrote. "But he also showed enough knowledge of the book, had lived with the book, made the book so much a part of him, that basically it *is* his book."

In his memoirs, Clifford said he believed that Pearson's conclusion in his diary was "pretty close" to the mark. "Kennedy had help, and plenty of it—but the book was his."

Parmet came to the opposite conclusion. Even without knowing that Joe's employees had conducted the research and written the first drafts, he said that Jack's role was "overseer, or, more charitably, as a sponsor and editor, one whose final approval was as important for its publication as for its birth."

In other words, just as Drew Pearson had said, the book had been ghostwritten for Jack. Within the family, Joe always counseled against filing libel suits, no doubt because he realized that, in the course of the proceedings, they could uncover his unsavory activities. While he never did file a suit, throughout his life Joe would use the threat of filing one to intimidate the press and suppress the truth about his pursuits. With the exception of Earle Looker's 1937 *Fortune* piece, which Joe had had killed, the press never did investigate him.

◆　◆　◆

Even if the press had had the courage to probe Joe, newspapers would have found it difficult to penetrate his activities. Gertrude Ball was always amazed at how well Joe compartmentalized his operations. Joe's New York office was the heart of his operations, yet Ball—who worked for Joe from 1952 to 1983—knew only a fraction of his interest.

The New York office consisted of some twenty employees who worked in carpeted quarters. The office administrator was Thomas J. Walsh, a certified public accountant who had been with Price, Waterhouse until he joined Joe in 1954. Paul Murphy oversaw the office as Joe's confidant. The work of the office was to manage the family investments and the finances of each family member.

Joe "got a report every three months on everything he owned," Ball said in the first interview she has ever given on the Kennedys. "Our office was like a switchboard. Everything came into the office. A small number of people could control a number of companies. The foundation had one desk. Oil investments, real estate, all were one desk. Stocks and bonds were another desk." Still another accountant handled the personal accounts of family members. "Everyone [in the family] was kind of on a budget," Ball said. "Whatever income came in, half went back into the trusts to be reinvested. Once they started getting married, some of their bills went to their homes, but some came to us."

Joe had compartments within compartments—the way the Central Intelligence Agency is supposed to operate. "Joe believed that no one person should know what was going on. Only one person knew what was going on, and that was Joe Kennedy," a confidant said. "He had a mind that could grasp all the details."

While Ball knew about the family's personal finances, she had no access to Joe's payroll records. Even Walsh, who kept the records in a ceiling-high safe, did not know about the payoffs Joe made in the political arena. Usually, these assignments were carried out by trusted people hired on a consulting basis. They did not mix with the New York office and did not know each other.

Within the New York office, gossiping about Joe's business was frowned upon. To make sure everyone was staying tight-lipped, Joe periodically ran his own tests. For example, one morning Joe came into the office and told Ball he wanted his pearl formal-wear studs from the office safe. Ball said she did not have the combination. When Murphy later delivered the studs, Joe said he did not need them after all. Ball took this to be an exercise to make sure she did not have the combination.

"If Mr. Kennedy gave an order, he wanted that order obeyed," she said. "Nobody ever really got close to Mr. Kennedy in the office. He was the boss. You wouldn't ask him personal questions. If he went to a show the night before, you might say, 'Was it a good show?' If he played golf, you might ask how it went. He would say it went well, but he wouldn't say what his score was."

The office rented space at a storage company that kept old files and hundreds of cases of Haig & Haig Pinch Bottle Scotch left over from Joe's ownership of Somerset Importers Inc. The files alone took up as much space as an average size house.

It was the job of Leo Racine to make sure cases of the Scotch were sent at Christmastime to such people as Arthur Krock and Sam Rayburn, the Speaker of the House, according to Ball. William Douglas received from Joe not only cases of Haig & Haig Pinch Bottle delivered to him in his chambers at the Supreme Court but a personal loan as well.

Joe was careful not to display his wealth. "Ninety percent of the people who came to that office wanted to take money from his pocket and put it into theirs," Ball said. Joe would go to lunch with Cardinal Spellman and remark to Ball, "This lunch is going to cost me $10,000." But when Joe thought Spellman had favored Richard Nixon over Jack for president, Joe cut off all contributions.

Ball recalled how eagerly the archdiocese sought to reestablish good relations. "One time in 1960, Mrs. [Rose] Kennedy wanted to go to a Christmas party given by the cardinal, and she wanted me to get a ticket for her," Ball said. "So I called the chancery office to get a ticket. I said I would send somebody to get it." But the chancery insisted on delivering it, and the person who was sent was a monsignor. "It was obvious he [the cardinal] was trying to get him [Joe] back. If you're crossed off the list, you're off. He had friends that, right or wrong, he was with them. It would take years before he trusted you that much."

For years, Joe kept his main bank accounts at Morgan Guaranty Company. One day, he walked into the bank's Paris office to cash a $1,000 check. "He had to wait a half an hour while they verified who he was, and they charged him $3.75 to cash it," Ball said. "He said, 'Thank you very much,' walked out, got on the phone, and said, 'Take every cent out of that bank.' Morgan Guaranty almost died," Ball continued. "They had representatives coming into the office. Paul Murphy said there was nothing he could do. 'My instructions are to take every cent out.' " Joe switched the accounts—which Ball thought had average balances of more than $1 million—to Bankers Trust Company.

Joe paid only average salaries, but he made up for it with small favors for the staff. For example, he gave them tickets to charity dinners, which generated loyalty. One night, when Joe attended a charity ball for retarded children at the Plaza Hotel, Ball found him watching the dancing through a concealed window above the ballroom. Joe claimed he did not want to disrupt the party by dancing himself, but Ball said, "He was there for an hour and a half. He loved to see them doing the twist. I'm sure he liked watching the girls."

Yet in the twenty-nine years Ball worked for Joe, she said she never saw any indication that Joe had girlfriends. She often dealt with Janet Des Rosiers, Joe's secretary in Hyannis Port, but had no idea she was his mistress.

"We never knew about girlfriends," Ball said. "I never knew what they did after 6 P.M. I might know they had bought two tickets for the theater. I didn't know who he was going with." As far as Ball could tell, Joe was an "honest and fair man."

◆ ◆ ◆

When in New York, Joe arrived at the office just after 9 A.M., always wearing a blue suit that accentuated his blue eyes. He would lunch at Le Pavillon or La Caravelle and return by 3 P.M. He left the office by 4:30 or 5 P.M. "Sometimes he said, 'I have half a day's work done before you people get to work,' " Ball said. "That was true. He was up at 6 A.M."

"He liked to see everybody busy," Ball said. "He didn't want you sitting around." Yet Joe was considerate. "We were giving a party for someone getting married," Ball said. "It was to begin at 2 P.M. They said come and have something to eat. I said, 'Let me finish this letter.' Mr. Kennedy took the letter and said, 'Come.' If it was party time, it was party time. If it was work time, it was work time."

Eventually, Ball's job was to act as liaison between the office and family members. She made sure they registered their vehicles, renewed their driver's licenses, and paid their bills. It was a difficult job because, as rich kids, the family had little sense of responsibility. "You would get the license plates and give instructions for which plate to put on which car," Ball said. "They would mix it up. I would warn them you will get the whole family down on you if you don't sign that form. They would send it to me instead of to the Motor Vehicle Administration. Invariably, things would come to me instead of to where I told them to send it. It was frustrating."

Joe insisted that employees refer to each member of the Kennedy family by his or her first name. Otherwise, he said, he wouldn't know which person was being discussed. "He was Mr. Kennedy and Rose was Mrs. Kennedy. If we talked about the children, he said call them Eunice or Teddy or Jack. Otherwise, 'I don't know whom you are talking about.' If Ethel called, and you called her Mrs. Kennedy, you got bawled out," Ball said.

One day, Eunice sent Ball two boxes of personal bills. Ball called her and asked what she was supposed to do with them. Apparently, over a period of months, Eunice's secretary had been throwing all of Eunice's bills into the box, neglecting to pay them. "What can you make of them?" Eunice asked Ball.

"It took me six months to straighten things out with all these merchants and department stores. It was terrible," Ball said.

Because of her role as liaison with the family, Ball wound up acting as confidant. One day, Rose called her from Hyannis Port. "Gertrude, I can't ask everybody this question, but what is inflation?" Rose said. "I said, 'It's kind of hard to explain,'" Ball said. "'I can give you an example better. . . . When I first came here, you used to buy evening gowns that cost $350. I used to think that was an awful lot of money.' She said, 'Yes, I did.' I said, 'Today, for the same dress, you would have to spend $1,500.' She said, 'Yes, that's right.' I said, 'That's inflation.' 'Oh,' she said, 'that's what they are all talking about.'"

Rose confided to Ball that she was going into New York Hospital to have a "female problem" addressed. Rose was embarrassed to tell the family, so she only told Ball and checked in under an assumed name. When no one came to visit Rose at the hospital, Rose's doctor told Ball to let the family know where Rose was.

Before family members made investments or major purchases, the office checked them out. If word leaked out that a Kennedy was looking at a piece of property, the price invariably went up. The office would have the property appraised, and if the price were too high, the office would advise against the purchase. In effect, the accountants had veto power over the children's finances. As in everything else, the children did as they were told.

The job of telling the children bad news fell to Ball. She found that if she broke bad news gently to them, they were understanding. "The men would say, 'Will you tell Jean this or Pat that?'" Ball said. "I would say, 'I'm the bearer of bad news.' If you prepared them, you could work it out with them. If I blurted it out, I would get a balling out."

Like Rose, Joe was frugal. He had two apartments at 270 Park Avenue. He used his apartment for Rose if she was visiting, Des Rosiers, or other girlfriends. One afternoon, he told Leo Racine that he was having some friends over for dinner. They included Carroll Rosenbloom, the owner of the Baltimore Colts, and Morton Downey. As Joe's errand boy, Racine would sometimes mimic himself: He would salute, click his heels, and say, "I'm from Ambassador Kennedy's office." This time, Joe wanted Racine to buy lemons for the drinks he planned to serve. Not knowing how many people were coming, Racine bought twelve.

The morning after the dinner, Joe walked into the office and asked for Racine. "We thought, 'What's Leo done now?'" Ball said.

"What did you buy all those lemons for?" Joe wanted to know. "I only needed three."

"How did I know how many he needed?" Racine said later.

"That's how he was," Ball said. "He would tell us to turn off lights in offices when no one was in the room. He would say, 'Are we working for the electric company?'"

In fact, "None of the Kennedys is free with money," Ball said. "They never had much in their pockets. Sometimes, they would borrow from me and say, 'Take it out of petty cash.'" Jean Kennedy Smith, who married Stephen Edward Smith in May 1956, would borrow $10 for a taxi. She would not repay the loan, and she would instruct Ball to deduct the amount from her account.

◆ ◆ ◆

One of the recommendations of the first Hoover Commission, on which Joe served, was that Congress establish a joint committee to oversee the operations of the intelligence community. The existing congressional committees gave the agencies little oversight. Because of fear of leaks from Capitol Hill, Dwight Eisenhower, who was elected president on November 4, 1952, instead established the Board of Consultants on Foreign Intelligence Activities, now called the President's Foreign Intelligence Advisory Board. The board was to investigate problems at the Central Intelligence Agency and other intelligence agencies and report to the president on how to improve intelligence operations.

After ordering the FBI to conduct a background check, Eisenhower appointed Joe to the new board on February 6,

1956. Joe had become an enthusiastic supporter of Richard M. Nixon, who was vice president under Eisenhower and probably had recommended him. Joe wrote to his friend William Douglas that Nixon was being treated "lousy." He suggested it was because of Nixon's "conviction" of Alger Hiss, a former State Department employee said by *Time* editor Whittaker Chambers to have been a Communist spy. As chairman of the House Un-American Activities Special Subcommittee, Nixon investigated the charge. Joe told Douglas there couldn't have been "any other good reason" for criticism of Nixon.

Nine days after his appointment, Joe had lunch with J. Edgar Hoover. As a special service contact, Joe had used his periodic debriefings by FBI agents to flatter Hoover. After a typical visit with Joe at Hyannis Port in August 1953, J.J. Kelly, the special agent in charge of the FBI's Boston field office, reported to Hoover that Joe was very high in praise of "you personally and the bureau generally." Joe stated "unequivocally" that if it were not for the FBI, the "country would go to hell."

Kelly quoted Joe as dismissing a recent newspaper column by Westbrook Pegler criticizing Hoover. Joe insisted it was merely an effort to please the "Jews, Negroes, and the Communist element behind the civil liberties outfit, as well as the NAACP." This compliment, in turn, rated a letter back from Hoover commending Joe.

Later, Joe told the Boston FBI office that Ted Kennedy had relayed the fact that Edward Bennett Williams, the Washington criminal lawyer, had "unfavorably slanted" against the FBI a talk he gave at the University of Virginia Law School. Joe suggested that the FBI send a speaker to the campus, where Ted was a student, to give the FBI's side. Clyde Tolson, Hoover's deputy, wrote, "Good idea" on the internal memo. It turned out Williams was scheduled to speak at the university but had not yet done so.

For all the mutual backslapping, the FBI recommended against giving Joe a meritorious service award. After all, he had "not affirmatively actually done anything of special value to the bureau," a bureau official wrote. By 1954, Joe's status as a special service contact had been terminated. Yet Joe continued to ingratiate himself with the director, enhancing his own prestige and virtually guaranteeing that the FBI would not investigate him.

By 1955, Joe was urging Hoover to run for president. He told Hoover he had heard Walter Winchell mention the FBI director as a possible candidate, and he said that it would be "the most wonderful thing for the United States." If Hoover ran, Joe said he would "guarantee" him the "largest contribution that you would ever get from anybody . . . I think the U.S. deserves you. I only hope it gets you."

Joe wrote to Hoover, "I think I have become too cynical, but the only two men I know in public life today for whose opinion I give one continental* both happen to be named Hoover—one John Edgar and one Herbert—and I am proud to think that both of them hold me in some esteem."

Now that Joe was a member of the intelligence board, he asked Hoover for his advice. Hoover always sought to expand the FBI's jurisdiction and was only too happy to share with Joe some of the CIA's failings in order to show that the FBI should assume more of its job overseas.

Joe told Hoover that he had recommended that the members of the intelligence board move to Washington and work full-time on problems like the overlapping operations of intelligence agencies. He had found no support for the idea.

In Palm Beach, Joe had lunch with Allen W. Dulles, then the CIA's deputy director for plans, a euphemism for the clandestine operations of the spy agency. Afterward, Joe wrote to Hoover, "I asked what he thought of Marilyn Monroe, Jayne Mansfield, and Anita Ekberg," referring to the three top sex goddesses of the time. "He said that he had never heard of the last two, and then I asked him how he liked Perry Como, and he asked me what he did."

---

*A piece of paper money issued by the Continental Congress during the Revolutionary War.

Joe took advantage of his intelligence position to ask the CIA to help arrange his overseas travel. F. Mark Wyatt, a CIA officer based in northern Italy, recalled that Joe asked Gerald M. Miller, the chief of the CIA's station in Rome, to "set up the golf games and reservations" when Joe attended the wedding of Grace Kelly and Prince Rainier of Monaco.

The job of dealing with Joe fell to Wyatt. "He wanted to embark on the *Andrea Dorea* or something like that," Wyatt said. "He wanted the best service. He was extremely demanding. He wanted to live this up to the hilt. He was on the president's intelligence board, and I had no choice but to go along."

◆ ◆ ◆

As a movement grew in the summer of 1956 to nominate Jack for vice president on the Democratic ticket with Adlai E. Stevenson, Joe warned Jack that Stevenson would never win and advised against running with him.

"I told him it was a terrible mistake," his father later said. "I knew Stevenson didn't have a chance." But once Jack was in the running, Joe, who was on the Riviera, "spent the next eighteen hours calling everybody he knew at the convention to help Jack," Ted Kennedy said.

Jack went on CBS' *Face the Nation* to say he was not a candidate for president or vice president but would accept if he were nominated. On August 16, on the first ballot at the Chicago convention, Stevenson won the Democratic nomination for president. After Eleanor Roosevelt let it be known that she had misgivings about Jack because he had failed to condemn Joe McCarthy, Jack lost the vice presidential slot to Senator Estes Kefauver of Tennessee. Jack came within thirty-nine votes of winning.

Furious, Joe later said this was the only time Jack had not taken his advice. But the exposure gave Jack more national prominence.

A week after the convention, Jack was on a cruise in the

Mediterranean when Jackie, pregnant for the first time, gave birth to a stillborn child at Newport, Rhode Island. She was staying at the family's twenty-eight-room estate set on seventy acres overlooking Narragansett Bay. The *Washington Star* interviewed the boat's skipper, who said "several young women" were on the cruise.

Meanwhile, Joe was staying with Janet Des Rosiers at the Hotel Raphael in Paris when he began experiencing extreme pain in his lower abdomen. Des Rosiers and an American doctor accompanied Joe on a flight to Boston, where he checked into the New England Baptist Hospital for a week.

Joe insisted that Des Rosiers check into the hospital with him to keep him company. Des Rosiers had a slight case of strep throat, so she exaggerated the symptoms.

"The doctors and nurses were fussing over me," she said. "But I think they knew. This was an indication of his need to not be alone. I think the thought of being alone in the hospital was more than he could tolerate."

On September 13, 1956, Joe, then sixty-eight, had a prostatectomy—removal of the prostate gland. Rose did not visit Joe in the hospital, Des Rosiers said. But J. Edgar Hoover wrote to Joe to say he was "pleased" to hear that he was making a rapid recovery.

Rose continued to pretend that she did not know Des Rosiers was having an affair with her husband. On May 19, 1956, she wrote to Des Rosiers on TWA stationery. Rose said she wanted to let Des Rosiers know how much the Kennedys appreciated "your thoughtfulness, your willing cooperation under all circumstances, your light and cheerful disposition, besides many other sterling qualities of mind and heart which you have displayed to us so often during the last few years."

In writing to her, Rose established dominion over her. Des Rosiers may have been Joe's mistress, but Rose was still her employer. "It's remarkable that she had no feelings," Des Rosiers said. "Any woman would be jealous to some degree. She never was."

Joe meanwhile continued to pose as a moral arbiter. On December 27, 1956, the Boston papers reported that he had banned from his theaters the film *Baby Doll*, a sizzling Tennessee Williams tale about a child bride, because it was "immoral.

"I have been in this business forty-five years, and I think this is the worst thing that has ever been done to the people and to the industry," Joe huffed.

24

The Cardinal

In November 1957, Joe had lunch with Francis Cardinal Spellman at the cardinal's residence at 452 Madison Avenue in New York. Cardinal Spellman, who had officiated at the weddings of three of Joe's children, knew that the beautiful young women Joe introduced as his "nieces" were, in fact, his girlfriends. Indeed, just the night before Joe came to lunch at the cardinal's residence, Ned Spellman, the cardinal's nephew, had reported to his uncle that he had once again seen Joe that evening dining at the sumptuous Le Pavillon with a well-sculpted blonde.

From the pulpit, Spellman would rail against immodesty in the movies and magazines, calling for government censorship. He began a crusade against the "immoral and indecent" attitude toward marriage presented in *Two-Faced Woman*, starring Greta Garbo. But in private, Spellman was tolerant of the man who had given so many millions of dollars to the church. Between Spellman and his nephew, the fresh-faced young things always in Joe's company were a joke. The sighting on the night before the luncheon was no exception.

"I said, 'Uncle Frank, I saw Joe Kennedy last night having dinner at Pavillon,'" Ned Spellman recalled. "He said, 'Was he with his niece?' He had a big smile on his face, meaning . . . 'Is he with his girlfriend?' Niece was just a codeword."

The main meal of the day at the cardinal's residence was always lunch, served promptly at 1 P.M. Joe had just finished a fruit salad and was beginning the main course of roast beef when he mentioned his latest activities. "I just bought a horse for $75,000," Joe told the cardinal. "And for another $75,000, I put Jack on the cover of *Time*."

Ned Spellman, who was at the lunch, recalled that Joe was "very proud of the fact that he had spent $75,000, and now he would not have to spend as much [on advertising]." The sum was equivalent to $385,676 today. "He did not say whether he paid it directly to [Henry] Luce," who was editor-in-chief and principal stockholder in Time Inc., Spellman said.

On December 2, 1957, Jack's smiling face appeared for the first time on *Time*'s cover. As ordained by Joe, he had just begun his bid for the presidency.

"As far as I know, Luce had nothing to do with it," said Otto Fuerbinger, who was assistant managing editor in charge of covers at the time. "The point was, who is going to run? He wasn't much of a senator. That cover story gave him fairly high marks for his ideas. We had him to lunch in New York before we did that. I remember he talked about how low his name recognition was then. He really wasn't all that well known."

Fuerbinger said, "You wouldn't have to pay anyone to get him on the cover." Moreover, he said, Luce by then had largely ceded the magazine to the editors.

Yet the evidence is that well into the 1960s Luce continued to exercise editorial control of the magazines he had founded. In 1956, Luce was staying with Joe on the Riviera when he cabled his editors that they might devote more space to Jack, who was emerging as a national figure. But Luce had mixed feelings about Jack. He thought him too liberal and not tough enough on Communism. Stanley Karnow, then a *Time* correspondent, recalled Luce's saying after Jack won the Oregon primary, "Well, it looks like we'll have to stop Jack."

Editorially, *Life*—which had earlier run a cover on Jack— endorsed Nixon for president while praising Jack as comparable to Theodore Roosevelt. Luce was not directly involved in that decision. But when Jack heard that *Life* was going to run a story saying that evangelist Billy Graham was coming out for Nixon, Jack called Luce to complain that the story would be unfair. According to what Luce told his mistress Lady Jean Campbell, he then ordered the story killed.

"Maybe Joe Kennedy called Harry and put the pressure on, too," she told Ralph G. Martin. "The double-whammy. But he only told me about the Jack-whammy, not the Joe-whammy. Maybe because he knew how I felt about old slimy Joe."

"My understanding of that [Jack's appearance on the cover of *Time*] was Joe saw Luce in front of Le Pavillon, and Joe said, 'Why don't you give Jack a break?'" Joe's confidant Frank Morrissey said. "I don't know if he paid money."

"Joe had a good deal to do with getting Luce to put Jack on the cover," George Smathers said. "Jack had not made any great record as a congressman or senator. It was nothing outstanding in terms of what others were doing. Lots of congressmen had more legislative accomplishments than Jack."

Joe could not help boasting about the cover story to his friend Max Beaverbrook, the London publisher. "Weren't you a little surprised that *Time* went as far out as it did for Jack in his article?" he asked. "I'll bring you up to date on this when I see you."

While Joe routinely lied to the media, he was not in the habit of inventing stories for confidants such as Spellman. Moreover, he routinely paid off publishers and public officials to get what he wanted. While Jack eventually would have been a candidate for *Time*'s cover, giving such prominence to a fledgling candidate was unusual. The piece gave the "Democratic Whiz of 1957," as the cover story called him, a tremendous boost. Jack was gratified by the story and phoned Marshall Berges, the author, in the middle of the night to express his pleasure.

If Joe had one area of expertise, it was manipulating the media. Long before spin doctors and political gurus talked of "packaging" presidential candidates, Joe shaped Jack's image more effectively than any Madison Avenue executive. "We're going to sell Jack like soap flakes," Joe said.

Already, Joe had persuaded a top television executive in New England to give Jack lessons in going before a camera. "He was consumed by the fact that TV would make the difference in the presidential election," the executive said. "Jack was the fastest read I ever saw. He mastered TV production. He was very natural. Jack was himself. We taught him the techniques. We had him look through the camera lens. He was formidable. This guy did his homework. He worked at it."

Al Lehmann, an aide to John A. Volpe when Volpe was governor of Massachusetts, thought Joe's chief contribution was bringing "electronics to politics." He said, "The old politicians used rule of thumb [experience], but Joe and his boys left nothing to chance." Joe "learned a lot of tricks" from the movies during his days in Hollywood, Lehmann said.

Lehmann decided the "mystique of the Kennedys" has to do with the fact that "the Irish worship kings. . . . They can believe anything the king tells them, and today the Kennedys are kings."

In an unusually frank interview, Joe told the *Saturday Evening Post* that he wanted Jack to be president, Bobby to be attorney general, and Ted to be a senator. The September 7 story included David Hackett's "Rules for Visiting the Kennedys." "Now for the football field," Hackett said. "It's 'touch,' but it's murder if you don't want to play . . . don't let the girls fool you. Even pregnant, they can make you look silly. . . ."

The yarns of touch football made good copy, but Richard Harwood, then a *Washington Post* reporter, gave a more telling description of how the game was played. Bobby "jammed his palm into his face in a deliberate foul," according to an account by Jack Newfield. After scoring a touchdown anyway, Harwood turned to Bobby and said, "You're a dirty player, and a lousy one, too."

Joe's disclosure of his plans for his sons was out of character. Most of the time, Joe concealed his role. "It would be silly," Joe had earlier told a *Time* correspondent, "to pretend that we're unaware of all the talk about Jack being a presidential candidate in 1960, and it would be just as silly to pretend that we don't even think about the possibility." Joe said he was in Europe during the Chicago convention. "I still don't understand it all," he said.

Joe maintained that Jack became interested in politics by listening to his two grandfathers talk at Sunday gatherings. "Aside from that, I don't think you could say that anyone ever took him by the hand and led him politically," Joe said. Indeed, he never counseled Jack on his career, Joe said. What was important, he averred, was instilling in his children a sense of "responsibility."

Joe told Bill Cunningham of the *Boston Herald*: "I guess it's no secret that Jack and I don't see eye-to-eye on some things. . . ." He said he did not want to fuel a story about "dissension in the Kennedy family."

The real secret to the efficiency of Jack's organization was simple, Stewart Alsop revealed in the *Saturday Evening Post*: "Jack Kennedy himself makes all the major decisions and most of the minor ones." Alsop quoted an unnamed Kennedy aide as saying, "We just do what Jack asks us to do." This, then, was behind what Alsop called "Kennedy's Magic Formula."

Based on what he had been told, James MacGregor Burns wrote that "Kennedy won his first big race mainly on his own." He said his father's activities "probably had only a small effect on the outcome."

Dave Powers, Jack's aide, contended that there was practically no Kennedy money in Jack's campaigns. He said Jack "deftly moved his father's cigar-smoking friends into the background and replaced them with new young faces." Kenneth O'Donnell, another aide, said that Joe Kennedy "no longer knew a goddamn thing about what was going on in Massachusetts."

But Joe Timilty said Joe was, quite simply, the "mastermind" of all Jack's campaigns. Without his father, he "never would have entered politics."

"Joe knows he's controversial, so he stays out of the way," Ralph Lowell, his Harvard friend, said. "He's sort of like a caterpillar—couldn't become a butterfly, but his boys were going to fly at any price."

That price would be high. In November 1957, *Fortune* listed Joe as one of the sixteen wealthiest people in the country, with a net worth of $200 to $400 million. Only J. Paul Getty appeared in the top category of $700 million to $1 billion; seven others were in the $400 to $700 million range. Eight, including Joe, were in the $200 to $400 million range.

Joe let a business associate know that *Fortune* had overestimated. "The figure Joe wanted tossed around was $200 million," said a confidant.

By April 1960, *Fortune* had downgraded Joe to a mere $200 to $300 million in assets, in the same category with David Rockefeller. Whatever the figure, Joe was willing to devote a good chunk of it to Jack's campaign. "What's $100 million if it will help Jack?" Joe asked Landis.

◆ ◆ ◆

After more than nine years as his mistress, Janet Des Rosiers left Joe in March 1958. During the previous winter, when they were having "cook's night out" in the butler's pantry in Palm Beach, Joe had said to her, "Ann Gargan is going to come and live with us at the Cape." Des Rosiers responded, "If that happens, the two of you are going to end up alone, miserable."

Ann Gargan's mother, Agnes, was Rose's sister. Both her parents died before she was eleven. After high school, Ann decided to enter the convent. When Joe visited her at St. Mary's Convent in Notre Dame, Indiana, he noticed that her hands shook. He had her diagnosed at the Lahey Clinic, which said she had multiple sclerosis.

Since she had not taken her final vows, she had to leave the convent. (To discourage those who might want to take advantage of free room and board, no one with an incurable disease was allowed to join a convent.) Joe set up a small trust fund to support her for the rest of her life. Later, doctors said she probably had not had the disease after all.

Soon, Rose's niece became Joe's "constant companion," as Ted Kennedy put it in *The Fruitful Bough*. She said she began living with the Kennedys and traveling with Joe in 1957. But Gargan said Joe "never made a pass at me. Ridiculous. There was great warmth and affection. He was a father figure to me."

For her part, Des Rosiers had decided long ago she did not want to stay with Joe forever. As Joe grew older, sex with him had become less frequent. Then it had dwindled to almost nothing in the previous six months. "It was mutual," she said. "I had lost interest. If you reach ten years [with someone], you either stay for life or you go. . . . I just wanted my own life. I didn't want to be in this situation any longer."

As cold winds blew outside, Des Rosiers told Joe in the living room one morning that she was leaving. He asked what she planned to do. She said she hadn't yet decided. "I want to start a life of my own," she said.

When Des Rosiers told Joe that she planned to tour Europe with her female cousin, Joe wished her well and threw a going-away party for her and twenty family members at Le

Pavillon. Des Rosiers' family stayed at Joe's two Park Avenue apartments, and he gave her two cases of Dom Pérignon champagne for the voyage.

After she left, Rose wrote several warm notes of appreciation to Des Rosiers. In one letter, she imparted one of the secrets to her perpetually youthful-looking hair—brown Roux Color Curl 21. In another, she asked how to address a letter to an ambassador. "My love to you," she said. In a third, she enclosed perfume and closed by saying, "My deep appreciation for all you have done throughout the years for all of us."

In January 1962, William "Bill" H. Lawrence, a former *New York Times* reporter then at ABC-TV, wrote to Des Rosiers to say that on New Year's Eve he was at a party with Jack, Jackie, and Rose at the home of Charles B. Wrightsman. The dinner conversation began with questions about what Janet was doing and whether she was happy. After the first toast, "Rose raised her glass up to mine and said she thought we should have a toast to you, and to a happy 1962."

After she sent him a card, Joe wrote to Des Rosiers on April 10, 1958, in Spain. Unlike some of his other letters to her, this one had been dictated to a secretary. Careful about saying anything incriminating, Joe told Des Rosiers that any husband she might find would have to meet with the approval of "Cavanaugh, Houghton, and Kennedy. If he gets by the three of us, you're home safe."

Since Des Rosiers had said nothing about finding a husband, she thought the remark an attempt by Joe to come up with an acceptable reason for why she had left him.

"It must be a great satisfaction to you to have such a congenial traveling companion," he wrote. "I am looking for one of those myself."

But Joe did not lack for companions. Marianne Strong, a literary agent, recalled seeing Joe at La Caravelle one night. "I could see that he had these two very young girls, and his hands were everywhere, pinching their cheeks," she said. "I don't know what he was doing under the table, but I have a good imagination. He was diddling with them and fondling them, with them, at them."

Strong said the girls "looked like high school girls. They were not sophisticated or elegantly dressed. . . . It was so unattractive that my husband, who was a prosecutor, was appalled."

In interviews for this book, Des Rosiers expressed mixed emotions about the affair. At times, she said she felt she was used and manipulated. "He picked me out. A young girl like I was at the time can be easily overwhelmed by such a dynamic personality. If I had known what I know now, I probably would not have done it," she said. "I was a young girl taken advantage of. Absolutely. It is easy to manipulate someone if you are a powerful tycoon with a lot of practice. He was very authoritative in a nice way. There will never be a man like Kennedy." Yet at other times, she professed love for Joe and said she wished he could see her today. "He did love me," she said. "This wasn't just a fling. He didn't want me out of his sight."

As for Rose, Des Rosiers is perplexed. "I just don't understand that woman," Des Rosiers said. An incident related by Cynthia Stone Ray, who was later Rose's secretary, is instructive: Almost every day, Rose insisted on going swimming, and she wanted Ray to accompany her. "In Hyannis Port, the water was sixty-two degrees, and I didn't want to go swimming with her," Ray said. "I went into the water, and then she said she was going out of the water." So Ray hid behind the dunes, figuring Rose would assume she had continued to swim. Rose played along. "Later, she said, 'How did you like the water?'" Ray recalled. "I said, 'It was neat.' She said, 'I can see over the dunes.'"

But if Rose knew what was going on and chose to overlook it, she was not as stoic as she appeared to be. Her secret, like that of some of her children and grandchildren, was drugs. Not alcohol or illegal drugs, but rather prescription tranquilizers. Her prescription records over the years show that at various points she took five different tranquilizers to relieve nervous tension or stress. They included Seconal, Placidyl, Librium, and Dalmane. For her nervous stomach, she took Lomotil, Bentyl, Librax, and Tagamet.

"She [Rose] has a history of irritable colon [causing abdominal pain and often caused by stress] going back to 1933," wrote Dr. Russell Boles in a September 1976 medical report.

◆ ◆ ◆

On December 11, 1958, Jack wrote to Eleanor Roosevelt to berate her for a statement she had made four days earlier on ABC-TV. She had said that "Senator Kennedy's father has been spending oodles of money all over the country, and probably has a paid representative in every state by now."

Saying she had received "misinformation," Jack challenged her to name one representative, or even one example of such spending. On December 18, she replied that she had been told that Joe would spend "any money" to make his son the first Catholic president. Many people had told her of money spent by Joe on Jack's behalf. "Building an organization is permissible, but giving too lavishly may seem to indicate a desire to influence through money," she said.

Still not satisfied, Jack wrote back, again asking for proof or, if she had none, a correction. In her syndicated newspaper column, she referred to Jack's denial. That didn't satisfy Jack, who wrote her again. Finally, she outfoxed him by asking if he would like her to write another column on the subject. On January 22, 1959, Jack said he thought "we can let it stand" for the present.

Yet Joe's payoffs had just begun. "He slammed money [into the campaign] in the beginning," Tommy Corcoran said. "It was a long-shot risk. What family would do this?"

As Jack began a second term in the Senate and moved to a three-story house at 3307 N Street NW in Georgetown, Joe solicited author William Bradford Huie to distribute cash to politicians who would help Jack, according to what Huie later told a *Time* reporter. Huie said he made payoffs of $1,000—the equivalent of $4,800 today. Huie promised he would reveal more details, but he died before he could.

About the same time, Bobby, who became Jack's campaign manager, offered to pay Harry Golden, author of *For Two Cents, Plain*, to give speeches on behalf of Jack. "We need you to get the Jewish vote and other minority votes in certain geographic areas," he said. Golden declined, according to what his son told a *Time* reporter before he died.

Although it was well known, the press never raised the issue of Joe's anti-Semitism. However, a group calling itself the Lest We Forget Committee took out ads listing some of Joe's anti-Semitic statements. The ads warned that if Jack were elected, "Joseph P. Kennedy will be the most powerful man in America."

Two months before the Democratic convention, Joe was asked to speak at a reunion of his Harvard class. He declined, because he thought he might say something that would hurt Jack. "By that time, his own advancement didn't concern him," Landis said.

Joe lined up the support of key old-line political bosses such as Charles A. Buckley in the Bronx and Peter Crotty of New York. He got John McCormack, by then the House Democratic majority leader, to push for Jack with Edmund G. "Pat" Brown of California and William J. Green Jr. of Philadelphia. And he won the support of Chicago mayor Richard J. Daley.

Joe knew "instinctively who the important people were, who the bosses were behind the scenes," New York congressman Eugene Keogh said. "From 1958, he was in contact with them constantly by phone, presenting Jack's case, explaining and interpreting his son, working these bosses."

Meanwhile, the Kennedys cranked up their media campaign. In October 1959, *Look* began running a series of articles by journalist Joe McCarthy. Prepared with the family's cooperation, they might as well have been written by Joe himself. Jack was said to be in excellent health: "He says that he feels no pain worth mentioning." In fact, Jack had been diagnosed in 1947 as having Addison's disease, a failure of the adrenal glands, which accounted for Jack's weight loss and gaunt appearance. Jack joked that it was "just a result of Jackie's cooking" and told reporters that his condition was left over from a bout of malaria. When a Boston reporter suggested to his aide Ted Reardon that Jack should disclose his health history, Reardon replied, "No, old Joe doesn't want that to be done. We can't do it now."

In one of the *Look* magazine articles, McCarthy quoted Rose as saying she did not know why Jack was running for the presidency, since he could have a "nice, interesting life in the Senate." Joe was said to have little influence over his son and to have no interest in spending money on political campaigns. "In political circles, the Kennedys are not regarded as big spenders," McCarthy wrote.

If she pretended to be mystified about why Jack wanted to run for the presidency, Rose was savvy enough to know what not to say. After confiding to a *Time* reporter that she bought her dresses from Dior and other expensive Paris designers, she said, "You mustn't print that. It would cost Jack votes. Hubert Humphrey, you know, tried to hurt Jack with stories about how the Kennedys flew all around in private planes and were so very rich. No, some people wouldn't like to hear that Jack's mother bought her clothes from those expensive dressmakers in Paris."

Having already lined up support, Jack formally announced his presidential candidacy on January 2, 1960. Before three hundred cheering supporters in the Senate Caucus Room, he said he would not accept the vice presidential nomination. His agenda would emphasize foreign policy and moral ideals. He declared that the White House must be "the center of moral leadership."

A month later, Jack's friend Frank Sinatra introduced Jack to Judith Exner, a tall, black-haired, blue-eyed former actress, at the Sands Hotel in Las Vegas. On March 7, 1960, he began an affair with her at the Plaza in New York. Jack's "attitude was that he was there to be serviced," Exner said in her book. After Jack was elected, White House telephone logs would record seventy calls between them.

While seeing Jack, Exner was also seeing Sam Giancana, the Mafia boss. In a *People* magazine story, she claimed she introduced Giancana to Jack, who asked for the mob's help in financing the campaign. While that is not documented, it is clear Giancana gave money to the campaign. After the election, an FBI wiretap picked up Giancana talking with Johnny Roselli, a mob associate. He said his donation had been "accepted," yet complained that Bobby, whom Jack had appointed attorney general, was cracking down on organized crime. He had expected that "one of these days, the guy will do me a favor. . . ." Instead, as Roselli summed it up, "If I ever got a speeding ticket, not one of these fuckers would know me."

Giancana responded, "You told that right, buddy."

Meanwhile, Joe was funneling money to politicians to swing the West Virginia primary, a critical test of whether a Protestant, largely anti-Catholic state would come out for a Catholic candidate for president. Tip O'Neill recalled that Eddie Ford, a successful Boston real estate man, "went out there [with] a pocket full of money." O'Neill said Ford would "see the sheriff, and he'd say to the sheriff, 'Sheriff, I'm from Chicago. I'm on my way south. I love this young Kennedy boy. He can help this nation, by God. He's got the feeling for it, you know. He'll do things for West Virginians. I'll tell you what. Here's $3,000.'" Or, "'Here's $5,000. You carry your village for him or your county for him, and I'll give you a little reward when I'm on my way back.' And they passed money around like it was never seen."

O'Neill said Joe made all the arrangements. "Although Jack certainly knew that his father was spending a lot of money, he wasn't always aware of the details," O'Neill said in his memoirs. "But during the campaign, he was able to defuse the criticism about all his father's money by repeating one of his famous jokes." Jack would say, "I have just received the following telegram from my generous father: 'Dear Jack: Don't buy a single vote more than is necessary. I'll help you win this election, but I'll be damned if I'm going to pay for a landslide!'"

◆　◆　◆

When Des Rosiers returned from Europe in 1958, Joe called her. "You pick the job you want in New York City, and I'll get it for you," he said. Des Rosiers thanked him but said she would find her own job. "I didn't want to be indebted to anyone," she explained.

Des Rosiers began working for the president of General Dynamics Corporation. After a year and a half, a company that sold Convair airplanes offered her a job demonstrating the planes to potential buyers. She took the job, which paid a commission, and called Jack's office to see if he wanted a demonstration. Jack and an entourage flew with her from Washington to New York on the twin-engine turboprop. Impressed, he told her he would lease the plane from her for his presidential campaign.

A few days later, Joe called Des Rosiers. "Hell, Janet, Jack isn't going to rent a plane from you. We're going to buy him one," he said.

On September 22, 1959, Stephen Smith, whom Joe had placed in charge of investments at his New York office, announced the "family" was about to purchase a Convair for $385,000. The plane was named the *Caroline*, for Jack's daughter. After Jack announced his candidacy, it would be the first personal plane ever used by a presidential candidate. Jack was said to have leased it from his father for the ridiculous sum of $1.75 a mile.

As her commission, Des Rosiers received a lump sum payment of six months' salary, plus additional cash. At Jack's request, Des Rosiers became his stewardess and secretary on the forty-four-seat plane, which had been converted to a plush executive interior. She flew a quarter of a million miles with him.

On the plane, Des Rosiers often massaged Jack's feet and hands behind closed doors. Many reporters thought she must have been having sex with him. In fact, he had made a pass at her, giving her a printed napkin that said, "Don't you think it's about time you found me attractive?" But Des Rosiers was not interested.

"A lot of my friends said, 'Why don't you get a Kennedy boy?' I said, 'I wouldn't marry one of them for anything.' I wasn't impressed by their wealth. They didn't appeal to me. I didn't want to be in that group."

During the West Virginia primary campaign, when Jack lost his voice, a speech therapist told him to write notes on a yellow legal pad instead of talking. Des Rosiers kept some of them and later sold them, creating publicity about some of the unusual instructions and comments. "I got into the blonde," was one.

25

A TIP OF THE HAT

In providing the cash for Jack's campaign, Joe used the Catholic Church and, in particular, Cardinal Cushing. One of the couriers told author Peter Maas how it worked: If Boston area churches had collected $950,000 on a particular Sunday from collections, for example, Joe would write a check for $1 million to the diocese, deduct it as a charitable contribution, and receive the $950,000 in cash. Thus, in this example, the church got a contribution of $50,000, Joe could deduct the entire amount on his income tax, and he could use the money to pay off politicians without fear that it would be traced. Naming Joe, Maas included this account in his novel *Father and Son*.

"The cash is untraceable," Maas said. "Part of the money goes to the diocese. He gets a contribution from Joe Kennedy for more than what the cash is. It's brilliant. Nobody can trace the money."

In 1966, Cushing admitted that he had played a role in

making payoffs to ministers. He told Hubert Humphrey, the Minnesota senator who was Jack's Democratic opponent, "I'll tell you who elected Jack Kennedy. It was his father, Joe, and me, right here in this room." The prelate explained that he and Joe decided which Protestant ministers should receive "contributions" of $100 to $500. Cushing smiled as he described the tactic. "It's good for the church. It's good for the preacher, and it's good for the candidate."

Maas recalled that as a writer for the *Saturday Evening Post* he interviewed a political operative in one dirt-poor town in West Virginia who told him his county was for Humphrey. "A few weeks later, I interviewed him again, and he said the county was for Jack. I asked what had changed, and he said with a smile, 'My workers each got $20, and I got $150. We're for Kennedy.'"

In a June 30, 1960, interview with *Time*, Joe denied that he had paid off anyone in West Virginia. For that *Time* cover story, Jack attributed the claims that Joe was anti-Semitic to the incident involving Pat Gardner Jackson, who had wanted Jack to oppose Senator Joe McCarthy back in 1952 and faced Joe's wrath as a result. Jack said it was "unfair" to say his father was anti-Semitic based on that incident. And, sounding a familiar theme, he said his differences with his father on policy were "total."

Echoing his son, Joe responded when asked by a United Press reporter whether he was in touch with Jack's campaign activities by saying that he "read the newspapers." Yet Joe's supervision was so all-encompassing that Jack himself attributed his frenetic efforts to his father. Charles Spalding recalled being at Palm Beach when Rose urged Jack to stay over. Jack said he didn't have time. Then he turned to Joe. "If you hadn't pushed me so hard, I wouldn't be leaving," he said.

Jack beat Humphrey in West Virginia and in other key primary states. Joe was in awe. "We were standing at the pool at Palm Beach," said Spalding. "We were going to one of the primary states. The president-to-be was in the pool. Joe said, 'Look at him. He's a scrawny kid. He's going to do it. I tried all my life, and I couldn't do it. But he's going to do it.'"

♦ ♦ ♦

In the final days of the campaign for the Democratic candidacy, Jack suggested a threesome with Judith Exner in Peter Lawford's Beverly Hilton Hotel suite.

"He assured me the [other] girl was safe, that she would never talk about it to a single soul, that there was nothing wrong with a *ménage à trois*," Exner recalled. In tears, she rejected the arrangement.

Jack was a "tremendous risk taker," Exner said. "Jack felt that he could do as he pleased, and he did as he pleased."

Like his father, Jack compartmentalized his life. "No one ever knew John Kennedy, not all of him," said Charles Bartlett, his friend.

"This was obviously the way Kennedy wanted it," Richard Reeves wrote. "All his relationships were bilateral. He was a compartmentalized man with much to hide, comfortable with secrets and lies. He needed them because that was part of the stimulation; things were rarely what they seemed."

While "vigor" was his motto, Jack was in reality sick much of the time. Besides Addison's, he had persistent complications from a case of gonorrhea he contracted at Harvard. Like his father, Jack had a "Kennedy stomach." He restricted his diet to bland foods all his life.

Jackie knew about Jack's philandering and developed a visceral dislike of politics. When talk turned to politics at a party columnist Roscoe Drummond gave, "She almost literally took a chair, turned it towards a corner, and sat there for the entire evening without bothering to talk to anybody," Drummond said.

"Politics was sort of my enemy as far as seeing Jack was concerned," she once explained. "My theories for a successful marriage? I was afraid you'd ask that," she said grimly to an interviewer. "I can't say I have any yet."

"She was ready to divorce Jack, and Joe offered her $1 million to stay until Jack entered the White House," said Igor Cassini. "Then she got a taste of being first lady. But she knew of all these infidelities. He paid $1 million for her to stay with Jack until he was elected. . . . He didn't tell me, but my brother and I learned about it."

Reporter Fred Sparks overheard Jack and Jackie arguing at La Caravelle. Asking for the check, Jackie said, "I'm going to walk out on you. Every Kennedy thinks only of the family! Has anybody ever thought about my happiness?"

But then, like Rose and her daughters, Jackie never expected men to be faithful. "I don't think there are any men who are faithful to their wives," she said. "Men are such a combination of good and bad."

Nor was Jackie interested in sharing her life with the public. Once in the White House, she instructed her press secretaries to say as little as possible, with maximum politeness. Even photos of the White House were not to be given out, according to Barbara Coleman, an aide to press secretary Pierre Salinger.

Later, Jackie pressured Jack's friend Red Fay to cut two thousand words from *The Pleasure of His Company*, his book about Jack. She went to court to demand major deletions from William Manchester's *Death of a President*. And she urged Random House not to publish Jim Bishop's *The Day Kennedy Was Shot*. In the years after her husband's death, she gave only one interview, to *Publishers Weekly*.

In that respect, she mirrored the rest of the Kennedys, whom Joe had taught to control their image as carefully as Communist Party leaders.

◆ ◆ ◆

During the Democratic Convention in Los Angeles, Joe stayed at the home of Marion Davies, Hearst's mistress. The Spanish-style Beverly Hills estate sat on twelve secluded acres.

Joe never set foot on the convention floor but directed Jack's campaign through his operatives.

"Joe was the mastermind of everything," Joe Timilty said. "I was carrying out the instructions of Joe. That's what I did in all the campaigns; I represented Joe." In a nationally televised appearance, Truman tried to block Jack's nomination before the convention. He made a slip, referring to Jack as Joseph Kennedy.

When Krock suggested that if Jack didn't get the presidential nomination, he could be vice president, Joe said, "For the Kennedys, it's the castle or the outhouse. Nothing in between."

Jack won the presidential nomination on July 13, 1960. The next morning, Joe had breakfast at Davies' home with Jack, Rose, Frank Morrissey, and Timilty. They began discussing vice presidential candidates.

"Joe said, 'What about Lyndon?' " Timilty recalled. "Joe said, 'We need Texas. . . . ' Lyndon was good in the Senate. He had plenty of influence in the South."

"The ambassador insisted that Jack take Johnson as vice president because otherwise he wouldn't make it," said Morrissey, who had Jack's power of attorney. "Of course he was right. . . . At crucial points in the president's career, his judgment prevailed. . . . On all important decisions, Jack would still call the father. He gave his advice great weight."

"Jack did what Joe wanted him to do," George Smathers said. That included becoming president. "Joe had all the money and was the number one power. Even after Jack was president, he still had to be reckoned with. You could tell that Jack had great respect for what Joe thought."

The decision made, Jack called Bobby and asked him to see Johnson about the vice presidency. That day, Joe flew to New York and called Henry Luce, saying he wanted to see him. Joe timed his visit so he had to be invited to dinner, Luce recalled.

Luce knew that Joe would never hang back from anything that would advance his son's ambitions. "He didn't come just for a free meal," he said. So after a lobster dinner at his Waldorf suite, Luce decided to beat Joe to the punch. Luce laid it on the line: He realized that Jack had to appear to be left of center on domestic affairs to get the Democratic nomination, but if Jack turned soft on Communism, *Time* would slit his throat, Luce said.

Joe retorted: "How could a son of mine be a goddamned liberal?" He added, "Don't worry about him being a weak sister." That said, the two settled down to watch Jack's acceptance speech on television.

Joe retreated to the Riviera, where he told a *U.S. News & World Report* writer, "Since 1952, when Jack went to the Senate, I've never campaigned for him, never made any speeches. You know, I've never even heard Jack make a speech on television." He later claimed he had been on the Riviera during the convention.

"Jack and Bobby will run the show/While Ted's in charge of hiding Joe," a popular couplet went.

Hugh Sidey of *Time* was interviewing Jack when the subject of Joe's influence came up. Sidey turned to Red Fay and asked his opinion. Fay began to give an honest evaluation, saying, "I think that Mr. Kennedy has been the most vital force in the careers of the Kennedy men and women, particularly after they left grade school and entered high school and college."

Grimacing, Jack slid a finger across his throat. Fay quickly added that he didn't know that much about the relationship. Later, Jack chided him. "This is just the material *Time* magazine would like to have—that I'm a pawn in Dad's hands. . . . That Joe Kennedy now has the vehicle to capture the only segment of power that has eluded him. . . ."

During the campaign, Krock wrote critically of Jack, pointing out that he had never known him to associate with blacks or to express any concern about their plight. After each column, Joe would call him and say, "Why don't you give Jack a fair break?"

Krock's position quickly led to a falling out with Joe. Krock came to realize that all along Joe had only been using him.

Self-pityingly, Krock reflected that Joe "never liked me at all," but rather "found me useful and thought he might be able to use me." Joe and Krock talked only once more, when Joe called him on the phone before the inauguration and we had a "friendly talk," Krock said later.

After prostituting himself for more than two decades by using his *New York Times* column to further Joe's career, Krock had finally come to realize that he was but a pawn in Joe's empire. For his part, Joe no longer needed Krock. In 1953, James Reston had succeeded him as the chief Washington correspondent of the *New York Times*. Reston's column, not Krock's, was the most influential in Washington.

By November 1961, Krock had written to Milton S. Kronheim, Washington's preeminent liquor wholesaler, to ask that his name be dropped from the list of people who received a case of Haig & Haig Pinch Bottle at Christmas from Joe.

Joe routinely sent gifts and cash to other journalists. Thomas Winship, the editor of the *Boston Globe*, recalled that Joe routinely "gave two or three bottles of Pinch Bottle to press people—to people at the *Globe*, to political writers, and to a lot of people in Washington."

Joe sent expensive jewelry to female columnists, a confidant said, and gave cash to others. "He distributed a substantial amount to journalists," the confidant said. "He knew when to give them a full set of Tiffany sterling silver, and he knew when to say don't fuck around with me." In addition, "Reporters took consulting assignments. Some of these guys were pretty amenable to consulting fees and gifts." Columnists, especially, were "for sale"—not to mention politicians. For such purposes, Joe always kept large stashes of cash.

Dave Farrell, then managing editor of the *Boston Herald*, recalled having lunch in 1972 at Anthony's Pier 4 restaurant in Boston with Frank Morrissey and Billy Sutton. Morrissey related that Joe had once called him to Hyannis Port to help him move $1 million in cash from the basement of his home.

"A big northeast storm was coming up," Farrell said, reading from his notes of the conversation. "The old man was afraid a lot of the cash would get wet. Morrissey said he had $1 million in cash."

Morrissey said Joe entrusted valuable papers to him, but he declined to comment on whether he moved cash for him.

In 1965, Ted and Bobby would persuade Lyndon Johnson to nominate Morrissey as a federal judge. Earlier, at Joe's urging, Massachusetts governor Foster Furcolo had appointed Morrissey to the Boston Municipal Court. As a local judge, he got high marks as fair and objective. But the American Bar Association protested that Morrissey was not qualified to be a federal judge, and Morrissey asked to have his nomination withdrawn.

◆ ◆ ◆

Francis Cardinal Spellman held the fifteenth annual Alfred E. Smith Memorial Foundation Dinner at the Waldorf-Astoria on October 19, 1960. Named after the former governor of New York, the dinner ostensibly was a way to raise money for Catholic charities. But under Spellman, the dinner had become a portentous political event and a way for Spellman to show off his powerful friends.

This dinner was no exception. Among the guests were Henry Luce, Bernard Baruch, New York governor Nelson A. Rockefeller, New York City mayor Robert F. Wagner, Tammany Hall boss Carmine De Sapio, and United States Senator Jacob K. Javits.

Spellman had chosen to have both Jack and his opponent Richard M. Nixon speak. While Nixon had accepted the invitation at once, Jack had vacillated. He was trying to balance his need for Catholic votes against his fear that too much identification with the church would drive non-Catholics away.

Even though Spellman had officiated at three Kennedy weddings and received millions in donations from Joe, he was offended by the fact that Jack had said the church should not expect special favors from him. Yet at the dinner, most thought Spellman displayed impartiality.

In introducing the two candidates, Spellman said, "Both are completely dedicated to the welfare of our countrymen. Both are endowed with brilliant minds and the ability to face and solve crises. Both are men of good will."

Joe was not there, but others told him that they detected more enthusiasm for Nixon. Moreover, Joe knew that Spellman had passed the word that he preferred Nixon.

"They were trying to get money from the federal government for education," Gertrude Ball, Joe's secretary, said. "They felt with a Catholic president in there, they would not get any funds for parochial schools. He [Spellman] even had some of the priests . . . preach against it. I heard it myself. I almost fainted."

After the dinner, Joe called the cardinal. "Lo and behold, we got home and the phone rang in the private den behind the office," Ned Spellman recalled. "It was Joe Kennedy. It was around 11:15 P.M. He [the cardinal] had had a drink, I had a drink, and the phone rang. The ambassador told the cardinal in no uncertain terms that he had favored Nixon over his son, which was not true."

"That is a truly evil man," Spellman said of Joe after a subsequent conversation with him, Monsignor Eugene Clark remembered.

Quickly Joe struck Spellman from guest lists. He reneged on a pledge he had made to contribute $400,000 toward a new school. When Jack won, Spellman was not invited to the inauguration, the first time he had not attended one in twenty years. Instead, Cardinal Cushing, who had introduced Jack at one dinner as "the next president of the United States," would be seated in a place of honor.

Yet even Cardinal Cushing's obeisance was not good enough for Joe, who asked why his bishops did not come out more openly for Jack. Cushing told him their passive role was not a sign they were against Jack. "I'm not sure Joe was convinced," Cushing later said.

◆ ◆ ◆

When Joe awoke in Hyannis Port on November 9, 1960, Jack had been elected president by a margin of a tenth of one percent. For Joe, it was the culmination of a lifetime of effort.

Now he consented to being photographed with his son. "There are no accidents in politics," he said. "I can appear with him any time I want now."

As Joe predicted, television had been a decisive factor. By then, some 90 percent of American households owned television sets, and 13 percent owned more than one. Meanwhile, the number of daily newspapers had dropped. The televised debates between Jack and Nixon had given Kennedy the edge that enabled him to defeat the vice president.

But so had Joe's money. Looking back, Jack told his friend Ben Bradlee, "I spent $13 million in 1960." Of that sum, $4 million went "to buy the nomination," according to what Harry Truman told his daughter, Margaret.

Eunice would later tell a *Time* reporter that except for Jack himself, her father had been "the most important factor" in winning the election. "They didn't agree on many things, but on political tactics, my father was extremely able. The president listened to him; some of the young men around him did not."

Eunice said it was Joe who had influenced Jack to run for Congress instead of for lieutenant governor of Massachusetts, which he had wanted to do. When Jack ran for the Senate in 1952, it was Joe who told him television was the way to reach people.

"Don't spend your time talking on street corners. Get on TV," Joe told Jack. Joe also urged his daughters to come up with a way to help, leading to the receptions and teas. "Father never cared about credit," Eunice said. "He knew he could be a handicap. But up in that top floor room, nobody was better."

Having orchestrated and paid for his son's election, Joe

continued to exercise dominion over him as president. Senator Smathers recalled sitting with Jack at one end of the pool in Palm Beach one morning after the election. At the other end of the pool, Joe was reading the papers.

Jack was perplexed. "I don't know what to do with Bobby," Jack said. "He busted his tail for me."

"I said, 'Why don't you think about making him an assistant secretary of defense?' " Smathers said. "He hadn't done anything. He was just a young boy. He hadn't practiced law. He said, 'The old man wants him to be attorney general.' I said, 'He never had a case in his life.' He had never argued in a courtroom. I said, 'If you make him assistant secretary of defense, he'll have a lot of power. It's an appropriate job for a guy who has never done a damn thing.' He said, 'Why don't you tell the old man?' "

Smathers said, "Excuse me, Mr. Ambassador. Jack and I have just been talking about Bobby. He wants to do something with Bobby. I thought he could be assistant secretary of defense, and then in a year or so, he could move up."

Without hesitating, "Joe said, 'Jack, come here,' " Smathers recalled. "Jack walked over. He said, 'I want to tell you, your brother Bobby busted his ass for you. He gave you his life blood. You know it, and I know it. By God, he deserves to be attorney general of the U.S., and by God, that's what he's going to be. Do you understand that?' Jack said, 'Yes, sir.' So Bobby became attorney general."

◆ ◆ ◆

On a freezing winter day, January 20, 1961, Jack was sworn in as thirty-fifth president of the United States. In his famous oration, he said, "And so, my fellow Americans, ask not what your country can do for you. Ask what you can do for your country."

As Jack's limousine drove past the White House, the new president tipped his hat to Joe, who was seated in the stands. Joe returned the gesture.

After the inauguration, Joe gave a luncheon at the May-flower Hotel for his family and Jackie's. "Who are all these people?" Joe demanded of Letitia Baldrige, a White House staffer who had organized the affair.

"Your family, Mr. Ambassador," she said.

"They are *not*," he said. "Just who are all these freeloaders? I want to know exactly why you asked them."

Furious, he went up to four of the guests and asked who they were. After satisfying himself that they were either Kennedy-Fitzgerald or Bouvier-Auchincloss cousins, he told Baldrige she was right. "They *are* all family. And it's the last time we get 'em all together, too," he said.

Meanwhile, some of Joe's old friends—like Joe Timilty—felt slighted. "Joe never saw him anymore," according to Joe Dinneen.

Being president helped Jack's love life. He visited Bing Crosby's home in Palm Springs, where the pool was "full of naked starlets all over the place," recalled Red Fay. A bar-tender "was there serving bull shots to the girls in the pool." Later that night, "Jack was in bed with two girls [from the White House staff] at the same time," Fay said.

At a dinner at the White House, Jack pounced on Marlene Dietrich, who later told movie director Joshua Logan that she deflected the attack. As he walked Dietrich to the elevator on the way out of the White House, Jack said he had a question for her. "What is it?" she said. "Have you ever slept with my father?" he asked. "He always claimed you did."

"After Jack had been nominated in 1960," Krock recalled, "I called his father and said, 'I think Jack had better watch his step. He keeps taking these young girls to El Morocco, and so forth, and it might hurt him.' And he said that the American people don't care how many times he gets laid, and he was right. That was his reprise, cold as you can imagine. No concern."

Yet Joe became so concerned about Jack's and Bobby's affairs with Marilyn Monroe that he asked Washington law-yer James McInerney, a Fordham University graduate and ex-FBI agent, to spy on her. McInerney consulted his friend Edward Bennett Williams, the legendary Washington lawyer, about whether he should comply. Williams' advice is not known.

Earlier, when Jack was a member of Congress, Joe had hired detectives to watch his own son. "I represented Joe when he wanted private detectives to keep a watch on Jack in Georgetown," said Nick Chase, a Washington lawyer who hired the William J. Burns Agency for the purpose. "He used a private eye or two to check Jack's conduct. The old man wanted to know what he was doing and who he was horsing around with because he figured it would affect him politically. He made him, and he felt he owned him."

After Jack, Joe was now the most powerful man in the country. At first, he enjoyed his newfound celebrity. "One day sitting by his pool in Palm Beach, he placed calls to Mayor [Richard] Daley, [James] Scotty Reston, Frank Sinatra, Janet Leigh, Jack Warner, Chet Huntley, and two of his sons"— the president and attorney general. "Now who else can we call?" he asked his secretary, Diane Winter D'Alemberte.

Just weeks after the inauguration, Igor Cassini called on Joe at Palm Beach to warn that the Dominican Republic was on the verge of exploding in a left-wing revolution. Since the United States had broken off relations with the country, Cassini suggested that Jack send an emissary to meet secretly with dictator Rafael Trujillo. Joe passed the information on to his son.

Jack asked Robert D. Murphy, who had retired as undersecretary of state, to visit Trujillo. Afterward, Luis R. Mercado, Dominican consul general in New York, wrote to Trujillo to report what Cassini had told him. He said that according to Joe, Jack had been "very well impressed" by Murphy's report on his meeting with the dictator. In another letter, Mercado said Joe had reported that Jack would help Trujillo. The White House later said Murphy had recommended no action.

Peter Maas broke the story of the secret meeting in the

Saturday Evening Post. In February 1963, Cassini was arraigned in federal court on a charge of failing to register as an agent of a foreign country. Cassini pleaded no contest.

Meanwhile, Jack appointed James Landis a special presidential assistant and later named him to a board that was to coordinate regulatory functions of the government. Because Landis had been appointed by the president, the Internal Revenue Service checked his tax returns. The agency found he had not filed an income tax return for five years. Knowing that Landis worked in Joe's office, Ken Moe, the IRS' district director in New York, called Joe's office to find out if the accountants there had a copy of Landis' returns. When Joe's accountants discovered that Landis had not filed, they filed his returns, and Joe loaned him some of the money to pay his back taxes, according to an account by Mortimer M. Caplin, then the IRS commissioner. Caplin discussed the case with Bobby, then attorney general, who recused himself from the case. Deputy Attorney General Nicholas Katzenbach recommended Landis' prosecution. The fact that Landis was depressed and had a drinking problem could not be used as an excuse, he felt.

Landis eventually pled guilty to five counts of filing late federal income tax returns. At the time of his sentencing, he paid $94,492 in back taxes, penalties, and interest but still owed $76,401. Because he was suffering convulsive attacks, Landis was placed in a Public Health Service Hospital instead of prison. Bobby then ordered him sent to Columbia Presbyterian Hospital, where two armed guards watched over him for the remainder of his thirty-day sentence.

On July 30, 1964, Landis was found dead in the swimming pool at his home on the grounds of the Westchester Country Club in Harrison, New York. The medical examiner attributed his death to drowning, possibly caused by a heart attack. At his death, Landis owed Joe $40,000 on a loan collateralized against $11,875 in securities.

◆ ◆ ◆

After celebrating his forty-fourth birthday in May 1961, Jack stood in front of the family home in Hyannis Port waiting for the marine helicopter that would take him to the airport. After groping in his pockets, he turned to his father.

"Oh, Dad. I don't have a cent of money," the president said. Joe had his secretary give Jack a wad of bills. Jack took the cash, and with a grin said, "I'll get this back to you, Dad." As Joe watched Jack depart, he muttered, "That'll be the day."

Frank Saunders, Joe's chauffeur, recalled a party Joe gave for Frank Sinatra at the Hyannis Port home just after Jack became president. "The women they had trucked in that afternoon looked like whores to me," he said. In the middle of the night, Saunders remembered that he had not returned Joe's riding boots, which he had polished. Leaving his apartment over the garage, he entered the main house through a back door.

"I could hear party noises," he said. Then he saw a woman with Joe. As Frank got closer, he saw that her dress consisted of see-through netting. "She was giggling," he recalled. "Mr. Kennedy was pressing her against the wall. Then he stood away from her, his arms extended, hands against her breasts, fingers tickling. Her silhouette showed big tits."

"I have your riding boots, Mr. Kennedy," Saunders said.

"My riding boots! Just in time!" Joe laughed. The woman giggled.

Joe would order ice cream from Louis Sherry's in New York and kept caches of Fanny Farmer chocolates. Periodically, he went on Metrecal.

Newspaper photographers caught Joe on the golf course in Biot, France, with a twenty-two-year-old blonde caddy built like Brigitte Bardot. "Pa Joe's Nifty Caddy" was the headline over their photo in the *New York Daily Mirror* in August 1961. "I was a caddy [for him] for about seven years," Françoise Pellegrino recalled. "I started at age eleven."

For all the money spent on vacations, Joe refused to maintain his homes. The furniture at the Palm Beach home looked like Salvation Army castoffs, the concrete steps were crumbling, and huge water bugs took over at night. The house had neither air conditioning nor central heat—only a few space heaters downstairs.

"The house was falling apart," Ann Downey, a top interior decorator and wife of Morton Downey, said of the Palm Beach home. "It was terrible. . . . They never did anything to it. Joe could never understand Morton fixing up the house. He never put anything back into his. It's just the way they believed."

Most of the children never liked the Palm Beach home, and they later put it up for sale. In May 1995, they sold the Palm Beach house to New York merchant banker John Castle and his wife, Marianne. The couple paid $4.9 million, roughly $2 million less than the asking price of $7 million.

While better maintained, the Hyannis Port home was often in need of a paint job and contained well-worn furniture. It is the largest of three houses in what has become known as the Kennedy compound. The main house at the end of Marchant Avenue on the bay was Joe's. Situated on 2.43 acres, it is assessed at $2.3 million and is currently owned by Ted. The home could probably fetch far more if sold. Another sliver of land along the bay, amounting to just over half an acre, was owned by Rose and is assessed at $280,000. To the west of the main house, fronting on Irving Avenue, was Jack's house. It sits on 1.39 acres, is assessed at $553,000, and is owned by Jackie's children. To the west of Jackie's house is Bobby's. It sits on 1.19 acres and is assessed at $701,000. While Ethel lives in it, the property is still in Bobby's name. Jackie insisted that a high fence be constructed at the rear of the houses, giving the appearance that they were part of a compound. In fact, other residents' homes are located on the same dead-end street.

Ted's home on Squaw Island is about a quarter of a mile away. Assessed at $1 million, it sits on 1.18 acres and is now owned by Ted's former wife, Joan.

Rose delighted in her new role as first mother. She constantly asked Secret Service agents to perform chores beyond their assignment. Rose would "come down and suggest this should be done and that should be done," said Stanley B. Galup, a Secret Service agent assigned to Jack. "She would say this needs to be fixed up. . . . She wanted me to take care of the drapes in the JFK house [the house that belonged to Jack]. She would suggest changing the drapes."

As Frank Saunders drove, she would throw newspapers out the car window one at a time as she finished reading them. Saunders would warn her that they could be fined for littering, but she would laugh. "Oh, Frank," she would say. "They know who we are!"

Rose would have Saunders stop the car to pick up hitchhikers so she could see their startled expressions when they realized who she was. But one day, Saunders picked up a man who did not recognize Rose.

"Guess who I am!" Rose said to him.

The hitchhiker looked at Saunders and shrugged.

"Go ahead now. Guess who I am," she said.

The man looked more closely at her.

"I really don't know who you are," he said.

"You really don't? Really?" she said.

"No, lady," he said.

"I am the president's mother!" Rose said.

The hitchhiker looked over at Saunders, who was staring straight ahead at the road. Then the man turned to Rose.

"The president of what?" he asked.

Drawing out the words dramatically, Rose said, "The president . . . of the . . . United States!"

There was a long pause. Saunders looked in the rearview mirror and saw Rose beaming.

Finally the hitchhiker said, "No shit, lady!"

"We drove in silence," Saunders recalled. "I had to bite my lip to keep from laughing. She kept a scowl on her face for a long time after that."

◆　◆　◆

After Jack became president, he asked Janet Des Rosiers to work for him as one of his secretaries in the White House. But she was unhappy with her position, which required working from 8:30 A.M. to 10 P.M. After a few weeks, she told Jack she wanted to leave. "He said, 'You know, Janet, if I had known what this job was like, maybe I wouldn't have worked so hard for it.'"

Jack asked Des Rosiers what she planned to do. She told him she was going to Paris for a year. The daughter of French parents, Des Rosiers said she had always wanted to live in France. "He said, 'Would you like to be secretary to the American ambassador in Paris? I've just appointed him.' So he made an appointment with James E. Gavin. In five minutes I had the job," she said.

Soon she was working for the ambassador in France. The Kennedy family—especially Jackie—would ask her to pay for French dresses or pieces of furniture they had ordered. "She [Jackie] was supposed to be buying Americana to refurbish the White House," Des Rosiers said. "But she didn't. She bought these French antiques. The antique store would call, and I would have a military cargo plane fly them to the White House. . . . She was supposed to be dressed American, but she would buy from French couturiers."

On September 27, 1961, Joe wrote to Des Rosiers to tell her about a dinner he had had with Jack and Ambassador. Gavin and his wife at Hyannis Port. "He and his wife were very enthusiastic about you, and the ambassador told the president that you were taking care of the important people," Joe wrote to her. "The president said no one could do it better, and Mrs. Gavin chirped in with her boasts also." Joe said that he was sure there was "no question in their minds" how Des Rosiers stood with the Kennedy family.

Joe informed Des Rosiers that money had been deposited in her account to cover bills of $896.67 from Sulka & Co. and $2,036 from Nina Ricci, which had supplied clothes to

Eunice. Joe asked his former mistress to have A. Sulka "make up for me eight bow ties in the same style as before and mail them over to me whenever they are finished."

Joe had achieved everything he had wanted, but still he was not satisfied. "It is a hectic world now—not too much fun," Joe told Des Rosiers mournfully in the September 27 letter.

On December 3, Joe checked into the Ambassador East Hotel in Chicago. At 7 P.M., he called the local FBI field office to say he thought his suite was bugged.

"His reason for believing it 'bugged' was because five minutes after he checked in, all kinds of people arrived in his room," an FBI report said. At 11:55 P.M., the FBI complied with Joe's request that the bureau send in sound technicians. No bugs were found.

26

STROKE

On the morning of December 19, 1961, Ann Gargan drove Joe to see off Jack at the Palm Beach International Airport. After the plane left at 9:14, they took Caroline, who had been riding with Jack in a Secret Service car, back to Joe's Palm Beach home. Gargan and Joe then drove to the Palm Beach Golf Course.

Since the two arrived later than their usual 9:30 A.M. starting time, the first nine holes were already crowded, so they played the back nine. "We finished the sixteenth, and, as Uncle Joe picked up the ball, he said he felt rather faint," she said. His balance seemed off as well.

Gargan asked Red Crowther, their caddy, to get a cart. Meanwhile, she got her car, had Joe get in, and then drove him home.

"Caroline and Jackie were swimming. He talked to them but said he didn't feel up to a swim right now," Gargan said. "He went to his room. He apparently lay on his bed with his clothes and golf shoes on." A secretary then told Gargan that Bobby was calling. Joe was not picking up the line. "So we went, and the bedroom door was open," she said. "He was just laying there. We called the doctor, and then we went to the hospital. He couldn't pick up the phone."

It was 2 P.M. by the time Joe was admitted to St. Mary's Hospital. He had suffered a stroke—an intracranial thrombosis, a blood clot in an artery of the brain.

That night, Jack flew back from Washington, and the rest of the family began to gather. Joe's arm and leg were almost totally paralyzed. Beyond some guttural sounds, he was unable to speak. His right facial muscles were frozen, and his mouth dropped on that side. He could not control his saliva.

"In some ways he could make himself understood, but you couldn't be sure. We would think he was thinking this, but you didn't know. No way," Gargan said. "He would say 'no, no, no,' and some other words were clear, too, swear words."

Yet soon the press picked up on the family line: "Kennedy Heart Block Leaves No Ill Effects," said the *Boston American*. "Joseph Kennedy Gains, Takes Walk Each Day," the *Boston Globe* said. If Kennedys don't cry, they certainly are not felled by strokes.

"Son of poor Irish immigrants, this bright and eager chap rose through his own efforts to become one of the wealthiest men in America," Ruth Montgomery wrote in a column distributed by Hearst. "In any free country, Joe Kennedy would be counted among the national assets. Here in America . . . Joe Kennedy has earned the congratulations of his countrymen."

Des Rosiers went to see Joe in Hyannis Port. By then, she had married and had a son. (She would later divorce.) "I saw him on the porch after the stroke, and all he did was go, 'Uh, uh, uh' and cry. It was pathetic," Des Rosiers said. Joe kept pointing at his former mistress. Des Rosiers thought he was trying to say to her, "You were right." She thought of how she had told him that he and Gargan would be alone and miserable.

Gloria Swanson sent Joe a telegram, signing it "Kelly." Just after seeing him, Cardinal Cushing told the press that he had assured Joe he was going to be all right. "I know I am," the cardinal told newspapers Joe replied. But later the cardinal recounted seeing Joe and praying for him. "Whether he understood me or not, I do not know. . . ." he said.

Jack told Ben Bradlee that Joe had Ann Gargan call the White House regularly. Jack would "grit his teeth" and "rattle on," while the voice on the other end said, "No, no, no."

"I saw him after the stroke," recalled Oleg Cassini. "He recognized me. I looked into his eyes, and there were moments when he was desperate to communicate, but he couldn't."

Joe had told Des Rosiers that the one thing he feared most was being incapacitated, unable to exercise control. Now his worst fear had been realized. Aware of his surroundings but unable to speak, he was imprisoned in a torture chamber. And, having worked much of his life to get his son in the White House, he had been able to enjoy the fruits of his efforts for only eleven months.

"Joe used to tell me there is no such word as 'can't,'" Des Rosiers said. "The suffering at the end was the one thing he could not control."

◆ ◆ ◆

If Joe could not speak, he could still express anger. With his strong left hand, he would throw whatever he could find at the object of his wrath. His "Hickey eyes" would narrow and turn steel gray, and he would bellow, "Nooo, nooo, nooo." Yet at other times, Joe placidly devoured the *New York Times*. He liked to watch *I Love Lucy* reruns. At the end of the day, he watched *Perry Mason*.

Joe had a staff of around-the-clock nurses headed by Rita Dallas. Dallas would call Joe's New York office and put Joe on the line. He would speak gibberish to the people on the other end. As instructed by Steve Smith, they would respond, "You always come up with the right decision, chief."

Once a year, Joe visited the Merchandise Mart, staying in Chicago for a week. He would stay three or four days at a time in New York.

"He couldn't look at books, but they could discuss them with him," Ann Gargan said. "In Chicago, Wally Ollman went over a changeover of elevators at the Merchandise Mart. Wally was good about it and found out what he would like and thought he was right."

When Joe visited the White House one day, Jack, Bobby, Jackie, and Caroline came down a hall to greet him. Suddenly, Joe began bellowing and shaking his fist at them. Dallas whispered to Bobby that perhaps he was thinking the boys should get to work. Bobby told Jack, who said, "Yes, Dad, we can't stand around entertaining you all day. I think it's time for me to get to my office and start running the country."

Joe smiled and put his hand out to his sons. Bobby bent to kiss him on the forehead, then winked at Dallas.

If Joe did not like Rose around the house before his stroke, now he wanted her around even less. Joe's children said as much to Dr. Henry Betts, a fellow at the Rusk Institute, who treated him. The doctor related that Joe "did not like having her around before his stroke. She made him nervous. That's what I've been told, because she always had something else— she was always upset about something else, and she wanted to change something."

When Rose came into Joe's bedroom, Joe would scream, "Nooo! Nooo! Nooo!" It was clear from the ferocity of his outburst that he meant it. He would start flailing at her, swinging his left arm like a sword. She would say, "I'm going, dear. I'm going."

One Halloween, Frank Saunders decided he would dress up as a girl. When Joe saw him standing there, he panicked. "Gggggaaaah!" he screamed.

"It's me, chief, it's Frank," Saunders said.

Saunders yelled for Gargan to get the oxygen. Joe seemed

to be choking. Finally, Joe understood. He convulsed with laughter. Tears streamed down his cheeks. With his good hand, he kept pointing at Frank, apparently appreciating the humor.

Joe wanted to hold his grandchildren, but they were afraid of him. With his good left arm, he would reach out for them, but "they'd cry and run away," Saunders said. "Then Mr. Kennedy would cry. He had only wanted to hold the child."

Before his stroke, Joe would clap his hands in steady rhythm to accentuate his admonition to his steadily multiplying grandchildren: "No crying in this house! No crying in this house!"

The children learned their lesson well. Joe "used such phrases as 'Kennedys never cry,'" Joseph P. Kennedy II recalled. "We all just sort of grew up with the idea that Daddy [Bobby] never cried or gave up when he was young, so we wouldn't."

Undoubtedly, the suppression of emotions contributed to the multiplying problems of Joe's children, and of their children: Before his recent marriage to Washington lawyer Victoria Anne Reggie, Ted would consume a bottle and a half of wine in a quarter of an hour, following that with large glasses of Scotch. He suffered blackouts, gained enormous amounts of weight, and neglected his personal hygiene.

"One thing I am struck by is the tremendous capacity the man has for doing his job," K. Dun Gifford, his former aide, said. "I think they were all like that. That is something that comes from the old man. No matter what he did the night before, Ted Kennedy was up reading the memos from his staff before he went to work. He got to work at 8:45 A.M., sometimes shaking like a leaf and ashen. There is a strength that comes from the old man."

Pat also had a problem. "I think everyone knows that Pat Lawford drinks," said Mary Lou McCarthy, the daughter of Joe's sister Loretta. "She has for years. Peter Lawford cheated on her and was cruel. She worshipped him. She has just never been the same."

Among Bobby's children, Joe II, Bobby Jr., and David abused drugs. In 1984, David, twenty-eight, would be found dead in Room 107 at the Brazilian Court Hotel in Palm Beach. In his wallet were 1.3 grams of cocaine. A combination of three drugs was later blamed for his death. Christopher Lawford was caught with heroin. Teddy Kennedy Jr., one of Ted's sons, announced that he was an alcoholic, as did Michael Kennedy, another son of Bobby's. Kara Kennedy, Ted's daughter, attended Alcoholic Anonymous meetings. Patrick Kennedy, his other son, became a drug addict. William Kennedy Smith was accused of raping a woman in Palm Beach. After he was found not guilty, he got into a fight in a bar in Arlington, Virginia. He pleaded no contest to a charge of assault and battery.

"The kids hold AA meetings at the weddings. Half of them are alcoholics," said television producer James K. Langan, a friend of Pat's.

"I've been at weddings with them in the past year where the boys would get up and leave and hold AA rah-rah meetings," Gifford, Ted's former aide, said. "God bless them. It's fabulous. They go outside where the reception is held, where everyone is getting loaded, and they support each other."

◆　◆　◆

One morning, Rose came into the kitchen in Hyannis Port and saw Dallas drinking coffee.

"Mrs. Dallas, how many times a day do you come in here and have coffee?" Rose asked the nurse.

Before Dallas could answer, she said, "It isn't that I mind, my dear, but coffee does keep going up, and expenses can get out of hand, if we're not careful."

Rose asked her to post a note on the bulletin board asking all the nurses to confine their coffee drinking to one cup a shift. Or, she suggested, they might bring their own coffee to work in a thermos.

Aside from her cheapness, the staff had to put up with

Rose's prissiness. When Dallas referred to Evelyn Jones one day as the housekeeper, Rose felt threatened. "I am the only housekeeper in this house," she corrected Dallas.

"But you are the mistress, Mrs. Kennedy," Dallas said.

"A housekeeper, I am," she said firmly. "A mistress, I am not."

When Rose noticed another aide reading a book, she said, "Young man, is that a good book you're reading?"

"Well . . . yes," he stammered.

Peering at the title, she asked, "Is Portnoy a town?"

"No," the man said, turning beet red. "It's a man's name."

"Well," Rose said. "I guess I'd better see what he's complaining about."

Rose ordered the book, in which the main character obsesses on masturbation, from a local bookstore. Later, the amazed owner asked Dallas who had recommended *Portnoy's Complaint* to Rose. "I never saw a book come back so fast in my life," the owner told Dallas, who related the story in her book, *The Kennedy Case*.

One morning, Rose confronted Dallas after the nurse had stepped out of a walk-in closet where fresh linens were stored.

"So you're the one," Rose said. "You're the one who leaves the lights burning. I saw you!"

"Mrs. Kennedy," Dallas said. "Let me explain."

"There's nothing to explain," Rose said.

Dallas then showed her that when the door to the closet closed, the light inside went out.

"You don't mean it?" she said in disbelief.

Rose ordained that none of the children could use the family car, a Chrysler. Joe preferred Chryslers because the company sponsored *The Lawrence Welk Show*, always one of his favorites. One day, Bobby, who was in a hurry, asked Frank Saunders, the chauffeur, for the keys.

"I can't, Mr. Kennedy," he told the attorney general.

Bobby was incensed. "The keys!" he shrieked, as he stuck out his hand.

"Mr. Kennedy, you know what your mother's orders are," Saunders said. "No one is to use that car."

"It's my father's car, and I want the keys," Bobby said. "I need a car right now!"

"No," Saunders said. "If you want the keys, ask your mother."

Bobby made an exasperated noise and stalked off. He never came back.

Rose, with her queasy stomach, invariably had the same thing for lunch: "Boiled chicken, white meat only, plain with no salt, pepper, or dressing of any kind, between two crustless pieces of white bread," Saunders said. "For dessert, she had a piece of angel food cake with no frosting. The help had beef, pork, or lamb roasts with all the trimmings."

Rose often went shopping but "never seemed to know what she wanted," Saunders said. "And then, after she'd decided, she'd never be sure of her choice. In the back seat on the way home, she'd express doubts to me about whether she had bought the right pair of stockings."

Rose developed the habit of insisting that Saunders return clothes—including underwear—after she had worn them. Usually, she had no receipt. "Tell them they don't suit me," she would say.

When the washing machine broke down, Rose said she would have to discuss it with "the boys"—meaning the president, the attorney general, and Ted, who was then an assistant district attorney in Boston's Suffolk County.

When Rose's television set broke, Saunders lent her his. She commented that his was color, while hers was black and white. She questioned how he could afford it. "I can't afford a color TV," she complained.

When Rose invited Rita Dallas to play golf one day, Dallas told her she could not afford the fees.

"What do you mean, afford?" Rose said quizzically. "I don't pay a thing."

Rose explained that she slipped in on the fifth hole and played through the eighth.

"You could do it, too," she said.

When Saunders tried to throw out some mildewed furniture from his quarters above the garage at the Palm Beach house, Rose told him to offer it to nuns. They refused the items.

Rose was like a Polaroid lens, filtering out anything she did not want to acknowledge. "Her formula for survival seemed to be based on: 'See what you want to see, and hear only what you want to hear,' " Dallas said.

◆ ◆ ◆

Early on, friction developed between Dallas, who thought Joe's condition would improve if he were pushed more aggressively, and Ann Gargan, who became convinced that his condition was hopeless. Dallas thought overindulging a patient was the worst thing that could be done.

"Ann Gargan wanted to keep things the way they were, and I was trying to get him to exert himself," Dallas said. "Ann was family. At that time, the family did not believe much in medicine or rehabilitation. Now they do."

"Rita Dallas saw things her way," Gargan said. "We tried both theories. . . . It wasn't my decision. I wasn't in charge. The children were." In any case, she said, "We tried to get him out as much as possible."

Dr. Saul Rotter, Joe's Palm Beach cardiologist, found that Rose took little interest in Joe. While Joe's children were "attentive," he said, "his wife, I didn't see much of her. She was a religious person, and pretty much wrapped up in that. She didn't contribute."

In April 1962, Joe began treatment at the New York Institute of Physical Medicine and Rehabilitation, founded by Dr. Howard Rusk. Joe lived in his own ranch-style bungalow at the institute, ten yards off East 34th Street near the corner of First Avenue.

The family decided it was time to generate more fairy tales.

The White House issued a statement that Joe's "speech has begun to return, he is mentally alert, and there is beginning to be improvement in the paralyzed (right) side." By December 3, 1962, the *Boston Globe* was saying that Joe had made a "remarkable recovery," although "some effects [of the stroke] linger." On at least one occasion, Joe had given "orders" to his son, the president. "He is doing well, and carrying on his activities as usual," a family spokesman was quoted as saying. And on June 4, 1964, the *Boston Traveler* reported that Joe was "taking an active part in plans for the John F. Kennedy Memorial Library" in Boston.

In fact, Dr. Betts, the fellow at the Rusk Institute, said Joe was "fully able to understand, but unable to speak." He said Joe could communicate only with his eyes, facial expression, and strong left hand.

"He was aphasic and paralyzed on one side and extremely frustrated, and a very angry man because of that," Dr. Rotter said. "The crying spells were related to frustration. He was angry and couldn't express himself," he said. "One of the problems was that every attempt to do any kind of rehabilitation was foiled by his refusal to cooperate. That was abetted by his niece, Ann Gargan, who really took care of him. She just said, 'Uncle Joe, if you don't feel like doing it, you don't have to do it.'"

Yet both the Rusk Institute and Dr. Robert Watt, the family doctor, agreed that when Joe did not respond to the more aggressive therapy in New York, it meant little could be done. "My attitude was more aggressive rehabilitation was not warranted at that time [after the New York treatment]," Dr. Watt recalled. "I felt they should maintain what they had. I felt that after more than a year, we were not going to bring him back."

On November 7, 1962, Dr. Joseph M. Wepman of the University of Chicago Medical School Department of Surgery agreed. A consultant to the Rusk Institute, he wrote to Rose recapitulating what he had told her in a conference about efforts to improve Joe's speech with therapy. He said Joe's stroke originally had left him with "almost a total incapacity to communicate," at least verbally. Since then, he said, some indications of improvement had been noticed, including "his present use of relatively well-organized jargon speech" and his "evident ability to understand when spoken to, especially and perhaps only when the subject matter relates to his condition, his state of well being, his family, or his possessions." However, he wrote, Joe had "much less ability" to understand "external events that do not relate directly to him."

About half the time, Dr. Wepman judged, Joe used "yes" and "no" appropriately. Given that more than a year had elapsed since the stroke, the limited speech Joe had managed to master represented "minimal gains." Thus "a very long convalescence" should be expected, and only "a limited amount of recovery" could be foreseen. Further, he wrote, "After observing Mr. Kennedy in speech therapy, it is my considered opinion that this phase of his therapy should be discontinued, at least for a time. He is not profiting from it, in fact, just barely endures it." Dr. Rusk agreed.

Dr. Wepman advised that the family should not respond to Joe's "emotional outbursts," which occurred when certain topics were mentioned. "These outbursts will increase if sympathy is extended to him at that time," he said. "They should be ignored and not reinforced. Treated that way, they will tend to disappear."

Dr. Wepman also advised Rose and the family to avoid discussing with Joe "external events not relating to himself, his family, or his possessions." Such discussions are "less frustrating to him," since "most of his present thought is concerned with these topics and not the outside world."

Meetings between the family and Joe should last less than half an hour, he said. "Most of the time should be spent with the nurses and Ann Gargan, his constant companion."

In April 1964, Joe was flown to the Institute for Achievement of Human Potential in Philadelphia to try a controversial treatment that entailed forcing arms and legs into normal movement to restore the brain's normal brain patterns. It did no good whatsoever.

Given the hopelessness of Joe's condition, Dr. Watt was always mystified by the way the family insisted on covering it up. Eunice and the others would pick up Joe and drive him to a shop, later reporting that he had "picked out" a sweater. In reality, said Dr. Watt, Joe often did not know what was going on.

"Eunice is another one of these optimistic people," Dr. Watt said. " 'You have to keep them moving. You have to keep mother moving. . . . ' As far as bringing back something that has been permanently damaged, forget it. Once a year has gone by, forget it."

◆ ◆ ◆

If Joe could not be brought back, at least his physical condition could be maintained. Dr. Rusk asked Janet Jeghegian to give Joe physical therapy.

A pretty woman with a good figure and dark hair, Jeghegian arrived at Joe's Hyannis Port home and knocked at the front door. A servant let her in. "I remember getting to the second floor, and Rose Kennedy appeared with wings, which was to get rid of facial lines," said Jeghegian. "They were similar to butterfly bandages. It was like out of the movies in the 1920s. Rose was in a robe. She asked me what I was doing. I said I was the ambassador's physical therapist."

Rose pointed brusquely to a rear corridor and said, "Henceforth, don't use the front door."

Over the next three years, Jeghegian, who later ran against Ted in a primary election campaign for the Senate, came to realize that Rose's relationship with her husband was cold. "I never really saw anything that could be construed as loving or caring," she said. Rose's main interest was shopping, which produced the only interaction between her and her husband. "After she would come back from Paris, she would model her clothes for him," Jeghegian said. "Like Loretta Young, she would make a 'ta-da' appearance for him in the doorway. She would spin around. He was almost disgusted. He would go 'uh, uh.' But she would keep coming back, showing all the clothes she had gotten."

Other wives with husbands similarly stricken would hold their hands. With Rose and Joe, "You didn't see that kind of intimacy," Jeghegian said. "She patted him on his shoulder, but it was never a demonstration of love."

On the other hand, Ann Gargan was "very loving toward him. Of all of them, she really knew how to talk to him in a caring way," Dallas said. "She put her arm around him and kissed him on the cheek, and chatted with him and whispered something and laughed in his ear. He seemed to enjoy her presence." It was clear that "Ann was the person in charge," she said. "To get anywhere with Mr. Kennedy's treatment, you had to get through Ann."

Among the children, Dallas thought Joe seemed to enjoy Ted the most, while Jeghegian thought Bobby was most caring with him. Jackie and Joan spent a lot of time with him as well.

Several friends still visited. "Downey and Morrissey were there almost once a week," she said. "Carroll Rosenbloom came on weekends."

Rose would take her French lessons, play golf, walk on the beach, and go to church every morning. "She was a strong woman, very into herself and self-absorbed," Jeghegian said. Like Rita Dallas, Jeghegian was amazed at her cheapness. One morning, Rose walked over to the nurses' station. "In shocked disbelief, I heard her say 'Oranges are now a dollar a dozen, so please dilute Mr. Kennedy's orange juice.' I couldn't believe it."

Jeghegian was equally shocked by the way members of the family walked around the house nude. "They often were nude walking around the house," she said. "Jack was the same way. There was nothing sacred about being private. That was rather different. A door would be open, and you would walk through, and they would be getting out of a bathing suit into some clothes. It was Eunice or Pat or the president."

On the *Marlin*, Jack would "jump in the water and go swimming, and come back on the boat and take the wet bathing suit off and put on something dry. He would go up to the bridge and talk to Frank Wirtanen [the captain], and strip his bathing suit off and stand naked for a while and put something on." Jeghegian, who was married, would turn her back. "It was amazing. I was just shocked."

Joe developed affection for Jeghegian. He lunged at her only once when he was angry. She ducked, and he missed. Other nurses refused to work for him because they feared his blows.

Jeghegian would coax Joe to walk with the help of a brace. "But he hated that brace, you could tell," she said. "He resisted my having to put it on him every day."

For Easter 1963, Jack arranged for Joe to be in Palm Beach. Red Fay recalled that Joe seemed to be fuming because cocktail hour was going on too long.

"Mr. Kennedy wanted to have things on time," Fay said. "We were taking too long during the cocktail party. . . . He liked a short cocktail period, and then move right into dinner. But anyway, we were maybe five minutes late, so the steaks were a little more done than he liked. It really irritated him. He was easily irritated after the stroke."

Then a butler served Dom Pérignon, which was flat.

"He just got furious," Fay said. "Because he couldn't articulate, he just got so goddamned mad. The president got up and said, 'Dad, you've done it again. I'd be willing to challenge anybody that there's nobody else tonight in Palm Beach drinking Dom Pérignon champagne that is flat.' It brought a smile to the senior Kennedy. He forgot all his problems relative to the champagne."

As Joe was flying on the *Caroline* from New York to Hyannis, he became enraged when he read in the paper that the plane was being put up for sale. Howard Baird, the pilot, recalled that it "took us two hours to get him to leave the airplane." As a result of his objections, the sale was canceled. The family eventually sold the plane in 1967 after it had carried the Kennedys 650,000 miles.

◆ ◆ ◆

In early November 1963, Herbert Hoover invited Joe to dinner at the Waldorf Towers. Ann Gargan recalled that Hoover carried on a monologue, trying to make Joe feel comfortable.

Three weeks later, on the afternoon of November 22, Dora Lawrence, one of the maids at the Hyannis Port house, began screaming. She had been watching television, and she ran up the stairs. "The president's been shot! My God!" she shrieked.

Rose's eyes clouded. Without making a sound, she turned and started back to her room. Her hand trembled slightly as she pressed her fingers against her temples.

"Don't worry," she said to Rita Dallas. "We'll be all right. You'll see."

Rose walked to her room and closed the door.

Joe had been asleep, but all five telephone lines in the house were ringing, waking him up. Bobby called to say that Jack was not expected to live. Then came the news that he had died. Rose came out of her room and told Dallas not to tell Joe anything. The children were coming. "I want them to tell him," she said.

Rose later explained, "In our household, many long years before, Joe and I had adopted as a general principle that if there was bad news to be faced, it should be given in the morning, not late in the day, for otherwise there would be a sleepless night, which would only make the debility worse."

Ann Gargan had already begun to tell Joe: "Uncle Joe, there's been a terrible accident," she said. When Dallas whispered that Rose did not want her to say anything, Gargan claimed she had been talking about the gardener, who would be all right.

"It's so hard," Rose said. But her eyes were dry.

After Hammond "Ham" Brown, a Secret Service agent, unplugged the television sets, everyone made up stories about why they were not working.

The next morning, Ted and Eunice told Joe.

"Daddy," Eunice whispered. "Daddy, there's been an accident. But Jack's okay, Daddy. Jack was in an accident, Daddy. Oh, Daddy, Jack's dead. He's dead. But he's in heaven."

Ted dropped to his knees and buried his face in his hands. "He's dead, Daddy. He's dead," he said.

"Joe's eyes darted back and forth, a streak of panic discoloring them," Dallas recalled. "Mr. Kennedy looked up at me, and I saw a sea of sorrow seep over his face as he laid his hand on Eunice's buried head."

When Dallas later brought Joe his juice, she noticed that the front page of the morning newspaper was lying face up on the floor. Black banner headlines reported more details of the assassination. Dallas looked back at Joe, who was sitting in bed. He had gripped the sheet in a tight knot. His eyes were closed, and two tears ran down his cheeks.

Two days after the funeral, Jackie brought Jack's American flag to Joe.

"Grandpa," she said. "Jack's gone, and nothing will ever be the same again for us. He's gone, and I want to tell you about it."

Without pausing, Jackie told Joe the entire story, from Jack's arrival in Dallas to the funeral in Washington.

Now Joe's constant admonition, "Kennedys don't cry," became the watchword. During Thanksgiving dinner, the family was boisterous. Afterward, someone started singing "Heart of My Heart," one of Jack's favorites. Bobby fled the room. But later, the family played a game of touch football on the lawn, while Rose took a walk.

"When I got there, the family in Hyannis Port was buoyant," Jeghegian said. "Not laughing, but getting ready to go to Florida. I thought, 'I can't believe this.' I had been so down for a whole week, and these people are behaving like that. They were really strong people. I don't know what it means. I was devastated by JFK."

After three years, Jeghegian left the job to teach. She decided the family's jocular attitude was but another act. Camelot existed only in the minds of the press.

"I didn't think there was true happiness there," Jeghegian said. "It was devoid of warmth. Maybe they didn't know how to be warm. You never saw them hug, or put their arms around each other."

Soon, the Secret Service protection was withdrawn, and the direct line to the White House was removed. The weekend after Thanksgiving, Cardinal Cushing came to the house to repeat for Joe the eulogy he had given for Jack.

Rose refused to see him. "Oh, Lord, no," she said. "Tell him I'm not doing well."

Joe kept his eyes glued to the ceiling as the cardinal delivered the eulogy in his nasal twang.

◆　◆　◆

On June 19, 1964, Ted asked Howard Baird, the captain of the *Caroline*, to fly him to Springfield for the Massachusetts Democratic Convention. The pilot refused, saying severe fog in the area would make flying dangerous. So Ted chartered a plane for the trip. Baird told Rita Dallas he was upset by Ted's decision.

Ted's plane crashed in Southampton on its way to Springfield. The Weather Bureau reported visibility was less than two and a half miles, conditions described as "marginal" even for instrument landings. The forty-eight-year-old pilot, Edwin J. Zimny, was killed, along with Ted's administrative aide Edward Moss. Ted was injured and semiconscious. Also injured were Senator Birch Bayh and his wife.

Ted's recklessness was but another example of a family trait. While it usually harmed only them, it sometimes affected others.

After a cookout on Nantucket, Joe II, now a congressman, borrowed a recreation vehicle and crammed six others into it. With two teenagers standing in the open back, he went driving wildly though the woods, careening on and off the road. When he swerved violently to avoid another car, all seven occupants were thrown from the vehicle. Pam Kelley, one of those standing in back, severely injured her spine.

A judge fined Joe II $100, saying he had a "great father and a great mother." Kelley was paralyzed from the waist down for life.

Nancy Tenney Coleman, whose house is on the water directly across the street from Ethel's, said being a member of Congress did little to improve Joe's judgment. She vividly recalled seeing Joe in the summer of 1993 trying to sail in the middle of winds that were just under hurricane force. "Young Joe went out on a sunfish, and the wind was fifty knots. The waves were crashing in. He was taking six little kids," she said. "He has no common sense. I prayed the boat would not break in half. Luckily, he couldn't take it out. Nobody had life preservers."

"These people are jumping all over the place," Dr. Watt, the family physician who treated Ted, said of the Kennedys. "Joe Jr. was warned that his plane had a problem. Kathleen was on a small plane. Ted tried to find a pilot who would fly in the bad weather when his crash occurred."

"They were always told they were better than everyone else," Mary Lou McCarthy said. "Just like Hollywood starlets who say, 'I can get in this car and go 150 miles an hour if I want to and the officer won't give me a ticket if I give him an autograph,' they think they can get away with anything. It's pitiful. A girl was paralyzed for life in a jeep driven by Joe II. Chappaquiddick was the same. A beautiful life was lost, and there's no excuse for it."

Yet there were compensations to being a Kennedy.

"I couldn't begin to tell you the parties," said James Langan, who lived with Pat in New York. "Whatever big party there is, if your name is Kennedy, you are summoned. . . .

With her sister Jean, now ambassador to Ireland, they have a social secretary out of the Joseph P. Kennedy Foundation. The secretary would come over to her apartment once a week on Sutton Place, and the invitations would be culled politically and socially by the staff people, and whatever they wanted to go to, they would go to."

While he was in the hospital, Ted asked 160 people—including Gloria Swanson and Janet Des Rosiers—for their recollections of Joe for *The Fruitful Bough*, a privately published book. Realizing they would have to lie to conceal their true relationships, neither Swanson nor Des Rosiers contributed.

"The family seemed to be still living with Rose's mythology when they asked for a statement from Gloria for *The Fruitful Bough*," said William Dufty, Swanson's last husband.

In the mid-1970s, Rose "made the comment that it was his business, meeting with stars and starlets like Gloria Swanson, and she was raising her family and couldn't be with her husband all the time, so people would talk," recalled Dennis B. Spear, the caretaker at the Palm Beach home.

By 1966, Joe had begun to suffer periodic heart seizures. A December 1964 medical report had said he had had "cardiac [heart] irregularity for 25 years in the form of atrial [the two upper chambers of the heart] premature contractions. Atrial fibrillation had been the pattern for 14 years."

Joe's prescription records show that at various points he took Digitoxin, which is used to control the rhythm of the heart; Dilantin and phenobarbital, which control seizures or convulsions; Taractan, used to treat nervous or emotional conditions; Ritalin, a stimulant now used to treat hyperactive teenagers and depressed adults, but then considered helpful in increasing "pep"; Placidyl, a tranquilizer used to treat insomnia; four anti-allergy pills; Lomotil, for diarrhea; Donnatal for stomach cramps; and several eye medications.

The first seizure came at 11:30 A.M. on January 5, 1966, in Miami. To the family, it was a signal to write another script. This time, Ann Gargan told the *Boston Globe* in an "exclusive" interview that Joe shaved himself and read balance sheets. "He makes decisions by telephone with his business associates, and his schedule calls for him to go both to New York and to Chicago this winter for business talks," she told the paper. Despite slurring of speech, Joe "can be understood, and on the phone he can be understood more clearly than in ordinary conversation." Gargan later told the author she had been misquoted.

27

DELIVER US FROM EVIL

On June 5, 1968, Bobby Kennedy, who had become a senator from New York and was campaigning for the presidency, was shot in Los Angeles. Joe lay on his back as the television set flickered with reruns of a tape of the shooting. Joe covered his eyes, and Dallas could see tears trickling down his face.

The *New York Times* quoted a family spokesman as saying Joe accepted the news "bravely."

Stoically, Rose attended mass, but returned crying. After Bobby had died on June 6, she was heard to say, "Oh, why did it have to be Bobby? Why couldn't it have been Joe?"

On the evening of Thursday, July 18, 1969, Ted threw a party on Chappaquiddick Island on the western end of Martha's Vineyard for the "Boiler Room" girls, who had worked for Bobby on his campaign. Sometime after midnight, Ted drove his car off Dike Bridge. His passenger, Mary Jo Kopechne, drowned.

After the accident, Ted returned to the cottage where the party was being held and rounded up Joe Gargan and Paul Markham, another lawyer who was his friend. They drove back to the scene, and both Gargan and Markham tried to rescue Kopechne, without success.

"The conversation was brief about having to report," Joe Gargan said. "I was insistent on it. Paul Markham was backing me up on it. Ted said, 'Okay, okay, Joey, okay. I've got the point, I've got the point.' Then he took a few steps and dove into the water, leaving Markham and me expecting that he would carry out the conversation."

But Ted did not report the matter until later in the morning. In his statement to police, Ted claimed he was driving Kopechne to the ferry to take her back to Edgartown at 11:15 P.M. He said he was "unfamiliar with the road" and had made the mistake of turning right onto Dike Road from Main Street. After he "fully realized" what had happened, he went back to his hotel room and contacted police. But Edgartown District Court Judge James A. Boyle, in a report after an inquest, noted that Ted had been driven over Dike Bridge twice on July 18. He concluded that Ted and Kopechne "did not intend to return to Edgartown" and that his turn onto Dike Road was "intentional." He said Ted knew of the hazard that lay ahead of him on Dike Bridge and had driven "negligently."

Ted later pled guilty to leaving the scene of an accident and was given a two-month suspended sentence and a year of probation. The incident dashed his presidential aspirations.

After making the report to police, Ted climbed the stairs of the family home in Hyannis Port and walked into his father's bedroom. "Dad, there was an accident," he said. "There was a girl in the car, and she drowned."

Joe tilted his head forward as he listened to Ted. Then his head dropped back. Ted sat down and held his face in his hands. "I don't know, Dad, I don't know."

After that, Rita Dallas noticed a deterioration in Joe's condition. "I saw him go downhill after Chappaquiddick," Dallas said. "Every time something happened, his bounce back would be less. After Chappaquiddick, he just couldn't bounce back."

Even before Chappaquiddick, a May 1968 medical report had noted that Joe's left hand had become more deformed, probably from another small stroke, and that a loss of muscular tone and strength were evident.

"My suggestion," wrote Dr. Russell Boles, who, with Dr. Watt, took care of Joe, "is to encourage physical activity, with short sessions in the pool if he can cooperate. He could then enjoy a trip to New York. My prediction, however, is his progress in this endeavor will be minimal if at all, and trips for a change or pleasure are no longer feasible. They may trigger an embarrassing sequence of events which would make all close to him, as well as himself, suffer needlessly."

By May 1969, Dr. Boles reported that Joe was "essentially blind," and he could no longer get out of bed. He said that "the effort should be to make him comfortable, and nothing should be done that would cause pain. The family understood."

Joe's freckles had become big liver splotches all over his face and balding head. He stopped wearing his glasses. He wasn't interested in seeing movies or television. The smile that had opened so many doors for him was gone. In its place was a crooked look brought on by the stroke.

By the end of the summer, Joe had lost his appetite. He also began rubbing his eyes. He could only make out shapes. His throat tightened, and he could no longer swallow. His vocal cords made a low, almost inaudible noise in his throat.

Joe had always hated the wind. Now he seemed frightened by it even more. The banshee wail meant death was coming.

◆ ◆ ◆

On November 15, Joe suffered another mild heart attack. The family agreed with the doctors that no extraordinary methods should be used to prolong his life. His skin had begun to deteriorate, and his veins were fragile. He was completely unconscious and had lost all voluntary motion. The next day, Rose sat with Joe all day and into the night. By November 17, Joe's vital signs were poor, and he was comatose. Jackie sat with him that night.

On the morning of November 18, the family began arriving—Ted and Joan, Pat, Jean and Stephen Smith, Jackie, Ethel, Eunice and Sargent Shriver. Ann Gargan kept in the background. The weather was clear, windy, and mild. Yardmen were clearing leaves from neighboring lawns.

"Senator, you should bring your mother in now," Rita Dallas told Ted. He returned to Joe's second-floor bedroom with his arm around his mother. Rose put her head against Joe's hand and wept. He no longer had the strength to chase her away.

Eunice began praying: "Our Father, Who art in Heaven . . ."

At 11:05 A.M., Rose finished: "And deliver us from evil. Amen." It was then that Joe died.

Joe Gargan asked his sister Ann for the rosary beads. "Hail Mary, full of grace, the Lord is with thee," Joe Gargan intoned. "Blessed art thou among women and blessed is the fruit of thy womb Jesus. Holy Mary, mother of God, pray for us sinners now and at the hour of our death. Amen."

Dr. Watt was called. "They were still praying when I got there to pronounce Joe dead," he said. "I stayed outside the room until they were finished praying. I listened to his heart. It was obvious he was dead. He had been dying for some time. He had just decided this is it, and I don't care."

Dr. Watt pronounced Joe dead and signed the death certificate. The official announcement said he had died of cerebrovascular thrombosis due to arteriosclerosis. Joe Kennedy was eighty-one.

A gray Mercury hearse from Doane Beal and Ames funeral home in Hyannis took the body away. That evening, Father Cavanaugh, president emeritus of Notre Dame, celebrated a special mass at the century-old St. Francis Xavier Church, a simple white colonial structure on South Street at High School Road.

The next morning, Cardinal Cushing, who had loyally continued to visit Joe, offered a funeral mass, highlighting the message of life after death, at the same church. He was assisted by Terence Cardinal Cooke, who replaced Cardinal Spellman after his death in 1967.

All of Joe's children and his twenty-eight grandchildren attended the service. Among friends who came in rain-streaked limousines were Morton Downey, Joseph Timilty, Carroll Rosenbloom, Father John Cavanaugh, and Frank Morrissey.

Ted eulogized his father, who lay in a copper-colored casket. Reading from a piece Bobby had written about him in *The Fruitful Bough*, Ted began, "I don't believe he is without faults. But when we were young, perhaps because of his character or the massiveness of his personality, they were unobserved or at least unimportant."

In his booming voice, Cardinal Cushing delivered a fourteen-minute eulogy. He quoted Joe as saying, "My ambition in life is not to accumulate wealth but to train my children to love and serve America for the welfare of all people."

Downey sang "Panis Angelicus." The Kennedy children sang the recessional, "Holy God We Praise Thy Name."

Sheets of rain blew in the stiff wind as the mourners walked outside. Some five hundred spectators lined the street.

Later that day as the skies cleared, Joe was buried in the family plot at Holyhood Cemetery in Brookline, some two miles from the former family home. The plot was at the end of a road called O'Connell Avenue.

The wind whipped away the sound of the cardinal's words as he knelt by the coffin to say good-bye to his friend. As the twenty funeral cars moved away, "a woman in black, appearing to be in her 60's, knelt alone in front of the grave," the *Boston Herald* reported. "She remained there for several minutes. The woman, who was well-dressed, walked alone and declined to give her name."

Only the word "Kennedy" would be carved on Joe's large granite tombstone.

◆ ◆ ◆

A *Boston Herald* story hailed Joe as a "devout Catholic." Another quoted Timilty as saying, "We would be in Paris or Rome, but every night at 7 o'clock he would call Rose. He'd say, 'Get ahold of Rose!' and he'd talk to her on the telephone."

A *Boston Globe* obituary claimed Joe had made a "substantial recovery" after his stroke and "was able to walk with a cane and regained limited powers of speech." A *Boston Herald* editorial said Joe "rose from modest beginnings to the pinnacles of financial power and political eminence by adhering to old-fashioned American virtues that have been somewhat discounted in today's society: devotion to family, loyalty to friends, strength of character, and the will to win." But the *New York Times* said Joe would go down in history primarily as the founder of a powerful and distinguished family. As a public official, he rated only a "footnote," which was "not more than half favorable."

When newspapers reported the terms of Joe's will, his sisters were embarrassed. In a final act of meanness, Joe had willed only $25,000 each to Loretta and Margaret. Yet the Kennedy family's wealth was $400 to $500 million, according to a December 1979 *New York Times* estimate. With accountants and lawyers on his payroll, Joe's slap in the face to his two sisters, who had always adored him, could not have been an oversight, any more than his refusal to attend his father's funeral. Joe had updated the will with a codicil as recently as June 1958.

"My parents never expressed bitterness about the will," Mary Lou McCarthy said. "When Kerry [her daughter] put it to Aunt Rose, she said he was always going to change that. She [Kerry] said he was in his seventies. When would it have been a proper time to change it? She said, 'I don't know. He was human. He made mistakes.' It was embarrassing to

Mommy because it was in the papers. Everyone thought it was $250,000, which it should have been. Mommy and Daddy just let them think that, because they didn't want people to think he wasn't generous."

In addition to the trust funds, Joe's 1955 will, witnessed by Des Rosiers, left Rose $500,000 plus a building in Albany, New York, valued at $1 million. Any remaining assets were willed to the Joseph P. Kennedy Jr. Foundation. The assets included an interest in the Merchandise Mart, the Palm Beach home, $36,374 in cash, $100 in clothing, a Movado pocket watch, and a 1969 Chrysler Imperial. In 1984, the Hyannis Port home had been deeded to Ted.

After the patriarch's death, the National Archives took what were supposed to be his papers—some 140 boxes of them—and carted them to Boston, where they eventually were placed in the John F. Kennedy Library. The papers represented only a fraction of his records, according to Joe's former secretary Gertrude Ball, who said the rest were in storage in Manhattan. Moreover, family lawyers had reviewed the papers before they went to the archives. According to what archivists were told, they removed some of the material. Even then, the family retained ownership of the papers. After they were placed in the archives, the family allowed access to only one nonfamily author, Doris Kearns Goodwin. Goodwin is married to Richard Goodwin, who wrote speeches for Jack in the Kennedy White House.

In keeping with their usual practice, Joe's children declined to be interviewed for this book. Describing the routine when an independent book on the Kennedys is being prepared, Mary Lou McCarthy, the daughter of Joe's sister Loretta, said Ted puts out the word within the family not to say anything. "Marnee [the daughter of Joe's sister Margaret] is a bright child, but she will say, 'Someone is coming to interview me, what should I say?' I say, 'Say what you want.' She says, 'Well, Teddy always says don't say anything.' That's his problem. He has so damn much to cover up that he's a wreck," McCarthy said. "Within the family, there has been an element of fear because the family is so powerful, there are so many of them, and they control many things in government and business. Someone might not get a good job because someone might not put in a good word for them. Power corrupts, and some have not handled it well. Uncles and aunts are intimidated."

Yet, like any children, Joe's family knew little about his business activities in any case. And the question remained: If they spoke, would they tell the truth?

"The poor man, he does not know truth from fiction anymore," McCarthy said of Ted. "He really doesn't anymore. How can you when you've spent the last twenty-five years doing what he's been doing? No wonder the younger boys have all gotten in trouble at one time or another. With that as an example, my God."

◆　◆　◆

After two strokes, one in 1974 and one in 1984, Rose rarely uttered a word. A September 1989 medical report from Massachusetts General Hospital said, "In lucid moments, she will make some response to a question that seems appropriate and will utter a coherent phrase. This appears to vary with her degree of alertness, which at times is so low that she makes hardly any response at all. Occasionally she will make known to her nurse something that she wants or needs."

The report said "there is no indication" that recent incidents led "to the formation of memories thereto. Her left eye is closed much of the time. . . . Evidently she sees something, but it is difficult to evaluate her visual field. Knee and ankle jerks virtually unobtainable. Some grasp in her left hand. Sensation difficult to judge."

Since that time, Rose had become "semicomatose," according to Dr. Watt, who continued to consult with Rose's doctor. Sedated with Valium or Xanax, she received food through a stomach tube. "When the weather was good, they would bundle her up and put her in the chair and waltz her around the compound and down to the dock and back," Dr. Watt said.

"Every now and then, Rose says a monosyllable, and you don't know why," he said when she was alive.

"Rose is out of it now," said Nancy Tenney Coleman when Rose was 103. "I'm sure she didn't know who I was. They talk to her like you and I. She is alive. She doesn't talk. Her eyes are closed. She appears to be sleeping."

In a replay of what they had done for Joe, her children covered up her true condition. In July 1990, Ted told the *New York Times* that when he had last visited her, Rose said when he took out his tennis racket, "Are you sure that is yours, Teddy? I've been looking all around the house for mine."

On her 101st birthday, Melody Miller, Ted's spokesperson, said, "She is as well as can be expected at 101" and is "still a dynamic spirit in the household." On her 103rd birthday, the family put out the word that she still called the shots and had "requested that all gifts be homemade."

"She has her good days and her bad days," Melody Miller said just before Rose's 104th birthday, "but she's very much a dynamic presence in the house."

"She has everything money can buy to keep her alive," Janet Des Rosiers said. "No one would want that. It's so sad. She has no dignity left. They claim she watches TV. That's so pathetic. It's the same as with Rosemary. They won't admit something is not perfect or negative. Everything is for the public."

"If it were up to her, Rose Kennedy wouldn't want to be alive," said Larry Newman, a neighbor. "They treat her as though she were a normal person. . . . I saw Rose two years ago at a mass at the house. She was totally out of it. This is part of the Kennedy mystique. She is the symbol of it."

◆ ◆ ◆

Rose died at 5:30 P.M. on Sunday, January 22, 1995, at the age of 104 from complications of pneumonia. Just as they had mythologized Joe, the press and politicians mythologized her. She was described as having the grace, character, and courage of a saint.

"Very few Americans have endured as much personal sacrifice for their country as Rose Kennedy," President Bill Clinton said. "She played an extraordinary role in the life of an extraordinary family."

To be sure, Rose imposed discipline on her children and encouraged them to learn and be curious. She endured more tragedies than any human should have to bear. But it was also true that she was tranquilized much of the time, that she could be stingy, that she devoted much of her life to shopping, that she displayed no interest in marital sex, and that she lived her life in denial. While many wives of her era may have suffered in silence as she did, denial is not a trait to be admired.

"She has gone to God," Ted told eight hundred mourners at St. Stephen's Church in Boston's North End, where she had been baptized. "She is home. And at this moment, she is happily presiding at a heavenly table with both of her Joes, with Jack and Kathleen, with Bobby and David."

Ted repeated the anecdote about Rose asking in 1990 where her tennis racket was. Gullible as ever, the press picked it up. Every member of the family knew it was another fabrication. "It represented what she was like when she was in her eighties," said Kerry McCarthy, Rose's grandniece.

Besides the senator, the one hundred members of the Kennedy family at the service included two members of Congress—Joseph P. Kennedy II of Massachusetts and Patrick Kennedy of Rhode Island—Kathleen Kennedy Townsend, the lieutenant governor of Maryland; and Mark Kennedy Shriver, a member of the Maryland House of Delegates.

The impressive assembly was testimony to a remarkable achievement: No family in American history had produced so many members elected to high public office. Indeed, if the calculations of *Washingtonian* magazine were correct, based on the progressively larger number of Kennedys in public office, 256 Kennedys will be running for office by the year 2050 and 4,096 by the end of the next century.

"Boys," Joe told the other commissioners back at the SEC, "I've got nine kids. The only thing I can leave them that will mean anything is my good name and reputation. I intend to do that, and when you think I'm not doing so, sound off."

If Joe seriously thought his legacy would be an honorable reputation, he was wrong. "Blessed are the pure in heart, for they shall see God," the Catechism of the Catholic Church says. "Pure in heart" refers to those who have demonstrated "charity, chastity or sexual rectitude, love of truth, and orthodoxy of faith," according to the Catechism. While Joe had been charitable, he had failed to meet the other three tests.

After reading the manuscript of this book, Janet Des Rosiers expressed shock and dismay at some of the revelations. She decided she had been among the many Joe had fooled. "I'm mad at myself for giving myself to this man," she said. "It was because of my ignorance."

For all his wealth and power, "Joe was not a happy man," Des Rosiers said. "He didn't seem to think enough of himself to live with himself." William Hazlitt, the English essayist, said, "A hypocrite despises those whom he deceives, but has no respect for himself. He would make a dupe of himself too, if he could."

This, then, was the cost of Joe's deception and manipulation, a cost exacted not only on himself but on members of his family. Rosemary, who was not at Rose's funeral, was a living symbol of Joe's need to control, to cover up, and to engage in savage competition. The "Kennedy stomach," the tranquilizers, illicit drugs, and alcohol were but manifestations of the culture of deceit that Joe created.

If Joe was not truly happy, he also had no shame. Thus, for all his pronouncements, he did not care about his reputation. What he cared about was having power. Through the political dynasty that he founded, Joseph P. Kennedy achieved that for generations to come. If he hurt and corrupted others in the process, it was because no one had the courage to challenge him.

For that, they have only themselves to blame.

NOTES

AM   Academy of Motion Picture Arts and Sciences
BU   Boston University Mugar Memorial Library
CU   Columbia University Oral History Collection
FBI Federal Bureau of Investigation records, obtained under the Freedom of
     Information Act
FDR Franklin Delano Roosevelt Library
GU   Georgetown University Lauinger Library
HI   Hoover Institution
HU   Harvard University
JFK John F. Kennedy Library
LC   Library of Congress
MH   Massachusetts Historical Society
NA   National Archives
PU   Princeton University Seeley Mudd Library

PROLOGUE

1 Joe was "very proud": Interview on December 16, 1993, with Ned Spellman.
2 The pictures never showed: Des Rosiers, now Janet Fontaine, was interviewed
on July 10 and 17, 1994. On August 14, 1994, she confessed that she had been
Joe's mistress. More than a dozen additional interviews were held with her.
3 Jack Kennedy's friend: Interview on April 12, 1994, with Charles Spalding.

Dave Powers attributed the same comment to Jack in *The American Experience,* "The Kennedys," Part II, WGBH-TV, September 21, 1992.

3 "Joe was always watching": Not-for-attribution interview on October 18, 1962, with Thomas G. Corcoran, by Richard J. Whalen researcher, Nigel Hamilton papers, MH.

CHAPTER 1: NODDLE ISLAND

5 "In his own right": *Boston Herald,* November 19, 1969.

5 The first article: *Boston Record-American,* November 20 and 21, 1969.

5 Fifty miles south: *New Bedford Standard-Times,* November 19, 1969.

6 The cottage had four rooms: Davis, John H., *The Kennedys,* page 4.

6 Patrick decided to leave: Davis, John H., *The Kennedys,* page 6; and Rachlin, Harvey, *The Kennedys,* page 5.

7 Patrick made his way: Passenger lists of vessels arriving at Boston, Massachusetts, 1820–1891, NA. The Kennedy family believes Patrick arrived in 1849, and the manifest for the vessel that arrived on April 21, 1849, lists "Patrick Kennedy, laborer, age 29." Patrick's year of birth is commonly listed as 1823, which would have made him twenty-six. However, his actual date of birth is not known.

7 The company laid out streets: *Noddle Island Illustrated, Argus-Advocate,* May 1897; *East Boston: 200 Neighborhood Series,* 1976; Sumner, William, *History of East Boston; The Bostonian,* April–September, 1985; Bacon, Edwin M., and Arthur P. Gay, *The East Boston Ferries and the Free Ferries Issue,* 1909.

7 In her memoirs: Kennedy, Rose, *Times to Remember,* page 5.

8 He was said to have received strong backing: Leamer, Laurence, *The Kennedy Women,* page 99.

11 In one of his earliest: Whalen, Richard J., *The Founding Father,* page 20.

11 "He was a Robin Hood type": Interview on August 11, 1994, with Kane Simonian.

12 "Joe did not come in": Interview on February 13, 1994, with Mary Lou McCarthy.

CHAPTER 2: FAILING GRADES

14 Psychologists say: *Psychology Today,* February 1988, page 52.

14 "As a child": Interview on January 16, 1994, with Mary Lou McCarthy.

15 "It wasn't a case": *Boston Record-American,* January 8, 1964, page 5.

15 To increase their store: Whalen, Richard J., *The Founding Father,* page 21.

16 Besides the rags-to-riches: Loretta Connelly account, in Kennedy, Edward M., editor, *The Fruitful Bough,* page 5.

16 The transcript of his grades: JPK student folder, HU.

18 "The only reason": Interview by Ralph Martin of Joseph Kane, Nigel Hamilton papers, MH.

18 Owing to a little blackmail: Hamilton, Nigel, *JFK: Reckless Youth,* page 20.

19 "My father refused": Kennedy, Rose, *Times to Remember,* page 58.

19 "There was nothing": Kennedy, Rose, *Times to Remember,* page 61.

21 But Joe did make: JPK responses to Harvard College questionnaire, HU.

21 In his freshman year: JPK transcript, HU.

21 "We try to make": Letter of October 14, 1911, from Harvard to P.J. Kennedy, HU.

22 Joe would later boast: *Time* dispatch of May 7, 1957, Nigel Hamilton papers, MH.

22 As unimpressive as his grades were: Interview on March 2, 1994, with Kerry McCarthy. The granddaughter of Joe's sister Loretta, Kerry McCarthy obtained the information from a classmate of Joe's when she was preparing a paper on P.J. Kennedy.

22 During vacation: Drew Pearson, *Washington Post*, July 6, 1960, attributed to a former bookkeeper for Colonial.

23 The manager: Whalen, Richard J., *The Founding Father*, page 28.

23 Knowing that: Whalen, Richard J., *The Founding Father*, page 27; and Blanchard, John A., editor, *The H Book of Harvard Athletics*: 1852–1922, page 286.

24 "I don't think any": Interview on October 30, 1994, with Janet Des Rosiers.

25 "He talked himself": Not-for-attribution interview by Richard J. Whalen on October 12, 1962, with Arthur Goldsmith, Nigel Hamilton papers, MH.

25 His classmates: Secretary's first report, Harvard College, Class of 1912, HU.

25 But Hugh Nawn: Nawn account, *The Fruitful Bough*, page 14.

CHAPTER 3: THE BRAHMINS

26 In September 1912: FBI report of February 14, 1956, FBI; and *Boston Herald*, January 8, 1938, which said JPK's father got him the job as state bank examiner.

26 "That bank examiner's job": Interview by Richard J. Whalen on October 5, 1962, with Ralph Lowell, Nigel Hamilton papers, MH.

28 A later FBI: FBI report of February 14, 1956, FBI.

28 "Bank President at the Age": *Boston Herald*, January 21, 1914.

28 If it took Joe: Account of Joe's Harvard classmate Thomas J. Campbell, *The Fruitful Bough*, page 20. Campbell said Joe told him the story and quoted Joe as saying, "Of course, he [the bank clerk] was dead right."

29 "I found money": Interview on March 2, 1994, with Kerry McCarthy.

29 He could be "extremely charming": Interview on July 19, 1994, with Gertrude Ball.

29 "Joe's a hard-headed": Interview by Richard J. Whalen on October 5, 1962, with Ralph Lowell, Nigel Hamilton papers, MH.

29 During his three-year tenure: Goodwin, Doris Kearns, *The Fitzgeralds and the Kennedys*, page 302.

30 On October 7, 1914: *Boston Herald*, October 8, 1914.

30 Rose loved: Rose Kennedy account, *The Fruitful Bough*, page 197.

31 "He knew art": Interview on November 14, 1994, with Anne Anable.

31 "Do you know": Interview by Richard J. Whalen on September, 25, 1962, with James Fayne, Nigel Hamilton papers, MH.

32 In October 1917: FBI report of March 2, 1956, FBI. In addition, a story in the October 16, 1917, *Quincy Patriot Ledger* reported that JPK had resigned as president of Columbia Trust Company and would become assistant manager at the Fore River shipyard.

32 When the board turned down: Goodwin, Doris Kearns, *The Fitzgeralds and the Kennedys*, page 327.

32 Joe would later boast: Beschloss, Michael R., *Kennedy and Roosevelt*, page 45; and Whalen, Richard J., *The Founding Father*, page 49.

33 "Joe was just": Interview on November 1, 1994, with Daniel Strohmeier.
33 For example, Fitzgerald called: Whalen, Richard J., *The Founding Father*, page 55.
34 "What was unusual": Interview by Richard J. Whalen on October 5, 1962, with Ralph Lowell, Nigel Hamilton papers, MH.
34 Yet Joe also told his friend: Interview by Richard J. Whalen on October 10, 1962, with Oscar Haussermann, Nigel Hamilton papers, MH.
34 While he was no longer: Interview with Timothy McInerny on October 4, 1962, by Richard J. Whalen researcher, Nigel Hamilton papers, MH.
36 Costello was allied: Messick, Hank, and Burt Goldblatt, *The Mobs and the Mafia*, pages 105 and 133; and Hammer, Richard, *Playboy's Illustrated History of Organized Crime*, page 65.
36 "The way he": Katz, Leonard, *Uncle Frank*, page 68.
36 "Frank Costello said": Interview on November 29, 1993, with Peter Maas.
36 When the story: *New York Times*, February 27, 1973, page 39.
36 However, Joseph "Joe Bananas" Bonanno: Bonanno, Joseph, *A Man of Honor*, page 308.
37 Besides importing Scotch: Interview on May 12, 1994, with a former Jacob Kaplan relative who did not want to be named; and Trager, James, *The People's Chronology*, page 904.
37 The best Scotch cost: Katz, Leonard, *Uncle Frank*, page 62.
38 "On and off": Memo of October 21, 1938, from JPK to Cordell Hall, R.G. 84, London Embassy, General Records, NA.
38 "How could I": Interview by Laura Bergquist with Rose Kennedy, Laura Bergquist papers, BU.
38 "It was mostly": *Time* memo of June 4, 1960, Nigel Hamilton papers, MH.

CHAPTER 4: THE TRIBE

40 "Your children": Goodwin, Doris Kearns, *The Fitzgeralds and the Kennedys*, page 357.
40 However, Louis Eaton: *Patriot Ledger*, June 24, 1995, page 11.
40 "People would barely": Interview on August 22, 1994, with Augustus Soule.
41 "Everything was figured": Interview on January 16, 1994, with Mary Lou McCarthy.
41 "When Joe spoke": Interview on December 16, 1993, with Edward McLaughlin.
41 Tag football was played: Oral history of Thomas Bilodeau, page 9, JFK.
41 "I myself used to play": Interview on December 15, 1993, with Dave Farrell.
42 "Dinner at Uncle Joe's": Joe Gargan account, *The Fruitful Bough*, page 174.
42 "The right side": Interview on January 9, 1994, with Joe Gargan.
43 Joe wanted the children: Ted Kennedy account, *The Fruitful Bough*, page 203.
43 He inquired: McTaggart, Lynne, *Kathleen Kennedy*, page 37.
44 "Mrs. Kennedy didn't say": Leamer, Laurence, *The Kennedy Women*, page 153.
44 "It's solitary": *Time* memo of June 6, 1960, Nigel Hamilton papers, NH.
45 "Timilty was a disgrace": Interview on November 23, 1993, with Robert Tonis.

45 "I hope you": Goodwin, Doris Kearns, *The Fitzgeralds and the Kennedys*, page 354.

45 At least part: A letter of February 6, 1942, from JPK to Will H. Hays, president of the Motion Picture Producers' Association, makes it clear the association was paying Houghton's salary. Will H. Hays papers on microfilm, GU.

46 "My collateral": Morton Downey account, *The Fruitful Bough*, page 35.

46 "They owned": Interview on May 4, 1994, with Ann Downey.

46 In 1957, it was revealed: *New York Times*, June 13, 1957; and Hammer, Richard, *Playboy's Illustrated History of Organized Crime*, page 262.

46 According to Arthur Stryker: Interview on May 5, 1994, with Stryker.

47 "Joe Kennedy's feeling": Interview on October 4, 1993, with Morton Downey Jr.

47 "Dad was known": Ted Kennedy account, *The Fruitful Bough*, page 205.

47 "We never discussed": Martin, Ralph G., and Ed Plaut, *Front Runner, Dark Horse*, page 124.

47 "I don't know": Fay, Paul B., Jr., *The Pleasure of His Company*, page 10.

48 When Joe first told: Interview on July 8, 1994, with William Mulcahy.

48 To Bernard Baruch: Draft of Bernard Baruch speech of January 26, 1965, Bernard Baruch papers, PU.

48 The first trust: Summary of JPK irrevocable trust, 1926, James M. Landis papers, LC.

49 While the size: *Forbes*, October 21, 1991, page 34.

50 In Arthur Krock's view: Interview by Joan and Clay Blair Jr. with Krock, Nigel Hamilton papers, MH.

50 "Joe analyzed": Not-for-attribution interview by Richard J. Whalen on October 18, 1962, with Thomas Corcoran, Nigel Hamilton papers, MH.

CHAPTER 5: ROBBER BARON

52 In return for a commission: Goodwin, Doris Kearns, *The Fitzgeralds and the Kennedys*, page 398.

52 "You had to be sharp": Interview by Richard J. Whalen on October 10, 1962, with Oscar Haussermann, Nigel Hamilton papers, MH.

54 That involved the camera: Fernett, Gene, *American Film Studios*, page 162.

54 For his work at Pathé alone: Letter of July 16, 1934, from JPK to Krock, Arthur Krock papers, PU.

55 Stockholders filed suit: Koskoff, David E., *Joseph P. Kennedy*, page 33.

55 "He did not behave": Interview on July 3, 1994, with Anne Anable.

55 Lucy P. Steinert: Interview on November 14, 1993, with Steinert.

55 More than ten years later: *Congressional Record*, January 18, 1940, page 493.

56 Another congressman: *Congressional Record*, May 12, 1933, page 3351.

56 He called for: Hays, Will H., *The Memoirs of Will H. Hays*, page 460.

56 "This seems hardly": Goodwin, Doris Kearns, *The Fitzgeralds and the Kennedys*, page 490.

56 After playing golf: Oral history of Edward M. Gallagher, page 17, JFK.

58 Pantages was booked: Anger, Kenneth, *Hollywood Babylon II*, page 29.

58 "We were both seated": *Los Angeles Times*, October 5, 1929, page 1.

58 "He was kissing": Giesler, Jerry, *The Jerry Giesler Story*, page 21.

59 On her deathbed: Wolf, Marvin J., and Katherine Mader, *Fallen Angels*, page 107.

59 For their perjured testimony: *Los Angeles*, November 1989, page 128. In a July 14, 1994, letter to the author, Andy Edmonds, who wrote the piece, said her sources included an attorney who worked for Giesler.

CHAPTER 6: GLORIA

61 "For this subject": Swanson, Gloria, *Swanson on Swanson*, page 305.

62 "Gloria was a fiendishly": Interview on April 28, 1994, with William Dufty.

63 "Now, listen, Rosie": Goodwin, Doris Kearns, *The Fitzgeralds and the Kennedys*, page 455, quoting Ann Gargan.

63 "Wherever you went": Hamilton, Nigel, *JFK*, page 45.

64 "He didn't resemble": Swanson, Gloria, *Swanson on Swanson*, page 327.

68 "Take Boston": Swanson, Gloria, *Swanson on Swanson*, page 339.

72 "He moved so quickly": Swanson, Gloria, *Swanson on Swanson*, page 356.

73 "Soon after Mrs. Kennedy": Leamer, Laurence, *The Kennedy Women*, page 188. While Swanson says nothing in her memoirs about going to Hyannis Port, William Dufty, her sixth husband, said she was often confused about where she had been. While she said in her memoirs that Joe asked her to attend a Halloween party at his Bronxville home, the time sequence indicates that the home she was referring to was actually in Riverdale.

76 According to Simonian: Interview on November 4, 1993, with Kane Simonian.

77 On August 20, 1929: Swanson, Gloria, *Swanson on Swanson*, page 385. Doris Kearns Goodwin's *The Fitzgeralds and the Kennedys*, on pages 480 and 481, straightens out the chronology.

78 "Your uncle thought": Interview on March 2, 1994, with Kerry McCarthy.

79 "I think she knows": Interview on May 3, 1994, with Cynthia Stone Ray.

79 "Clothes, jewels": Martin, Ralph G., *A Hero for Our Time*, page 34.

CHAPTER 7: CRASH

80 Currier warned Joe: Goodwin, Doris Kearns, *The Fitzgeralds and the Kennedys*, page 487, citing Guy Currier's letter of May 6, 1929, to JPK, and JPK's letter of May 7, 1929, to Currier. The letters are in JPK's papers under the control of the Kennedy family at the John F. Kennedy Library.

80 "It looks to me": Goodwin, Doris Kearns, *The Fitzgeralds and the Kennedys*, page 487, quoting from Louis Kirstein's papers.

82 "When the time comes": Asked by James Fayne if the story of the shoeshine boy was true, Joe said, "It happened just that way," according to Richard J. Whalen's interview on September 25, 1962, with Fayne, Nigel Hamilton papers, MH.

82 Nor was Joe: Klingaman, William K., *1929*, page 188.

84 "I am here": Swanson, Gloria, *Swanson on Swanson*, page 394.

85 Geraldine Hannon: Goodwin, Doris Kearns, *The Fitzgeralds and the Kennedys*, page 459.

87 "She wanted to see": Interview on July 19, 1994, with Gertrude Ball.

88 Years later, Joe bragged: Hamilton, Nigel, *JFK*, page 68.

88 "I'm sure Joe": Interview on April 28, 1994, with William Dufty.

88 "If Joe and Ben Smith": Interview on May 23, 1994, with Charles Spalding.
89 The price rose: *Hearings on Stock Exchange Practices*, Committee on Banking and Currency, United States Senate, 73rd Congress, Second Session, 1934, pages 6218–6231.
89 With Bernard Baruch: Grant, James, *Bernard M. Baruch*, pages 264–265.
89 Joe lost money: Whalen, Richard J., *The Founding Father*, page 132.
89 "Today people": Interview on August 31, 1994, with Irwin Borowski.
90 "There weren't any regulations": Interview on January 11, 1994, with Charles Burke.
90 As Goldsmith told: Not-for-attribution interview by Richard J. Whalen on October 12, 1962, with Arthur Goldsmith, Nigel Hamilton papers, MH.

CHAPTER 8: I'M FOR ROOSEVELT

94 In fact, Joe eventually: Interview by Ralph Martin with Joseph Kane, Nigel Hamilton papers, MH.
96 "W.R.": Oral history of Arthur Krock, page 7, CU.
97 "Do you know": Swanson, Gloria, *Swanson on Swanson*, page 426.
98 To others, he confided: Letter of July 12, 1932, from Roy Howard to Newton D. Baker, Nigel Hamilton papers, NH.
99 "It is pleasant": Letter of May 19, 1933, from JPK to FDR, FDR.
99 Joe reminded Moley: Moley, Raymond, *The First New Deal*, page 381.
100 Williams described Joe: Oral history of James P. Warburg, page 405, CU.
101 Joe was impressed: Interview by Richard J. Whalen researcher on October 18, 1962, with Thomas Corcoran.
101 "Why you perfect": Amory, Cleveland, *The Proper Bostonians*, page 166.
101 Eventually, the "energy": Adams, Brooks, *The Law of Civilization and Decay*, page 34.
102 President Roosevelt himself: Interview on December 11, 1994, with Walter Trohan.
102 Even after war: *Time*, April 18, 1994, page 83.
103 On June 30, 1933: Palm Beach County assessor records.
104 Already, he had gotten: Goodwin, Doris Kearns, *The Fitzgeralds and the Kennedys*, page 515. JPK confirmed in a June 30, 1938, *New York Times* article that he imported liquor during Prohibition using medicinal permits.
104 President Roosevelt told: Letter of July 2, 1939, from FDR to James Roosevelt, FDR.
105 He wrote that he saw: Roosevelt, James, *My Parents*, page 255.
105 Recognizing that Jimmy was: Not-for-attribution interview with Arthur Goldsmith, on December 26, 1962, by Richard J. Whalen researcher, Nigel Hamilton papers, MH. On May 19, 1933, James Roosevelt thanked JPK for steering additional insurance business to him.
105 "Outside of Massachusetts": Letter of July 24, 1933, from James Roosevelt to FDR, James Farley papers, LC.
106 Jimmy told Joe Kennedy biographer: Koskoff, David E., *Joseph P. Kennedy*, page 52, citing an interview by the author with James Roosevelt on March 20, 1962.
106 According to a major Boston: The promised 25 percent cut was also reported in the *Boston Sunday Advertiser*, January 26, 1964.
107 In his memoirs: Roosevelt, James, *My Parents*, page 210.

107 "I was on a plane": Martin, Ralph G., *A Hero for Our Times*, page 24, citing an interview with Franklin D. Roosevelt Jr.

107 As Joe set up Somerset: FBI report of February 26, 1955, FBI.

108 "Well, Doctor Hammer": Hammer, Armand, *Hammer*, page 254.

108 In November 1934: *Boston Post*, November 15, 1934.

108 "It has been clearly established": Minutes of board meeting of Haig & Haig Limited, Edinburgh, Scotland, May 5, 1939, page 62.

109 By overstocking: Interview on September 9, 1994, with Dr. Nicholas Morgan, United Distillers PLC.

109 Joe called the charge: Transcript of a May 1944 interview of JPK provided by Joseph Dinneen to Richard J. Whalen and verified as accurate by Lawrence Spivak on December 12, 1966, Nigel Hamilton papers, MH.

110 During Prohibition: Marrus, Michael R., *Mr. Sam*, page 146.

110 The board concluded: Haig & Haig Limited board minutes of January 10, 1946, page 108.

110 The total price: *Forbes*, October 21, 1991, page 36.

110 "I don't think the parting": Interview on January 2, 1995, with Richard O'Leary.

111 "He was this extraordinary": *The American Experience*, "The Kennedys," WGBH-TV, Part I, September 20, 1992.

111 At the time: Hamilton, Nigel, *JFK*, page 105.

111 "She was a loner": Interview by Nigel Hamilton of Paul Fay, Nigel Hamilton papers, MH.

111 For her fortieth birthday: Rose Kennedy account, *The Fruitful Bough*, page 199.

112 From the Ritz in Paris: Goodwin, Doris Kearns, *The Fitzgeralds and the Kennedys*, page 495.

112 Jack, who was now: Interview by James MacGregor Burns on March 22, 1959 with JFK, Nigel Hamilton papers, MH.

113 "I don't know how the church": Goodwin, Doris Kearns, *The Fitzgeralds and the Kennedys*, page 547.

CHAPTER 9: THE FOX IN THE CHICKEN COOP

114 What he did not write down: Moley, Raymond, *The First New Deal*, page 519.

116 "With a burst": Moley, Raymond, *After Seven Years*, page 288.

117 "The president has": Diary entry of June 30, 1934, of Ickes, Harold L. Ickes papers, LC.

117 *The New Republic*: *New Republic*, July 11, 1934, page 220.

117 Krock called Joe: Beschloss, Michael R., *Kennedy and Roosevelt*, page 91.

118 When Joe later thanked: Letter of July 1, 1937, from Krock to JPK, Arthur Krock papers, PU.

120 "He spoke these words": William Douglas account, *The Fruitful Bough*, page 73.

120 "I knew the details": Interview by Richard J. Whalen researcher on September 21, 1962, with James Landis, Nigel Hamilton papers, MH.

120 "I thought he relied": Interview on January 15, 1994, with Orval DuBois.

121 "If he stops liking you": Interview by Richard J. Whalen on September 25, 1962, with James Fayne, Nigel Hamilton papers, MH.

121 Early on, Joe: de Bedts, Ralph F., *The New Deal's SEC*, page 97.
122 During Joe's tenure: Seligman, Joe, *The Transformation of Wall Street*, page 113.
122 Dan T. Moore: Interview on June 21, 1994, with Moore.
123 During Prohibition: Goodwin, Doris Kearns, *The Fitzgeralds and the Kennedys*, page 512.
123 When first hired: Reports of June 19 and 24, 1935, of the Treasury Department, and diary entry of July 1, 1935, of Henry Morgenthau Jr., FDR.
124 Pecora became so frustrated: Ritchie, Donald A., *James M. Landis*, page 66.
125 "Joe worked on us": Interview on December 4, 1994, with Walter Trohan.
126 At 11:55 A.M.: Memo of February 18, 1935, from JPK to the file, FDR.
127 The next day: Memo of February 19, 1935, from FDR to JPK, FDR.
127 On the recommendation: White House memo of October 18, 1934, FDR.
128 "The trouble with Kennedy": Diary entry of April 15, 1935, of Henry Morgenthau Jr., FDR.
128 "At 7 p.m.": Memo of July 1, 1935, from Krock to the file, Arthur Krock papers, PU.
129 The company claimed: Letter of September 4, 1935, from JPK to FDR; and *Chattanooga Times*, September 3, 1935, FDR.
129 Two days later: Letter of September 6, 1935, from JPK to FDR, FDR.
129 When Joe's resignation: de Bedts, Ralph F., *The New Deal's SEC*, page 106.
130 "Joe is the kind": Interview by Richard J. Whalen researcher on October 18, 1962, with Thomas Corcoran, Nigel Hamilton papers, MH.

CHAPTER 10: PROFITEERING

132 In the November 1935 issue: Manchester, William, *The Last Lion*, pages 148–149.
133 "Joe was fascinated": Beschloss, Michael R., *Kennedy and Roosevelt*, citing an interview with James Roosevelt.
133 Referring to him as "that bastard": Diary entry of November 15, 1935, of Ickes, Harold L. Ickes papers, LC.
134 For $8 million: Hammer, Armand, *Hammer*, page 17.
134 In Hyannis Port, Joe's schedule: Oral history of Edward M. Gallagher, page 24, JFK.
134 One of Joe's favorite practices: Interview on October 4, 1993, with Morton Downey Jr.
135 "I was a great friend": Interview on December 4, 1994, with Walter Trohan.
135 Krock responded: Letter of June 24, 1936, from Krock to JPK with notation by Krock, Arthur Krock papers, PU.
135 Krock recalled that he gave Joe: Interview by Joan and Clay Blair Jr. with Arthur Krock, Nigel Hamilton papers, MH.
136 "I am not being boastful": Letter of September 18, 1936, from James Roosevelt to JPK, FDR.
136 Besides Raymond Moley: Diary entry of October 9, 1936, of Ickes, Harold L. Ickes papers, LC.
136 Then a Boston bishop: Diary entry of October 24, 1936, of Francis Joseph Spellman; Gannon, Robert I., *The Cardinal Spellman Story*, page 111.

136 Joe provided a special train: Francis Joseph Spellman account, *The Fruitful Bough*, page 135.
137 When he was assigned to the Vatican: Gannon, Robert I., *The Cardinal Spellman Story*, page 154.
138 The next day: Gannon, Robert I., *The Cardinal Spellman Story*, page 119.
138 "If it's all the same": Beschloss, Michael R., *Kennedy and Roosevelt*, page 129.
139 Ultimately, the Justice Department decided: Letters of March 19, 1937, from Justice Department to James Roosevelt, and of March 3, 1937, to FDR; letter of March 12, 1937, from JPK to Senator Royal S. Copeland, chairman of the Senate Commerce Committee, FDR.
139 Meanwhile, Joe told James Roosevelt: Farley diary entry of March 12, 1937, James A. Farley papers, LC.
140 When Roosevelt suggested: de Bedts, Ralph F., *Ambassador Joseph Kennedy*, page 12.
140 At one of the first meetings: James Fayne account, *The Fruitful Bough*, page 84.
141 Joe was a "genius": *The American Experience*, "The Kennedys," Part I, WGBH-TV, September 20, 1992.
141 "He was responsible": Admiral Emery Scott Land account, *The Fruitful Bough*, page 79.
141 Meanwhile, the commission's staff: United States Maritime Commission report of October 25, 1937, to Congress.
142 "No, Mr. President": Interview by Richard J. Whalen on October 10, 1962, with Oscar Haussermann, Nigel Hamilton papers, MH; and Oscar W. Haussermann account, *The Fruitful Bough*, page 81.
142 For the twenty-fifth anniversary report: JPK's draft of his twenty-fifth anniversary Harvard College report, HU.
143 If he forgot: Interview by Richard J. Whalen on October 5, 1962, with Ralph Lowell, Nigel Hamilton papers, MH.
144 "So he read it": Interview on February 12, 1994, with Dimitri Kessel.
144 After weeks of exhaustive research: Martin, Ralph G., *Henry and Clare*, page 194; and Goodwin, Doris Kearns, *The Fitzgeralds and the Kennedys*, page 582.

Chapter 11: Reward

146 Jimmy baldly proposed: Morgan, Ted, *FDR*, page 463.
146 "I'd like to be": Roosevelt, James, *My Parents*, page 208.
146 "He tried to get me": Oral history of Arthur Krock, page 4, JFK.
148 Tommy Corcoran did "everything": Diary entry of March 17, 1938, of Ickes, Harold L. Ickes papers, LC.
149 When Morgenthau asked: Diary entry of December 8, 1937, of Henry Morgenthau Jr., FDR.
150 Apparently not aware: Memo of December 23, 1937, from Krock to the file, Arthur Krock papers, PU.
150 "Kennedy has probably": Diary entry of December 18, 1937, of Ickes, Harold L. Ickes papers, LC.
151 "It is almost done.": Telegram of February 7, 1938, from James Roosevelt to JPK, James Roosevelt papers, FDR.

151 To soften the expected ribbing: Interview on December 4, 1994, with Walter Trohan.

151 "I don't know": Telegram of January 13, 1938, from JPK to FDR, Nigel Hamilton papers, MH.

152 "If the king himself": de Bedts, Ralph F., *Ambassador Joseph Kennedy*, page 32.

153 Joe explained to Chamberlain: Memo of March 4, 1938, from JPK to Cordell Hull, NA.

154 The British official was "quite stunned": Letter of March 3, 1938, from JPK to James Roosevelt, Cordell Hull papers, LC.

154 In his unpublished memoirs: Untitled Joseph P. Kennedy memoirs, written with James Landis, Chapter 2, page 2, Nigel Hamilton papers, MH. The memoirs were finished in 1961. Joe told friends they would be published "after Jack leaves the White House."

155 For fifteen minutes: de Bedts, Ralph F., *Ambassador Joseph Kennedy*, page 34.

155 "The ceremony": Memo of March 8, 1938, from JPK to Cordell Hull, NA.

157 In an ebullient mood: Letter of March 22, 1938, from FDR to JPK, Nigel Hamilton papers, MH.

157 Instead of saying: Telegram of March 11, 1938, from Cordell Hull to JPK, Stanley G. Hornbeck papers, HI.

158 Before leaving for London: Diary entry of January 28, 1938, of Moffat, Jay Pierrepont Moffat papers, HU.

158 After receiving Hull's revisions: Letter of March 14, 1938, from JPK to FDR, Cordell Hull papers, LC.

159 Joe sounded the same theme: Letter of March 21, 1938, from JPK to Baruch, Bernard Baruch papers, PU; a duplicate letter went to Roy Howard, Roy W. Howard papers, LC.

159 "You must be a Jew": Dalton diary entry of April 7, 1938, Hugh Dalton papers, London School of Economics, London.

160 In his diary: Lindbergh, Charles A., *The Wartime Journals of Charles A. Lindbergh*, page 26.

160 When Nazi documents: Manchester, William, *The Last Lion*, page 315.

CHAPTER 12: THE JEWISH QUESTION

161 Joe told the German ambassador: Letter of June 13, 1938, from Dr. Herbert von Dirksen to Ernst von Weizsäcker, state secretary, *Documents on German Foreign Policy, 1918–1945*, Part I, United States Government Printing Office, 1951, page 713.

163 Upon reading Dirksen's cables: Telegram of November 2, 1939, from Hans Dieckhoff to Herbert von Dirksen, *Documents on German Foreign Policy, Part IV*, page 637.

164 Referring to Joe Jr.: Memo of May 5, 1938, from JPK to Cordell Hull, NA.

164 "He said, 'You're a friend'": Interview on December 4, 1994, with Walter Trohan.

165 "He went to my boss": Interview on December 11, 1994, with Walter Trohan.

166 Sulzberger was unconvinced: Beschloss, Michael R., *Kennedy and Roosevelt*, page 169.

166 On the same day that Trohan's: *New York Times*, June 23, 1938.
167 During the visit, Joe confided: Diary entry of June 26, 1938, of Ickes, Harold L. Ickes papers, LC.
167 Roosevelt told Ickes: Diary entry of July 3, 1938, of Ickes, Harold L. Ickes papers, LC.
167 "He wants him to attack": Diary entry of July 3, 1938, of Ickes, Harold L. Ickes papers, LC.
168 Arthur Sulzberger had just told: Letter of October 10, 1941, from JPK to Krock, Arthur Krock papers, PU. What editing job Joe and Ickes were referring to was not clear. Upon the death of Edwin L. James in 1951, Sulzberger chose Turner Catledge, Krock's protégé, to run the paper as managing editor.
168 Among other things: *Saturday Evening Post*, July 2, 1938, written by Alva Johnston.
169 Then in a letter: *Boston Traveler*, July 20 and 29, 1938.
169 Three weeks after arriving: Letter of July 20, 1938, from Herbert von Dirksen to Baron von Weizsäcker, *Documents on German Foreign Policy*, Part I, page 721.
169 "This morning his manner": Memo of July 20, 1938, from JPK to Cordell Hull, NA.
170 Morgenthau called Hull: Diary entry of June 14, 1938, of Henry Morgenthau Jr., FDR.
170 "Why, when he was here": Diary entry of July 13, 1938, of Henry Morgenthau Jr., FDR.
171 Gently, Hull suggested: Telegram of September 1, 1938, from Cordell Hull to JPK, *Foreign Relations of the United States: Diplomatic Papers*, page 569.
171 After the column ran: Beschloss, Michael R., *Kennedy and Roosevelt*, page 175, citing *National Issues*, February 29, 1939, page 22.
172 After meeting him: Memo of September 17, 1938, from JPK to Cordell Hull, NA.
172 "Without doubt": Cable of September 22, 1939, from JPK to the Secretary of State [Cordell Hull], *Foreign Relations of the United States*, page 72; and Lindbergh, Charles A., *The Wartime Journals of Charles A. Lindbergh*, page 72.
173 As they talked: Heymann, C. David, *Poor Little Rich Girl*, page 168.
175 "He loses his amiability": Memo of October 28, 1938, from Moffat to Cordell Hull, NA.
176 The paper called the idea: *New York Post*, October 21, 1938, page 18.
176 Writing in: *Wall Street Journal*, October 21, 1938.

CHAPTER 13: THE KENNEDY PLAN

177 But Joe "did not": Oral history of George Rublee, page 284, CU.
179 "They brought it on themselves.": *The Independent*, July 31, 1992, page 24, based on interviews Philip Whitehead conducted with Harvey Klemmer before his death in 1992.
179 When a reporter asked him: *New York Times*, December 17, 1938.
179 "The Jews are kicking": Letter of July 3, 1946, from JPK to Max Beaverbrook, Nigel Hamilton papers, MH.
180 After the offending: Diary entry of November 25, 1938, of Ickes, Harold L. Ickes papers, LC.

181 Farley felt Joe: Diary entry of May 15, 1935, of Farley, James A. Farley papers, LC.

182 "He attributes this largely": Diary entry of December 16, 1938, of Phillips, William Phillips papers, HU.

182 Ironically, Arthur Krock: Letter of October 6, 1938, from Krock to JPK, Arthur Krock papers, PU.

182 "It's a shame": Letter of October 20, 1938, from JPK to Krock, Arthur Krock papers, PU.

182 Only a Roman Catholic: Interview by Joan and Clay Blair Jr. with Arthur Krock, Nigel Hamilton papers, MH.

183 While Rose and eight: Beschloss, Michael R., *Kennedy and Roosevelt*, page 182.

183 He had Dr. Sara M. Jordan: Letter of December 13, 1939, from Jordan to FDR, Nigel Hamilton papers, MH.

183 Finally, Moffat: Diary entry of February 9, 1939, of Moffat, Jay Pierrepont Moffat papers, HU.

185 Soon, Spellman received: Cooney, John, *The American Pope*, page 75, quoting from Spellman's diary.

186 "He has no money": Transcript of transatlantic call between JPK and Hull, April 24, 1939, Cordell Hull papers, LC.

186 Joe himself told William Phillips: Diary entry of March 14, 1939, of Phillips, William Phillips papers, HU.

186 He later complained: Letter of August 9, 1939, from JPK to FDR, FDR.

186 While it was true: Diary entry of March 29, 1939, of Ickes, Harold L. Ickes papers, LC.

188 Joe was interested: Undated synopsis of Mooney, James D. Mooney papers, GU.

188 After Joe proposed the visit: Telegram of May 4, 1939, from Sumner Welles to JPK.

189 The Germans resolved: Memo of March 5, 1940, from Hans Dieckhoff to Herbert von Dirksen, *Documents on German Foreign Policy*, Part VIII, page 865.

189 "I'm coming home": Interview by Ralph Martin with Joseph Kane, Nigel Hamilton papers, MH.

189 With Britain's reserves: Interview by Richard J. Whalen on October 10, 1962, with Oscar Haussermann, Nigel Hamilton papers, MH.

189 At a dinner at his home: Diary entry of April 29, 1939, of Ickes, Harold L. Ickes papers, LC.

190 Frankfurter would later say: Oral history of Felix Frankfurter, page 6, JFK.

190 Indeed, Joe told Lippmann: Oral history of Walter Lippmann, pages 183–184, JFK.

190 Churchill assured Lippmann: Manchester, William, *The Last Lion*, pages 437–438.

191 "I have arrived at the point": Letter of May 12, 1939, from JPK to Reid, Helen Ogden Reid papers, LC.

191 Through a friend: Letter of June 14, 1939, from W.L. Colze to FDR, Nigel Hamilton papers, MH.

192 When Roosevelt read: Diary entry of July 2, 1939, of Ickes, Harold L. Ickes papers, LC.

192 On July 3, Ickes had lunch: Diary entry of July 15, 1939, of Ickes, Harold L. Ickes papers, LC.

192 After a meeting with Halifax: de Bedts, Ralph F., *Ambassador Joseph Kennedy*, page 84.
192 "Wohlthat thinks": Memo of July 20, 1939, from JPK to Cordell Hull, NA.
194 When Arthur Krock wrote: Letter of July 22, 1939, from FDR to JPK, Nigel Hamilton papers, MH.
194 "Of course, the purpose": Diary entry of August 12, 1939, of Ickes, Harold L. Ickes papers, LC.
194 He wrote Roosevelt: Letter of July 20, 1939, from JPK to FDR, Nigel Hamilton papers, MH.
194 Seeking to humor: Letter of August 5, 1939, from FDR to JPK, Nigel Hamilton papers, MH.
194 Klemmer "resented": Interview on December 1, 1993, with Page Huidekoper.
195 From London sources: Diary entry of July 24, 1939, of Ickes, Harold L. Ickes papers, LC.

CHAPTER 14: THE PARTY IS ON

197 "It's the end": de Bedts, Ralph F., *Ambassador Joseph Kennedy*, page 147.
197 He blamed the U.S. failure: Koskoff, David E., *Joseph P. Kennedy*, page 212.
197 The king thought that Joe: Dilks, David, editor, *The Diaries of Sir Alexander Cadogan*, page 215.
197 "As I see it": Wheeler-Bennett, John W., *King George VI: His Life and Reign*, page 419.
198 Above all, he said: Telegram of September 10, 1939, from JPK to FDR, Nigel Hamilton papers, MH.
198 Roosevelt directed Hull: Memo of September 11, 1939, from Cordell Hull to JPK, NA.
199 "Kennedy has been": Israel, Fred L., editor, *The War Diary of Breckinridge Long*, page 10.
200 Sumner Welles: *Diaries of Henry Morgenthau Jr.*, pages 112–113, FDR.
200 Baron Erik Palmstierna: de Bedts, Ralph F., *Ambassador Joseph Kennedy*, page 159.
200 For the second time: Whelan, Richard J., *The Founding Father*, page 275.
200 Luce was aware: Not-for-attribution interview by Richard J. Whalen on June 11, 1962, with Henry Luce, Nigel Hamilton papers, MH.
201 On September 30, 1939: Letter of September 30, 1939, from JPK to FDR, Nigel Hamilton papers, MH.
202 In mid-October 1939: Koskoff, David E., *Joseph P. Kennedy*, page 220.
202 When Ickes showed Roosevelt: Diary entry of September 27, 1939, of Ickes, Harold L. Ickes papers, LC.
204 "Joe was prospectively": Interview on December 12, 1994, with Robert Crowley.
204 To Columbia Pictures: Letter of November 17, 1939, from JPK to Harry Cohn, Columbia Pictures, Arthur Krock papers, PU.
205 On November 18: Telegram of November 18, 1939, from Cordell Hull to JPK, NA.
205 This time, he insisted: Letter of November 30, 1939, from JPK to FDR, Nigel Hamilton papers, MH.

206 Roosevelt expressed horror: Terkel, Studs, *The Good War: An Oral History of World War Two*, page 318.
206 At the Navy Department: Diary entry of December 15, 1940, of Moffat, Jay Pierrepont Moffat papers, HU.
207 Krock would later confirm: Interview by Joan and Clay Blair Jr. with Arthur Krock, Nigel Hamilton papers, MH.
207 Cheerfully, Joe entered: Diary entry of March 10, 1940, of Ickes, Harold L. Ickes papers, LC.
208 An angry letter-writer: *New York Times*, March 14, 1940, page 22.
209 Joe relied more: FBI report of February 26, 1955, FBI, and Hersh, Burton, *The Old Boys: The American Elite and the Origins of the CIA*, page 64.
210 "Take the workman": Diary entry of March 13, 1940, of Moffat, Jay Pierrepont Moffat papers, HU.
210 "What went wrong": Diary entry from the 1960s of Luce, Clare Boothe Luce papers, LC.
210 To conceal the purpose: *New York Times*, April 3, 1940, page 14.
210 In her diary entry: Diary entry of April 2, 1940, of Luce, Clare Boothe Luce papers, LC.
211 Through Beaverbrook: Martin, Ralph G., *Henry and Clare*, page 342.

Chapter 15: Democracy Is All Done

213 "Every move he makes": Transcript of the April 29, 1940, meeting, FDR.
213 Included were the coded: Stevenson, William, *A Man Called Intrepid*, page 80.
214 Joe told Hull: Telegram of May 27, 1940, from JPK to Cordell Hull, *Foreign Relations of the United States*, page 233.
215 "Kennedy at the time": Maisky, Ivan M., *Memoirs of the Soviet Ambassador*, page 454; translated from the German by Willi R. Korte.
215 On June 30: Memo of June 30, 1940, from Ernst von Weizsäcker to subordinates, *Documents on German Foreign Policy*, Part X, page 68.
216 Gleefully, Thomsen: Telegram of June 19, 1940, Part IX, from Hans Thomsen to German Foreign Ministry, *Documents on German Foreign Policy*, page 525.
216 Thomsen told the ministry: Cable of August 26, 1939, from Hans Thomsen to the German Foreign Ministry, Political Archives of the German Foreign Office, translated by Willi R. Korte.
216 Clare Booth Luce tried: Telegram of July 8, 1940, from Luce to JPK, Clare Boothe Luce papers, LC.
216 In her diary: Diary entry of August 5, 1940, of Luce, Clare Boothe Luce papers, LC.
217 Even as Donovan: Memo of July 31, 1940, from JPK to Cordell Hull, NA.
218 James A. Rousmanière: Interview by Nigel Hamilton on April 6, 1989, with Rousmanière, Nigel Hamilton papers, MH.
219 Joe asked Harvey Klemmer: Martin, Ralph G., *A Hero for Our Time*, page 40.
219 Once Klemmer had finished: Oral history of Arthur Krock, page 5, JFK.
219 As Krock later put it: Interview by Joan and Clay Blair Jr. with Arthur Krock, Nigel Hamilton papers, MH.

220 In a good university: Letter of August 21, 1940, from Harold Laski to JPK, Nigel Hamilton papers, MH.
220 "Here's this young guy": Interview on May 23, 1994, with Charles Spalding.
220 "We were playing golf": Interview on May 23, 1994, with Charles Spalding.
221 There, Joe had a special cache: Inventory of supplies as of May 29, 1940, James W. Seymour papers, JFK.
222 Besides spending inordinate amounts: *The Independent*, July 31, 1992, page 24, based on interviews Philip Whitehead conducted with Harvey Klemmer before his death in 1992.
222 In another cable: Telegram of September 30, 1940, from Hans Thomsen to Ernst von Weizsäcker, *Documents on German Foreign Policy*, Part XI, page 227.
223 On October 1: Letter of October 1, 1940, from JPK to Luce, Clare Boothe Luce papers, LC.
223 Joe had been plotting: Martin, Ralph G., *Henry and Clare*, page 204.
224 That day, Roosevelt had lunch: Memo of May 5, 1965, from Krock to the file, Arthur Krock papers, PU.
224 Joe blew up: Memo of December 1, 1940, from Krock to the file, Arthur Krock papers, PU.
225 Joe told her: Ketchum, Richard M., *The Borrowed Years*, page 523.
225 "He feels, as we do": Lindbergh, Charles A., *The Wartime Journals of Charles A. Lindbergh*, page 420.
225 But according to Elliott: Roosevelt, Elliott, and James Brough, *An Untold Story: The Roosevelts of Hyde Park*, page 298.
225 On the morning of Friday: *Boston Globe*, March 18, 1972, by Louis Lyons.
226 "I would give him": Interview on March 17, 1994, with Bobby Young.
227 Using circular reasoning: Letter of April 21, 1965, from Ralph Coghlan to Richard J. Whalen, Nigel Hamilton papers, MH.
227 Coghlan later conceded: Letter of November 12, 1940, from Ralph Coghlan to Krock, Arthur Krock papers, PU.
228 As might have been expected: Oral history of Arthur Krock, page 8, JFK.
228 Krock later wrote: Letter of November 12, 1940, from Krock to JPK, Arthur Krock papers, PU.
228 Krock knew full well: Letter of April 22, 1940, from JPK to Krock, Arthur Krock papers, PU.
228 Nonetheless, Joe issued a denial: *New York Times*, November 30, 1940, page 3.
228 Then Joe denounced: "Statement to the Press" by Joseph P. Kennedy, Will H. Hays papers, microfilm at GU.
228 In private: Oral history of Edward M. Gallagher, page 8, JFK.
229 Ickes wrote that Roosevelt: Diary entry of December 1, 1940, of Ickes, Harold L. Ickes papers, LC.
229 Roosevelt fully believed: Diary entry of December 10, 1939, of Ickes, Harold L. Ickes papers, LC.
229 From four different people: Letter of November 19, 1940, from Douglas Fairbanks Jr. to FDR, Nigel Hamilton papers, MH.
230 "I never want to see": Beschloss, Michael R., *Kennedy and Roosevelt*, page 229.
230 In the mid-1930s: *The Nation*, March 5, 1977; and Seldes, George, *Even the Gods Can't Change History*.
231 Without revealing that he had already: Letter of November 26, 1940, from JPK to William Randolph Hearst, Nigel Hamilton papers, MH.

232 The poem ended: Felix Frankfurter papers, LC.

232 Looking back many years later, Joe insisted: Untitled Joseph P. Kennedy memoirs, written with James Landis, Chapter 28, page 3, Nigel Hamilton papers, MH.

233 "Despite the fact that Kennedy": Diary entry of December 13, 1940, of Ickes, Harold L. Ickes papers, LC.

235 "Some use the argument": *New York Herald Tribune*, January 19, 1941.

235 "There ain't a gut": Not-for-attribution interview by Richard J. Whalen on October 22, 1962, with Walter Trohan, Nigel Hamilton papers, MH.

235 The president then penned: Goodwin, Doris Kearns, *No Ordinary Time*, page 211, citing John Boettiger papers, FDR.

236 "When the going gets tough": *Oxford Dictionary of Quotations*, 1992, page 394; also Safire, William, *New York Times*, December 24, 1973.

237 Even as he was preparing: Diary entry of January 19, 1941, of Ickes, Harold L. Ickes papers, LC.

237 After visiting London: Morgan, Ted, *FDR*, page 378; FBI report of May 2, 1941, FBI.

CHAPTER 16: LOBOTOMY

239 She wrote that, as a baby: Kennedy, Rose, *Times to Remember*, page 151.

239 After the family returned: Kennedy, Rose, *Times to Remember*, page 286.

239 "She stayed for many years": Interview on October 23, 1994, with Ann Gargan.

240 He thought of him: Interview on December 1, 1993, with Frank Waldrop.

241 "Every time one": McTaggart, Lynne, *Kathleen Kennedy*, page 100.

241 "That's what all men": McTaggart, Lynne, *Kathleen Kennedy*, page 62.

241 As Lynne McTaggart described: McTaggart, Lynne, *Kathleen Kennedy*, page 98.

242 The lobotomy era: *Washington Post*, April 7, 1980, page A-1.

243 The doctors claimed: *Psychosomatic Medicine*, April 1941, page 117.

243 Yet they said others: *Psychosurgery*, May 1942, page 805.

243 At the time Joe asked the doctors: Interviews on October 13 and 14, 1994, with Dr. James Watts; *Psychosomatic Medicine*, April 1941, page 111.

243 "We went through the top": Interview on October 13, 1994, with Dr. James Watts.

244 "It may have been agitated": Interviews on October 13 and 18, 1994, with Dr. James Watts.

244 As described in one of the papers: *Sonderdruck aus dem Zentralblatt für Neurochirurgie*, 1940, number 3, page 8.

245 In a later paper: *Southern Medical Journal*, July 1943, table 1.

245 According to a review: *American Journal of Psychiatry*, April 1995, pages 505 and 508.

245 As now defined, depression: *Diagnostic and Statistical Manual of Mental Disorders: DSM IV*, American Psychiatric Association, 1994, pages 320–322 and 339–341.

245 Typically, patients are disoriented: *Yale Journal of Biology and Medicine*, May 1939, page 530.

245 A 1962 report: *Washington Post*, April 6, 1980, page A-1.

246 "They knew right away": Goodwin, Doris Kearns, *The Fitzgeralds and the Kennedys*, page 744.

246 At the age of nine: Goodwin, Doris Kearns, *The Fitzgeralds and the Kennedys*, page 418.

246 At the age of sixteen, she wrote to her father: Kennedy, Rose, *Times to Remember*, page 156.

247 "Rosemary's name": Interview on July 10, 1994, with Janet Des Rosiers.

247 "The old man": Interview on April 23, 1994, with Nellie McGrail.

247 Joe orchestrated an elaborate cover-up: Blair, Joan, and Clay Blair Jr., *The Search for JFK*, page 21.

248 In the same way: Blair, Joan, and Clay Blair Jr., *The Search for JFK*, page 25.

248 "I used to think": *Time*, July 11, 1960, page 22.

249 Contrary to what Joe had said himself: *Newsweek*, December 15, 1969, page 14D.

250 A smaller Kennedy foundation: Internal Revenue Service Form 990 return of private foundation for Park Foundation, 1992.

250 For "many years": FBI report of February 21, 1956, FBI. While the FBI redacted the attorney's name from copies of files provided under the Freedom of Information Act, Brickley was the only person who fit the description in the reports of JPK's Boston attorney.

250 During any given year: *Update*, National Institute of Mental Health, August 1993, page 35; and *Fact Sheet*, January 1992, Special Olympics International. Mentally retarded individuals manifest subnormal mental development. Traditionally, this shows up in lower than normal scores in intelligence tests. Other characteristics such as social maturity and ability to sustain personal and social independence are also used to evaluate whether an individual is mentally retarded.

251 According to Dr. Brown: Interviews on October 14 and 24, 1994, and February 1 and March 8, 1995, with Dr. Bertram Brown. Dr. Brown is co-author with Dr. Thomas F. Courtless of *The Mentally Retarded Offender*, National Institute of Mental Health, 1971.

After a draft of the manuscript of this book had been completed, the author showed Dr. Brown the material pertaining to Rosemary Kennedy's condition. On March 8, 1995, Dr. Brown said the material was "technically accurate" and, from a psychiatric standpoint, "professionally sound."

251 "In my experience": Interview on February 11, 1995, with Dr. Rene Parmar. Dr. Parmar was not initially told that the subject of the inquiry was Rosemary Kennedy. Similarly, Dr. Melvyn Semmel, who was interviewed on the same day, was not initially told the subject of the inquiry. On February 14, 1995, Paula Hirt, director of Programs and Services, American Association on Mental Retardation, confirmed that mental retardation is defined as an IQ of 75 or below.

251 "I've see an awful lot of families": Interview on February 1, 1995, with Dr. Bertram Brown.

252 Confirming Dr. Brown's analysis: Interview on January 9, 1995, with Luella Hennessey.

253 When asked for comment, Melody Miller: Interview on December 6, 1994, with Miller.

255 She cannot wash or dress herself: Leamer, Laurence, *The Kennedy Women*, page 760.

255 "She is very quiet": Interview on July 21, 1994, with Nellie McGrail.

CHAPTER 17: BINGO

256 "I was so stupefied": Interview by Joan and Clay Blair Jr. with Arthur Krock, Nigel Hamilton papers, MH.

257 Jack told his friend: Interview by Nigel Hamilton with Paul Fay, Nigel Hamilton papers, MH.

257 In a memoir: Hamilton, Nigel, *JFK*, page 421.

258 Born on October 6, 1913: Interview by Nigel Hamilton with Ronald McCoy, Nigel Hamilton papers, MH.

259 "She made no secret": Interview on December 2, 1993, with Pat Munroe.

263 "One day the FBI": Interview by Nigel Hamilton on December 16, 1991, with William Sutton, Nigel Hamilton Papers, MH.

263 "Distrust is a funny": Letter of January 27, 1942, from Inga Arvad to JFK, Nigel Hamilton papers, MH.

264 "Inga Arvad was a great": Interview on May 24, 1994, with Charles Spalding.

264 To make sure Jack: Davis, John H., *The Kennedys*, page 93.

264 "She thought it was": Interview by Nigel Hamilton with Ronald McCoy, Nigel Hamilton papers, MH.

265 "He was in control": Interview on July 13, 1994, with Ronald McCoy.

265 But on May 4, 1942: Note of May 4, 1942, from FDR to J. Edgar Hoover, Nigel Hamilton papers, MH.

CHAPTER 18: MERCHANDISE MART

266 "I don't want to appear": Letter of March 4, 1942, from JPK to FDR, Nigel Hamilton papers, MH.

267 In his reply to Joe: Letter of March 7, 1942, from FDR to JPK, Nigel Hamilton papers, MH.

267 "I know that the president": Diary entry of March 29, 1942, of Ickes, Harold L. Ickes papers, LC.

267 Such speculation received: Memo of April 20, 1942, from J. Edgar Hoover to Edwin M. Watson, secretary to FDR, Nigel Hamilton papers, MH.

268 "So Joe Kennedy": *PM*, April 21, 1942.

269 "Of course, they'd like": Letter of January 25, 1943, from JPK to Luce, Clare Boothe Luce papers, LC.

269 As he put it to his friend: Beschloss, Michael R., *Kennedy and Roosevelt*, page 251.

270 "One day Jack": Interview on August 22, 1994 with Henry James Jr.

272 "I have twenty-four points": Interview on November 2, 1994, with Harold Clancy.

272 About another proposed investment: Letter of August 4, 1949, from James Landis to Corcoran, Thomas G. Corcoran papers, LC.

273 "We had it right": Interview by Richard J. Whalen on September 25, 1962, with James Fayne, Nigel Hamilton papers, MH.

273 He might buy: Interview by Richard J. Whalen on November 29, 1962, with James Landis, Nigel Hamilton papers, MH.

273 Asked for comment: *New York Times*, September 29, 1944.

274 "I used to go to races": Interview by Nigel Hamilton with Fred Good Jr., on December 19, 1991, Nigel Hamilton papers, MH.

274 "Joe Kennedy just thought": Interview on May 14, 1994, with Margot Prendergast.
275 The Joseph P. Kennedy Jr. Foundation bought: *Boston Herald*, March 22, 1947.
275 At the time, government agencies: Wallace Ollman account, *The Fruitful Bough*, page 47.
276 "They were sort of outdated": Blair, Joan, and Clay Blair Jr., *The Search for JFK*, page 519.
276 Meyer advised the family: Reich, Cary, *Financier*, page 356.
276 "It became such a success": Interview on April 23, 1994, with Nellie McGrail.
276 It was "simply a case": Letter of June 21, 1994, to author from Michael Reynolds.
276 James T. Lee, a friend: Interview on December 30, 1994, with James Auchincloss.
277 "Who says it?" Transcript of a May 1944 interview of JPK provided by Joseph Dinneen Sr. to Richard J. Whalen and verified by Lawrence Spivak on December 12, 1966, Nigel Hamilton papers, MH.
278 "You've got to take out": Interview by Richard J. Whalen on November 9, 1962, with Joseph Dinneen, Nigel Hamilton papers, MH.
279 Joe tried to get some sort: Cooney, John, *The American Pope*, page 101.
281 Once at a restaurant: Interview on April 6, 1994, with Igor Cassini.

Chapter 19: Pappy's Eyes

282 At about 2 A.M.: Rachlin, Harvey, *The Kennedys*, page 88; and Hamilton, Nigel, *JFK*, page 563.
283 "I talked to everyone": Martin, Ralph G., *A Hero for Our Time*, page 43.
283 Jack's friend Red Fay: Reeves, Thomas C., *A Question of Character*, page 66.
284 "The ambassador was about to turn": Interview by Ralph Martin with Joe Kane, Nigel Hamilton papers, MH.
284 "No, that's Joe's department": Interview by Ralph Martin with Joe Kane, Nigel Hamilton papers, MH.
285 Olsen urged Joe: Davis, John H., *The Kennedys*, page 105; and Hamilton, Nigel, *JFK*, page 660.
285 "I was there when they showed up": Interview on January 9, 1994, with Joe Gargan.
285 ". . . Roosevelt told many people": Interview by Joan and Clay Blair Jr. with Arthur Krock, Nigel Hamilton papers, MH.
286 "Joe's death has shocked": Letter of September 5, 1944, from JPK to Forrestal, James Forrestal papers, PU.
286 "For a fellow who didn't want": Letter of October 23, 1944, from JPK to Max Beaverbrook, Nigel Hamilton papers, MH.
286 Joe told Krock afterward: Memo of October 26, 1944, from Krock to the file, Arthur Krock papers, PU.
287 "Harry, what are you doing": McCullough, David, *Truman*, page 328; and Beschloss, Michael, *Roosevelt and Kennedy*, page 259.
287 "I got Jack into politics": Blair, Joan, and Clay Blair Jr., *The Search for JFK*, page 356.

288 Just six months after Joe: Interview on December 13, 1993, with James Reed; and oral history of Reed, page 13, JFK.

288 Rose was in Paris: *Palm Beach Post*, March 11, 1995, page A-1.

289 "I still can't see": Letter of May 13, 1946, from JPK to Max Beaverbrook, Nigel Hamilton papers, MH.

289 Two years later, Joe recalled: Letter of January 3, 1948, from JPK to Max Beaverbrook, Nigel Hamilton papers, MH.

290 "My judgment to the ambassador": Interview on June 30, 1994, with Frank Morrissey.

290 "Give the kid": Goodwin, Doris Kearns, *The Fitzgeralds and the Kennedys*, page 820, citing Rose Kennedy's papers.

291 "Curley knew that he was in trouble": Interview by Ralph Martin, with Joe Kane, Nigel Hamilton papers, MH.

291 Joe paid Curley: Hamilton, Nigel, *JFK*, page 674.

291 To Joe, this was standard operating: Martin, Ralph G., and Ed Plaut, *Front Runner, Dark Horse*, page 133.

292 "The gifts from the foundation": Oral history of Joseph Casey, page 9, JFK.

292 "It was the strangest": Goodwin, Doris Kearns, *The Fitzgeralds and the Kennedys*, page 825, quoting from an interview with David Powers.

293 "Joe's people in New York": Interview on May 16, 1994, with William Sutton.

293 "It was his money": Transcript of interview with William Sutton by David A. Farrell for *Boston Globe* story that appeared November 22, 1973, page 1.

293 "I never thought too much": Interview on July 8, 1994, with William Mulcahy.

293 "They gave me favors": *Boston*, June 1993, page 82, by Steve Buckley. Mary Gigante, one of Joseph Russo's daughters, confirmed Buckley's account.

293 "They didn't leave": Interview on December 20, 1993, with Joseph A. Russo.

294 Once he came to a decision: Not-for-attribution interview by Richard J. Whalen on October 9, 1962, with John Dowd, Nigel Hamilton papers, MH.

294 "Joe said, 'Jack, I think you should attack'": Interview on November 5, 1993, with John Galvin.

295 "He compared the stories": Interview by Nigel Hamilton with Peter Cloherty, Nigel Hamilton papers, MH.

295 Yet Fay recalled how cheap: Interview by Nigel Hamilton with Paul Fay, Nigel Hamilton papers, MH.

295 Joe called in his chits: Reeves, Thomas C., *A Question of Character*, page 82.

296 "I don't know why I'm so dumb": Not-for-attribution interview by Richard J. Whalen on June 11, 1962, with Henry Luce, Nigel Hamilton papers, MH.

297 "The one thing about him": Interview on November 3, 1993, with Mark Dalton.

297 Joe spent $300,000: O'Neill, Tip, *Man of the House*, page 77.

297 "Although he lived in New York": O'Neill, Tip, *Man of the House*, page 81.

CHAPTER 20: PHILANDERING

299 An "almost incestuous": Heymann, C. David, *A Woman Named Jackie*, page 148.

299 "I think it's Dad's idea": Hamilton, Nigel, *JFK*, page 116.

300 "Jack had no respect": Hamilton, Nigel, *JFK*, page 172.

300 "The first thing": An anonymous campaign aide quoted in Hamilton, Nigel, *JFK*, page 737.

300 "Whenever he was at home": Hamilton, Nigel, *JFK*, page 830.

301 "I can remember going up": Interview by Joan and Clay Blair Jr. with Mary Pitcairn, Nigel Hamilton papers, MH.

301 One of Jack's girlfriends: Interview by Nigel Hamilton with Kay Stammers, Nigel Hamilton papers, MH.

302 "He asked me how much": Blair, Joan, and Clay Blair Jr., *The Search for JFK*, page 354.

303 "When I joined them": Martin, Ralph G., *A Hero for Our Time*, page 54.

303 In Hyannis Port, Joe would insist: Hamilton, Nigel, *JFK*, page 161.

304 "It was a Cézanne show": Interview on December 3, 1993, with William Walton.

305 "His manner was always": Cassini, Oleg, *Oleg Cassini*, page 319.

305 "Girls were an ego trip": Interview on June 15, 1994, with Oleg Cassini.

306 "We have to discuss": Cassini, Oleg, *Oleg Cassini*, page 281.

306 "There was no doubt": Interview on June 15, 1994, with Oleg Cassini.

306 "I'm like Bobby": Interview on June 15, 1994, with Oleg Cassini.

306 Bobby, as Arthur Krock put it: Interview by Joan and Clay Blair Jr. of Krock, Nigel Hamilton papers, MH.

307 "One of the young women": Interview on February 17, 1994, with George Smathers.

307 "I attempted to do": Oral history of George A. Smathers, page 47, JFK.

308 "The door opened": Interview on May 12, 1994, with Carmen dell'Orefice. The August 14, 1981, issue of *People* quoted her as saying of Joe, "I was so naive. . . . He took me right home."

308 "I was sophisticated enough": Interview on May 12, 1994, with Margaret dell'Orefice.

308 "I like it": Fontaine, Joan, *No Bed of Roses*, page 267.

309 Slim Aarons: Weiss, Murray, and Bill Hoffman, *Palm Beach Babylon*, page 126.

309 "Joe Kennedy represented": Heymann, C. David, *A Woman Named Jackie*, page 140.

310 "When I was a young fellow": Letter of February 4, 1948, from Corcoran to James Landis quoting JPK, Thomas G. Corcoran papers, LC.

310 "See what a principality": Letter of July 30, 1948, from Corcoran to JPK, and August 7, 1948, from JPK to Corcoran, Thomas G. Corcoran papers, LC.

311 Before Kravis could say: Raymond Kravis account, *The Fruitful Bough*, page 56.

311 Indeed, Joe expected: Letter of January 27, 1948, from James Landis to Corcoran, Thomas G. Corcoran papers, LC.

312 Meanwhile, they made plans: Goodwin, Doris Kearns, *The Fitzgeralds and the Kennedys*, page 853.

312 "Wasn't that just like": McTaggart, Lynne, *Kathleen Kennedy*, page 239.

CHAPTER 21: JANET

315 "He was very taken": Des Rosiers, now Janet Fontaine, was interviewed on July 10 and 17, 1994. On August 14, 1994, she confessed that she had been Joe's mistress. More than a dozen additional interviews were held with her.

318 "The only thing Rose": Heymann, C. David, *A Woman Named Jackie*, page 141.

320 "She went to mass": Interview on January 9, 1994, with Joe Gargan.

323 "The Irish versus the WASPs": Interview on November 2, 1993, with K. Dun Gifford.

329 "Mr. Kennedy had stomach problems": Interview on January 10, 1994, with Dr. Robert Watt.

330 "I was attacked": Interview on February 27, 1994, with Nancy Tenney Coleman.

CHAPTER 22: PAYOFF

333 "Actually, twenty-one": John Cavanaugh account, *The Fruitful Bough*, page 161.

334 "He gave me an education": Interview on October 1, 1994, with Donald Senich.

335 "I suppose it was also": Interview on February 14, 1994, with Henry Luce III.

335 Later, Joe suggested to the elder Luce: Interview by Richard J. Whalen on October 1, 1962, with Henry Luce, Nigel Hamilton papers, MH.

335 On November 10, 1950: Parmet, Herbert S., *Jack*, page 211.

335 In a speech to the University of Virginia Law School Forum: Advance copy of text of December 12, 1950, speech at the University of Virginia School of Law, H.A. Smith papers, PU.

336 "There was talk": Eunice Shriver account, *The Fruitful Bough*, page 237.

336 "Joe said some way": *Time* memo of June 4, 1960, Nigel Hamilton papers, MH.

336 "That's what Jack needs": Eunice Shriver account, *The Fruitful Bough*, page 239.

337 "The old man hovered": Letter of April 21, 1965, from Ralph Coghlan to Richard J. Whalen, Nigel Hamilton papers, MH.

337 "There's no stopping the Kennedys": Interview on April 28, 1994, with William Dufty.

338 Even though the Massachusetts Supreme Judicial Court: *Boston Globe*, January 23, 1985, page 17.

339 Indeed, Fox's doctor: Interview on June 17, 1994, with Dr. Julius Siegel.

339 "The rumors were": Oral history of Robert L. Lee, page 11, JFK.

339 In response to a question, Fox: Special Subcommittee on Legislative Oversight, House Committee on Interstate and Foreign Commerce, June 27, 1958, page 4115.

340 Joe issued a statement: Parmet, Jack S., *Jack*, page 242.

340 "It was part of the package": Interviews on June 18 and 23 and on August 19 and November 19, 1994, and on February 25, 1995, with Raymond Faxon.

340 "The whole thing": Interview on February 25, 1995, with Raymond Faxon.

341 Always known for having a pint: *Boston* magazine, December 1973, page 120.
341 "You know, we had to buy": Laura Bergquist oral history for the JFK Library, December 8, 1985, page 10, BU.
342 In December 1952, Joe called: Schlesinger, Arthur M., Jr., *Robert Kennedy and His Times*, page 107.
342 "We were dragging": Interview on January 9, 1994, with Joe Gargan.
343 Yet, under the Senate rules, Jack could have: *Boston Globe's New England* magazine, November 20, 1983.
344 "I prepared a newspaper ad": Martin, Ralph G., *A Hero for Our Time*, page 63, citing an interview with Pat Gardner Jackson.
344 Jackie had "all the social ingredients": Heymann, C. David, *A Woman Named Jackie*, page 117.
345 Lem Billings said that Jack and Jackie: Collier, Peter, and David Horowitz, *The Kennedys*, page 241.
346 "I was getting a divorce": Interview on May 23, 1994, with Charles Spalding.
346 Jack's sisters made fun: Heymann, C. David, *A Woman Named Jackie*, pages 143 and 166.
346 Photographers at the *Washington Times-Herald*: Martin, Ralph G., *A Hero for Our Time*, page 77.
346 He rented an apartment: Collier, Peter, and David Horowitz, *The Kennedys*, page 242.
347 "Jack kept assuring": Collier, Peter, and David Horowitz, *The Kennedys*, page 242.

CHAPTER 23: COMPARTMENTS WITHIN COMPARTMENTS

348 "Mr. [James] Fayne": Interview on July 19, 1994, with Gertrude Ball.
349 Joe then persuaded Arthur Krock: Interview by Joan and Clay Blair Jr. with Krock, Nigel Hamilton papers, MH.
349 He described Jack's writing: Parmet, Herbert S., *Jack*, page 320.
349 "Jack told me Joe got people": Interview on August 22, 1994, with Henry James Jr.
350 By now, Jack was a member of the prestigious: Oral history of Hugh Sidey, page 9, JFK; and oral history of George A. Smathers, page 157, JFK.
350 It soon became clear: Clifford, Clark, *Counsel to the President*, page 307.
352 In his memoirs: Clifford, Clark, *Counsel to the President*, page 310.
352 The office administrator: Interview on February 26, 1995, with Thomas Walsh.
354 William Douglas received: Supreme Court of the United States memo of December 2, 1955, from Edith Allen, Douglas's secretary, and handwritten note of December 2, 1955, from Douglas to Allen inquiring if there was a record of the amount of the loan, William O. Douglas papers, LC.
359 Joe wrote to his friend: Letter of January 14, 1955, from JPK to Douglas, William O. Douglas papers, LC.
359 Kelly quoted Joe: FBI report of August 28, 1953, FBI.
359 Later, Joe told: FBI memo of December 18, 1957, FBI.
360 If Hoover ran: Felt, W. Mark, *The FBI Pyramid*, page 195, quoting JPK's letter of October 12, 1955, to Hoover.

361 "He wanted to embark": Interviews on January 10 and November 8, 1994, with F. Mark Wyatt.

CHAPTER 24: THE CARDINAL

365 "I said, 'Uncle Frank' ": Interview on July 15, 1994, with Ned Spellman.
365 Ned Spellman, who was at the lunch: Interview on December 16, 1993, with Ned Spellman.
365 "As far as I know": Interview on November 2, 1994, with Otto Fuerbinger.
365 In 1956, Luce was staying: Martin, Ralph G., *Henry and Clare*, page 359.
366 Stanley Karnow, then a *Time* correspondent: Interview on September 28, 1994, with Karnow.
366 "Maybe Joe Kennedy called Harry": Martin, Ralph G., *Henry and Clare*, page 361.
366 Joe could not help boasting: Letter of December 9, 1957, from JPK to Max Beaverbrook, Nigel Hamilton papers, MH.
367 Jack was gratified: Prendergast, Curtis, *The World of Time Inc.*, page 21.
367 Al Lehmann: Interview by Richard J. Whelan on November 9, 1962, with Lehmann, Nigel Hamilton papers, MH.
368 Bobby "jammed his palm": Richard Harwood said of the quote on February 6, 1995, "I don't recollect saying that, but the basic idea is correct."
368 "It would be silly": *Time* dispatch of May 7, 1957, Nigel Hamilton papers, MH.
368 Joe told Bill Cunningham: *Boston Herald*, April 7, 1957.
369 Dave Powers, Jack's aide: Reeves, Thomas C., *A Question of Character*, page 77.
369 But Joe Timilty said: Interview by Joan and Clay Blair Jr. with Timilty, Nigel Hamilton papers, MH.
369 "What's $100 million": Koskoff, David E., *Joseph P. Kennedy*, citing an interview with James Landis on March 3, 1962.
370 "If that happens": Interview on October 23, 1994, with Janet Des Rosiers.
370 But Gargan said Joe: Interview on October 23, 1994, with Ann Gargan.
371 Careful about saying anything: Letter of April 10, 1958, from JPK to Des Rosiers, courtesy of Janet Des Rosiers.
371 "I could see that he had these": Interview on July 8, 1994, with Marianne Strong.
372 "In Hyannis Port, the water": Interview on May 3, 1994, with Cynthia Stone Ray.
373 Saying she had received "misinformation": Letter of December 11, 1958, from JFK to Eleanor Roosevelt, and letter of December 27, 1958, from Eleanor Roosevelt to JFK, Bruce Biossat papers, BU.
373 As Jack began a second term: The information about William Bradford Huie and Harry Golden came from confidential sources.
374 "By that time": Interview by Richard J. Whelan on September 21, 1962, with James Landis, Nigel Hamilton papers, MH.
374 Joe lined up the support: Oral history of Anthony B. Akers, page 11, JFK.
374 He got John McCormack: Oral history of John W. McCormack, page 26, JFK.
375 In one of the *Look* magazine articles: Reeves, Thomas C., *A Question of Character*, page 156.

375 After confiding to a *Time* reporter: *Time* memo of June 4, 1960, Nigel Hamilton papers, MH.
375 A month later, Jack's friend Frank Sinatra: Exner, Judith, *My Story*, page 86.
376 After the election, an FBI wiretap: Fox, Stephen, *Blood and Power*, page 338; and *Newsday*, February 23, 1988, page 6.
376 Tip O'Neill recalled that Eddie Ford: *The American Experience*, "The Kennedys," Part I, WGBH-TV, September 20, 1992; and O'Neill, Tip, *Man of the House*, page 92.
377 After Jack announced: *Cape Cod Standard Times*, September 21, 1967, page 3.

Chapter 25: A Tip of the Hat

379 One of the couriers told author Peter Maas: Interview on November 29, 1993, with Maas, who cited the method in his novel *Father and Son*, on page 65 of the 1990 HarperCollins reprint.
380 "It's good for the church": Reeves, Thomas C., *A Question of Character*, page 165.
380 "A few weeks later, I interviewed him": Interview on September 27, 1994, with Peter Maas.
380 Echoing his son, Joe responded: *Boston Herald*, September 4, 1960. The wire service is now called United Press International.
380 "We were standing at the pool": Interview on April 12, 1994, with Charles Spalding.
381 "He assured me": Exner, Judith, *My Story*, page 162.
381 "No one ever knew John Kennedy": Reeves, Richard, *President Kennedy*, page 19.
381 Besides Addison's: Hamilton, Nigel, *JFK*, page 342, citing Jack's medical history from navy medical records.
381 When talk turned to politics: Martin, Ralph G., *A Hero for Our Time*, page 102.
382 "She was ready to divorce Jack": Interview on June 18, 1994, with Igor Cassini.
382 Later, Jackie pressured: Reeves, Thomas C., *A Question of Character*, page 5.
383 "Joe was the mastermind": Interview by Joan and Clay Blair Jr. with Joseph Timilty, Nigel Hamilton papers, MH.
383 When Krock suggested: Oral history of Arthur Krock, page 14, JFK.
383 The next morning, Joe had breakfast: Interview by Joan and Clay Blair Jr. with Joseph Timilty, Nigel Hamilton papers, MH.
383 "The ambassador insisted": Interview on June 30, 1994, with Frank Morrissey.
383 "Jack did what Joe wanted": Interview on March 9, 1994, with George Smathers.
383 "He didn't come just for": Not-for-attribution interview by Richard J. Whalen on October 1, 1962, with Henry Luce, Nigel Hamilton papers, MH; and oral history of Henry R. Luce, pages 9–12, JFK.
384 Grimacing, Jack slid: Fay, Paul B., Jr., *The Pleasure of His Company*, page 33.

384 During the campaign, Krock wrote: Interview by Joan and Clay Blair Jr. with Arthur Krock, Nigel Hamilton papers, MH.

385 By November 1961, Krock had written: Letter of November 21, 1961, from Krock to Milton Kronheim, Arthur Krock papers, PU.

385 Thomas Winship: Interview on April 21, 1994, with Winship.

385 Dave Farrell: Interview on February 8, 1994, with Farrell.

387 In introducing the two candidates: Cooney, John, *The American Pope*, page xix.

387 "Lo and behold": Interview on December 16, 1993, with Ned Spellman.

387 "That is a truly evil": Cooney, John, *The American Pope*, page 265.

387 Cushing told him their passive: Cutler, John Henry, *Cardinal Cushing of Boston*, page 220.

388 Looking back, Jack told his friend: Bradlee, Benjamin C., *Conversations with Kennedy*, page 201.

388 Of that sum, $4 million: McCullough, David, *Truman*, page 970.

389 Senator Smathers recalled sitting: Interview on February 17, 1994, with George Smathers.

390 "Who are all these people?": Baldrige, Letitia, *Of Diamonds and Diplomats*, page 153.

390 He visited Bing Crosby's home: Interview by Nigel Hamilton with Paul Fay, Nigel Hamilton papers, MH.

390 "Have you ever slept with my father?": Heymann, C. David, *A Woman Named Jackie*, page 287.

390 "After Jack had been nominated": Interview by Joan and Clay Blair Jr. with Arthur Krock, Nigel Hamilton papers, MH.

390 Yet Joe became so concerned: Thomas, Evan, *The Man to See*, page 163.

391 "I represented Joe when he wanted": Interview on November 23, 1993, with Nick Chase.

391 "Now who else": Diane Winter D'Alemberte account, *The Fruitful Bough*, page 263.

391 Just weeks after the inauguration: Interview on April 7, 1994, with Igor Cassini; and Whalen, Richard J., *The Founding Father*, page 472.

391 Peter Maas broke the story: PR Newswire, May 31, 1984; and *Boston Herald*, July 23, 1962.

392 Cassini pleaded no contest: *New York Times*, October 9, 1963.

392 Caplin discussed the case: IRS oral history interview of Mortimer Caplin on February 7, 1961, page 54; and Ritchie, Donald A., *James M. Landis*, page 196.

392 On July 30, 1964: *Washington Star*, July 10, 1964; and *Washington Post*, August 3, 1963, and July 31, 1964.

392 At his death, Landis owed: Accounting of May 1, 1965, of Estate of James M. Landis; and letter of April 8, 1965, from Landis, Cohen, and Singman to Stanley Gewirtz, Esq., Thomas G. Corcoran papers, LC.

393 "She was giggling": Saunders, Frank, *Torn Lace Curtain*, page 84.

393 "I was a caddy": Interview on November 2, 1993, with Françoise Pellegrino.

394 Situated on 2.43 acres: Barnstable Board of Assessor records.

395 Rose would "come down": Interview on January 15, 1994, with Stanley Galup.

395 "We drove in silence": Saunders, Frank, *Torn Lace Curtain*, page 146; and Dallas, Rita, *The Kennedy Case*, page 70.

396 Joe informed Des Rosiers: Letter of September 27, 1961, from JPK to Janet Des Rosiers, courtesy of Des Rosiers.
397 "His reason for believing": FBI report of December 4, 1961, FBI.

CHAPTER 26: STROKE

398 "Caroline and Jackie": Interview on September 23, 1994, with Ann Gargan; and oral history of Rose Kennedy, February 1, 1968, Herbert Hoover Presidential Library, page 8, HI.
399 "He would say 'no, no, no' ": Interview on September 23, 1994, with Ann Gargan.
400 "Whether he understood me": Richard Cardinal Cushing account, *The Fruitful Bough*, page 156.
400 Jack told Ben Bradlee: Bradlee, Benjamin C., *Conversations with Kennedy*, page 146.
401 As instructed by Steve Smith: Dallas, Rita, *The Kennedy Case*, page 71.
401 When Joe visited the White House: Dallas, Rita, *The Kennedy Case*, page 211; and Dr. Henry Betts account, *The Fruitful Bough*, page 275.
401 Joe's children said as much: Leamer, Laurence, *The Kennedy Women*, page 351.
402 Before his stroke, Joe would clap: Diane Winter D'Alemberte account, *The Fruitful Bough*, page 265.
402 Joe "used such phrases": Joseph P. Kennedy II account, *That Shining Hour*, page 288.
402 Before his recent marriage: David, Lester, *Good Ted, Bad Ted*, page 243.
402 "I think everyone knows that Pat Lawford": Interview on March 1, 1994, with Mary Lou McCarthy.
403 Among Bobby's children: Gibson, Barbara, *The Kennedys: The Third Generation*, pages 10, 279, 280, and 281; *New York Times*, May 17, 1984; *Washington Post*, February 14, 1995, page B-3; *People*, February 27, 1995, page 52.
403 William Kennedy Smith was accused: *People*, November 8, 1993, page 137; and *Washington Post*, November 23, 1993, page E-1.
403 "The kids hold AA meetings": Interview on December 20, 1993, with James Langan.
404 "You don't mean it?": Dallas, Rita, *The Kennedy Case*, page 158.
405 Rose, with her queasy stomach: Saunders, Frank, *Torn Lace Curtain*, page 93.
406 "Her formula for survival": Dallas, Rita, *The Kennedy Case*, page 47.
406 "Ann was family": Interview on November 14, 1993, with Rita Dallas.
406 "Rita Dallas saw things": Interview on October 23, 1994, with Ann Gargan.
406 Dr. Saul Rotter: Interview on May 5, 1994, with Dr. Rotter.
407 In fact, Dr. Henry Betts: Betts account, *The Fruitful Bough*, page 271.
407 "He was aphasic": Interview on May 5, 1994, with Dr. Saul Rotter.
409 "Eunice is another one": Interview on February 7, 1994, with Dr. Robert Watt.
409 Rose pointed brusquely: Interview on February 9, 1994, with Janet Jeghegian.
411 "He just got furious": Oral history of Paul Fay, November 9, 1970, MH.
411 Howard Baird, the pilot: Baird account, *The Fruitful Bough*, page 279.
412 "The president's been shot!": Dallas, Rita, *The Kennedy Case*, page 12.

412 Rose later explained, "In our household": Kennedy, Rose, *A Time to Remember*, page 442.
414 Baird told Rita Dallas: Dallas, Rita, *The Kennedy Case*, page 280.
415 A judge fined Joe II: Barbara Gibson, with Ted Schwarz, *The Kennedys*, page 14.
415 "Young Joe went out": Interview on February 27, 1994, with Nancy Tenney Coleman.
416 In the mid-1970s, Rose "made the comment": Interview on May 5, 1994, with Dennis Spear.
417 "He makes decisions": *Boston Globe*, January 16, 1966.

CHAPTER 27: DELIVER US FROM EVIL

418 After Bobby had died: Reeves, Thomas C., *A Question of Character*, page 314.
419 "The conversation was brief": Interview on October 15, 1994, with Joe Gargan.
419 In his statement to police: Damore, Leo, *Senatorial Privilege*, page 23; and report of Judge James Boyle, February 18, 1970.
419 Ted later pled guilty: Damore, Leo, *Senatorial Privilege*, page v.
419 "Dad, there was an accident": *The American Experience*, "The Kennedys," Part II, WGBH-TV, September 21, 1992.
421 At 11:05 A.M., Rose finished: Dallas, Rita, *The Kennedy Case*, page 352.
421 "I stayed outside the room": Interview on June 26, 1994, with Dr. Robert Watt.
423 A *Boston Globe* obituary: *Boston Globe*, November 18, 1969.
423 A *Boston Herald* editorial: *Boston Herald*, November 19, 1969.
423 In a final act of meanness: Last will and testament, Joseph P. Kennedy, dated December 30, 1955, codicil added June 9, 1958, and filed December 22, 1969, Palm Beach County Probate Court, folio 535, page 652.
424 The assets included: Inventory, estate of Joseph P. Kennedy, Palm Beach County Probate Court, dated November 4, 1970, folio 460, page 629.
424 In keeping with their usual practice: The author made written requests for interviews or comment on September 25, 1993, and April 5, August 15, and December 15, 1994. Discussions were also held with Melody Miller, Ted's press secretary, about the book in general and Rosemary Kennedy's condition in particular. On August 1, 1994, Miller said that Ted "has instructed me that he and the family will not be giving further interviews on family members. He will do his own book and does not want to give it away." On August 25, 1994, she said, "He has not changed his mind, and neither have his sisters. They just really don't feel they want to sit down and talk with any people writing any books. They've just been burned too many times."
426 In a replay of what they had done: *New York Times*, July 13, 1990, page A-8.
428 "Boys," Joe told the other commissioners: Goodwin, Doris Kearns, *The Fitzgeralds and the Kennedys*, page 522, citing *Philadelphia Record*, November 1934.

BIBLIOGRAPHY

Adams, Brooks. *America's Economic Supremacy*. Harper and Brothers, 1947.
———. *The Law of Civilization and Decay: An Essay on History*. Books for Libraries Press, 1896.
Amory, Cleveland. *The Proper Bostonians*. E.P. Dutton, 1947; Dutton reprint.
Anger, Kenneth. *Hollywood Babylon II*. Dutton, 1984.
Baldrige, Letitia. *Of Diamonds and Diplomats*. Houghton Mifflin, 1968.
Bearse, Ray, and Anthony Read. *Conspirator: The Untold Story of Tyler Kent*. Doubleday, 1991.
Beatty, Jack. *The Rascal King: The Life and Times of James Michael Curley, 1874–1958*. Addison-Wesley, 1992.
Beschloss, Michael R. *Kennedy and Roosevelt: The Uneasy Alliance*. W.W. Norton, 1980.
Blair, Joan, and Clay Blair Jr. *The Search for JFK*. Berkley, 1976.
Blanchard, John A., editor. *The H Book of Harvard Athletics: 1852–1922*. Harvard Varsity Club, 1923.
Blum, John Morton, editor. *From the Morgenthau Diaries*. Houghton Mifflin, 1959 and 1965.
Bonanno, Joseph, with Sergio Lalli. *A Man of Honor: The Autobiography of Joseph Bonanno*. Simon and Schuster, 1983.
Bradlee, Benjamin C. *Conversations with Kennedy*. W.W. Norton, 1975.
Brown, Anthony Cave. *C: The Secret Life of Sir Stewart Menzies, Spymaster to Winston Churchill*. Macmillan, 1987.
Brownlow, Kevin. *The Parade's Gone By*. Alfred A. Knopf, 1969.

Bryant, Traphes, with Frances Spatz Leighton. *Dog Days at the White House*: *The Outrageous Memoirs of the Presidential Kennel Keeper*. Macmillan, 1975.

Burke, Richard E., with William and Marilyn Hoffer. *The Senator*: *My Ten Years with Ted Kennedy*. St. Martin's, 1992.

Burns, James MacGregor. *John Kennedy*: *A Political Profile*. Harcourt, Brace, 1960.

Cadogan, Sir Alexander. *The Diaries of Sir Alexander Cadogon*: *1938–1945*. David Dilks, editor. G.P. Putnam's Sons, 1971.

Cassini, Oleg. *Oleg Cassini*: *In My Own Fashion*. Pocket Books, 1987.

Chellis, Marcia. *The Joan Kennedy Story*: *Living with the Kennedys*. Simon and Schuster, 1985.

Chernow, Ron. *The House of Morgan*: *An American Banking Dynasty and the Rise of Modern Finance*. Atlantic Monthly Press, 1990.

Clifford, Clark, with Richard Holbrooke. *Counsel to the President*. Random House, 1991.

Collier, Peter, and David Horowitz. *The Kennedys*: *An American Drama*. Summit, 1984; Warner reprint.

Colville, John. *The Fringes of Power*: *10 Downing Street Diaries, 1939–1955*. W.W. Norton, 1985.

Cooney, John. *The American Pope*: *The Life and Times of Francis Cardinal Spellman*. Times Books, 1984.

Costello, John. *Ten Days to Destiny*: *The Secret Story of the Hess Peace Initiative and British Efforts to Strike a Deal with Hitler*. William Morrow, 1991.

Cutler, John Henry. *Cardinal Cushing of Boston*. Hawthorn, 1970.

———. *"Honey Fitz"*: *Three Steps to the White House*. Bobbs-Merrill, 1962.

Dallas, Rita, with Jeanira Ratcliffe. *The Kennedy Case*. G.P. Putnam's Sons, 1973.

Damore, Leo. *The Cape Cod Years of John Fitzgerald Kennedy*. Four Walls Eight Windows, 1993.

———. *Senatorial Privilege*: *The Chappaquiddick Coverup*. Regnery Gateway, 1988.

David, Lester. *Good Ted, Bad Ted*: *The Two Faces of Edward M. Kennedy*. Birch Lane Press, 1993.

Davis, John H. *The Kennedys*: *Dynasty and Disaster*. McGraw Hill, 1984.

de Bedts, Ralph F. *Ambassador Joseph Kennedy, 1938–1940*: *An Anatomy of Appeasement*. Peter Lang, 1985.

———. *The New Deal's SEC*: *The Formative Years*. Columbia University Press, 1964.

Delaney, Mary Murray. *Of Irish Ways*. Crown, 1985.

Dinneen, Joseph F. *The Kennedy Family*. Little, Brown, 1959.

Eisenberg, Dennis, Uri Dan, and Eli Landau. *Meyer Lansky*: *Mogul of the Mob*. Paddington Press, 1979.

Exner, Judith, with Ovid Demaris. *My Story*. Grove, 1977.

Fay, Paul B., Jr. *The Pleasure of His Company*. Harper and Row, 1966.

Felt, W. Mark. *The FBI Pyramid*. G.P. Putnam's Sons, 1979.

Fernett, Gene. *American Film Studios*: *An Historical Encyclopedia*. McFarland, 1988.

Fontaine, Joan. *No Bed of Roses*. William Morrow, 1978.

Fox, Stephen. *Blood and Power*: *Organized Crime in Twentieth Century America*. William Morrow, 1989.

Gannon, Robert I. *The Cardinal Spellman Story*. Doubleday, 1962.

Giancana, Antoinette, and Thomas C. Renner. *Mafia Princess: Growing Up in Sam Giancana's Family*. William Morrow, 1984; Avon reprint.

Gibson, Barbara, with Caroline Latham. *Life with Rose Kennedy: An Intimate Account*. Warner, 1986.

Gibson, Barbara, with Ted Schwarz. *The Kennedys: The Third Generation*. Thunder's Mouth, 1993.

Giglio, James N. *The Presidency of John F. Kennedy*. University Press of Kansas, 1991.

Gilbert, Martin. *Winston S. Churchill: Volume VI, The Finest Hour, 1939–1941*. Houghton Mifflin, 1983.

Goodwin, Doris Kearns. *The Fitzgeralds and the Kennedys: An American Saga*. Simon and Schuster, 1987. Endnotes refer to the 1988 St. Martin's reprint.

———. *No Ordinary Time: Franklin and Eleanor Roosevelt*. Simon and Schuster, 1994.

Grant, James. *Bernard M. Baruch: The Adventures of a Wall Street Legend*. Simon and Schuster, 1983.

Hamilton, Nigel. *JFK: Reckless Youth*. Random House, 1992.

Hammer, Armand, with Neil Lyndon. *Hammer*. G.P. Putnam's Sons, 1987.

Hays, Will H. *The Memoirs of Will H. Hays*. Doubleday, 1955.

Hersh, Burton. *The Education of Edward M. Kennedy: A Family Biography*. William Morrow, 1972.

———. *The Old Boys: The American Elite and the Origins of the CIA*. Charles Scribner's Sons, 1992.

Heymann, C. David. *Poor Little Rich Girl: The Life and Legend of Barbara Hutton*. Lyle Stuart, 1984.

———. *A Woman Named Jackie: An Intimate Biography of Jacqueline Bouvier Kennedy Onassis*. Lyle Stuart, 1989.

Higham, Charles. *American Swastika*. Doubleday, 1985.

Hull, Cordell. *The Memoirs of Cordell Hull*, Volume I. Macmillan, 1948.

Johnson, Paul. *Ireland: A Concise History from the Twelfth Century to the Present Day*. Granada, 1981.

———. *Modern Times: The World from the Twenties to the Eighties*. Harper and Row, 1985.

Katz, Leonard. *Uncle Frank: The Biography of Frank Costello*. Drake, 1973.

Kennedy, Edward M., editor. *The Fruitful Bough: A Tribute to Joseph P. Kennedy*. Privately printed by Halliday Lithograph Corporation, 1965.

Kennedy, John F. *Profiles in Courage*. Harper and Row, 1956; Pocket Books reprint.

Kennedy, Rose Fitzgerald. *Times to Remember*. Doubleday, 1974.

Ketchum, Richard M. *The Borrowed Years: America on the Way to War*. Random House, 1989.

Koskoff, David E. *Joseph P. Kennedy: A Life and Times*. Prentice-Hall, 1974.

Krock, Arthur. *Memoirs: Sixty Years on the Firing Line*. Funk and Wagnalls, 1968.

Lange, James E.T., and Katherine DeWitt Jr. *Chappaquiddick: The Real Story*. St. Martin's, 1992.

Laqueur, Walter. *The Terrible Secret: The Suppression of the Truth About Hitler's "Final Solution."* Little, Brown, 1980.

Lash, Joseph P. *Dealers and Dreamers: A New Look at the New Deal*. Doubleday, 1988.

Lasky, Victor. *JFK: The Man and the Myth*. Macmillan, 1963.

Lawford, Patricia, editor. *That Shining Hour.* Privately printed by Halliday Litho-graph Corporation, 1969.

Leamer, Laurence. *The Kennedy Women: The Saga of an American Family.* Villard, 1994.

Lindbergh, Charles A. *The Wartime Journals of Charles A. Lindbergh.* Harcourt Brace Jovanovich, 1970.

Long, Breckinridge. *The War Diary of Breckinridge Long.* Fred L. Israel, editor.

Madsen, Axel. *Gloria and Joe: The Star-Crossed Love Affair of Gloria Swanson and Joe Kennedy.* William Morrow, 1988.

Maheu, Robert, and Richard Hack. *Next to Hughes.* HarperCollins, 1992; HarperCollins reprint.

Maisky, Ivan M. *Memoirs of the Soviet Ambassador.* East Berlin; Dietz Verlag, 1975.

Manchester, William. *The Death of a President: November 1963.* Harper and Row, 1963.

———. *The Glory and the Dream.* Little, Brown, 1974; Bantam reprint.

———. *The Last Lion.* Little, Brown, 1988; Laurel reprint.

Marrus, Michael R. *Mr. Sam: The Life and Times of Samuel Bronfman.* Penguin, 1991.

Martin, Ralph G. *A Hero for Our Time.* Macmillan, 1983.

———. *Ballots and Bandwagons.* Rand McNally, 1964.

Martin, Ralph G., and Ed Plaut. *Front Runner, Dark Horse.* Doubleday, 1960.

———. *Henry and Clare: An Intimate Portrait of the Luces.* G.P. Putnam's Sons, 1991.

McCullough, David. *Truman.* Simon and Schuster, 1992.

McTaggart, Lynne. *Kathleen Kennedy: Her Life and Times.* Doubleday, 1983.

Messick, Hank, and Burt Goldblatt. *The Mobs and the Mafia.* Thomas Y. Crowell, 1972.

Moley, Raymond. *After Seven Years.* Harper and Bros., 1939.

———. *The First New Deal.* Harcourt, Brace and World, 1966.

Morgan, Ted. *FDR: A Biography.* Simon and Schuster, 1985.

Morrison, Samuel Eliot. *One Boy's Boston: 1887–1901.* Riverside Press, 1962.

Nevins, Allan, and Henry Steele Commager. *Pocket History of the United States.* Pocket Books, 1992.

Ney, John. *Palm Beach: The Place, the People, Its Pleasures and Palaces.* Little, Brown, 1966.

O'Donnell, Kenneth P., and David F. Powers with Joe McCarthy. *"Johnny, We Hardly Knew Ye."* Little, Brown, 1972.

Olsen, Jack. *The Bridge at Chappaquiddick.* Little, Brown, 1970.

O'Neill, Tip, with William Novak. *Man of the House: The Life and Political Memoirs of Speaker Tip O'Neill.* Random House, 1987.

Parmet, Herbert S. *Jack: The Struggles of John F. Kennedy.* Dial Press, 1980.

Parris, Barry. *Louise Brooks.* Alfred A. Knopf, 1989.

Prendergast, Curtis, with Geoffrey Colvin. *The World of Time Inc.: The Intimate History of a Changing Enterprise, 1960–1980.* Time Inc., 1986.

President's Commission on the Assassination of President Kennedy. *The Warren Report.* Government Printing Office, 1964.

Rachlin, Harvey. *The Kennedys: A Chronological History.* World Almanac/Pharos Books, 1986.

Reedy, George. *From the Ward to the White House: The Irish in American Politics.* Charles Scribner's Sons, 1991.

Reeves, Richard. *President Kennedy: Profile of Power.* Simon and Schuster, 1993.

Reeves, Thomas C. *The Life and Times of Joe McCarthy.* Stein and Day, 1982.

————. *A Question of Character: A Life of John F. Kennedy.* Free Press, 1991. Endnotes refer to the 1992 Prima reprint.

Reich, Cary. *Financier: The Biography of André Meyer.* William Morrow, 1983.

Ritchie, Donald A. *James M. Landis: Dean of the Regulators.* Harvard University Press, 1980.

Roberts, Gary Boyd. *Ancestors of American Presidents.* Carl Boyer III and New England Genealogical Society, 1989.

Roosevelt, Elliott, and James Brough. *An Untold Story: The Roosevelts of Hyde Park.* G.P. Putnam's Sons, 1973.

Roosevelt, James, with Bill Libby. *My Parents: A Differing View.* Playboy Press, 1976.

Saunders, Frank, with James Southwood. *Torn Lace Curtain: Life with the Kennedys.* Holt, Rinehart and Winston, 1982.

Schlesinger, Arthur M., Jr. *Robert Kennedy and His Times.* Houghton Mifflin, 1978. Endnotes refer to the 1979 Ballantine reprint.

————. *A Thousand Days: John F. Kennedy in the White House.* Houghton Mifflin, 1965.

Seligman, Joel. *The Transformation of Wall Street: A History of the Securities and Exchange Commission and Modern Corporate Finance.* Houghton Mifflin, 1982.

Shackleton, William. *The Book of Boston.* Penn, 1916.

Shirer, William L. *The Rise and Fall of the Third Reich: A History of Nazi Germany.* Simon and Schuster, 1960; Ballantine reprint.

Smith, Cecil Woodham. *The Great Hunger.* New English Library, 1962.

Smith, Page. *John Adams: 1735–1784.* Doubleday, 1962.

Spada, James. *Peter Lawford: The Man Who Kept the Secrets.* Bantam, 1992.

Stevenson, William. *A Man Called Intrepid: The Secret War.* Harcourt Brace Jovanovich, 1976.

Swanson, Gloria. *Swanson on Swanson.* Random House, 1980.

Talese, Gay. *The Kingdom and the Power: The Story of the Men Who Influence the Institution That Influences the World.* World, 1966.

Teresa, Vincent, with Thomas C. Renner. *My Life in the Mafia.* Doubleday, 1979; Fawcett reprint, 1973.

Thomas, Evan. *The Man to See: Edward Bennett Williams, Ultimate Insider, Legendary Trial Lawyer.* Simon and Schuster, 1991.

Thomas, Gordon, and Max Morgan-Witts. *The Day the Bubble Burst: A Social History of the Wall Street Crash of 1929.* Penguin, 1980.

Trager, James. *The People's Chronology.* Henry Holt, 1979.

Troy, Thomas F. *Donovan and the CIA: A History of the Establishment of the Central Intelligence Agency.* Aletheia, 1981.

United States Department of State. *Documents on German Foreign Policy, 1918–1945: From the Archives of the German Foreign Ministry.* Government Printing Office, 1949 and 1954.

————. *Foreign Relations of the United States: Diplomatic Papers.* Government Printing Office, 1956.

Weiss, Murray, and Bill Hoffman. *Palm Beach Babylon: Sins and Scandals of America's Super-Rich.* Pinnacle, 1993.

Whalen, Richard J. *The Founding Father: The Story of Joseph P. Kennedy.* New American Library, 1964.

Wheeler, Burton K., with Paul F. Healy. *Yankee from the West*. Doubleday, 1962.
Wolf, Marvin J., and Katherine Mader. *Fallen Angels: Chronicles of L.A. Crime and Mystery*. Facts on File, 1986.
Wyman, David S. *The Abandonment of the Jews: America and the Holocaust, 1941–1945*. Pantheon, 1984; Pantheon reprint.

INDEX